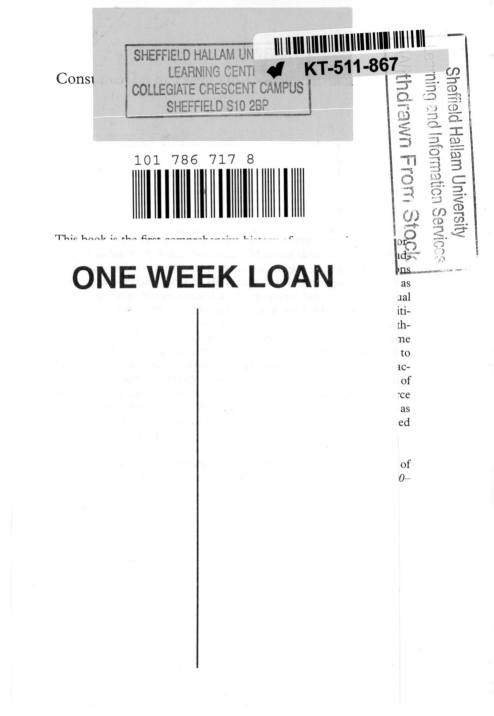

KT-511-867

Cons...

This book is the first comprehensive history of ...

ONE WEEK LOAN

...or
...nd-
...ns
...as
...ial
...iti-
...th-
...ne
...to
...ac-
...of
...ce
...as
...ed

...of
...0–

Consumerism in Twentieth-Century Britain

The Search for a Historical Movement

Matthew Hilton

University of Birmingham

CAMBRIDGE
UNIVERSITY PRESS

PUBLISHED BY THE PRESS SYNDICATE OF THE UNIVERSITY OF CAMBRIDGE
The Pitt Building, Trumpington Street, Cambridge, United Kingdom

CAMBRIDGE UNIVERSITY PRESS
The Edinburgh Building, Cambridge, CB2 2RU, UK
40 West 20th Street, New York, NY 10011–4211, USA
477 Williamstown Road, Port Melbourne, VIC 3207, Australia
Ruiz de Alarcón 13, 28014 Madrid, Spain
Dock House, The Waterfront, Cape Town 8001, South Africa

http://www.cambridge.org

First published 2003

Printed in the United Kingdom at the University Press, Cambridge

Typeface Plantin 10/12 pt.   *System* LATEX 2ε   [TB]

A catalogue record for this book is available from the British Library

ISBN 0 521 83129 6 hardback
ISBN 0 521 53853 X paperback

For Doris and Jim Buckley

Contents

Illustrations

Acknowledgements

This book has been several years in the making and I am indebted to many people. Martin Daunton provided support and encouragement when it all began in London in the mid-1990s and his assistance has been vital right through to the end as he commented on several chapters of the manuscript. I have relied on the wit and judgement of Margot Finn whose close reading of some early drafts was crucial to the development of my arguments. At the University of Birmingham, numerous friends and colleagues have offered help of all kinds and I have depended on many for their insights, ideas and inspiration. In particular, I would like to thank John Breuilly, Nick Crowson, George Lukowski, Graeme Murdock and Chris Wickham in the History department, Jonathan Reinarz in the Centre for the History of Medicine, Ian Cook in Geography, Helen Laville and Scott Lucas in American Studies, Conrad James in Hispanic Studies and Frank Webster and Ann Gray in Cultural Studies and Sociology, the latter of whom created a thriving interdisciplinary seminar in consumption studies just prior to their department's 'restructuring' in 2002. Also at Birmingham, several students have shaped the themes of the book. Matthew Anderson, Kathryn Eccles and especially Matthew Schofield were often the best audience to test many early ideas and a special subject class in 2001–2 provided a great forum for debate and discussion. The History department further provided me with a period of study leave in the latter half of 2000 which, together with the funding provided by the British Academy and the Nuffield Foundation, was crucial to the completion of the bulk of the research.

I am grateful for the many questions and comments received from several seminar and conference audiences over the last few years, especially those at Birmingham, Lancaster University, the Open University, the universities of Bristol and Warwick, the Institute for Contemporary British History, the North American Conference on British Studies in Pasadena, the Institute for Social Sciences in Amsterdam, the Economic History Society Conference in Glasgow, the 'Material Politics' colloquium at Churchill College, Cambridge, the International Economic

History Society Pre-Conference in Lille, and the series of three workshops on consumption in Sussex, Berlin and Tel Aviv. Many individuals at these events and elsewhere have further provided me with important references, advice and encouragement or have allowed me to see unpublished work and materials. I cannot thank them all but must mention Chris Beauchamp, Maxine Berg, Hartmut Berghoff, Lawrence Black, Gisela Bock, James Chapman, Christoph Conrad, Gary Cross, Hanna Hodacs, Billie Melman, Michael Mertens, Avner Offer, Pat Thane, Nick Tiratsoo, Frank Trentmann, John Walton and Michael Zakim.

Several consumer policy workers and veterans of the consumer movement agreed to be interviewed or to correspond on specific points and I am indebted to their many frank assessments on the state of consumerism, past and present. I am particularly grateful to Len Tivey, Rachel Waterhouse, Maurice Healy and Jeremy Mitchell who went on to read the manuscript as well, but I cannot value too highly the recollections, opinions and interpretations of Anna Bradley, Alastair Macgeorge, Sheila McKechnie, Rosemary McRobert, Janet Upward, and the late Michael Young.

For access to archival sources I wish to thank the staff of the Information Services department at the Consumers' Association and Julian Edwards of Consumers International, as well as the staff at the British Library, the British Library of Political and Economic Science, the Public Record Office, Kew, and the Labour History Archive, Manchester. For permission to reproduce the front cover and Figure 2 I am grateful to Punch and to the Consumers' Association for Figure 5.

It has seemed a never-ending project and I could not have finished it without a number of close friends. But most of all, Barbara Lehin lived through the writing of this book. I will never be able to repay her for all her support in that time, but wish to thank her especially for everything she gave to me.

Abbreviations

AGM	Annual General Meeting
AIC	Advertising Inquiry Council
ASA	Advertising Standards Authority
BEUC	Bureau Européen des Unions de Consommateurs
BSI	British Standards Institution
CA	Consumers' Association
CAB	Citizens' Advice Bureau
CAC	Consumer Advisory Council, BSI
CAFOD	Catholic Agency for Overseas Development
CAI	Council for Art and Industry
CAP	Common Agricultural Policy
CBI	Confederation of British Industry
CCC	Consumers' Consultative Committee
CI	Consumers International
CID	Council for Industrial Design
CND	Campaign for Nuclear Disarmament
CNS	Consumer Needs Section, Board of Trade
CPAC	Consumer Protection Advisory Committee
CSAC	Consumer Standards Advisory Committee
CU	Consumers' Union
CWS	Co-operative Wholesale Society
DCCC	Domestic Coal Consumers' Council
DPCP	Department of Prices and Consumer Protection
DSIR	Department of Scientific and Industrial Research
DTI	Department of Trade and Industry
ECRA	Ethical Consumer Research Association
EPI	Ethical Purchasing Index
FBI	Federation of British Industries
GATT	General Agreement on Tariffs and Trade
GHI	Good Housekeeping Institute
ILP	Independent Labour Party
IMF	International Monetary Fund

IOCU	International Organisation of Consumers' Unions (later CI)
LETS	Local Exchange Trading Schemes
MRC	Modern Records Centre, University of Warwick
NCC	National Consumer Council
NCF	National Consumer Federation
NCW	National Council of Women
NEDC	National Economic Development Council
NFCG	National Federation of Consumer Groups
NGO	Non-Governmental Organisation
NHS	National Health Service
OECD	Organisation for Economic Co-operation and Development
OFT	Office of Fair Trading
PEP	Political and Economic Planning
PIRC	Public Interest Research Centre
P. P.	Parliamentary Papers
PRO	Public Record Office
RICA	Research Institute for Consumer Affairs
RTSA	Retail Trading Standards Association
SDP	Social Democratic Party
SJC	Standing Joint Committee of Industrial Women's Organisations
TUC	Trades Union Congress
WAC	Women's Advisory Committee, BSI
WCG	Women's Co-operative Guild
WEC	War Emergency: Workers' National Committee
WI	Women's Institute
WTO	World Trade Organisation

Introduction: luxury's shadow

Consumption, consumerism, consuming, price and material culture are all crucial to our understandings of twentieth-century history. They must be accorded the same historical significance as notions of production, work, the wage and perhaps all the ideologies associated with a productivist mentality. In the final analysis, they are perhaps more important: as one recent historian of twentieth-century American commercialism put it, 'consumerism was the "ism" that won'.[1] We are all consumers now. Yet to herald the triumph and all-pervasive nature of consumer society is not to deny the diversity of consumerist visions of society and culture, as well as of the economy, the state, politics and government. Smith's adage that 'consumption is the sole end and purpose of all production' is oft repeated to remind us of the centrality of the commodity to modern life, but it actually misses its true significance.[2] Consumption has been one of the most recurring means by which citizens have moulded their political consciousness and shaped their political organisations, as well as being one of the main acts around which governments have focussed their policies and interventions. In twentieth-century Britain, the politics of consumption has offered itself as a persistent 'middle' or 'third way' solution to a party political system dominated by the interests of manufacturers and workers. This is what unites all the individuals, groups and institutions to be covered within this book, most of whom can be located under the admittedly large umbrella of social democracy and democratic socialism. Consumption has inspired an important socio-political movement over the last one hundred years, though it has not followed the same shape or trajectory as those usually associated with labour and capital.

Consumerism therefore does not simply involve the story of the success of one culture, one economy or one way of life. Consumerism is a mobilising force at the heart of twentieth-century social and political history.

---

[1] G. Cross, *An All-Consuming Century: Why Commercialism Won in Modern America* (NY, 2000), p. 1.

[2] A. Smith, *The Wealth of Nations* (1776; Chicago, 1976), vol. 2, p. 179.

1

Ideas about consumption and knowledge of prices shaped much early socialist thought. The demand for reasonably priced and good quality household necessities was central to the co-operative and labour movements. Consumer activism manifested itself in the Women's Co-operative Guild, in the Consumers' Council of the First World War, in the critique of profiteering led by the Labour Party, in the struggles for price regulation in Parliament throughout the inter-war period and in the cost-of-living campaigns within the trade union movement. Ideas about consumption and basic needs are crucial to understanding Free Trade and liberal economics, government rationing schemes and food control in two world wars, the fights for a living wage conducted principally by the Independent Labour Party, and the whole range of culturalist critiques of commerce from John Ruskin and William Morris to J. B. Priestley, F. R. Leavis and George Orwell. Though often criticised for being ineffectual, consumer representation has existed within the state infrastructure since the First World War Consumers' Council in institutions such as the Food Council, set up in 1925, and the consumer committees of the Agricultural Marketing Boards in the 1930s. Consumer consultative machinery was also established within the nationalised industries in the 1940s, and since the 1950s a whole range of government-funded consumer bodies have emerged: the Consumer Council of 1963–70, the Office of Fair Trading from 1973 and the National Consumer Council from 1975, together with direct government representation through various Ministers of Consumer Affairs. In its middle-path pragmatism, consumerism has often become the site upon which battles over new forms of citizenship and political expression have been fought. Most obviously, consumption offered the Co-operative movement a socio-political path beyond the formal institutions of the state. For women – socialist and conservative – consumption has often been the means by which they have entered political debate. For the poor, consumption has provided an alternative focus to the wage to understand the day-to-day difficulties of getting and spending. And for ambitious professionals and intellectuals, especially in the 1930s and 1950s, consumption was the point of entry for freeing the state, society and the economy from the supposedly narrow-minded stranglehold of both business and the trade unions.

If the various consumer activists in this book have sought to revise the contours of the political sphere, then so too must their actions force the historian to examine the twentieth century in a new consumerist light. When social history examined the history of the working class through political suffrage organisations and the creation of the Labour Party, it was the trade unions that were located firmly within the dynamism of change. There was good reason for such studies, especially of a movement whose membership reached over 10 million in the 1960s.[3] But organised consumers saw such membership rates too; slightly earlier, in fact, in the 1940s, as the Co-operative Union reached its zenith. Since that time, the Co-operative movement has fallen into a seemingly irreversible decline, but consumerism changed direction and the Consumers' Association came to spearhead the interests of organised consumers, its own membership peaking at over 1 million in the late 1980s.[4] Qualifications to such statistics are, of course, necessary. The vast majority of co-operators were interested only in the financial return of the dividend payment and not the utopian ideals of the Co-operative Commonwealth,[5] and many hundreds of thousands of mainly middle-class *Which?* readers, committed only to 'Best Buy' purchasing, would no doubt be surprised to learn of some of the political campaigns launched by the Consumers' Association financed by their annual subscriptions. But not all trade unionists have been committed to the lead taken by the Trades Union Congress (TUC) and not all have been Labour Party supporters either. Consumerism has its tremendous limitations as a social and political movement, in the immense gulf between the aims of its leaders and the apathy of its rank and file, and this book will cover many of them, but this is not to deny the sheer importance of the politics of purchasing suggested by the membership figures of organised consumer groups alone.

This book is an attempt to write a systematic account of these consumer movements, ideologies and official institutions in Britain. It emphasises that in the early twentieth century, the abstract monetary contents of the pay packet were only made real when they had been transferred to the purse. Wages were thought of in terms of the commodities that they could be used to purchase. The politics of industrial disputes were intricately tied in with the politics of price and the two ought not to be separated, as indeed they were not for many working-class radicals in this period of poverty. In an age of relative affluence after the Second World War, consumerism needs also to be brought centre stage. New social movements, from the Campaign for Nuclear Disarmament to Greenpeace and Amnesty, have received recognition for their tremendous impact on late twentieth-century political culture, but the apparently less radical and the less overtly ideological consumerism of the consumer groups ought also to be included here. Indeed, while its more socially and often politically respectable nature has perhaps made it less attractive to historians, its relative conservatism has enabled many of its leaders and its campaigns

[3] H. Pelling, *A History of British Trade Unionism* (1963; Harmondsworth, 1971), p. 283.
[4] Consumers' Association, *Thirty Years of 'Which?' 1957–1987* (London, 1987).
[5] P. Gurney, *Co-operative Culture and the Politics of Consumption in England, 1870–1930* (Manchester, 1996).

to have a direct impact on mainstream politics. Modern consumerism has been largely middle class, but it has also been much more than a 'minority movement' both in its impact on specific Acts of legislation and in its contribution to the development of single-issue political campaigning.[6]

Consumerism: cultural or political phenomenon?

For too long consumerism has been studied separately from politics, an implicit – and often explicit – assumption being that the two are mutually exclusive. While recent studies have shown the inherently political nature of material culture and everyday life, especially on questions of identity and social group dynamics, consumption has still received little attention in terms of its impact on politics in every sense of the term. It must be remembered that the term consumerism has several meanings. On the one hand it invokes the doctrine of continually increasing rates of consumption as the basis for a sound economy, which in turn triggers a series of cultural effects, principal among these being the absorption of social life into the world of commodities. This can be interpreted as either a positive phenomenon, in the sense that it is equated with full participation in modern society, or as a negative expression, such as it was first used in 1960 in Vance Packard's *The Waste Makers* where it was equated with excessive materialism.[7] This critique was clearly the latest manifestation of a centuries old unease with consumption, especially in its luxurious forms, but another definition of consumerism, specific to the twentieth century, captures the desire for self-empowerment expressed by consumer activists. This definition also originated in the US and refers to the campaigns to protect the interests of consumers through either comparative testing organisations such as the US Consumers' Union or the aggressive political campaigning of consumer rights advocates such as Ralph Nader, especially as embodied in his original critique of the motor industry in 1965.[8] Initially, it was a term of abuse thrown at consumer advocates by US businessmen. In 1968 Nader wrote in the *New York Review of Books*: ' "Consumerism" is a term given vogue recently by business spokesmen to describe what they believe is a concerted, disruptive ideology concocted by self-appointed bleeding hearts and politicians who find it pays off to attack the corporations. "Consumerism," they say,

[6] It is Arthur Marwick who has most recently described such US figures as Ralph Nader and Rachel Carson as the champions of what were really 'minority movements': A. Marwick, *The Sixties* (Oxford, 1998), p. 258.
[7] V. Packard, *The Waste Makers* (New York, 1960), p. iii.
[8] R. Nader, *Unsafe at any Speed: The Designed-in Dangers of the American Automobile* (NY, 1965).

undermines public confidence in the business system [and] deprives the consumer of freedom of choice . . .'[9] Subsequently, the term came to be used more positively, by the consumer movement itself, as it began to notice a series of campaigning successes in the early 1970s. Today, however, these political and critical elements associated with the campaigning side of consumerism are rarely suggested in the use of the term, perhaps in a classic example of containment at the linguistic level, as consumerism becomes a mere category of description for an increasingly commodified culture, which only suffers a mild sense of rebuke by the employment of the term.

As a history of organised consumer movements and consumer politics, this book is an attempt to re-politicise consumerism, both as a category of analysis and a field of historical study. Consumerism is thus recognised as a movement, a part of consumer society which consumers themselves have been actively involved in making. But the political dimensions of the term need to be expanded to incorporate not only the consumer movements associated with comparative testing in an age of affluence, but also the fight for basic needs in an age of poverty. Consumerism thus includes discussions of bread and butter, as it does assessments of cars and kettles. The two socio-political movements of consumer poverty and consumer affluence may seem worlds apart, but as will be seen, there have been important crossovers between the two which now, in a global political environment, are once again coming together.

The division between politics and consumption manifests itself in the scholarship on late modern Britain, where consumer society is studied according to often arbitrary disciplinary divisions between economic, social and cultural history. There are economic accounts of the mass market, social accounts of class and consumer society and culturalist interpretations of advertising and marketing, studies of the material culture of single commodities and some well-researched but ultimately exaggerated interpretations of the importance of the department store.[10] While these divisions between the sub-specialisms of consumption are now less

---

[9] Quoted in R. Swagler, 'Evolution and applications of the term consumerism: themes and variations', *Journal of Consumer Affairs*, 28:2 (1994), 350. For other definitions see the Oxford English Dictionary; D. A. Aaker and G. S. Day (eds.), *Consumerism: Search for the Consumer Interest*, 3rd edn (Basingstoke, 1978), p. 2; Y. Gabriel and T. Lang, *The Unmanageable Consumer: Contemporary Consumption and its Fragmentation* (London, 1995), pp. 7–9.

[10] Contrast, for instance, the approaches found in L. A. Loeb, *Consuming Angels: Advertising and Victorian Women* (Oxford, 1994); T. Richards, *The Commodity Culture of Victorian England: Advertising and Spectacle, 1851–1914* (London, 1991); W. H. Fraser, *The Coming of the Mass Market, 1850–1914* (Basingstoke, 1981); J. Benson, *The Rise of Consumer Society in Britain, 1880–1980* (London, 1994); E. Rappaport, *Shopping for Pleasure* (Princeton, 2000). The literature on department stores is often impressive, though

.pparent, together they share the absence of a sustained and detailed treatment of the interaction of consumption with the political sphere, understood in all its possible meanings. The peculiarity of this situation must be made clear, since work on the eighteenth century does not share this problem. Consumption here has been shown to be central to discussions of gender, to cultural critiques of luxury, the rise of the bourgeoisie, the development of the modern nation state, the emergence of political economy and the commercialised marketplace, the end of both aristocratic clientage and the moral economy, and the development of modern subjectivities through the categorisation of individuals as consumers.[11] Likewise, studies of consumer society in America, perhaps coming out of an academic arena in which the intellectual left does not share quite the same ascetic disdain for commodity culture as its European counterparts, has produced works demonstrating the richness and varied nature of consumerism. In a country where material abundance has frequently been equated with nationhood and citizenship, it is no surprise to discover that labour activists were as concerned with what wages were spent on as to how they were earned.[12] And following such traditions, social historians have perhaps been more willing to see how consumption can become a site for grass-roots political activity. Dana Frank has argued that 'consumer tactics have been at the core of the labour movement in all periods of US history', her case study in Seattle showing how trade unions politicised consumption 'through boycotts, co-operatives, labour-owned businesses and promotion of the union label and shop card'.[13]

even here leading scholars doubt the significance of their own subject: G. Crossick and S. Jaumain (eds.), *Cathedrals of Consumption: The European Department Store, 1850–1939* (Aldershot, 1999); L. Tiersten, 'Redefining consuming culture: recent literature on consumption and the bourgeoisie in Western Europe', *Radical History Review*, 57 (1993), 116–59.

[11] J. Brewer, 'Commercialisation and politics', in N. McKendrick, J. Brewer and J. H. Plumb, *The Birth of a Consumer Society: The Commercialisation of Eighteenth-Century England* (London, 1982); M. Berg and H. Clifford (eds.), *Consumers and Luxury: Consumer Culture in Europe, 1650–1850* (Manchester, 1999); J. Brewer and R. Porter (eds.), *Consumption and the World of Goods* (London, 1993); A. Bermingham and J. Brewer (eds.), *The Consumption of Culture 1600–1800: Image, Object, Text* (London, 1995); D. Winch, *Riches and Poverty: An Intellectual History of Political Economy in Britain, 1750–1834* (Cambridge, 1996); J. Brewer, *The Pleasures of the Imagination: English Culture in the Eighteenth Century* (London, 1997).

[12] L. B. Glickman, *A Living Wage: American Workers and the Making of Consumer Society* (Ithaca, 1997); L. B. Glickman, 'Workers of the world, consume: Ira Steward and the origins of labor consumerism', *International Labor and Working Class History*, 52 (1997), 72–86; C. McGovern, 'Consumption and citizenship in the United States, 1900–1940', in S. Strasser, C. McGovern and M. Judt (eds.), *Getting and Spending: European and American Consumer Societies in the Twentieth Century* (Cambridge, 1998), pp. 37–58.

[13] D. Frank, *Purchasing Power: Consumer Organising, Gender, and the Seattle Labour Movement, 1919–1929* (Cambridge, 1994), pp. 4–5.

Likewise, Lizabeth Cohen's inter-war Chicago workers had a far more nuanced relationship with consumption and mass culture than one of denial in the pursuit of the appropriation of the means of production.[14] Studies of ethnicity have demonstrated the varied forms of consumerism, for some immigrant groups consumption enabling assimilation into the American dream, while for others the boycotting of certain goods and stores served as a rallying point for civil rights, such as black Americans' 'Don't buy where you can't work' campaigns.[15] In 1993 Jean-Christophe Agnew called for consumption history to be combined with social and political history, especially since 'a far-reaching ideological redefinition of polity and society did begin to take hold during the 1930s and 1940s: the promotion of the social contract of cold-war liberalism, which is to say a state-sponsored guarantee of private consumption'.[16] Recently, other historians have begun to develop this argument, pointing to the implications for citizenship when politics imagined the consumer interest purely in terms of private, individual or family-based acquisitiveness. At the same time, though, historians have also uncovered consumer-citizenship promoted, for example, during the Progressive and the New Deal eras.[17]

It is through such studies that we can reach a better understanding of both consumer society and consumerism and which embraces both positive and negative attitudes to the world of goods. An older literature, if not always outrightly condemning consumer culture, did believe that the twentieth-century shift from a producer to a consumer mentality resulted in a decline in class politics: 'many who might have chosen the socialist way went instead with the hope of the culture of abundance'.[18] Consumers were not necessarily to blame for this decision, since they

---

[14] L. Cohen, *Making a New Deal: Industrial Workers in Chicago, 1919–1939* (Cambridge, 1990).

[15] A. Heinze, *Adapting to Abundance: Jewish Immigrants, Mass Consumption and the Search for American Identity* (NY, 1990); C. Greenberg, *Or Does it Explode? Black Harlem in the Great Depression* (Oxford, 1997).

[16] J-C. Agnew, 'Coming up for air: consumer culture in historical perspective', in Brewer and Porter (eds.), *Consumption*, p. 32. See also W. Susman, *Culture as History: The Transformation of American Society in the Twentieth Century* (NY, 1984).

[17] Cross, *All-Consuming Century*; L. Cohen, 'Citizens and consumers in the United States in the century of mass consumption', and M. Jacobs, 'The politics of plenty: consumerism in the twentieth-century United States', in M. Daunton and M. Hilton (eds.), *The Politics of Consumption: Material Culture and Citizenship in Europe and America* (Oxford, 2001), pp. 203–21, 223–39; M. Jacobs, ' "How about some meat?": the Office of Price Administration, consumption politics, and state-building from the bottom up, 1941–1946', *Journal of American History*, 84:3 (1997), 910–41.

[18] W. Susman, quoted in R. W. Edsforth, *Class Conflict and Cultural Consensus: The Making of a Mass Consumer Society in Flint, Michigan* (New Brunswick, 1987), p. 224. See also T. J. Lears, 'From salvation to self-realisation: advertising and the therapeutic roots of the consumer culture, 1880–1930', in R. W. Fox and T. J. Lears (eds.), *The Culture of Consumption: Critical Essays in American History, 1880–1920* (NY, 1983), pp. 1–38;

had in any case been manipulated by advertising and the mass media, according to a body of opinion shared by both marxists and the liberal left.[19] If this was seen as too crude a denial of human agency, consumption scholars then began to find everywhere diversity within the mass, and the ability of consumers to appropriate, mediate and reject the dominant meanings of goods: denim jeans became a favourite example of the creative imaginary canvas that had become clothing and material culture.[20] Similarly, an early postmodern scholarship which had pointed to the self-referential 'logic of signs' within which consumers were as embroiled as the commercial images themselves, developed into an emphasis on the *bricoleur*, the consumer who could forever play out, adapt and experiment with the signs and imagery of commodity capitalism.[21] Influential here was the work of Michel de Certeau, whose expression *poiësis* referred to the moment of active re-creation, to the ways of using products, to the strategies and tactics of resistance in which consumption itself becomes a form of cultural production.[22] It is not difficult to see the attraction of such theoretical frameworks. In a modernist scholarship that positions the consumer as either the entirely free agent of the neo-liberal market or the passive dupe of the overly deterministic structures of capitalism, postmodern pastiche and poaching offer a genuine sense of liberation through the exploration of alternative lifestyles and subaltern identities. This has been either through the breaking down of existing boundaries or through the anti-hierarchical values implicit in much consumer appropriation of commodity meanings.[23]

T. J. Lears, *Fables of Abundance: A Cultural History of Advertising in America* (NY, 1994). And for the seminal Frankfurt School formulation: M. Horkheimer and T. Adorno, *Dialectic of Enlightenment* (1944; London, 1973), pp. 120–67. See also A. Gorz, 'Work and consumption', in P. Anderson and R. Blackburn (eds.), *Towards Socialism* (London, 1965), pp. 317–53.

[19] For two exemplary accounts see V. Packard, *The Hidden Persuaders* (1957; Harmondsworth, 1960); S. Ewen, *Captains of Consciousness: Advertising and the Social Roots of the Consumer Culture* (NY, 1976).

[20] R. Laermans, 'Learning to consume: early department stores and the shaping of modern consumer culture, 1860–1914', *Theory, Culture and Society*, 10 (1993), 79–102; J. Fiske, *Understanding Popular Culture* (Boston, MA, 1989).

[21] J. Baudrillard, 'Consumer society', in M. Poster (ed.), *Jean Baudrillard: Selected Writings* (Oxford, 1988), pp. 29–56; J. Baudrillard, *The Consumer Society: Myths and Structures* (London, 1998); F. Jameson, 'Postmodernism and consumer society', in H. Foster (ed.), *Postmodern Culture* (London, 1985). For good accounts of these intellectual developments see R. Bocock, *Consumption* (London, 1993); M. Featherstone, *Consumer Culture and Postmodernism* (London, 1991); C. Lury, *Consumer Culture* (Oxford, 1996); D. Slater, *Consumer Culture and Modernity* (Oxford, 1997).

[22] M. de Certeau, *The Practice of Everyday Life* (London, 1984); M. Poster, 'The question of agency: Michel de Certeau and the history of consumerism', *Diacritics* (Summer 1992), 94–107.

[23] S. Lash and J. Urry, *The End of Organised Capitalism* (Cambridge, 1987), p. 15.

Introduction 9

Two problems with this approach have quickly become apparent. Firstly, many of these consumer strategies are inner-directed: 'consumption for the presentation of the self has the self as a primary audience in modern times'.[24] Without wishing to deny the importance of constructing self-identities in an increasingly globalised and distant world,[25] for many this focus on the self has resulted only in intellectual exasperation. Naomi Klein has recently argued that her turn towards anti-corporatism and the economics of globalisation was a direct consequence of her frustration with the narrow focus of the identity politics of the late 1980s and early 1990s.[26] Secondly, it has been suggested that in response to the manipulation thesis, academics have come to celebrate any act of appropriation by consumers, even among the most oppressed groups, thereby suggesting that consumer empowerment is available for all: 'the triumph of the will of the consumer can overcome any scarcity, where budget constraints don't exist (and where love never dies)'.[27] For Daniel Miller, postmodern critics have performed a similar feat as the neo-liberal economists: that is, they have created a 'virtual' consumer who bears little or no relation to the realities of consumers' everyday lives.[28] The consequence of this can only be that the account of consumer behaviour loses its critical objective, consumption scholars championing the freedom of the creative consumer in a manner similar to that which business leaders and marketing experts have been doing for decades. More generally, Richard Hoggart has bemoaned the fate of cultural studies as it has abandoned many of its founding conceptual frameworks, but Thomas Frank takes the attack much further.[29] He suggests that with both business and cultural studies communities there was 'a populist celebration of the power and "agency" of audiences and fans, of their ability to evade the grasp of the makers of mass culture, and of their talent for transforming just about any bit of cultural detritus into an implementation of rebellion'.[30] This ideological convergence has enabled many former hippies and counter-cultural innovators to become leading acolytes of the new economy, while some cultural studies scholars, claims Frank, are happy to leave the academic

[24] J. Friedman, 'Introduction', in J. Friedman (ed.), *Consumption and Identity* (London, 1994), p. 10.
[25] A. Giddens, *Modernity and Self-identity: Self and Society in the Late Modern Age* (Cambridge, 1991), p. 5.
[26] N. Klein, *No Logo* (London, 2000), p. xix.
[27] J. de Vries, 'The industrial revolution and the industrious revolution', *Journal of Economic History*, 54:2 (1994), 255; Cross, *All-Consuming Century*, p. 240.
[28] D. Miller, 'Conclusion: a theory of virtualism', in J. G. Carrier and D. Miller (eds.), *Virtualism: A New Political Economy* (Oxford, 1998), pp. 187–215.
[29] R. Hoggart, *The Way We Live Now* (London, 1995).
[30] T. Frank, *One Market Under God: Extreme Capitalism, Market Populism and the End of Economic Democracy* (London, 2001), p. 282.

arena and write for what he sees as business-sponsored neo-liberal publications.[31] Because the personal was political for the 1968 generation, it opened up every aspect of individual behaviour to intellectual scrutiny. While there was a clear radicalism to such an enterprise in the focus on the individual, wider political structures were too often taken for granted or simply ignored.

In terms of the future development of consumption studies, more likely is it that there will be a turn away from purely cultural accounts as scholars consider the wider economic and political issues concerned with consumer society – shifts which might be seen as part of a wider 'institutional turn' identified within recent scholarship.[32] This implies a turn away from the humanist explorations of 'the social life of things', but it is clearly a move which many consumers themselves are demanding. It is significant that one book pilloried as the epitome of the manipulationist school, Stuart Ewen's *Captains of Consciousness*, has now been re-issued twenty-five years after it first came out, its anti-advertising critique perhaps appealing to a new generation of students. Ewen's publishers must have been encouraged by a new trend to re-question the limits of consumption. Juliet Schor asks *Do Americans Shop Too Much?*, Daniel Miller urges the consumer and the housewife to make 'consumption the vanguard of history', artists seek to break down the informational barriers between developing world production and western consumption, while economists and sociologists seek to explore alternative frameworks to control the economy.[33] It is as though the older agendas of J. K. Galbraith, Vance Packard, Rachel Carson and Ralph Nader are enjoying a new fashionability, perhaps spurred on by the anti-corporate exposés of Naomi Klein and George Monbiot, together with the headline-grabbing activities of such organisations as Adbusters.[34]

If not yet in the academic field, consumption is being re-politicised by a new generation of activists who are taking on board conceptual

[31] 'Agency, that cult-stud staple, was recast by *Reason* into the silver bullet of corporate defence': *ibid.*, p. 299. Frank's favourite villain is the anthropologist Grant McCracken, author of *Culture and Consumption: New Approaches to the Symbolic Character of Consumer Goods and Activities* (Bloomington, 1988).

[32] B. Jessop, 'Institutional re(turns) and the strategic-relational approach', *Environment and Planning A*, 33 (2001), 1213–35.

[33] Schor, J. B., *Do Americans Shop Too Much?*, Boston, MA, 2000; D. Miller, 'Consumption as the vanguard of history: a polemic by way of an introduction', in D. Miller (ed.), *Acknowledging Consumption: A Review of New Studies* (London, 1995), pp. 1–57; I. Cook, 'Social sculpture and connective aesthetics: Shelley Sacks' "Exchange Values"', *Ecumene: A Journal of Cultural Geographies*, 7:3 (2001), 338–44; N. Goodwin, F. Ackerman and D. Kiron (eds.), *The Consumer Society* (Washington, DC, 1997).

[34] Klein, *No Logo*; G. Monbiot, *The Captive State: The Corporate Takeover of Britain* (London, 2000); K. Lasn, *Culture Jam: The Uncooling of America* (NY, 1999).

frameworks that an older collection of scholars was surprised to have seen disappear in the first place. Yet in the search for a new politics of consumption or a new agenda for radical consumers to follow, there is much that remains missing. In a recent criticism of the lack of imagination of the political Left, David Harvey has employed Gramsci's expression, 'pessimism of the intellect and optimism of the will' to describe the failure to find a real theoretical alternative to the free market.[35] Instead, and extending Harvey's use of Gramsci's phrase, we see in the new anti-globalisation movement a site for the projected hopes of various writers. Thus, Klein's *No Logo* does not offer a 'manifesto for the global age' as its ridiculous publicity suggests and Monbiot provides only an extremely weak response to 'the corporate takeover of Britain'.[36] Elsewhere, anti-consumerists have resorted to older Situationist techniques of subversion and the celebration of the absurd. These are potentially powerful attacks but they ought also to be seen as distinct from the positive instruments for the construction of alternatives. Yet, such fingers-crossed critiques pervade the writing on the subject. Firat and Dholakia suggest that the diversity of lifestyles thrown up in the plurality of postmodernity will lead to a 'theatre of consumption' creating new sites of non-confrontational resistance which will eventually replace the nation state.[37] It is all incredibly vague as to how this will happen, just as current consumer and anti-consumer activists continue to focus, sometimes successfully, on the specifics of single issues, without ever creating, or perhaps even desiring, a theory of general action or an idea of the ends beyond the means.

It is unlikely that anybody will ever produce a coherent consumerist agenda or ideology that can unite all consumers behind a political cause. Yet it is clear that throughout the twentieth century there has been a persistent and ever-apparent consumer consciousness. The consumer might never have been made, in the same sense that an earlier generation of social historians argued a working class was made, but it does not follow that all must necessarily adopt the same consuming ideology. 'The search for a historical movement' of this book's title is therefore important. It refers to both the efforts of historians to locate the politics of consumption within a specific set of social contexts and the attempts of consumers themselves to establish a third political force. If it is the case that our consuming identities are eclipsing other forms of selfhood as many argue, then it must follow that consumption will eventually find political as well as cultural expression. For some, this has enabled a deliberately

---

[35] D. Harvey, *Spaces of Hope* (Edinburgh, 2000), p. 17.
[36] Monbiot, *Captive State*, p. 360.
[37] A. F. Firat and N. Dholakia, *Consuming People: From Political Economy to Theaters of Consumption* (London, 1998).

'semi-utopian' agenda to emerge to do to consumption what socialism did for class and to place the consumer at the forefront of historical change. This masks the potential for division as well as unity in consumerism but it at least opens up the field of historical inquiry to include those instances when consumers have attempted to form a socio-political movement for themselves. It also imposes an impossible test upon their actions but which many consumer activists were happy to set themselves. Whether co-operator or comparative goods tester, many have believed they were developing a historical movement as potentially significant as socialism, trade unionism or any of the other ideologies traditionally associated with the Left. Their use of a rhetoric of a third or a middle way throughout the twentieth century makes clear their attempts to shift the nature of political debate away from the worker and towards the consumer.

Such strict and ambitious criteria for the existence of a historical movement suggests a narrative of failure as consumerism as activism has not replaced other political allegiances. But this is due to a central dilemma of which consumer groups themselves have been all too aware: that is, the consumer can always be everybody and yet nobody and consumption can always be everything and yet nothing. Especially when consumption is loosely and lazily interpreted as material culture, there is no end to its applicability. And notions of the consumer that stretch beyond either the shopper or the economic agent of commodity purchasing can quickly dilute so that commentators might find the more traditional political terms of voter or citizen more useful, with appeals being made to the public, rather than the consumer. When a political meaning or social relation does become embodied within a particular example of material culture, its very solidity, to borrow an expression, soon melts into air once one attempts to generalise to a wider class of goods or persons. But in terms of the history of consumerism, this is both the beauty and the dissatisfaction of the subject. While it evades a totalising narrative other than that found in economic theory (though even here this has always been strongly contested[38]), it is at least constantly re-shaped and re-invigorated through the diverse associations produced in the everyday interactions people have with goods, either within or beyond the marketplace. Consumerism is therefore like a kaleidoscope in the sense that its shape is never final and is always malleable yet unpredictable. It never fulfils the promise it always threatens to provide, but through its potential universal

---

[38] For some of the most sustained attacks on the notion of consumption and the consumer in economic theory see B. Fine, 'The triumph of economics; or, 'rationality' can be dangerous to your reasoning', in Carrier and Miller (eds.), *Virtualism*, pp. 49–73; *idem*, 'From political economy to consumption', in Miller (ed.), *Acknowledging Consumption*, pp. 127–63; B. Fine and E. Leopold, *The World of Consumption* (London, 1993).

scope, is always reinvigorated, creating new shapes, patterns and dynamics. It contains within it one of the central paradoxes within the history of modern consumer society. It can see its agendas slip from the profound to the trivial and its relevance to other political debates from the centre to the periphery. Consumption is the site for some of the richest political developments ever seen, yet the resultant inclusive rhetoric of consumption can often be empty and devoid of anything tangible.

This ambiguous approach to consumption is, nevertheless, more satisfactory than the assumptions of coherence imposed on earlier identifications of consumer consciousness. In 1971, E. P. Thompson saw a 'highly-sensitive consumer-consciousness' in the eighteenth-century 'moral economy' of the common weal: there was 'a popular consensus as to what were legitimate and what were illegitimate practices in marketing, milling, baking, etc. This in its turn was grounded upon a consistent traditional view of social norms and obligations, of the proper economic functions of several parties within the community, which, taken together, can be said to constitute the moral economy of the poor.'[39] Famously, this consumerism of necessity was said to have been replaced by an emerging political economy, though Thompson claimed it lingered on, particularly in the 'bowels' of the Co-operative movement. While focus on the institutions, state bodies and consumer groups of the twentieth century appears to lack the same empathetic concern with the lives of the ordinary man and woman found in the Thompsonian tradition it does not impose upon them a uni-dimensional political outlook. The quantity and richness of the sources for the late-modernist enables instead an uncovering of the diversity of consumer beliefs and actions. And following the criticisms of the original moral economy position – that too sharp a distinction has been made from political economy – greater attention can be paid to consumers' 'pragmatic economy', 'in which both rioters and magistrates acted with an eye to political calculation and experience, rather than hoary traditions'.[40] For, despite all the emphasis on the overhaul of existing political divisions found in much third force rhetoric, consumer advocates have consistently taken a pragmatic attitude to their relationship to the market. They have eschewed ideological proscription and explored varied solutions to perceived market failures. Consumer politics has been most

---

[39] E. P. Thompson, 'The moral economy of the English crowd in the eighteenth century', *Past & Present*, 50 (1971), 79.

[40] J. Bohstedt, 'The pragmatic economy, the politics of provisions and the "invention" of the food riot tradition in 1740', in A. J. Randall and A. Charlesworth (eds.), *The Moral Economy and Popular Protest: Crowds, Conflict and Authority* (Basingstoke, 2000), p. 55; I. Hont and M. Ignatieff, 'Needs and justice in *The Wealth of Nations*', in I. Hont and M. Ignatieff (eds.), *Wealth and Virtue* (Cambridge, 1983).

successful when, on the one hand, it has turned away from idealistic generalisations of the potential of the consumer and yet, on the other, has pitched itself at a level of abstraction above immediate practical concerns. It has therefore enabled intellectual links to be made between a range of single issue campaigns in a sufficiently adaptable worldview which has enabled consumerism to draw strength from the very number of specific concerns that can refuel and change the direction of an admittedly amorphous movement.

Luxury's shadow

In part, many of these contradictions reflect the debates over the relationship between consumption and the individual in modern liberal societies. To what extent is the individual free to make up his or her mind about what he or she can consume, or to what extent should the state intervene to determine and structure these decisions? It is a problem which many commentators have experienced considerable difficulty in steering an immense middle-ground somewhere between outright libertarianism and Stalinist proscription. In addition, if the consumer is to bear in mind politics, morality, ethics, culture – anything that is more than that which is ascribed to the utility maximiser of economic theory – then how far should these duties extend? How much responsibility ought to be expected of the individual in the exercise of his or her consuming duties and how much should the state seek to protect the rights of the collective mass of all consumers? The debate in part can never be resolved because of the dichotomous way in which discussions of consumption have been framed – we speak in terms of the binary dualisms between rights and duties, luxury and necessity, use and abuse, productive and unproductive, moderation and excess. Ultimately, we are forced into a choice between ethical absolutism or cultural relativism. We cannot make that choice at an overall level and yet if we also admit to the problem – as Bernard Mandeville did in the eighteenth century when he suggested that the private vices of individual consumption led to the public benefit of economic growth – then we stand condemned too for our moral passivity.[41]

In one sense, then, the debates over luxury which scholars have associated with the eighteenth century have cast a long shadow over subsequent periods, such that consumption today is still firmly located within a moral sphere. This is hardly surprising given the perennial problematisation of commerce that stretches as far back as Plato's worries over the lawless amusements of Athenian youth, the proscriptions over virtuous,

[41] B. Mandeville, *The Fable of the Bees* (NY, 1962).

non-covetous consumption found in St Paul's letters and the medieval development of sumptuary legislation across Europe, culminating in England in the 1563 Statute of Artificers.[42] With the proliferation of commodities throughout the early modern period, the critique against luxurious spending reached new heights in the pages of the *Tatler* and the *Spectator*, so that even Smith, usually held to have solved the Mandevillian paradox, maintained a personal disdain for the 'baubles' and 'trinkets' of commerce.[43] If we add a nonconformist conscience, then the vice and virtue of eighteenth-century luxury become the use and abuse, productive and unproductive, respectable and unrespectable of nineteenth-century liberalism. While early socialist writers such as William Thompson kept up the critique of the foibles of the rich who consequently steered production away from the manufacture of necessitous goods, John Stuart Mill performed the most thorough investigation of the terms productive and unproductive which Smith had formerly only applied to labour.[44] Mill defined consumption and wealth purely in economic terms, only to then overlay them with a moral condemnation of specific goods – in his case, gold lace, pineapples and champagne – which were held to contribute nothing to the production of wealth, being 'directly and exclusively for the purpose of enjoyment'.[45] Alfred Marshall would later admit to a less dogmatic attitude to consumption, accepting the need for social necessities and habitual comforts, but the polarised language surrounding commodities was apparent through a whole host of Victorian

---

[42] Plato, *The Republic* (Harmondsworth, 1955), p. 167; *Romans*, 13:12–14; J. Sekora, *Luxury: The Concept in Western Thought, Eden to Smollett* (London, 1977); C. Berry, *The Idea of Luxury: A Conceptual and Historical Investigation* (Cambridge, 1994).

[43] C. Shammas, *The Pre-Industrial Consumer in England and America* (Oxford, 1990); L. Weatherill, *Consumer Behaviour and Material Culture in Britain, 1660–1760* (London, 1988); E. Mackie (ed.), *The Commerce of Everyday Life: Selections from 'The Tatler' and 'The Spectator'* (Boston, MA, 1998); Winch, *Riches and Poverty;* P. Langford, *A Polite and Commercial People: England, 1727–1783* (Oxford, 1989); L. Klein, *Shaftesbury and the Culture of Politeness: Moral Discourse and Cultural Politics in Early Eighteenth-Century England* (Cambridge, 1994); J. Appleby, 'Consumption in early modern social thought', in Brewer and Porter (eds.), *Consumption*, pp. 162–73; N. de Marchi, 'Adam Smith's accommodation of "altogether endless" desires', in Berg and Clifford (eds.), *Consumers and Luxury*, pp. 18–36.

[44] W. Thompson, *An Inquiry into the Principles of the Distribution of Wealth most Conducive to Human Happiness* (London, 1824), pp. 183–203; N. Thompson, 'Social opulence, private asceticism: ideas of consumption in early socialist thought', in Daunton and Hilton (eds.), *Politics of Consumption*, pp. 53–4; J. S. Mill, *Principles of Political Economy, with Some of Their Applications to Social Philosophy* (1852; London, 1968), vol. 1, p. 64.

[45] J. S. Mill, 'III. Of the words productive and unproductive', in *Essays on some Unsettled Questions of Political Economy* (London, 1992), pp. 84–6. See also the essay, 'II. Of the influence of consumption on production', in the same volume, pp. 47–74; S. Hollander, *The Economics of John Stuart Mill, Volume 1: Theory and Method* (Oxford, 1985), pp. 264–72.

institutions[46]: in the Society for the Suppression of Vice and the Society for the Reformation of Manners; in the campaigns to ban cruel sports and popular festivities; in the rational recreation movement including the establishment of municipal parks and libraries and Henry Solly's Working Men's Club and Institute Union; in the codes of behaviour dictated by the popularly held notions of working-class respectability; in the campaigns against drinking, gambling and smoking; and in the literature surrounding 'self-help' with the Smilesian encouragement of discipline, patience, perseverance, moderation, providence, sacrifice, self-denial, honour, independence, economy, frugality, thrift, industry, honesty, prudence, forethought, self-respect and regularity.[47]

Liberalism's dichotomous attitude to consumption extended too to the rational and irrational, giving rise to a whole host of critiques of consumer society, with the masses being alleged to lack the necessary skills of discrimination to make clear, independent choices. The condemnation of the mass man has straddled the political and intellectual divide and has included within it the notions of irrationality ascribed to the crowd by Freud, Nietzsche and Spengler, the hatred of suburbia by the likes of H. G. Wells, D. H. Lawrence and Virginia Woolf, the contempt for the whims and excesses of fashion found in Veblen's *Theory of the Leisure Class* and the broad-ranging indictment of J. B. Priestley's 'admass' culture which 'you have to be half-witted or half-drunk all the time to endure'.[48] Contempt for Babbitt, Mickey Mouse and the cinema runs

[46] A. Marshall, *Principles of Economics* (1890; London, 1961); D. Reisman, *The Economics of Alfred Marshall* (London, 1986).

[47] G. Searle, *Morality and the Market in Victorian Britain* (Oxford, 1998); E. P. Thompson, 'Time, work discipline and industrial capitalism', *Past & Present*, 38 (1967), 59–91; R. W. Malcolmson, *Popular Recreations in English Society, 1700–1850* (Cambridge, 1973); J. M. Golby and A. W. Purdue, *The Civilisation of the Crowd: Popular Culture in England 1750–1900* (London, 1984); P. Bailey, *Leisure and Class in Victorian England: Rational Recreation and the Contest for Social Control* (London, 1978); H. Cunningham, *Leisure in the Industrial Revolution c.1780–c.1880* (London, 1980); M. Clapson, *A Bit of a Flutter: Popular Gambling and English Society, c.1823–1961* (Manchester, 1992); T. W. Laqueur, *Religion and Respectability: Sunday Schools and Working-Class Culture, 1780–1850* (New Haven, 1976); B. Hilton, *The Age of Atonement: The Influence of Evangelicalism on Social and Economic Thought* (Oxford, 1988); B. Harrison, *Peaceable Kingdom: Stability and Change in Modern Britain* (Oxford, 1982); F. M. L. Thompson, *The Rise of Respectable Society: A Social History of Victorian Britain, 1830–1900* (London, 1988); S. Smiles, *Self-Help* (1859; London, 1929); B. Harrison, *Drink and the Victorians: The Temperance Question in England, 1815–1872* (Keele, 1994); M. Hilton, *Smoking in British Popular Culture, 1800–2000* (Manchester, 2000).

[48] J. B. Priestley and J. Hawkes, *Journey Down a Rainbow* (London, 1957), pp. 43–4; G. Cross, *Time and Money: The Making of Consumer Culture* (London, 1993); T. Veblen, *The Theory of the Leisure Class* (1899; Harmondsworth, 1979); J. Carey, *The Intellectuals and the Masses: Pride and Prejudice Among the Literary Intelligentsia, 1880–1939* (London, 1992); D. L. LeMahieu, *A Culture for Democracy: Mass Communication and the*

through the pompous, proud, blinkered and self-congratulatory reviews of F. R. Leavis, Denys Thompson, D. W. Harding and L. C. Knights in the elitist pages of *Scrutiny*, while the response of the Left, or at least R. H. Tawney and Sidney and Beatrice Webb, was an ascetic, if not downright miserable, retreat from the life of material abundance. Indeed, George Orwell positively goaded socialists to accept 'that Socialism is a *better* way of life but not necessarily, in its first stages, a more comfortable one'.[49] In all of this the legacy of Ruskin and Morris has loomed large as the traditional critique of luxury came to be applied instead to the 'shabby gentilities' of the mass market.[50] This unease with luxury, though, should not be associated solely with the Left. Specific acts of consumption have continued to attract moral censure, be it in the 1920s with the discourses against cinemagoing and the fear of the flapper, through to a whole host of 'respectable fears' and 'moral panics' of the latter half of the twentieth century in which the tabloid media has, in turn, railed against the mods, rockers and punks.[51] Added to this is the increasingly health-conscious atmosphere of late-twentieth century life which has brought to morality an empowered medical and scientific authority against goods as diverse as tobacco, mobile phones, fast food and Ecstasy. Casting aside for the moment the validity or quality of the arguments against the particular

Cultivated Mind in Britain between the Wars (Oxford, 1988); D. Horowitz, *The Morality of Spending: Attitudes Towards the Consumer Society in America 1875–1940* (Baltimore, 1985); T. J. Lears, *No Place of Grace: Antimodernism and the Transformation of American Culture, 1880–1920* (Chicago, 1994).

[49] G. Orwell, 'London letter to *Partisan Review*', 15 August 1945, in S. Orwell and I. Angus (eds.), *The Collected Essays, Journalism and Letters of George Orwell, Volume 3: As I Please, 1943–1945* (Harmondsworth, 1970), p. 450; F. R. Leavis, *Mass Civilisation and Minority Culture* (Cambridge, 1930); M. Cole (ed.), *The Webbs and Their Work* (London, 1949); R. H. Tawney, *The Acquisitive Society* (1921; London, 1945); J. Tomlinson, 'The limits of Tawney's ethical socialism: a historical perspective on the Labour Party and the Market', *Contemporary British History*, 16:4 (2002), 1–16.

[50] J. Ruskin, *Munera Pulveris: Six Essays on the Elements of Political Economy* (1862–1863), in E. T. Cook and A. Wedderburn (eds.), *The Works of John Ruskin* (London, 1903– 12); J. Ruskin, *Sesame and Lilies* (1864; London, 1907); J. Ruskin, *Unto This Last: Four Essays on the First Principles of Political Economy* (1862; London, 1898); W. Morris, *News from Nowhere* (1890; London, 1970); A. Briggs (ed.), *William Morris: Selected Writings and Designs* (1962; Harmondsworth, 1977); N. Thompson, *The Market and its Critics: Socialist Political Economy in the Nineteenth Century* (London, 1998).

[51] K. Williams, *Get Me a Murder a Day! A History of Mass Communication in Britain* (London, 1998); J. Richards, *The Age of the Dream Palace: Cinema and Society in Britain, 1930–1939* (London, 1984); P. Miles and M. Smith, *Cinema, Literature and Society: Elite and Mass Culture in Inter-War Britain* (London, 1987); B. Melman, *Women and the Popular Imagination in the Twenties: Flappers and Nymphs* (NY, 1988); S. Cohen, *Folk Devils and Moral Panics: The Creation of Mods and Rockers* (London, 1972); S. Hall and T. Jefferson (eds.), *Resistance Through Rituals: Youth Subcultures in Post-War Britain* (London, 1976); T. Parssinen, *Secret Passions, Secret Remedies: Narcotic Drugs in British Society, 1820– 1930* (Manchester, 1983); M. Kohn, *Dope Girls: The Birth of the British Drug Underworld* (London, 1992).

vice, it is both clear that notions of luxury – social, cultural, moral, spiritual or psychological – continue to impinge on the freedom of neo-liberal economic man while consumption will never be free of its associations with taking away, eating up and wasting.[52]

In reaction to such moralising discourses, postmodernism has striven to subvert what it sees as the dichotomous hierarchies of modernity – self–other, ruler–ruled, black–white, rational–irrational, masculine–feminine, consumer–producer – in an attempt to free up subaltern voices. We might apply such a critique to consumerism as well, so that we no longer speak of manipulation versus agency, or expect the consumer to think in terms of rights and duties in every purchasing decision made. Consumerism would therefore recognise that the consuming body is imbricated in wider systems of power and thus consumer citizenship comes neither through informed individual purchasing nor through direct state prohibition or promotion. Instead, the duties often expected of a consumer who buys a good manufactured in the non-western world are not purely located in the direct act of purchasing, but in the other arenas of citizenship – the media, politics, protest, education and in the movement and presentation of self in everyday life – within which consumption is now intricately bound up. But consumer activists themselves have been dealing with these issues for several decades and have been offering varied solutions to the questions of citizenship, the role of the state, consumer rights and duties, the influence of the market and the gendered constructions of imaginary divisions between the public and the private. In the institutional solutions to the paradoxes of consumer society, we can trace a history of third force politics which lie between trade unions and employers, the state and the market, socialism and capitalism, modernism and postmodernism. Prior to the Second World War, the consumers' Co-operative movement attempted to build the Co-operative Commonwealth beyond the interference of business and government and according to a system that made the individual and collective good seem theoretically indistinguishable. In the latter half of the twentieth century, consumer activists sought to rectify the perceived inequities in the relationship between the seller and the buyer. As the structural problems of the state and the marketplace became more widely debated and understood many consumer activists turned to social democratic ideals to escape what were seen as the 'stagnant' politics of trade unions versus employers, collectivism versus individualism. The dualisms central to modern political consciousness have shaped the historical development of consumerism, but that is not

---

[52] R. Porter, 'Consumption: disease of the consumer society?', in Brewer and Porter (eds.), *Consumption*, pp. 58–81.

to say that consumers themselves have not offered sophisticated alternatives, recognising the limits of both state and market activity, of theories of consumer behaviour which seem over-deterministic or over-liberatory, and of the more complex workings of consumer-citizenship between individual duty and government responsibility.

This book traces these political ideas that have emerged between consumers and commodities and services. The central problem of the polymorphic meaning of the terms consumer and consumption can be overcome by categorising goods according to three distinct types: those associated with luxury, with necessity and with affluence. Although the distinction between the three is necessarily subjective and always changing, there is a long tradition of using the three categories. Political economists from Smith to Marshall discussed the nature of 'comforts', a middling range of 'semi-luxuries' and conveniences which are neither items crucial to everyday existence nor so opulent that they encourage moral censure as luxuries.[53] Today, they might be classified as 'ordinary' or 'normal' goods in introductory textbooks on economics, though this label belies the range of ideologies associated with their supply, distribution, purchase and use. They are likely to include the consumer durables usually associated with mass market affluence – refrigerators, cookers, electrical appliances, stereos – goods which have broken down the boundary between luxury and necessity and which have largely escaped moral censure, either because they have been consumed within the institution of the domestic sphere or because they have been de-politicised through commercial imagery.[54] Although scholars in disciplines beyond economics rarely categorise different types of commodity – and despite other disciplines' arguments that economics hardly theorises consumption at all – very different relationships between people and the three categories of good have emerged. While the subject of luxury is not the principal concern of this book, this is not to deny both its relevance to the following discussion of necessity and affluence, nor the opportunities for further research that might fruitfully be made in this area. But in focussing on the ability of consumers to speak and organise for themselves, as well as to interact with the institutions of the state, this history of twentieth-century consumerism concentrates on those goods that have given rise to more concrete and tangible policy proposals.

---

[53] J. E. Crowley, 'The sensibility of comfort', *American Historical Review*, 104:3 (1999), 749–82; M. Berg, 'New commodities, luxuries and their consumers in 18th century England', in Berg and Clifford (eds.), *Consumers and Luxury*, 63–85.

[54] M. Hilton, 'The fable of the sheep; or, private virtues, public vices. The consumer revolution of the twentieth century', *Past & Present*, 176 (2002), 222–56.

Accordingly, the first section is devoted to necessity. Chapter 1 provides the background to later political campaigns, outlining the concerns over necessitous consumption from the moral economy of the eighteenth century through to the rise of the Co-operative movement and the increasing attention given to consumption by labour organisations at the turn of the twentieth century. Chapter 2 examines a specific instance of consumer politics, in the form of the Consumers' Council of the First World War, when the state responded to growing consumer pressure for the fairer distribution of essential commodities. This is followed by two linked chapters on the inter-war period, one discussing the variety of consumer political thought which flourished in the 1920s and the 1930s, and the other on the practical political outcomes of consumer protest. A final chapter in the first section explores the politics of necessity in the 1940s and the opportunity given to the Labour Party to develop a politics of consumption which linked both the older consumer concerns of the labour movement and the consumer expectations of a post-war electorate. The second section of the book focusses on affluence and the growth of the organised, modern, comparative-testing based consumerism associated with *Which?* magazine. Chapter 6 demonstrates the range of business and women's organisations which set out to speak for the consumer in the 1950s, while chapter 7 explores the aims and ideas of consumers themselves who flocked to the 'professionalism' of the Consumers' Association (CA), established in 1956. Chapters 8 and 9 reflect on the institutionalisation of an individualist style of consumerism within state-sponsored bodies such as the 1960s Consumer Council and the Office of Fair Trading. In contrast, chapter 10 draws on an alternative strand equally apparent within modern consumerism: the social and even collective concerns expressed by many of the CA's early leaders and the work of the National Consumer Council from 1975. A final chapter highlights the growing importance of single-issue political campaigning to consumerism, using case studies of CA's international counterparts and the rise of ethical consumerism to demonstrate the many areas of intersection held by a diverse range of groups and individuals.

The historical narrative therefore leaves consumerism at a point at which many of the diverse threads of consumer politics are as ever relevant and enjoying as great a public prominence as at any other time over the last one hundred years. All of the concerns of consumer organisations today, as well as the politics of consumption articulated by spokespersons for the consumer within the institutions of the state, have firm precedents within British political culture of the past and remain as intellectually and ideologically broad as they have always been. What is apparent is the circularity of many consumer concerns as many of today's consumer radicals are returning to the ethical and political considerations expressed by leaders of the politics of necessitous consumption. Boycotts are motivated by the same politics as the creation of 'white lists' in the Consumers' League of the 1880s, anti-globalisation demonstrations reflect the same regard for the worker as found in the writings of Ruskin and Morris, the government's responses to BSE, genetically modified foods and the foot-and-mouth crisis mirror agricultural policy of the early twentieth century and the solutions proposed for the problems faced by developing world producers and consumers match some of the socialist agendas of the First World War Consumers' Council.

But the explanation for the re-emergence of various consumer politics is more than the fluctuating pattern of political agendas. Consumerism has always been fuelled from the everyday experiences of getting and spending by ordinary shoppers (though it does not follow that such grass-roots politics feed through into the policy agendas of political leaders). Thus consumerism is inevitably a product of the material circumstances in which the majority of consumers live. Regardless of the subjective boundaries between necessity and affluence, in the late nineteenth and early twentieth centuries, it straightforwardly followed that, on the whole, poverty focussed attention on the equal distribution, fair pricing and quality or adulteration of basic necessities or those commodities that made up the greatest proportion of the expenditure of the weekly income. Increased living standards in the latter half of the twentieth century shifted attention from the pantry to the parlour. The focus was on a new range of consumer durables often purchased for the first time by an expanding middle and professional class as well as an ever-increasing group of affluent workers. The two types of consumerism emerging around such categories of good, although requiring separate analytical treatment, are by no means entirely distinct. Both raise questions about the role of the state in individual purchasing and much of the history of the politics of consumption is the history of the piecemeal encroachment of government departments into everyday life. In the early twentieth century radical politicians of consumption called for the regulation of prices and supplies to protect the ordinary housewife. Left-wing unease with more luxurious forms of consumption often prevented the extension of this politics to other classes of good, but in the 1940s the trade unions, the Labour Party, Political and Economic Planning and many women's organisations, buoyed by the experiences of control and the Utility schemes of the Second World War, began to advocate the extension of state consumer protection to furniture, clothing, housing and the range of mass-produced technical goods which had appeared in the inter-war years but which were to be demanded by all in the democratic universalist spirit of the period of reconstruction. The Labour Party stood at the brink of developing a comprehensive consumer policy, only for productivist interests, ideological unease and electoral defeat to put an abrupt end to these investigations. Post-Second World War consumerism, therefore, emerged only around more expensive consumer goods and many of the connections to an older politics of consumption were subsequently lost. Affluent consumerism developed alongside, and as a handmaiden to, the post-war capitalist state, as it seemingly encouraged an individualistic acquisitiveness only differentiated from the hedonistic consumption of the 1960s by the rational scrutiny of the Consumers' Associaton's *Which?*-buying members. Only with the rediscovery of poverty in the late 1960s and 1970s did consumerism return to something of a politics of price which had been a mainstay of the labour and Co-operative movement up to the mid-twentieth century.

Cultural assumptions, stemming from the older critiques of luxury, have created an unease with consumption that has meant any form of consumerism has always existed within a wider moral discourse about the propriety of specific types of consumption. This perpetual unease with luxury, greed, avarice and vice has served to weaken any consumer politics as potential adherents have been put off by any positive critique which extended beyond the commodities commonly perceived as necessities. But this unease has also strengthened consumerism and made it a persistent third way in political culture. For those who accept some form of material abundance as a modern right of citizenship but question the freedoms to acquire such riches at only an individual and competitive level, consumerism has appealed as a type of liberalism at ease with both the state and the market, the spiritual and the material, and the rights and the duties of the consuming public. In this third-way dimension consumerism has been the collective self-help angst of the capitalist society. It has been the movement of the heretic who seeks not to reject the society he or she lives in, but to call into question and modify some of its fundamental principles through an incremental approach. Just as Galbraith's *The Affluent Society* is not a rejection of capitalism but a critique of the excesses of the free market, just as Solzhenitsyn's *One Day in the Life of Ivan Denisovitch* is not a rejection of communism, but a critique of the excesses of Stalinism, and just as Camus' *The Outsider* is not a rejection of individualism, but an exploration of its existential consequences for the self, so too is consumerism not a denial of material abundance but an attempt to negotiate through the relationship between the market, the individual and the state armed only with a set of loose-fitting social democratic principles. In a secular yet nevertheless evangelical age, consumers have turned to a series of penitential texts to assuage their guilt over consumption, whether it be in the writings of Samuel Smiles, John Ruskin, Vance Packard, E. F. Schumacher, Naomi Klein or whoever comes next with a guidebook on better spending.

Yet as this history will show, organisations such as the Co-operative movement, the Consumers' Association and the National Consumer Council have contained individuals within them who have sought to build on these popular feelings about goods and services to develop a middle path through the often polarised course of British politics. Any attempt to do so has inevitably encountered the problem faced by all: having identified the consumer as the potential for a new liberationist political direction, how does one satisfy the myriad interests, concerns and issues arising from individuals' infinite relationships with material culture? At this point, other groups have often entered the debate to speak for the consumer. Indeed, one of the persistent threads in what follows is the extent to which other groups – whether employers, workers, politicians or bureaucrats – have spoken for and consequently constructed the 'consumer interest'. Here, the narrative takes the form of a history of competing concepts of the consumer, though this prevents the consumer activist being placed centre stage. If this issue of who it is that speaks for the consumer was a problem faced by co-operative theorists, Labour Party advocates of a Consumers' Council and affluent consumer activists in the post-Second World War period, then so too must it be recognised that it was the sheer diversity of the everyday politics of consumption that revived, re-channelled and strengthened consumerism as a whole. If there is a lesson to be learnt from all of this for consumerism today, it is that any attempt to make consumerism the new basis of political action on its own, or any attempt to eclipse the worker, the voter and the citizen with an enriched notion of the consumer, is bound to encounter problems. Consumerism has shown its greatest potential as a movement for historical change when it has attached itself to a broad set of social democratic principles that coalesce with other interests in society. When it has attempted to unify everybody within society under the label 'consumer' it has slipped into idle platitude or utopian dreaming, yet when it has defined itself solely within the realm of purchasing it has had little to say to wider political debates. Consumerism has contributed most to socio-political discussion when it has attached itself to the wider interests of large numbers of citizens – in critiques over profiteering, in the lack of choice available to 'poor consumers', in the growing public prominence of a professional class of post-Second World War planners and in the concerns with globalisation today. At these points it has been about more than just shopping and individual materialism. It has put forward serious economic and social solutions to specific problems in a middle-way social democratic spirit that has increasingly created a space for itself between the interests of labour and capital. Consumerism as a historical movement might not have been the 'ism' that won, but it is fair to say that its organisations and proselytisers have been almost as crucial to the dynamo of change as workers, voters, employers and citizens.

Part I

Necessity

What I call poverty is when people are not able to secure for themselves all the benefits of civilisation; the necessaries, comforts, pleasures and refinements of life, leisure, books, theatres, pictures, music, holidays, travel, good and beautiful homes, good clothes, good and pleasant food.

R. Tressell, *The Ragged Trousered Philanthropists* (London, 1991), p. 29.

1 Socialism, co-operation, Free Trade and fair trade: the politics of consumption in the nineteenth century

How do people think about money? Are we more conscious of money as a financial return on our labour, or as the goods into which it can be converted? Are we wage-conscious or price-conscious? Do we produce to earn, or earn to spend? Are our identities structured around production or consumption? The answer must surely be that production and consumption are entirely intertwined in our economic lives, if not our social, political and cultural lives as well. We are what we eat and we are what we make. We have the potential to be creative, imaginative and intelligent subjects in the factory, the office, the shop and the home. Ultimately, we aim to share in the 'fables of abundance' of a rich and diverse material culture and we want to participate in the 'useful work' involved in creating such wealth. Yet formal political alliances, theoretical perspectives and economic classifications split our identities according to polarised divisions which do not correspond to our lived realities. For much of the twentieth century, politics at Westminster was based around one's position within production, whether trade union employee or trade association-affiliated employer, though the ability of Conservatives to marry a productivist mentality with a rhetoric of individual consumer gain perhaps accounts for much of their electoral success.[1] In cultural studies and sociological interpretations, modernist producer mentalities have given way to postmodern consumer subjectivities, the date for such a change being around 1968 or 1979, depending on where one lived. This literature has also tended to focus on the spectacular and the heavily advertised, ignoring the more mundane aspects of ordinary consumption and those goods which might be classified as necessities, rather than comforts, luxuries or status symbols.[2] But if we were to concentrate our attention on these less image-laden goods, then a different relationship between production and consumption might emerge. As the first part of this book will demonstrate, a much closer relationship has existed between the worker and the

---

[1] D. Jarvis, 'Mrs Maggs and Betty: the Conservative appeal to women voters in the 1920s', *Twentieth-Century British History*, 5:2 (1994), 129–52.
[2] A. Warde and J. Gronow (eds.), *Ordinary Consumption* (London, 2001).

shopper than previously thought, though it has been a relationship not without its tensions.

The most obvious point of reference is the politics of the 'living wage' in late nineteenth- and early twentieth-century America. In the rhetoric of the labour leader, Ira Steward (1831–83), Lawrence Glickman has identified a 'consumerist turn' in labour ideology and strategy in the years immediately after the civil war. The living wage was defined as an amount which enabled working-class wage earners to 'claim the rights and responsibilities of independent, freedom-loving citizens'.[3] Steward had clearly read his Mill, if not also his Ruskin, though he died too early to read his Morris. He divided consumption between the productive and the unproductive, the useful and the wasteful, thereby condemning the most popular amusements while at the same time believing that bourgeois criticisms of working-class extravagance were devices to downplay demands for higher wages. He held on to traditional critiques of luxury yet broadened his notion of necessities to include the 'human needs' associated with republican values of masculinity and independence. Wages, as Steward and an increasing number of labour activists in the twentieth century would argue, ought to be based not on the supply and demand of political economy, but the rights and needs of the 'natural laws' of 'social economy'.[4] This concept of the living wage was not without its problems. For many, it was a family wage, creating tensions between single- and multiple-earner households and Steward felt that workers from ethnic groups with lower living standards and expectations of consumption would dilute the efforts of established US trade unionists who had already reached a higher level. There were also difficulties in arriving at a precise monetary level in particular trade disputes. In the 1922 railroad shopcraft strike both employers and trade unionists recognised that real living standards 'depended in important ways upon the work and skills of the housewife, reflecting the family's relationship to the consumer marketplace rather than the individual worker's relationship to the means of production'.[5] Yet the living wage remained an important reference point, demonstrating both the consumer and producer consciousness held in American workers' notions of democratic citizenship and the role of consumption in politics: consumption could encourage forms of solidarity within working-class communities especially through

[3] L. B. Glickman, 'Workers of the world, consume: Ira Steward and the origins of labor consumerism', *International Labor and Working Class History*, 52 (1997), 75.

[4] L. B. Glickman, *A Living Wage: American Workers and the Making of Consumer Society* (Ithaca, 1997), pp. 71–3.

[5] S. Levine, ' "A bit of mellifluous phraseology": the 1922 railroad shopcraft strike and the living wage', in J. Belchem and N. Kirk (eds.), *Languages of Labour* (Aldershot, 1997), p. 83.

their own 'purchasing power' or the boycotting of firms that did not live up to trade union expectations.[6]

It seems less likely that the consumer- and producer-oriented living wage can be applied to Britain, where producer mentalities have held strong. Even taking account of the concerns of liberal political economy, the focus was ultimately on work, consumption being relegated to a subject that would take care of itself. Mill inverted Smith to argue that 'what a country wants to make it richer, is never consumption, but production'.[7] Morris' pastoral utopia ultimately rested on the dignity of production, not consumption.[8] And, for all those political movements inspired by Marx, consumption, desire and demand were not subjects to be explored at great length: 'The nature of . . . wants, whether . . . they spring from the stomach or from fancy, makes no difference.'[9] Nevertheless, notions of the living wage permeated British working-class politics, if never so clearly as in the US and often under the guise of a more abstract concept, such as Sidney Webb's 'national minimum'. While further chapters in this section will explore notions of a living wage in the inter-war period, this chapter will set out the politics of necessitous consumption prior to the First World War, an important point in the recognition of working-class consumer politics. It argues that consumption has informed radical political activity and practice, if not so much theory. For women especially, the practical day-to-day realities of 'getting and spending' have motivated people as consumers as much as producers. Beyond such grass-roots action, however, necessitous consumption has been one area of persistent government regulation, from the assizes to adulteration legislation. The politics of bread in particular has been central to the regulation of trade and its distribution and manufacture are central to understandings of the pre-industrial 'moral economy'.

This chapter therefore acts as an introductory survey of a whole range of politics of consumption all of which form the backdrop to the debates to be explored in greater detail on the twentieth century. It begins with a section which rejects the idea that the dominance of political economy led to the absence of a consumer awareness in the nineteenth century. Bread and other daily staples persisted as important symbols of political expression, from free trade rhetoric, adulteration legislation and even

---

[6] D. Frank, *Purchasing Power: Consumer Organising, Gender, and the Seattle Labour Movement, 1919–1929* (Cambridge, 1994); L. Cohen, *Making a New Deal: Industrial Workers in Chicago, 1919–1939* (Cambridge, 1990); G. Cross, *Time and Money: The Making of Consumer Culture* (London, 1993).

[7] J. S. Mill, 'Of the influence of consumption upon production', in *Essays on some Unsettled Questions of Political Economy* (London, 1992), p. 49.

[8] W. Morris, *News from Nowhere* (1890; London, 1970).

[9] K. Marx, *Capital, Volume 1*, in E. Kamenka (ed.), *The Portable Karl Marx* (Harmondsworth, 1983), p. 437.

municipal provision. A second section reviews some of the debates over the history of the Co-operative movement to detail the increased emphasis on the politics of consumption towards the end of the century. This, in turn, was linked to the wider politicisation of female consumers, the subject of a third section. The growing consumer consciousness of the Women's Co-operative Guild was, however, only part of a wider politicisation of consumption that had taken place within both radical working-class politics and the defensive concerns of an expanding middle class. By the First World War, then, there were a variety of political ideas about consumption which would come to fruition in the Consumers' Council, to be examined in chapter 2.

Taken together, these competing concerns over necessities did not represent the development of a coherent consumer consciousness. Consumption cannot be used in this instance as the site for the articulation of a revolutionary class consciousness by an otherwise politically disenfranchised marginal social group, though neither can any heightened concern over everyday getting and spending be dismissed as a simple 'bread and butter issue' as has been the case with earlier demonstrations over the cost of living. Rather, the debates over necessitous consumption prove, if not at the level of abstract political theory, then certainly at the level of practical political protest, that the politics of bread has been central to the development of many working-class movements and organisations. 'Consumerism', by the turn of the twentieth century, consisted of a body of ideas motivated by a set of demands for a decent standard of living, located somewhere well below the level of ideology, but substantially higher than that of gut reaction. Citizens and 'the people' have been inspired to political action, organisation and belief through their roles as consumers as well as producers and the poor especially have articulated a politics of necessitous consumption.

Fair trade and Free Trade

Just as luxury has always been regulated or politicised, so has necessity. The regulation of food has occurred in two main areas: adulteration and weights and measures. In Britain, the purpose of weights and measures legislation was to establish national standards which would both facilitate trade and protect the public. Much of it stretches back to the Magna Carta, the Assize System, which set down standards of measurement for bread and other staples, and local regulations, such as the control of prices and wages by guilds and the control of markets by municipalities.[10]

[10] J. Burnett, *A History of the Cost of Living* (Harmondsworth, 1969), pp. 30, 53; G. Borrie and A. L. Diamond, *The Consumer, Society and the Law* (1964; London, 1973), pp. 129–30.

There was of course resistance to the imposition of national standards and, as with sumptuary legislation, such close control of personal consumption was impossible.[11] The Assize of Bread, for instance, had fallen into 'desuetude' by the end of the seventeenth century, as had the Assize of Ale and, by 1815, the whole system collapsed as Free Traders opposed any 'interference in the free workings of the economy'.[12] Under the new system, laissez-faire often simply meant a licence to practise fraud. Short-weight, under-selling and false labelling were so common that in 1854 the editor of the *English Churchman* called for a system of 'detectives' to protect the poor from fraudulent trading practices.[13] The suggestion went unheeded until 1878 when the Weights and Measures Act eventually set up a national inspectorate, though employed by local authorities, to check the measuring equipment and selling techniques of retailers.[14] Even with the development of pre-packaging and branding, and the support given to the use of company labels under the Merchandise Marks Act 1887, traders continued to deceive customers and petitions were frequently sent to the government urging a reform of the law in the interests of the poor consumer.[15]

Added to these economic abuses, however, were the physical dangers presented by adulteration. Campaigns against the threat to public health caused by contaminated food began as early as the 1820s, though it was not until the results of Arthur Hill Hassall's microscopic investigations were published in the *Lancet* between 1851 and 1854 that an official investigation was launched. Subsequent legislation, in the form of the 1860 Act for Preventing Adulteration in Food and Drink, proved largely ineffective thanks to the imprecise definition of adulteration (a further Act had to be passed in 1870) and it took until the 1875 Sale of Food and Drugs Act to force local authorities to establish inspectorates. Even then, regulation was more the product of business 'capture' than popular pressure and was aimed mainly at retailers rather than manufacturers. By the end of the century a further spate of Acts and Orders had been passed while a Parliamentary Select Committee on Food Adulteration sat

---

[11] See the case of the Winchester bushel: R. Sheldon, A. J. Randall, A. Charlesworth and D. Walsh, 'Popular protest and the persistence of customary corn measures: resistance to the Winchester Bushel in the English West', in A. J. Randall and A. Charlesworth (eds.), *Markets, Market Culture and Popular Protest in Eighteenth-Century Britain and Ireland* (Liverpool, 1996), pp. 25–45.
[12] Burnett, *Cost of Living*, p. 209; S. Webb and B. Webb, 'The Assize of Bread', *Economic Journal*, 14 (1904), p. 200.
[13] PRO HO 45/5338: Frauds: *Necessity for Taking some Steps to Protect the Poor Against Short Weight, Short Measure and Adulteration, 1854.*
[14] Borrie and Diamond, *Consumer, Society and the Law*, p. 130.
[15] PRO BT 101/697: Weights and Measures Office: *Test and Inspection Code No. 14: Sale of Goods by Short Weight. Request for Legislation to Protect the Public, 1909.*

from 1894 to 1896.[16] Outbreaks of food poisoning were more the norm than the exception. Milk adulteration and bacteria caused considerable ill health well into the twentieth century and in the winter of 1900–1 at least seventy beer drinkers died through arsenic poisoning.[17] Added to these nationally reported events were the local scares which proliferated throughout the late nineteenth century: the Lancaster 'pepper scandal' of 1887; the Glasgow 'canned peas controversy' of 1891; the 'Kidderminster Coffee Case' of the same year; the Birmingham canned salmon panic of 1892; and the Sunderland lard case of 1895.[18] These scares resulted in the creation of a Foods Section within the Local Government Board in 1905 and the passing of the Public Health (Regulations as to Food) Act in 1907. This latter date also followed the scandalous food processing practices detailed in Upton Sinclair's *The Jungle*, published in 1906, the influence of which stretched to both sides of the Atlantic.[19]

It was against this backdrop of unhygienic, unhealthy and unethical trading practices that Sidney and Beatrice Webb searched for a fairer system of trading in the pre-industrial assizes. Their medievalism can be associated with the organic visions of Ruskin and Morris typical of the late nineteenth century, but others too have seen in pre-modern market relations alternative politics of distribution and consumption. The most famous interpretation is that of Thompson's moral economy and there is certainly much evidence to support the view that eighteenth-century consumers drew on collective notions of fairness to order the market.[20] Various writers have supported the Thompsonian position, stressing the ability of the crowd to act as moral arbiters.[21] Others, too, have either extended the concept to other periods or suggested that sections of the magistracy and an emerging urban bourgeois elite also retained commitments to social welfare in the market, despite their advocacy of Free

[16] M. French and J. Phillips, *Cheated Not Poisoned? Food Regulation in the United Kingdom, 1875–1938* (Manchester, 2000), pp. 40–64; J. Burnett, *Plenty and Want: A Social History of Diet in England from 1815 to the Present Day* (London, 1966), pp. 72–90.

[17] P. J. Atkins, 'White poison? The social consequences of milk consumption, 1850–1930', *Society for the Social History of Medicine*, 5:2 (1992), 207–27; J. Phillips and M. French, 'The pure beer campaign and arsenic poisoning, 1896–1903', *Rural History*, 9:2 (1998), 195–209.

[18] PRO DSIR 26/247–251: Laboratory of the Government Chemist: *Food Adulteration Press Cuttings*.

[19] U. Sinclair, *The Jungle* (1906; Harmondsworth, 1965); French and Phillips, *Cheated Not Poisoned*, p. 66; J. Phillips and M. French, 'Adulteration and food law, 1899–1939', *Twentieth Century British History*, 9:3 (1998), 350–69.

[20] E. P. Thompson, 'The moral economy of the English crowd in the eighteenth century', *Past & Present*, 50 (1971), 76–136; J. Stevenson, *Popular Disturbances in England, 1700–1870* (London, 1979), pp. 91–112.

[21] A. J. Randall, A. Charlesworth, R. Sheldon and D. Walsh, 'Markets, market culture and popular protest in eighteenth-century Britain and Ireland' in Randall and Charlesworth (eds.), *Markets*, pp. 1–24.

Trade in other arenas.[22] But the concept of the moral economy has come under sustained criticism over the last thirty years, either over details such as the role of women in the crowd, or more generally on issues such as the ability of plebeian culture to sustain a coherent moral framework.[23] Most importantly, several scholars have challenged the sharp distinction made between moral and political economy, suggesting instead the existence of a 'pragmatic economy' in which any conceivable moral economy existed alongside, and adapted with, a market economy over a considerable number of decades.[24]

In this chapter, what is important is not so much the challenge to the existence of a moral economy in the eighteenth century, but the examination of the other side of the conceptual coin: whether, in fact, the nineteenth century can be said to have been dominated solely by an amoral political economy. Thompson was correct to retain a tight definition of his notion of the moral economy, in order to better test it empirically in a historically specific period, but a consequence of this is to deny the possibility of alternative moralities within a market system undoubtedly increasingly dominated by capitalism. Indeed, it might well be argued that Free Trade held a moral agenda with the consumer's interest at heart. According to Frank Trentmann, Free Trade was not a policy, but a *Weltanschauung*: 'Free Trade meant free exchange and the libertarian rights of the consumer rather the free market.'[25] Whether this was interpreted either

[22] B. Sharp, 'The food riots of 1347 and the medieval moral economy', in A. J. Randall and A. Charlesworth (eds.), *The Moral Economy and Popular Protest: Crowds, Conflict and Authority* (Basingstoke, 2000), pp. 33–54; R. D. Storch, 'Popular festivity and consumer protest: food price disturbances in the Southwest and Oxfordshire in 1867', *Albion*, 14 (1982), 209–34; A. Charlesworth and A. J. Randall, 'Comment: morals, markets and the English crowd in 1766', *Past & Present*, 114 (1987), 200–13; S. Poole, 'Scarcity and the civic tradition: market management in Bristol, 1790–1815', in Randall and Charlesworth (eds.), *Markets*, pp. 91–114; D. Hay, 'The state and the market in 1800: Lord Kenyon and Mr Waddington', *Past & Present*, 162 (1999), 101–62.

[23] J. Bohstedt, 'Gender, household and community politics: women in English riots, 1790–1810', *Past & Present*, 120 (1988), 88–122; D. E. Williams, 'Morals, markets and the English crowd in 1766', *Past & Present*, 104 (1984), 56–73; J. Bohstedt, 'The moral economy and the discipline of historical context', *Journal of Social History*, 26:2 (1992), 265–84; J. Stevenson, 'The "moral economy" of the English crowd: myth and reality', in A. Fletcher and J. Stevenson (eds.), *Order and Disorder in Early Modern England* (Cambridge, 1985). On responses to these criticisms see A. Charlesworth, 'From the moral economy of Devon to the political economy of Manchester, 1790–1812', *Social History*, 18:2 (1993), 205–17; and Thompson's own reply in his *Customs in Common* (London, 1993), pp. 259–351.

[24] J. Bohstedt, 'The pragmatic economy, the politics of provisions and the "invention" of the food riot tradition in 1740', in Randall and Charlesworth (eds.), *Moral Economy*, p. 55; I. Hont and M. Ignatieff, 'Needs and justice in *The Wealth of Nations*', in I. Hont and M. Ignatieff (eds.), *Wealth and Virtue* (Cambridge, 1983).

[25] F. Trentmann, 'Wealth versus welfare: the British Left between Free Trade and national political economy before the First World War', *Historical Research*, 70:171 (1997), 70–98; F. Trentmann, 'National identity and consumer politics: Free Trade and Tariff Reform',

collectively through consumer co-operation or individualistically through the ideology of the Manchester liberals, 'cheap bread' could serve as a rallying cry for 'the people'.[26] In the Free Trade rhetoric of the Anti-Corn Law League from 1838 to 1846, 'the people' were imagined as 'the middle and industrious classes' against the pro-protection land-owning aristocracy. In a speech of 1845 John Bright claimed the high price of bread caused by the Corn Law was a 'great robbery' 'for the purpose of extorting from all the consumers of food a higher price than it is worth'.[27] He then extended his defence of low prices, consumers and the people by calling on the middle and working classes to end the domination of the hereditary peerage. Pickering and Tyrell rightly warn of the dangers of believing all this inclusive rhetoric, especially when voiced by Free Trade liberals whom the Chartists were eager to identify as notorious employers who treated their workers harshly.[28] Yet Free Trade was still more than self-interest. Pickering and Tyrell borrow A. J. P. Taylor's epithet for the likes of Cobden and Bright, 'The Trouble Makers', to describe the broadly defined Nonconformist and Dissenting challenge to government authority. Uniting consumers within a spirit of national identity, the anti-Corn Law agitation drew on a politics of bread that was prominent in the eighteenth-century food riots, the millers being replaced by the landlords as the 'objects of hatred': 'bread was an omnipresent theme in [the Anti-Corn Law League's] publications and speeches. Leaguers read the *Anti-Bread-Tax Circular*, over and over again they saw replicas of the three loaves that showed the British to be less well-fed than Poles and Frenchman.'[29]

Interpreting Free Trade as a consumer-based political economy opens the field for the further exploration of nineteenth-century consumer politics. We might, for instance, include the protests over the taxation of other commodities and the attempts to represent the consumer and the public interest in the municipalisation of public utilities, such as gas, electricity

---

in D. Winch and P. O'Brien (eds.), *The Political Economy of British Historical Experience, 1688–1914* (Oxford, 2002), pp. 215–42.

[26] M. Pugh, 'Women, food and politics, 1880–1930', *History Today*, 41 (1991), 14. On the rhetoric of 'the people' see E. J. Yeo, 'Language and contestation: the case of "the People"', in Belchem and Kirk (eds.), *Languages of Labour*, pp. 44–62; P. Joyce, *Visions of the People: Industrial England and the Question of Class, 1840–1914* (Cambridge, 1991).

[27] J. Bright, 'Free Trade', Covent Garden Theatre (19 December 1845), in J. E. T. Rogers (ed.), *Speeches on Questions of Public Policy by The Right Honourable John Bright* (London, 1869), pp. 417–18.

[28] P. Pickering and A. Tyrell, *The People's Bread: A History of the Anti-Corn Law League* (London, 2000), p. 8.

[29] *Ibid.*, p. 9. See also N. Longmate, *The Breadstealers: The Fight Against the Corn Laws, 1838–1946* (London, 1984); N. MacCord, *The Anti-Corn Law League 1838–1946* (London, 1958).

and water.[30] All suggest deeper discussions of the commodity or service than is usually associated with the concept of the fetish. As Marx famously explained, 'a commodity is . . . a mysterious thing' because it hides the social relations in production and presents them as a social relation between the products of labour. Capitalism does not produce 'things', but 'things *qua* commodities', the values of which 'have absolutely no connection with their physical properties and with the material relations arising therefrom'.[31] Instead, value relates to the fetishism of commodities, though Marx suggested that value 'converts every product into a social hieroglyphic' which we try to decipher to discover the labour that went into production. However, 'the determination of the magnitude of value by labour-time is . . . a secret, hidden under the apparent fluctuations in the relative values of commodities'.[32] The hieroglyphic remains indecipherable because the 'money form of the world of commodities' conceals 'the social character of private labour, and the social relations between the individual producers'.[33] This is an essentially pessimistic view of consumption, since it denies the possibility of the consumer discovering a deeper politics beneath the surface of the commodity. Politics, for Marx, of course, must therefore begin with production, but the rhetoric of Free Traders, the actions of food rioters, the campaigns of temperance reformers, the initiatives of rational recreationists, the cultural critiques of Ruskin and Morris, and even Mill's focus on the productive and unproductive aspects of consumption all suggest that the nineteenth-century consumer could get beyond the fetish and a politics of consumption could easily emerge without the need for a Rosetta Stone.

The Co-operative movement

The principal agency through which the commodity became a lens to view material circumstances was the Co-operative movement, long overlooked by social historians or dismissed as drab and dreary. Peter Gurney has recently sought to provide a revisionist account, arguing that for both co-operative leaders and ordinary working-class dividend hunters, the Co-op offered a viable alternative to capitalist economic relations.[34] However, if it was the case that such a coherent consumer-consciousness had

---

[30] J. Russell, *The Sugar Duties: A Consumer's Protest against a Scale of Duties on Sugar* (London, 1864); M. Daunton, 'The material politics of natural monopoly: consuming gas in Victorian Britain', in M. Daunton and M. Hilton (eds.), *The Politics of Consumption: Material Culture and Citizenship in Europe and America* (Oxford, 2001), pp. 69–88.
[31] Marx, *Capital*, p. 446.   [32] *Ibid.*, p. 450.   [33] *Ibid.*, p. 450.
[34] P. Gurney, *Co-operative Culture and the Politics of Consumption in England, 1870–1930* (Manchester, 1996); M. K. Hilson, 'Working-class politics in Plymouth, c.1890–1920', Ph.D. thesis, University of Exeter (1998).

emerged within co-operative thought and practice by the turn of the twentieth century, it was never so clear to the original Rochdale Pioneers in 1844. Even after the introduction of the dividend on purchases, which placed ownership in the hands of consumers, co-operation was still geared towards the building up of capital to purchase Owenite-style communities, the difference being that ownership of the means of production would ultimately rest with the workers rather than their middle-class benefactors and that funds would continue to build up for further expansion.[35] Consumer co-operation was to prove incredibly successful as a form of economic organisation, principally because it enabled working-class families to purchase better value, better quality goods while providing a form of saving through the quarterly payment of the dividend on purchases. But upon its introduction in 1844 it was always a means to an end: it was 'the device of despair – i.e., despair at failure of other stores to continue to grow'.[36] The aim was not for consumers to control economic relations, but for them to act as the providers of capital which would then be used to liberate the principal subject of industrial politics: the worker.

The shift in co-operation, from a producer to a consumer mentality, began in the 1870s. By this time, the Co-operative Wholesale Society (CWS) had been set up to co-ordinate supplies and distribution, and the umbrella organisation, the Co-operative Union, had been established, together with its Annual Congresses which met for the first time in the spring of 1869.[37] By the end of the decade individual membership would stand at around half a million, while the number of local societies approached 1,000.[38] A number of different strands of co-operative thought had also emerged, from the overtly Owenite traditionalists to the respectable Christian Socialists and on to the worker-controlled producer co-operators and the consumer-oriented Rochdale-inspired radicals within the CWS. At the 1873 Congress, differences became clear. Producer co-operators argued that 'consumption was merely the animal element, production the divine' and that 'Our Movement was not started with the object of making money or supplying cheap goods, but of making men. The other things were subordinate.'[39] According to an 1892

[35] G. J. Holyoake, writing in *The Movement* (1844) and *History of the Rochdale Equitable Pioneers* (1857), in G. D. H. Cole and A. W. Filson (eds.), *British Working Class Movements: Select Documents, 1789–1875* (London, 1951), pp. 427–9.

[36] G. J. Holyoake, *The History of Co-operation in England: Its Literature and Advocates, Volume 2: The Constructive Period, 1845–1878* (London, 1879), p. 38

[37] Gurney, *Co-operative Culture*, p. 19; M. Digby, *The World Co-operative Movement* (London, 1949), p. 23; P. Redfern, *The Story of the CWS: The Jubilee History of the Co-operative Wholesale Society Limited, 1863–1913* (Manchester, 1913).

[38] G. D. H. Cole, *A Century of Co-operation* (Manchester, 1944), p. 371.

[39] Cited in A. Bonner, *British Co-operation: The History, Principles, and Organisation of the British Co-operative Movement* (Manchester, 1961), p. 134.

pamphlet signed by E. O. Greening, the Christian Socialist E. Vansittart Neale and the prominent trade unionists Ben Tillett and Tom Mann, the relief of poverty would only come through a focus on production, income and the worker: 'The consumer's society cannot lift the consumer beyond the level attainable by the judicious use of his own income . . . The society may give the consumer more, and perhaps better things for the same income, but for an increase of this income he must look elsewhere.'[40]

Another signatory to this document and a principal proselytiser of co-operation in the movement's early decades was George Jacob Holyoake. Holyoake was sympathetic to the producer-co-operative strand of thinking and argued that 'co-operation was not complete so long as the servants of the store were left out'.[41] Yet he nevertheless criticised those producer co-operators who saw the consumer as either a mere 'guzzler – a person all throat and gastric juice' or even 'a child, a beggar, a madman, a thief and a murderer'.[42] Holyoake recognised the importance of the mass of consumers being enrolled into the co-operative store. Developing a co-operative politics of pragmatism, he urged his colleagues to recognise the capital brought to the movement by purchasers who only shopped at the stores for the gain of the dividend rather than any ideological commitment: 'It is mere feeble, unseeing sentimentality to be the friend of the producer, unless you provide to protect and sustain him by the confederation of the consumer.'[43] Holyoake therefore urged a union between consumer and producer co-operatives, though his ultimate sympathies would lie with the worker (he quoted George Eliot's Caleb Garth that work was 'poetry without the aid of the poets, . . . a philosophy . . . without the aid of philosophers, a religion without the aid of theology'[44]).

Holyoake's practical view of co-operation, in which the conditions of workers would be aided by the thrifty purchasing decisions of dividend-hunting shoppers, appealed to the Victorian liberal self-help tradition – the 'middle class embrace' as Gurney puts it.[45] For Holyoake, co-operation was the 'politeness of industry' and he expounded a notion of

---

[40] E. V. Neale and E. O. Greening, *Proposal for an International Alliance of the Friends of Co-operative Production* (Edinburgh, 1892), p. 3. See also R. Neville, *Co-operation* (London, 1901).

[41] Holyoake, *History of Co-operation, Volume 2*, p. 75.

[42] G. J. Holyoake, *The Policy of Commercial Co-operation as Respects Including the Consumer* (London, 1873), pp. 7–8.

[43] *Ibid.*, p. 15. On Holyoake generally see L. Grugel, *George Jacob Holyoake: A Study in the Evolution of a Victorian Radical* (Philadelphia, 1976); P. Gurney, 'George Jacob Holyoake: socialism, association, and co-operation in nineteenth-century England', in S. Yeo (ed.), *New Views of Co-operation* (London, 1988), pp. 52–72.

[44] Holyoake, *History of Co-operation, Volume 2*, pp. 143–4.

[45] Gurney, *Co-operative Culture*, pp. 143–68.

the mobilisation of self-interest which differed little from the civic-minded concerns of the Free Trader or a passage taken from Samuel Smiles.[46] Within this view of respectable co-operation, Holyoake suggested that state interference was 'repugnant to the spirit of independence' and that, following Herbert Spencer, socialism 'may prove a tyranny exacting and repressive'.[47] Although a secularist, Holyoake inscribed his co-operative rhetoric with a nonconformist conscience, preaching the virtues of self-interest as an organising principle in the 'business' of co-operation. It may have tended to de-radicalise the movement and situated the consumer solely as shopper, but it encouraged the support of 'famous promoters' such as John Stuart Mill, Harriet Martineau, Lord Brougham, Richard Cobden, Bright and Gladstone; figures who would be crucial in ensuring that capitalist business enterprises were unable to repeal the movement's legislative protection (that is, the Friendly Societies Act 1846, and the Industrial and Provident Societies Act 1852).[48]

Against the views of the producer co-operators stood J. T. W. Mitchell, a firm advocate of the Rochdale principles and chairman of the CWS. Mitchell felt that the movement had been too often 'let down' by producer co-operatives and that the best means of growth lay in the extension and development of consumer co-operation, to the extent that eventually all production would be organised on behalf of consumers who represented the 'universal interest'.[49] Beatrice Webb would later describe her first meeting with Mitchell, exalting him as a 'prophet', as he made it clear in a speech in 1889 that the profits of co-operation should go to consumers, not to the workers of the movement. Webb explained that the movement gradually came round to his views, realising 'the most essential element in the creation of "value" in the economic sense is neither labour nor capital, but the *correspondence* of the application of labour with actually felt specific desire'.[50] Co-operation resulted therefore in 'production for use' rather than 'production for profit'.

In her praise of Mitchell, Webb denied the importance of her own role in supporting consumer co-operation and for providing a firmer theoretical framework for its advocates. Her research into the movement in 1889 was vital in challenging the assumptions of triviality ascribed to the Co-op by political economists such as Alfred Marshall and even her fiancé of

[46] Holyoake, *History of Co-operation, Volume 2*, p. 88.
[47] G. J. Holyoake, *The Co-Operative Movement Today* (London, 1891), p. 152.
[48] Holyoake, *History of Co-operation, Volume 2*, pp. 167, 378–9. On Gladstone's views on co-operation see *The Co-operator*, 128, 11 January 1868, pp. 17–19, reprinted in N. Kirk, *Change, Continuity and Class: Labour in British Society, 1850–1920* (Manchester, 1998).
[49] Bonner, *British Co-operation*, p. 135; J. Birchall, *Co-op: The People's Business* (Manchester, 1994), p. 106.
[50] B. Webb, *The Discovery of the Consumer* (London, 1928), p. 13.

the time, Sidney Webb.[51] She polarised the debate within co-operation between what she identified as the 'Individualists' (those producer co-operators who favoured self-government for workers and profit-sharing) and the 'Federalists' (those who favoured the 'open democracy of the Store').[52] The problem with the Individualists, she believed, was that they had simply failed. Workers had too often inefficiently interfered in management or, if successful, had then become exclusive, retaining all the profits for themselves. In her 1891 book, Webb criticised the continual failure of producer co-operative experiments, a judgement she repeated in her joint work with Sidney in 1921.[53] Instead, Webb saw no reason why the democracy of consumers might not be extended into all areas of industry, such that the entire community (equated with all consumers) would be the ultimate employer. Here, the universal consumer shared none of the specific economic interests of the private producer and the community as purchaser and owner formed a new economic system: 'an organisation of labour whereby the immediate and ultimate welfare of the workers would be guarded by a representative personally uninterested in the question of wages and intent on a general high standard of effort and enjoyment in the class he represents – this fully-developed industrial democracy alone provides, in complete form, the economic basis for the future religion of humanity'.[54]

But just as worker co-operatives might ignore consumers in their self-interested pursuit of higher wages, so consumer co-operatives might ig-nore workers in their pursuit of lower prices. Webb therefore sought to introduce measures to protect producers, setting out a policy that looked after bread as well as wages: 'the citizens organised as consumers, and the workers organised as producers'.[55] With the potential to control all of industry, consumers had a 'moral obligation' to care for the manufac-turers of goods sold in co-operative stores. Co-operation could drive out the truck system, profiteering, fraud, the sweated trades and the wasteful methods of small capitalists, though trade unions were crucial to ensure that wages too were not also driven down. Ultimately, she hoped 'the people organised as consumers and the workers organised as profession-als might rapidly become an irresistible power', with the two seemingly separate interests recognised as one: 'their common object is to secure to themselves and their descendants the unearned income now received by other classes'.[56] Unity would come through a recognition of the economic

[51] M. Cole, 'Preface' to B. Potter, *The Co-operative Movement in Great Britain* (1891; London, 1987).
[52] Potter, *Co-operative Movement*, p. 188.
[53] B. Webb and S. Webb, *The Consumers' Co-operative Movement* (London, 1921), p. 463.
[54] Potter, *Co-operative Movement*, p. 221.   [55] *Ibid.*, p. 193.   [56] *Ibid.*, pp. 201–2.

wholeness of the family unit: 'it is suicidal folly for the wage-earning hus-band to raise prices on the housekeeping wife. And it is even more dis-astrous for the wife to beat down the husband's earnings to subsistence level, or to deprive him of employment.'[57]

Co-operation was to be part of a broader socialist and political project. Trade unions and the Co-operative movement ought to form a political alliance, she argued in 1891. Co-operators could help the Parliamen-tary Committee of the Trade Union Congress on questions such as the Factory Acts, Employers' Liability Act, the Truck Acts, technical edu-cation, liberty of combination and various safety and skill assurances. Trade unions, in turn, could help the Co-operative movement in their advocacy of Adulteration Acts, Merchandise Marks Acts, Weights and Measures Acts 'and in their steadfast opposition to any attempt on the part of landlords and capitalists to revert to protection as a method of increasing profits under the pretext of raising money wages'.[58] Later, her consumer politics were married more closely to the state socialist projects of her Fabian agenda. While voluntary co-operation was most appropri-ate for many goods, municipalisation was the better form of economic organisation for those goods and services which needed to be paid by all: education, libraries, the suppression of nuisances, gas and water. Others – the post office, mining, rail, timber, banking and insurance – were served better still under nationalisation and state socialism.[59] In the Webbs' joint vision, democracy would be based upon the combination of producers organised in trade unions, consumers organised in co-operatives, and both organised as citizens within the political state.[60] Democracies of consumers, however, extended beyond the organised Co-operative move-ment and the Webbs included within their definition building societies, housing associations, credit associations, social clubs and educational and recreational organisations.[61]

Most historians agree on the impact of Beatrice Webb on the Co-operative movement, her ideas helping to establish the Co-operative Union as an integral branch of a broader labour movement. Although the Co-operative movement's formal entry into politics would not take place until the end of the First World War, Webb provoked closer links with the trade unions, the Labour Party and socialist thought before 1914.[62] But her legacy is also much more problematic. On the one hand,

---

[57] *Ibid.*, p. 202.   [58] *Ibid.*, p. 203.
[59] B. Webb and S. Webb, *Consumers' Co-operative Movement*, pp. 401–39.
[60] B. Webb and S. Webb, *A Constitution for the Socialist Commonwealth of Great Britain* (London, 1920).
[61] Fabian Society, *Committee of Enquiry on the Control of Industry: Memorandum by the Chairman (Beatrice Webb)* (Letchworth, 1910), p. 9.
[62] Bonner, *British Co-operation*, p. 136.

she has been criticised by co-operative historians for failing to see the full potential of co-operation in and of itself, without the need for an alliance with either self-interested trade unionists or state socialist ideology. On the other, her criticisms of the active participation of most dividend hunters has established a dominant narrative within labour history of the limited appeal of consumer co-operation. In her 1891 survey she criticised the apolitical spending of most co-operators, whom she thought were motivated not by ideology but by the 'divi': 'a mechanical and unconscious device for saving or for forestalling quarterly expenses'.[63] Later, in 1921, she belittled those who 'took it for granted that the whole of this surplus ought, as a matter of course, to be distributed from the members, and thus *transformed from common property to individual property*'.[64] Likewise, co-operative managers and officers were accused of 'apathy and indifference', and were said to 'exist in vast numbers in the Co-operative democracy'.[65] While left-wing intellectuals and labour historians such as G. D. H. Cole have been quick to pick up on this observation, Webb herself felt the problem no worse than in trade unions or local and central government. Her pessimistic interpretation of both the revolutionary potential of consumers and producers acting on their own reflects the Leninist critique of the limited economic consciousness of trade unions and did, at least, force her to attempt to reconcile two branches of the labour movement within her own Fabian concerns. It also meant that the Webbs would reject other socialist strategies such as syndicalism and Cole's guild socialism with its focus on workers' control, seeking instead policies which recognised the consuming and producing role of each individual or family unit.[66] One has here a recognition that ordinary industrial life was dominated by both the factory and the shop and that a radical or socialist politics must recognise the relevance and interconnectedness of the two.

The female consumer

One crucial means by which the Webbs sought to politicise consumption was through the active participation of women. The local co-operative store, with all its attendant education and leisure facilities, management committees and topical discussion groups was an important training ground in citizenship for women as well as men. In 1891, Beatrice wondered whether the Co-operative movement would make women merely

---

[63] B. Potter, *Co-operative Movement*, p. 191.
[64] B. Webb and S. Webb, *Consumers' Co-operative Movement*, p. 297.   [65] *Ibid.*, p. 306.
[66] G. D. H. Cole, *Chaos and Order in Industry* (London, 1920); G. D. H. Cole, *Self-Government in Industry* (1917; London, 1919). For the critique see B. Webb and S. Webb, *Consumers' Co-operative Movement*, pp. 449–62.

better housekeepers or better citizens, though if it was to be the latter, she recognised the valuable work being done by the Women's Co-operative Guild.[67] That Webb believed women as family provisioners had an important political role to play should come as no surprise, given the frequency with which women have politicised consumption. Women as consumers had played an important role in the food riots of the eighteenth century, in the boycotts of sugar in the anti-slavery movement and in the bazaars, tea parties and temperance circles of the Anti-Corn Law League.[68] During the Chartist agitation, Female Political Associations urged the 'patriotic women of England' to attack the 'shopocracy' through exclusive dealing campaigns supporting only those retailers sympathetic to the Chartist cause.[69] Later, women realised their power as consumers in the rent strikes of the Jewish East End in 1904 and in Glasgow in 1915.[70] And, in the county courts, women manipulated their absence of legal rights in economic transactions under the law of coverture by avoiding paying debts for goods obtained on credit.[71]

In the Co-operative movement, the problem for many women was the few opportunities to participate in either the management of local societies or the institutions of the central bureaucracies of the Co-operative Union or the CWS. The Women's Co-operative Guild was a direct response to this. Set up in 1883 by Alice Acland who wished to create an

[67] Potter, *Co-operative Movement*, p. 193.

[68] K. Davies, 'A moral purchase: femininity, commerce, abolition, 1788–1792', in E. Eger and C. Grant (eds.), *Women and the Public Sphere: Writing and Representation 1660–1800* (Cambridge, 2000); C. Midgley, *Women against Slavery: The British Campaigns, 1780–1870* (London, 1992); C. Sussmann, 'Women and the politics of sugar, 1792', *Representations*, 48 (1994), 48–69; C. Sussmann, *Consuming Anxieties: Consumer Protest, Gender and British Slavery, 1713–1833* (California, 2000); E. J. Yeo, 'Introduction: some paradoxes of empowerment', in E. J. Yeo (ed.), *Radical Femininity: Women's Self-Representation in the Public Sphere* (Manchester, 1998), p. 2; Pickering and Tyrell, *People's Bread*; L. Davidoff and C. Hall, *Family Fortunes: Men and Women of the English Middle Class, 1780–1850* (London, 1987), p. 448; J. Vernon, *Politics and the People: A Study in English Political Culture, c.1815–1867* (Cambridge, 1993), p. 378; A. Clark, *The Struggle for the Breeches: Gender and the Making of the British Working Class* (Berkeley, 1995), p. 228.

[69] *Northern Star*, 8 December 1838, p. 6; D. Thompson, *The Chartists* (London, 1984), p. 137.

[70] M. van der Linden, 'Working-class consumer power', *International Labor and Working-Class History*, 46 (1994), 109–21; J. Melling, *Rent Strikes: People's Struggle for Housing in West Scotland, 1890–1916* (Edinburgh, 1983).

[71] M. Finn, 'Women, consumption and coverture in England, c.1760–1860', *The Historical Journal*, 39:3 (1996), 703–22; M. Finn, 'Working-class women and the contest for consumer control in Victorian county courts', *Past & Present*, 161 (1998), 116–54; E. Rappaport, ' "A husband and his wife's dresses": consumer credit and the debtor family in England, 1864–1914', in V. de Grazia and E. Furlough, *The Sex of Things: Gender and Consumption in Historical Perspective* (London, 1996), pp. 163–87; R. J. Morris, 'Men, women, and property: the reform of the Married Women's Property Act 1870', in F. M. L. Thompson (ed.), *Landowners, Capitalists and Entrepreneurs: Essays for Sir John Habakkuk* (Oxford, 1994), pp. 171–91.

opportunity for working-class women to express themselves, the original aims of the Guild were to enable women to strengthen the efforts to promote co-operation generally.[72] Membership figures remained in the hundreds throughout the 1880s until Margaret Llewelyn Davies became General Secretary. Securing greater funds from the Co-operative Union, Davies inspired 'the woman with the basket' to enter this 'trade union' for housewives. By the turn of the century, there were nearly 13,000 individual members and, by her retirement in 1921, over 50,000, together with 905 branch organisations.[73] Many of these women served to radicalise the aims of the Guild as it became explicitly committed to the general advancement of working-class women: 'the organisational expression of a wide-ranging feminist agenda'.[74] In the late nineteenth and early twentieth centuries, the Guild embarked on a series of campaigns which arguably materially assisted the lives of countless working-class women and served to politicise the Co-operative movement hierarchy. The Guild involved itself in charitable work for women, such as Clothing Clubs, Help-in-Need Funds, Outing Funds and Christmas Clubs, while it attempted to make the Co-operative Union more democratic through open membership (for men and women from the same family) and the abolition of entrance fees. Much emphasis was placed on education, the titles of lectures given to groups of working-class women ranging from political economy, municipal duties, money and the industrial revolution to food, ironing, health care and social purity.[75] Campaigns were fought against credit trading and high dividends and a famous victory was won in the establishment of a minimum wage for co-operative women employees.[76] It succeeded in getting more women involved in co-operation and in extending the trading ventures of the stores to poorer neighbourhoods.[77] More sustained efforts were made on questions of citizenship and the Guild was a principal agent in the extension of the suffragette campaign to working-class women.[78] It also helped change the nation's attitude to

---

[72] C. Webb, *The Woman with the Basket: The History of the Women's Co-operative Guild* (Manchester, 1926), p. 21.

[73] G. Scott, *Feminism and the Politics of Working Women: The Women's Co-operative Guild, 1880s to the Second World War* (London, 1998), p. xii; B. J. Blaszak, *The Matriarchs of England's Co-operative Movement: A Study in Gender Politics and Female Leadership, 1883–1921* (London, 2000). On the organisation of the Guild see Women's Co-operative Guild, *The ABC of the Women's Co-operative Guild* (Manchester, 1924); G. Goodenough, *The Central Board and the Grant to the Women's Co-operative Guild* (Manchester, 1914); Women's Co-operative Guild, *General Rules* (Manchester, 1921).

[74] Scott, *Feminism*, p. 3. See also M. L. Davies, *The Education of Guildswomen* (Manchester, 1913).

[75] Webb, *Woman with the Basket*, p. 54.   [76] *Ibid.*, p. 82.

[77] M. L. Davies, *Co-operation in Poor Neighbourhoods* (Nottingham, 1899); C. Webb, *The Women's Guild and Store Life* (London, 1892).

[78] Scott, *Feminism*, p. 20; L. S. Woolf, *The Control of Industry by the People* (London, 1915).

issues of motherhood as it advocated national state maternity centres, better provision of midwifery services, improved hospitals and a system of home helps. Here, the Guild achieved some notable successes, such as the provision for maternity benefits in social insurance legislation, despite the opposition of Labour men in Parliament.[79]

Undoubtedly, the Guild developed a strong feminist consciousness in the three decades of Margaret Llewelyn Davies' tenure as General Secretary. According to Gillian Scott, the Guild's radicalism subsequently declined as leaders in the inter-war period subsumed the advocacy of women's rights under a more general commitment to the policies of the Labour Party. Such a narrative of loss obscures the more general commitment to a consumption politics expressed by Davies and continued by leaders such as Eleanor Barton whom Scott claims 'abandoned these strongly held feminist convictions'.[80] Indeed, the inter-war focus on consumption is argued to have been a conservative rather than a feminist politics since the Co-operative's 'Push the Sales' purchasing campaigns 'did more to strengthen, than to challenge, the traditional domestic roles of married working women'.[81] Clearly, if feminism is defined through the concerns of the 1990s, the Guild's work did lose its radical edge in the inter-war period, but for those housewives committed to developing a political voice though their roles as consumers – and in tandem with their husbands as producers – persistent socialist and alternative feminist agendas are apparent in the Guild's publications. In 1890, just one year after taking office, Davies adopted a stance similar to Beatrice Webb, arguing that socialism and co-operation had similar aims and that they should therefore come together through Parliamentary action.[82] She urged a consumer consciousness calling on co-operators to think of themselves first as consumers, second as workers and third as citizens.[83] And women were to be at the vanguard of this movement since 'The woman with the basket . . . forms the corner-stone of the Co-operative Commonwealth . . . Under Co-operation her role as the buyer gives the married woman a place of supreme importance, where she can reinforce the claim of her Trade Unionist husband for better industrial conditions by buying goods made only under Trade Union conditions; and where she can

---

[79] Scott, *Feminism*, p. 111; Webb, *Woman with the Basket*, p. 133.

[80] Scott, *Feminism*, p. 177. On Eleanor Barton's consumer politics see E. Barton, *Through Trade to the Co-operative Commonwealth* (London, 1930); E. Barton, *Woman: In the Home, the Store and the State* (Manchester, c.1928).

[81] Scott, *Feminism*, p. 250.

[82] M. L. Davies, 'The relations between co-operation and socialistic aspiration', paper presented to 1890 Co-operative Congress, cited in Bonner, *British Co-operation*, p. 131.

[83] M. L. Davies, *Guild Work, in Relation to Educational Committees of Co-operative Societies* (Manchester, 1898), p. 9.

take part in forwarding the emancipation of the workers and the peace of the world . . . The power of the basket is a greater one than the power of the loom or of the vote.'[84] Women, the 'domestic chancellors of the exchequer', had the real power to transfer 'the power of capitalism into the hands of the people organised democratically as consumers'.[85] Such arguments might well have reinforced a domestic division between Mrs Consumer and Mr Breadwinner, but the purposes of her consumption are no less radical for that. This rhetoric persisted in Guild and co-operative circles throughout the twentieth century, so that even in the 1940s strong emphasis was placed on the 'community of consumers'.[86]

But Davies' feminisation of the politics of consumption was not confined to co-operation. Karen Hunt has recently demonstrated the extent to which women such as Clara Hendin and Dora Montefiore developed a consumer politics within the Social Democratic Federation. Their proposals to open a Socialist Trading Store in 1901 followed earlier initiatives to encourage socialists to shop at the Pioneer Boot Factory and the Red Flag Toffee Company.[87] Later, Margaretta Hicks of the Women's Council of the British Socialist Party attempted to mobilise the political power of ordinary women shoppers, educating them to develop a social as well as individual point of view. Building on the strategies of the Women's Co-operative Guild and the Women's Labour League, Hicks hoped to use boycotts and buycotts to combat the high cost of everyday commodities. In 1914, the Women's Council held a conference on the 'increased cost of living' with representatives attending from over one hundred societies, including the Women's Industrial Council, the Fabian Women's Group, the Independent Labour Party, the London Trades Council, the Women's Co-operative Guild and numerous trade unions. Their efforts were in part also inspired by the No Vote No Rent campaign organised in 1913 by Sylvia Pankhurst and other members of the East London Federation of the Women's Social and Political Union.[88]

The question to be asked of all these attempts to create a politics of consumption is whether a coherent theoretical framework emerged. The most important attempt to do so occurred in Teresa Billington Greig's *The Consumer in Revolt*, published in 1912. In this, the militant British feminist provided a highly gendered understanding of capitalism and the separation of the private and public spheres. Industrialisation, she argued,

---

[84] M. L. Davies, *Women as Organised Consumers* (Manchester, 1921), pp. 2–3.
[85] *Ibid.*, p. 4; M. L. Davies, *Inaugural Address, 54th Annual Congress of the Co-operative Union* (Manchester, 1922).
[86] Women's Co-operative Guild, *Woman of Tomorrow* (Manchester, 1943).
[87] K. Hunt, 'Negotiating the boundaries of the domestic: British socialist women and the politics of consumption', *Women's History Review*, 9:2 (2000), 389–410.
[88] K. Hunt, *Socialist Women* (London, 2001).

took away many aspects of women's production in the home and placed them in the factory and the world of men. Consequently, women's domestic work came to be undervalued and even held in 'contempt' as 'man' and 'producer' became synonymous.[89] Such gendered divisions of labour fed directly into the male control of the public sphere:

Public affairs have come to be the realm of man because man regarded himself as the breadwinner, the producer of wealth of the world; and public affairs naturally are now entirely dominated by the producer's point of view. Our politics are the politics of production . . . Capitalistic industry, that with its tongue in its cheek talks of the need of the consumer, is mainly concerned with making production useful to the small class that controls it.[90]

This economic and political division created a psychological split too. Woman, as the 'national purchaser', thought in terms of prices as opposed to wages, more interested in the economics of consumption than production. That she had not utilised this consciousness to protest against adulteration, under-selling and shoddy goods, was due to the 'segregation of women, each shut apart in her own home'. With appropriate education and training, women would realise their potential and end their 'exclusion from public life'. Greig urged a feminist liberation through the politics of consumption: 'Woman the consumer has been revenged for the degradation of woman the creature of sex. And it follows that the economic re-organisation of the world can only come when woman is active and free'.[91] Greig wrote with an independent mind in 1912. She headed no new consumer movement or organisation of women. She had few formal attachments to organisations of consumers or figures such as Davies, Hicks and Hendin and she had withdrawn from an active role in the suffragette campaign. *The Consumer in Revolt* consequently had no immediate impact on any consumer movement, despite some favourable if limited reviews in the press.[92] But despite its call to arms to women to use consumption as a means for political and economic enfranchisement, its main limitation was the absence of a programmatic formula for consumer politics or, as Brian Harrison puts it, the lack of a 'route-map to guide her readers towards her destination'.[93]

---

[89] T. B. Greig, *The Consumer in Revolt* (London, 1912), p. 19. See also K. Hunt, 'Fractured universality: the language of British socialism before the First World War', in Belchem and Kirk (eds.), *Languages of Labour*, pp. 65–80; M. Hilton, 'The female consumer and the politics of consumption in twentieth-century Britain', *The Historical Journal*, 45:1 (2002), 103–28.

[90] Greig, *Consumer in Revolt*, p. 57.   [91] *Ibid.*, p. 61.

[92] K. Hunt, *Socialist Women*, chap. 6.

[93] B. Harrison, *Prudent Revolutionaries: Portraits of British Feminists between the Wars* (Oxford, 1987), p. 60; E. Crawford, *The Women's Suffrage Movement: A Reference Guide, 1866–1928* (London, 1999), pp. 54–6.

The wider politics of consumption

Another problem confronted by Greig's feminist critique was the wider politicisation of consumption that had occurred in the late nineteenth century. It would have been a formidable task to bring together the many different strands of co-operation, socialism and feminism, but consumption was also being radicalised by many other groups, from the trade union movement to the suburban middle classes. Consumption was central to many people's understanding of increasing the quality and quantity of life, but its politicisation could take many forms. For many working-class women, in fact, consumption was not so much a means to feminist empowerment, but a tactic in the improvement of the working conditions of the industrial poor. The first self-styled consumers' movement in Britain was seen as a support to existing labour concerns rather than a radical reformulation of working-class politics. In August 1887, Clementina Black, Honorary Secretary of the Women's Trade Union Association, published an article in *Longman's Magazine*, calling for the creation of a Consumers' League. Inspired by the Knights of Labour in the United States, the intention was to mobilise shoppers to boycott the goods of employers 'who paid badly, had unsanitary workshops, or oppressed their employees'.[94] Consumers had the real power to ensure that wages were raised above starvation point by paying a fair price: 'such a price that the worker by working an eight-hours day can earn enough to live in decency and comfort'.[95] Together with labour reformers such as the Rev. H. C. Shuttleworth, F. C. Baum (of the London Trades Council) and Rev. H. Scott-Holland, Canon of St Pauls, Black organised a series of meetings from late 1887 to collect signatures for the new League. They emphasised that the purpose was to establish 'fair wages' and 'fair houses' of good practice, while not taking up a 'spirit of animosity towards any class'.[96] They created a list of 'fair' dressmakers, milliners, shirtmakers and upholsterers on Bond Street, Regent Street and Oxford Street, so middle-class consumers could more easily exercise their 'duties' to workers. Black recognised that 'such a league of consumers would never be strong enough entirely to remedy the poverty of the worker', but she believed it to be the first step towards a 'natural alliance' between consumers and trade unionists.[97] Given the paucity of sources on the League,

---

[94] The *Longman's Magazine* article of vol. 10 (1887), 409–20, was re-published as C. Black, *The Consumers' League: A Proposal that Buyers Should Combine to Deal only with Employers who Pay their Workers Fairly* (London, 1888), p. 6.
[95] *Ibid.*   [96] Consumers' League, *Prospectus* (London, 1887).
[97] Black, *Consumers' League*, p. 8; C. Black, *A Natural Alliance* (London, 1892). See also C. Black, *The Truck Acts: What They Do, and What They Ought to Do* (London, 1894).

it is difficult to gauge the extent of its activities, though it is unlikely that it ever really took off. Three years later, in November 1890, Black, Shuttleworth and Baum were still holding public meetings and resolving to set up a league to scrutinise employers' attitudes to wages, hours, sanitary conditions and meal-time provisions.[98] By 1892, Black seems to have given up on the project and she would later turn against the idea of the Consumers' League as a potent weapon of the labour movement. In 1907 she wrote that any such league must necessarily fail because of the practical difficulties in obtaining the appropriate information to guide civic minded-shoppers and that a league 'can never hope to be an economic remedy for underpayment'.[99] She did, however, acknowledge that the British organisation had been an inspiration for other consumers around the world. In the US, the Women's Trade Union League copied exactly the efforts of Black and decided to form a Consumers' League in May 1890, though it was not finally organised until 1891.[100] In 1898, the League became an incorprated body and launched its White Label Campaign, which inspired similar efforts in 1902 in France and Germany with the *Ligue Social d'Acheteurs* and the *Käuferbund Deutschland*. Other consumer movements appeared in Holland and Italy while in Berne, the Swiss League, concerned with the activities of the chocolate manufacturers, set up in 1904 a *type de la bonne fabrique*, with which the employers had to apply to obtain admission to *la list blanche*.[101] By 1908, the first International Conference of Consumers' Leagues was held in Geneva with delegates from France, Switzerland, Germany, Belgium, Italy, Austria, Spain and the US, all united behind the conference motto: '*Vivre, c'est acheter; acheter, c'est pouvoir; pouvoir, c'est devoir.*'[102]

That the League failed in Britain does not suggest the absence of a widespread critique against business practices from consumers as well as workers. The campaigns against trusts and the practice of 'profiteering' has usually been held within the province of work relations and labour history. But, just as with the fight against multinational capitalism today, objections were raised by both workers and consumers in the protests

[98] *The Times* (20 November 1890), p. 7.
[99] C. Black, *Sweated Industry and the Minimum Wage* (London, 1907), p. 211.
[100] M. Nathan, *The Story of an Epoch-Making Movement* (London, 1926), pp. 23–4.
[101] Greig, *Consumer in Revolt*, p. 93; K. K. Sklar, 'The consumer's White Label Campaign of the National Consumers' League, 1898–1918', in S. Strasser, C. McGovern and M. Judt (eds.), *Getting and Spending: European and American Consumer Societies in the Twentieth Century* (Cambridge, 1998), pp. 17–35; W. Breckman, 'Disciplining consumption: the debate on luxury in Wilhelmine Germany, 1890–1914', *Journal of Social History*, 24 (1991), 485–505; M.-E. Chessel, 'Aux origines de la consommation engagée: la Ligue sociale d'acheteurs, 1902–1914', *Vingtième siècle. Revue d'histoire*, forthcoming.
[102] Although the British League was long since defunct, representatives of the Anti-Sweating League did attend: Nathan, *Epoch-Making Movement*, p. 99–100.

against low wages and high prices. Henry Macrosty, for instance, in his calls for a programme of state regulation and nationalisation, was wary of a purely productivist mentality in opposing monopoly, emphasising instead that the state must represent more than just the sectionalism of the workers and aim at the good of the whole: 'its standpoint is that of the consumer, its purpose is the making of citizens'.[103] While within working-class politics consumers and producers most closely came together in the anti-trust movement in the First World War, the existence of large-scale business combines politicised other consumers as well. In a short-lived journal (1911–12) devoted to defending the interests of 'Mr Middle Class', *Watch Dog* condemned the 'shams, tyrants, sweaters, swindlers, rogues, and vagabonds' who exploited the consumer.[104] Begun as a populist and light-hearted weekly magazine for the likes of H. G. Wells' Kipps, *Watch Dog* soon developed a clearer political objective: 'the championship of the . . . oppressed middle classes'. This could take the form of bitter hatred against socialists and the labour movement ('several Labour leaders ought to decorate suburban lamp-posts'), racist rants against Jews by regular columnist 'Jim Crow', defensive eulogies to the 'tragedy of the suburban trader' and the perennial exposés of the London beggars who made a daily fortune.[105] Yet it could also result in campaigns typical of the Co-operative movement: *Watch Dog* fumed on several occasions over short-weight bread ('the biggest swindle of the day'), 'chemists and their tricks', the sweated trades of the Midlands and the false claims of the retail sale.[106] It set out many of the concerns that would be familiar to late twentieth-century consumer protection legislation. When the men went to work at the office, suburbia became a hunting ground for door-to-door salesmen who sold their wares to unprotected women: 'servant girls are the readiest victims of these men. The agents, of course, pursue special tactics for the benefit of Mary Ann, whose unsophisticated nature makes her an easy prey.'[107] Similar articles which played on the fears of the 'respectable classes' included revelations of the fraudulent methods of dating agencies ('matrimonial agents'), puppet shows, bogus charities, shoddy tailors ('the perils of the cheap suit'), unqualified opticians, theatre ticket traders and the 'blunders' of doctors.[108] With its articles on the sordid nocturnal activities in public parks, its calls for cinema censorship as early as 1912, its complaints about the tube and the commuter train

---

[103] H. W. Macrosty, *Trusts and the State: A Sketch of Competition* (London, 1901), pp. 308–9.
[104] *Watch Dog*, 1:1, 4 November 1911, p. 2.
[105] *Watch Dog*, 1:5 (1911), 130–1; 1:9 (1911), 262.
[106] *Watch Dog*, 1:2 (1911), 34; 1:4 (1911), 102; 1:5 (1911), 134; 1:6 (1911), 170; 1:11 (1912), 327; 1:13 (1912), 396.
[107] *Watch Dog*, 1:7 (1911), 209.
[108] *Watch Dog*, 1:8 (1911), 229, 242; 1:16 (1912), 490, 495; 1:18 (1912), 551, 559.

Figure 1   'The thrilling adventures of Mr Middle Class', *Watch Dog*, 1:10 (1912), 301.

and its statistics on the number of foreigners living in London, *Watch Dog* comes across as a parody of the petty-minded concerns of the lower middle class so condemned and ridiculed by the intellectuals of John Carey's thesis.[109] Yet for all that, the magazine demonstrates a growing consumer consciousness that might be individualist and self-serving in nature, but which had the potential to merge with other concerns about the state regulation of industry and the power relations of monopoly capitalism. In a series of cartoons, 'Mr Middle Class' may well have been pitted against organised labour interests, but he was much more the victim of the 'bread trust', the 'milk ring' and the 'coal trust' (see Figure 1).

The existence of *Watch Dog*'s consumerist concerns demonstrate the difficulty of outlining a coherent politics of consumption around the turn of the twentieth century. The 'consumer interest' might have been expressed through questions of adulteration, weights and measures legislation or even standard of living debates in social surveys. The Co-operative movement might have represented the most radical consumer movement, but proponents of Free Trade liberalism and the trade unions also claimed to speak for the consumer. And even among those who felt a focus on the consumer was the principal point of entry for a class politics, differences emerged over the extent to which this should be a woman's issue or a topic intricately bound up with work. Although historians of the same period in the United States have begun to suggest the development of a body of ideas of consumer-citizenship, often based around the notion of the 'living wage', this would perhaps be too sharp a focus to apply to Britain where there was a much more divergent body of consumerist thought. What is apparent is that in the late nineteenth century the consumer could mean everybody and yet nobody at the same time, as grand statements of consumer theory were insufficiently translated into specific programmes of consumer action. This marks the history of all types of consumer politics in all periods, and would seem to dilute the concerns of any movement of consumers. Yet the diversity of interests, issues and agendas attached to consumerism could also revitalise an emergent politics, and what is clear from the above is the richness of the ideas associated with consumption that refuelled and redirected many strands of the labour movement. This is because, in this period at least, a politics of bread was central to the development of political consciousness, citizens imagining themselves in the political arena as both consumers and producers. The variety of tactics deployed reflects the lack of an ideology of consumption pervading all aspects of the labour movement, but certainly we can discuss a politics of

---

[109] J. Carey, *The Intellectuals and the Masses: Pride and Prejudice Among the Literary Intelligentsia, 1880–1939* (London, 1992).

necessitous consumption at a level higher than that of a 'bread and butter' issue. There was a consumer consciousness around the turn of the twentieth century as people formulated a sense of what they earned in terms of what they could buy. If at any point the many strands of consumer thought did merge, it was over critiques of profiteering and in the sense of injustice people held over the perceived abuses of monopoly capitalism. In certain situations, notably times of poverty and extreme hardship, this issue had the potential to focus the politics of consumption. In the First World War, this situation would become apparent, as the Consumers' Council of the Ministry of Food positioned itself as the vanguard of a consumer society structured around necessities if not luxuries.

2 Revolutionary shoppers: the Consumers' Council and scarcity in World War One

Throughout the First World War, food shortages provoked a series of disturbances across the world and acted as catalysts for wider political discontent. Women, as family provisioners, were often foregrounded in demonstrations against the increasing cost of living, and a 'female consciousness' has been observed in the food protests that took place in 1917 in Melbourne, Barcelona and New York.[1] The phenomenon has been most systematically analysed in Berlin where Belinda Davis has suggested the sympathetic recognition of the political legitimacy of food protests may have delayed the revolution in Germany until 1918.[2] As soon as the British blockade became effective, shortages and price rises led to public anger being expressed on the streets. Women of lesser means led the calls for a 'food dictatorship' and the subsequent state system of rationing did alleviate some of the distribution problems of the private market. However, military control of the food supply was not sufficient to cope with the privations of the 'turnip winter' of 1917–18 and Berlin consumers soon gave up on their earlier social compact with the government. By November 1918 housewives had joined workers in attacking a régime they felt did not respond to the basic everyday needs of the populace.[3] Of other national food-shortage contexts the most spectacular is, of course, that of Russia in 1917. Although the implications for gender and consumerism have not been explored here, the food supply crisis has been recognised as 'both symptom and intensifier of the overall

---

[1] D. Frank, 'Housewives, socialists and the politics of food: the 1917 New York cost-of-living protests', *Feminist Studies*, 11 (1985), 255–85; J. Smart, 'Feminists, food and the fair price: the cost of living demonstrations in Melbourne, August–September 1917', *Labour History*, 50 (1986), 113–31; T. Kaplan, 'Female consciousness and collective action: the case of Barcelona, 1910–1918', *Signs*, 7 (1982), 545–66.

[2] B. J. Davis, *Home Fires Burning: Food, Politics and Everyday Life in World War I Berlin* (Chapel Hill, 2000).

[3] *Ibid.*, pp. 6–7. See also A. Offer, *The First World War: An Agrarian Interpretation* (Oxford, 1989), p. 2.

dislocation and then breakdown of national economic and social life' prior to the revolution.[4]

No crisis of such monumental proportions occurred in Britain. Certainly, the predominant fear throughout the war was that high prices, 'profiteering' and shortages, especially after the start of the German submarine blockade in 1917, would cause industrial unrest among workers and consumers in the major urban centres. The Increase of Rent and Mortgage Interest (War Restrictions) Act was a direct consequence of the Clydeside rent strike of 1915 and its further extension in 1919 was a reaction to the new rent strikes in Coventry and Woolwich.[5] More generally, though, part of the reason for the comparative absence of popular disturbances was the successful control of the food supply and the system of rationing introduced by the government in the final stages of the war. As Lloyd George wrote in his memoirs, the Allied victory was deeply dependent upon the efficient control of the civilian food supply, especially if compared to the serious damage done to morale through the Central Powers' failure to maintain supplies.[6] But moreover, and as this chapter will demonstrate, the creation of the Consumers' Council in January 1918 diluted much working-class tension that could have spilled over on to the streets. A deliberate attempt at political containment, the Council was intended to funnel much class antagonism through an official body and away from more radical and independent organisations. Yet the Council also became the means by which a socialist politics of consumption was articulated most consistently, bringing together the range of ideas and practices that had motivated working-class consumers throughout the nineteenth century. The wartime Cabinet recognised the importance of allowing the trade union movement to have a say in government and many of its leaders were only too willing to participate, acknowledging that moderation and the absence of confrontation would further improve the Labour Party's electoral prospects.[7] If such participation in government served to quash the aggressive spirit of this traditional seat of working-class radicalism, the ideas and policies of the Consumers' Council provides an alternative institutional focus for the examination of developments in socialist thought. By the time of the break-up of the Ministry of Food and the Council's resignation in 1921, a collectivist

---

[4] L. T. Lih, *Bread and Authority in Russia, 1914–1921* (Los Angeles, 1990), p. 1; E. Hobsbawm, *Age of Extremes: The Short Twentieth Century, 1914–1991* (London, 1994), pp. 60–1.
[5] D. Vincent, *Poor Citizens: The State and the Poor in Twentieth-Century Britain* (London, 1991), p. 53.
[6] L. M. Barnett, *British Food Policy During the First World War* (London, 1985), p. xiii.
[7] J. Hinton, *Labour and Socialism: A History of the British Labour Movement, 1867–1974* (Brighton, 1983), p. 115; Vincent, *Poor Citizens*, p. 55.

politics was being advocated with the consumer firmly in the vanguard of opposition to the capitalist system.

Avner Offer has demonstrated the importance of 'bread and potatoes' in winning the war: 'Germany did not run out of rifles or shells. It suffered badly from shortages of food.'[8] This chapter builds on the recognition of the centrality of day-to-day provisioning issues in times of war. It does so not by showing how food blockades could lead to the successful prosecution of war, but by outlining the political developments which emerged from the heightened regard for consumption in war. In the first part, attention will be given to the seriousness with which officials regarded consumer protests as a potential de-stabilising influence. Fear of industrial unrest led to the creation of Britain's first national compulsory rationing scheme and the mass mobilisation of the state apparatus in order to direct and control ordinary consumption. Consumers were here given direct representation within the Ministry of Food and the major part of this chapter will focus on the constitution and activities of the Consumers' Council, set up to advise and inform the Food Controller over working-class food concerns. In some respects, the Council was a vehicle for division, as seen in the splits between the socialists and the co-operators over Free Trade and protection, yet it also set an important precedent in consumer representation, the legacy of which would dominate food policy debate throughout the inter-war period. It also enabled the consumer voice to be mobilised in a consistent manner and, especially in the criticisms of profiteering, a radical working-class consumer consciousness emerged in accord with the other concerns of the labour movement. Ultimately, the Council was subservient to the interests of business in government, but this should not deny the focus it became for an aggressive and oppositional style of consumerism.

Prices and the fear of industrial unrest

Throughout the First World War, the government was concerned about political instability on the home front and the grievances caused by the rising cost of living. By June 1916, retail food prices were 59 per cent above the level of July 1914, provoking the government into appointing a Departmental Committee on Prices.[9] In the House of Commons, the Board of Trade was criticised for having a 'callous' attitude to the 'sufferings of consumers' and Members of Parliament such as Winston Churchill, Alfred Mond and Sir Edward Carson led the calls for the state

[8] Offer, *First World War*, p. 1.
[9] W. H. Beveridge, *British Food Control* (London, 1928), p. 19.

control of the food supply. In October 1916, the Royal Commission on Wheat Supplies, aware of the physical and symbolic importance of bread, recommended that wheat purchasing be taken over by the government. MPs renewed their demands for rationing and regulation and eventually the threat of working-class agitation was raised in Parliament. Throughout May and June of 1917, W. C. Anderson spoke of the privations of the poor while Sir G. Toulmin pointed out that 'a sense of injustice is a bitter condiment for food'.[10] In an important debate, all sides in the Commons acknowledged that profiteering was unpatriotic in wartime and needed to be stamped out, but Anderson further detailed the nature of the problem. In controlled industries, wages were fixed, yet the prices of the goods on which those wages were spent were still open to the fluctuations of the market and the exploitation of the opportunist. Nothing was more likely to cause industrial unrest, he argued, than when women sacrificed their sons on the Front only to be rewarded at home by increases in the cost of living.[11] Later, Anderson would persist with his threats of unrest emerging from the sense of hardship felt by women forced to queue for up to five hours a day. He contrasted their plight and those of the inmates of workhouses who were often at starvation point with the diets of the rich. In an emotive piece of impassioned rhetoric, Anderson first pointed to the meagre crusts that he alleged made up the diets of the working class, only to then list every item on the menu of a dinner held by a Masonic Lodge: 'Oysters, oxtail soup, tomato soup, boiled turbot (sauce Hollandaise), fried soles (sauce maître d'hotels), chicken cutlets, roast saddle of mutton, roast surloin [sic] of beef, Yorkshire pudding, a la Romaine, roast pheasant, Macedoine of fruit, Swiss creams, dessert, coffee.'[12] Each item was designed to increase the anger felt by the miners and munitions workers who had patriotically practised wage restraint only for rising prices to then magnify their plight in the sphere of consumption.

Such tensions in Parliament had forced the government to appoint a Food Controller in 1917.[13] But the pressure for intervention came not only from MPs, but from the streets. In June 1917, Lloyd George appointed a Commission of Enquiry into Industrial Unrest. The evidence from the eight regional committees was overwhelming. While most employers and employees were found to be patriotic and little 'revolutionary' fervour existed throughout the country, a number of grievances persistently caused industrial unrest: restrictions on personal freedom, lack of confidence in the government, the delayed settlement of

[10] *Parliamentary Debates, House of Commons* (hereafter *H. C. Deb.*), 96 (25 July 1917), col. 1297.
[11] *Ibid.*, cols. 1308–11.   [12] *H. C. Deb.*, 100 (17 December 1917), col. 1715.
[13] Beveridge, *British Food Control*, pp. 20–7.

industrial disputes and a whole range of smaller complaints arising from workplace conditions and benefits, including 'the inconsiderate treatment of women, whose wages are sometimes as low as 13s'.[14] However, all the regional Commissions 'put in the forefront', the rising costs of living and the unequal distribution of food:

Commissioners are unanimous in regarding this as the most important of all causes of industrial unrest. Not only is it a leading cause of unrest in itself, but its existence in the minds of the workers colours many subsidiary causes, in regard to which, in themselves, there might have been no serious complaint: and the feeling exists in men's minds that sections of the community are profiting by the increased prices.[15]

Recent historical work has suggested that shortages in the First World War were not as extensive as previously thought. While prices undoubtedly rose, especially for basic necessities, 'supplies of food remained sufficient to meet dietary needs'.[16] Those households with women and older children in well-paid work even experienced some improvement in living standards, being able to purchase certain luxury items, such as tobacco, in ever greater quantities. The experience of shortage was hardly uniform. Depending on contacts, goods were bought under the counter, soldiers on leave were treated with greater preference, loyal customers were looked after by local retailers and fair-minded butchers or retailers might introduce their own supply schemes according to their assessment of their neighbourhood's needs and ability to pay.[17] Yet working-class autobiographies attest to the anger felt with the growing length of queues throughout the war and with the amount of time that had to be devoted to the daily tasks of getting and spending.[18] There is even occasional evidence to point to how the practical difficulties experienced in the marketplace translated into more abstract political opinions. One working-class mother, writing bitterly to her sister in South Africa in March 1918, explained how she was ready to 'scream' on each occasion she queued for hours only to be told the shop had sold out when it reached her turn. She moved on to a more general anger at those who complained of shipyard workers who had to leave their work to take over from their exhausted wives and

[14] Commission of Enquiry into Industrial Unrest, *Summary of the Reports of the Commission*, Cd. 8696 (London, 1917), p. 6.
[15] *Ibid.* [16] J. Stevenson, *Social History of Britain* (1984; Harmondsworth, 1990), p. 81.
[17] E. Flint, *Hot Bread and Chips* (London, 1963), p. 95; J. Ayre, *The Socialist* (University of Brunel manuscript, 1980s), p. 10; J. Armitage, *The Twenty Three Years. Or the Late Way of Life – and of Living* (University of Brunel manuscript, 1974), pp. 64–70.
[18] G. C. Hughes, *Shut the Mountain Gate* (University of Brunel manuscript, 1980s), unpaginated; V. Austin, *[Untitled]* (University of Brunel manuscript, n.d.), p. 7; A. Linton, *Not Expecting Miracles* (London, 1982), p. 5; K. Pearson, *Life in Hull: From Then Till Now* (Hull, 1979), p. 91.

children in the food queues. Finally, such resentment spilled over into a consumer consciousness which became her primary political motivation: 'if you saw one of these crowds waiting for food you would see no rich or their maids or trades-people. No, that is all *managed*. I was always a bit of a Socialist but I am a rank one now and I've a vote at the next General Election. And I've a tongue and when I am waiting in mobs it is not quiet. Nothing will make my tongue wag more than want of a cup of tea.'[19]

The arguments of Labour politicians and the feelings of industrial workers all suggest a growing consumer consciousness provoked by the special conditions of the war. In her examination of First World War rationing, Margaret Barnett has argued that the labour movement's new consumer advocates were responsible for the government's shift towards food control from May 1917: 'compulsory price controls and rationing came about in direct response to popular demand and were effective because that demand existed'.[20] Indeed, she goes on to suggest that the government's consumer responsiveness also marked a shift away from the neglect that had previously marked consumer protection legislation. Perhaps underplaying the efforts of the Co-operative movement she nevertheless suggests 'the novelty of the situation during the First World War lay as much in the development of a cohesive consumer consciousness and the emergence of organised spokesmen and women who campaigned for consumer rights, as it did in the modification of the national philosophy of government'.[21]

The focus for this consumer politics was more often than not the War Emergency: Workers' National Committee (WEC). Formed in August 1914, the WEC was initially concerned with industrial relations and the problems of the worker, but it increasingly directed its attention to consumer affairs. Under the initial chairmanship of Arthur Henderson but influenced strongly by the ideas of Sidney Webb and the agendas of Robert Smillie, President of the Miners' Federation, and H. M. Hyndman, former leader of the Social Democratic Federation, the WEC campaigned for such consumer issues as the state control of the food supply, maximum prices, bread subsidies, the encouragement of agriculture and allotments, and special nutritional programmes for mothers and children.[22] Within a month of its establishment, the WEC had set up a Food Prices Sub-Committee, which included the Labour MPs Anderson, W. Brace and

---

[19] M. Todd, *Snakes and Ladders: An Autobiography* (London, 1960), p. 63.
[20] Barnett, *British Food Policy*, p. xvii.   [21] *Ibid.*, p. 127.
[22] *Ibid.* p. 131; R. T. Hyndman, *The Last Years of H. M. Hyndman* (London, 1923), pp. 85–7; J. M. Winter, *Socialism and the Challenge of War: Ideas and Politics in Britain, 1912–1918* (London, 1974); R. Harrison, 'The War Emergency Workers' National Committee, 1914–1920', in A. Briggs and J. Saville (eds.), *Essays in Labour History, 1886–1923* (Basingstoke, 1971), pp. 211–59.

Ramsay MacDonald, as well as Hyndman, Webb and Susan Lawrence of London County Council. By the beginning of October 1914 it was already urging the government to establish a Royal Commission on Wheat with the 'definite objects' of the state to commandeer all wheat stocks, to sell at fixed prices and to ensure that farmers put aside land for wheat production.[23] District Conferences on Food Prices were organised throughout England, mobilising working-class opinion behind resolutions that 'urged the Government to take immediate action to control supplies, to regulate food prices, and to prevent gambling with the means of life to the common people, and to prevent the community being exploited'.[24] A National Conference on Food Prices was held on 12 March 1915 and special investigations were made into coal and wheat prices and shipping freights, while women's particular consumer interests were researched by Lawrence, Mary Macarthur (General Secretary to the Women's Trade Union League), Margaret Bondfield (founder of the National Federation of Women Workers and active in the Women's Co-operative League) and Dr Marion Phillips of the Women's Labour League.[25] In addition, the WEC frequently published a *Memorandum on the Increased Cost of Living* which reportedly sold well throughout the country and led some trades councils to call for a Bread Act, setting down standard weights for the sale of the loaf.[26]

It should be of little surprise that historians have picked up on these calls for the regulation of bread and other staples as indicative of a resurgence of the 'moral economy'. Bernard Waites sees in the work of the WEC, rent strikes, the protests of co-operators and tenants' associations, and the response of the government through rent controls in 1915 and food controls from 1917, a widespread antipathy to profiteering that mobilised the working class against capitalism. Although there was no direct equivalent of the eighteenth-century bread riot, there was always the danger that the anger expressed in queues might spill over into the sort of protests being witnessed on the streets of Berlin. Furthermore, some strikes, such as that in Coventry in 1917, were directly attributable to higher food prices and absenteeism proliferated in times of shortage as workers were eager to relieve wives and family from the burdens of queuing.[27] But rather than

[23] War Emergency: Workers' National Committee, *Minutes of Executive Committee* (London, 1914–16), 5 October 1914 and 14 January 1915.
[24] *Ibid.*, 4 February 1915.   [25] *Ibid.*, 25 March 1915; *Dictionary of National Biography.*
[26] *Ibid.*, 16 September 1915; War Emergency: Workers' National Committee, *Memorandum on the Increased Cost of Living During the War, August 1914 – June 1916*, 3rd edn (London, 1916).
[27] B. Waites, 'The government of the Home Front and the "moral economy" of the working class', in P. H. Liddle (ed.), *Home Fires and Foreign Fields: British Social and Military Experience in the First World War* (London, 1985), pp. 175–93.

attempting to impose on the events of 1914–18 an analytical framework borrowed from the eighteenth century, it is perhaps more appropriate to see in wartime working-class radicalism a close attention to consumerist concerns which were, for this brief period at least, entirely in accord with the producer-centred interests of the worker. There is no doubt that the constitution of the WEC reflected the dominance of traditional labour movement interests. Of the initial fifteen Executive Committee members, three were from the Parliamentary Committee of the Trades Union Congress, three from the Labour Party Executive, three from the management committee of the General Federation of Trade Unions and there were a further six individual members such as Hyndman, Smillie and Webb.[28] The Executive soon expanded and had doubled in size by March 1916, incorporating three Co-operative representatives and the three prominent women members, Macarthur, Bondfield and Phillips.[29] But Labour interests dominated, the WEC's secretary, J. S. Middleton, also being the assistant secretary of the Labour Party. And, by 1917, believing that the WEC was becoming too closely recognised as Labour's voice on consumer issues, the Co-operative representatives withdrew in order not to have their distinctive voice eclipsed.[30]

What is perhaps most significant about the WEC was its attempt to develop a coherent consumer policy and the appeal this had with the public. The WEC became most effective when it turned away from a purely productivist mentality and began focussing on issues such as food and fuel prices, rent and taxes. According to J. M. Winter, Sidney Webb was able to use the WEC as a vehicle for his own ideas, though Webb's pro-war stance with Hyndman prevented the deliberate use of the hunger issue to disrupt the war effort.[31] Guided by Webb, the WEC's consumer policy advocated the government control of food supply and its distribution and the setting of maximum prices for all necessities. Conflating the citizen and the consumer, it proposed the establishment of Citizen Committees, assisted by all Labour, Socialist, Co-operative and Women's organisations, 'to guard against the exploitation of the people by unnecessarily high prices'.[32] These measures would be bolstered by public works programmes to maintain employment levels, adequate Labour and female representation on the local committees of the National Relief Fund and a series of legislative Acts to provide health and maternity benefits, meals, cheap rents, insurance and employment rights. Combining the consumer

[28] Winter, *Socialism*, p. 187.

[29] War Emergency: Workers' National Committee, *Report, August 1914 to March 1916* (London, 1916).

[30] Winter, *Socialism and the Challenge of War*, pp. 205–6. The Co-operative Societies later re-affiliated in the interest of Labour unity.

[31] *Ibid.*, p. 202.   [32] WEC, *Report*, p. 3.

concerns developed through Beatrice's co-operative investigation with the state Socialist measures of his Fabian outlook, Webb and the WEC recognised the importance of focussing as much on price as on the wage in the setting of any 'national minimum' for the relief of poverty. As a consequence, the WEC campaigned from the very beginning of the war for greater consumer and worker representation in government, especially on the Food Prices Committee within the Board of Trade which was made up of producer and distributor interests with no members of the Labour or Co-operative movements.[33]

In terms of success, the WEC played a crucial role in the establishment of food control from 1917. Rising prices and shortages in that year intensified labour protests of which the WEC became the focal point. Hyndman's advocacy of a bread subsidy (the '6d loaf') mobilised working-class anger and scared the authorities into believing that a riot triggered by high bread prices was inevitable. A bread subsidy was introduced in 1917 as the government began to extend its controls. The WEC also maintained the pressure for intervention, particularly in the latter half of 1917 when massive queues triggered popular resentment. In December over 3,000 people were alleged to have waited for margarine outside a southeast London grocery store and women in Sheffield threatened to raid the shops unless provided with tea and sugar. Queues provoked much rowdy and near-riotous demonstrations around the country and were taken seriously by the government, especially when the miners' leader and WEC member, Bob Smillie, suggested that the patience of working men was running out over the privations suffered by their wives in their everyday purchasing routines.[34] This labour unrest only ended once rationing had been introduced in November and had begun to be seen working, in the sense that queues were shortened and price rises checked, though in 1918 one minor riot did break out in Ipswich over the price of butter.[35] Furthermore, working-class resentment was contained and channelled through the establishment of the Consumers' Council within the Ministry of Food, a measure which satisfied many of the WEC's claims for greater representation of the concerns and interests of the ordinary shopper within the state apparatus.

Food control

Prior to the implementation of a full system of food control, the government's policy on consumption was one of propaganda, persuasion

---

[33] *Ibid.*, p. 13.   [34] Barnett, *British Food Policy*, p. 142.
[35] F. Trentmann, 'Bread, milk and democracy: consumption and citizenship in Britain, c.1903–51', in M. Daunton and M. Hilton (eds.), *The Politics of Consumption: Material Culture and Citizenship in Europe and America* (Oxford, 2001), p. 139.

and education. Voluntary bodies such as the National Food Economy League, the National War Savings Committee and the Patriotic Food League undertook the task of instructing the housewife in nutrition and the efficient use of scarce resources.[36] The government soon followed through its Ministry of Food, established in 1916 with Lord Devonport as the first Food Controller. A Women's Service was established which held Food Economy meetings in every town and village, set up approximately 1200 local Food Economy Campaign Committees and 'preached the gospel of food saving'.[37] Devonport was widely criticised for his Voluntary Economy campaign, even his own staff acknowledging that he 'sympathised more with the trader than with the consumer'.[38] Nevertheless, he persisted with the policy, appointing Sir Arthur Yapp of the YMCA as Director of Voluntary Food Economy. If one contrasts Yapp's efforts with the demands of the WEC, the experience of queuing and the calls for a more active role for the Co-operative movement in government, it is not difficult to understand the resentment many felt at his lectures. His own department eventually advised him to avoid speaking in the larger provincial cities for fear of attack and his schemes for voluntary rations for the poor were condemned by journalists who were quick to point out that no such rationing was visible on the menus of the Ritz.[39] Great expense was incurred on the voluntary scheme: 5 million leaflets were distributed of a Royal Proclamation urging the people to practise economy and frugality, as well as hundreds of thousands of pledges, certificates, memoranda, instructions and 'blue anchors' that were freely distributed.[40] Condemned by the media (see Figure 2) and criticised in Parliament, Yapp and the voluntary measures quietly disappeared, to be replaced by a more comprehensive policy of compulsory rationing.[41]

It was not until the unpopular Food Controller, Lord Devonport, was replaced by Lord Rhondda in June 1917 that policy shifted from the voluntary to the compulsory and regulations were implemented that led to the 'complete control over nearly everything eaten and drunk by 40,000,000 persons'.[42] Facing the potential crises of industrial unrest

---

[36] M. Teich, 'Science and food during the Great War: Britain and Germany', in H. Kamminga and A. Cunningham (eds.), *The Science and Culture of Nutrition, 1840–1940* (Amsterdam, 1995), pp. 213–34; M. Pugh, 'Women, food and politics, 1880–1930', *History Today*, 41 (1991), 17.

[37] C. S. Peel, *A Year in Public Life* (London, 1919), p. 25.   [38] *Ibid.*, p. 44.

[39] *Ibid.*, p. 167; Barnett, *British Food Policy*, p. 143.

[40] F. H. Coller, *A State Trading Adventure* (Oxford, 1925), p. 40; H. W. Clemesha, *Food Control in the North-West Division* (Manchester, 1922), p. 30.

[41] Coller, *State Trading Adventure*, facing p. 48; *H. C. Deb.*, 100 (17 December 1917), col. 1714.

[42] Beveridge, *British Food Control*, p. 3.

Figure 2   'Alimentary intelligence', *Punch*, 11 April 1917, p. 235.

and an effective submarine blockade, Rhondda was forced to reorganise the Ministry of Food and the entire system of distribution. Within a year, households had been registered for the rationing of most basic necessities, a government company had been set up to co-ordinate food purchasing in the US and a system of local Divisional Food Commissioners and Food Control Committees had been created. Whereas Devonport's notion of consumer policy involved publicity stunts such as the comedian Harry Lauder addressing a mass meeting of domestic servants in Drury Lane Theatre, Rhondda worked hard to abolish the inequalities that had caused so much resentment. Here, his agenda was already set, as detailed plans for food control had previously been worked out and the government had decided that the Food Controller had 'special responsibilities to the working classes': on 30 May 1917 a definite offer was even made to Robert Smillie to take over from Devonport.[43] Nevertheless, by the time of his death caused by the strains of overwork in July 1918, Rhondda had done much to restore the confidence of consumers in the government and he himself had become a popular and well-known figure.[44]

Rhondda's system of food control involved a massive expansion of the state. When Devonport resigned, his staff at the Ministry was just 400. In the first six months of his period of office, Rhondda appointed a further 3,000 staff and another 1,000 in the first months of 1918. Together with divisional employees and members of the 1,900 local food committees, 'about 26,000 men and women were involved in food administration at the end of the war'.[45] Rhondda, in peacetime a fervent advocate of Free Trade and liberal individualism, co-ordinated this enormous staff which ensured that '90 per cent of all food sold fell into one of the categories of control'.[46] It was he who received the credit for the introduction of a rationing scheme, though the WEC had long been calling for this and some towns, such as Gravesend, forced him to overcome his disinclination for rationing by pre-empting any national efforts when they introduced their own schemes from as early as November 1917.[47] The one successful measure introduced by Devonport, the bread subsidy, prevented this good from being rationed, but official procedures were started for most other staples, with special provisions being introduced for commodities such as milk to ensure adequate supplies reached mothers and children. Although the Ministry of Food was never able to stamp out profiteering, with many poor consumers not even being able to afford to buy their

[43] According to *ibid.*, p. 49; Barnett disagrees, *British Food Policy*, pp. 132–3.
[44] *Dictionary of National Biography*.
[45] Barnett, *British Food Policy*, p. 125.   [46] *Ibid.*, p. 136.
[47] A. J. Philip, *Rations, Rationing and Food Control* (London, 1918); Barnett, *British Food Policy*, pp. 146–7.

rationed amounts, Rhondda won public favour as the rationing measures were held to have been comparatively successful, with 'consumption of the average working person falling by only 3 per cent during the war'.[48]

Rhondda's popularity also rested very much on the attention he gave, or was seen to give, to the interests of the ordinary consumer. He made genuine attempts to foster good relations with the labour movement and won the respect of figures such as Smillie. He repeatedly claimed in public statements that he was 'on the side of the consumer'[49] and at official meetings he was keen to come across as a consumer advocate, telling senior ministers of his perceived role: 'I don't care a hang who suffers, whose interests go under, if I can make this job of the Ministry of Food a success for the consumer.'[50] He also listened to complaints about the lack of representation of the working-class consumer on local food committees. These consisted of twelve people appointed by the local authority for their knowledge of local affairs and trading conditions. They oversaw the local administration of rationing and distribution schemes, maximum prices, the enforcement of orders, the inspection of records of dealings and prices of the most controlled commodities, and the propaganda for voluntary economy and the prevention of waste. The problem for the WEC and other labour organisations was that the ordinary consumer was inadequately represented on the committees and the Co-operative movement had been deliberately excluded by local authority interests which ensured that the committees were packed with private farmers and retailers. In November 1917, of the 21,322 members of the 1,903 committees, 3,129 or 15 per cent were farmers and 2,572 or 12 per cent were traders, while only 584 or 2.5 per cent were from the Co-operative movement. Rhondda and others were sympathetic to the complaints about such figures and by June 1919 the proportion of members who were farmers had fallen to 9 per cent and food traders to 11 per cent, with Co-operative representation increasing to $5\frac{1}{2}$ per cent. In the same period the number of women on the committees had risen from 2,466 to 3,884 and that of labour representatives from 2,712 to 5,549.[51] However, as the more detailed figures for January 1919 in Table 1 show, the working-class consumer was still very much in the minority and something of the overall, pro-business and anti-co-operative tone of the committees can be seen in the first report of March 1918: in a discussion about falling supplies, it claimed most

[48] Barnett, *British Food Policy*, p. 152.
[49] *The Times* (2 July 1917), p. 3.   [50] Cited in Barnett, *British Food Policy*, p. 134.
[51] There is some overlap in the figures as the categories are not mutually exclusive: Beveridge, *British Food Control*, pp. 58–9. See also Clemesha, *Food Control*, p. 2.

Table 1. *Statistics of membership of Food Control Committees*

Total membership	16552	
Labour		
Nominated reps	2358	14.2%
Un-nominated reps	1787	10.8%
Total	4141	25.0%
Women		
Nominated reps	440	2.7%
Un-nominated reps	2509	15.2%
Total	2949	17.8%
Co-operative movement		
Nominated reps	678	4.1%
Un-nominated reps	274	1.7%
Total	952	5.8%
Food retailers/distributors	1822	11.0%
Farmers	1400	8.5%
Others	6873	41.5%

Source: Consumers' Council archive, Marion Phillips papers, Manchester Labour History Archive (hereafter CC) CP 3/7: *Food Control Committees*, 6 January 1919. These figures were compiled using data from 1,390 committees (449 did not respond). There is also some double counting: e.g., a female labour representative.

complaints came from colliery villages 'where discontent has been fermented by certain Socialist Demagogues, out to destroy individual retail trade'.[52] That there was a case for increased consumer participation was highlighted by the occasional prosecution of committee-member farmers and traders for offences against orders which they were supposed to administer.

The Consumers' Council

Given the anger felt by those who believed the consumer interest to be unheard and unrepresented, some official outlet was deemed necessary. Just as the *Kriegsernährungsamt* was instituted in Germany in 1916 to take account of the interests of the ordinary food consumer, so the Consumers' Council was to articulate the everyday concerns of the British working class.[53] Formed in January 1918 at the suggestion of the Labour MP and Parliamentary Secretary to Rhondda, J. R. Clynes, the Council

---

[52] Consumers' Council archive, Marion Phillips papers, Manchester Labour History Archive (hereafter CC) CR: *Commissioners' Reports*, 1 (23 March 1918).
[53] Davis, *Home Fires*, p. 114.

was set up to enlist the co-operation of the organised working classes in the task which lay before the Ministry of Food.[54] Clynes, first chairman of the Council, stated in Parliament that the representatives of women and the working class were to learn how the Ministry of Food operated and 'see with an eye on the consumer whether the interests and rights of consumers are being properly watched or not'.[55] It was to be independent of government and while the Food Controller was to retain all authority, the opinions of the Council were to be sought regularly on matters such as rationing, transport, administration and 'all questions arising from the shortage of certain articles of food'.[56] It was to represent no special interest, except that of 'the public at large' and the 'ordinary citizen', thereby explicitly making consumption an aspect of modern citizenship and an action falling within the legitimate sphere of state interference. There was much idealist rhetoric marking the creation of the Consumers' Council. Rhondda spoke of the alliance between producers and consumers and regarded the Council as a point of unproblematic direct access to the views of the ordinary consumer, while Food Ministry officials later reminisced about the 'concentration of massed endeavour and willing service that made light of almost insuperable obstacles'.[57]

Historians, more cynically, have seen the Council as a deliberate measure of political containment.[58] The work of the WEC on matters of consumption had become a threat to the government and this explains the overtures made by Lloyd George to Smillie to become the first Food Controller.[59] The Council was instituted as part of this broader attempt to bring the criticisms of labour away from more dangerous channels of political expression and into the sphere of official state bureaucracy. One civil servant went so far as to say that it was a 'powerful instrument for the prevention of industrial unrest', a body far more 'docile' than the angry Labour Congresses. Its purpose was far more of a propaganda device than the two-way exchange of information that Rhondda envisaged: 'The great point was to clear people's minds of suspicion; to convince them that a modest degree of privation was inevitable and that, so far as essential foodstuffs were concerned, rich and poor would share alike.'[60]

---

[54] CC CP 94/3: H. S. Syrett, *Report on the Constitution and Work of the Consumers' Council* (31 December 1919), p. 1.
[55] Beveridge, *British Food Control*, p. 71.   [56] CC CP 94/3: p. 2.
[57] Beveridge, *British Food Control*, p. 76; E. M. H. Lloyd, *Experiments in State Control at the War Office and the Ministry of Food* (Oxford, 1924), p. 1.
[58] P. Gurney, *Co-operative Culture and the Politics of Consumption in England, 1870–1930* (Manchester, 1996), pp. 215–16; M. French and J. Phillips, *Cheated Not Poisoned? Food Regulation in the United Kingdom, 1875–1938* (Manchester, 2000), p. 139.
[59] Winter, *Socialism and the Challenge of War*, p. 202
[60] Coller, *State Trading Adventure*, p. 127.

The arrogance of one official who compared the Council's complaints to that of a naughty child does at least make it clear how many civil servants regarded the entry of the working class into government. Of the general criticisms made by the Council of the government in the later stages of the war and in the period of de-control, Frank Coller wrote, 'while they [the members of the Council] violently abused the Ministry of Food themselves, they would allow no one else to abuse us, and instead that, for that worst of all things, a Ministry in a capitalistic State, we were comparatively decent and in rare cases almost worthy of consideration'.[61] The labour movement was not blind to such intentions. When the WEC was asked to send representatives to the Consumers' Council, Hyndman admitted that 'little, if any, good' would come out of its work, but, crucially, he thought that it at least put 'a few determined persons inside the enemy's entrenchments'.[62] Hyndman felt that this representation might be important at a critical moment and his attitude points to a more positive interpretation of the work of the Council. For all the deliberate attempts to contain working-class anger over food prices and shortages, the Council became an effective outlet for consumer concerns and, although it increasingly 'irritated' business and commercial interests in the moves to de-control after the war, it enabled a determined effort to be made for the articulation of a coherent politics of necessitous consumption.

Meeting weekly, the Council was constituted purely as an advisory body, though many of its recommendations were translated into policy and specific orders. It consisted of six representatives of the Co-operative movement, three representatives of the Parliamentary Committee of the Trades Union Congress, three figures from the WEC (including Hyndman) and three from the Standing Joint Committee of Industrial Women's Organisations (M. E. Cottrell, A. E. Reeves and Marion Phillips). Rhondda deliberately sought to dilute any radicalism that such organised labour and consumer representatives might develop and he appointed three figures to stand in for the 'unorganised consumer': the Countess of Selborne, Lord Rathcreedan and Sir William Ashley, first professor of business studies at Birmingham University.[63] The Council Secretary, Sydney Walton, and the Secretary to the Minister of Food, S. P. Vivian, felt that further 'safe' representatives were required. The Liberal social reformer and anti-suffragist, Violet Markham, was therefore asked to become a fourth unorganised consumer, specifically to tone

[61] Ibid., p. 131.   [62] Winter, Socialism and the Challenge of War, p. 155.

[63] CC CP 94/3: pp. 1–2. Conservatives often asked in Parliament why there were no middle-class consumers or even retailers on the Council: H. C. Deb., 112 (26 February 1919), col. 1766; 114 (26 March 1919), col. 424; 118 (14 July 1919), col. 45.

down the 'Bolshevik' element within the Council.[64] She declined, but concerns persisted and Rhondda deliberately took Selborne and Ashley aside and 'told them that their duty would be to moderate the zeal of the labour members, especially Hyndman'.[65] Such efforts at further containment were unsuccessful. Both Selborne and Rathcreedan proved ineffective and only Ashley was left to counter the aggression of Hyndman. Furthermore, a revealing letter from Walton to Markham points to the areas of chaos within the Ministry of Food. Rhondda was accused of not knowing 'one single word of his job', a power battle existed between the senior secretaries, Stephen Tallents, W. H. Beveridge and Vivian, and consequently the whole place was 'a congress of disconnected sections with no top grip of it as a whole anywhere'. Despite his public image, the Cabinet was allegedly considering sacking Rhondda because of his 'ignorance' and replacing him with Andrew Weir, 'some rich Unionist business man'. Within this confused situation, the Consumers' Council was able to exert some influence. A representative of the Ministry was not always at the meetings of the Council, allowing Hyndman to take over the Chair from Clynes. Accordingly, ' "decisions" were adopted and . . . subsequently *published* as the *decisions* of the Council, that became virtually imposed on some Food Committees as orders from the Ministry of Food'.[66] If true, this power vacuum certainly explains some of the successes of the Council, as its resolutions met little resistance. Judging success by its own terms, in 1918 it was responsible for legislation covering pure food and accurate weights and measures and its campaigns to get subsidies and controls extended may well have slowed down price increases towards the end of the war.[67]

The range of topics the Council covered demonstrates the commitment to the consumer cause of many of its members. Sub-committees were set up to deal with issues concerning such specific products as fruit, jam, meat, milk, potatoes, sugar, national kitchens and rationing. In November 1918, immediately following the Armistice, a Reforms Sub-Committee was set up to deal with the wider issues concerning the permanent regulation of food and consumption and the legislative provisions to ensure fairer trading régimes. And Council members sought to put forward the consumer view in the various advisory committees over specific food items within the Ministry of Food. Despite many of the major decisions

---

[64] British Library of Political and Economic Science, Violet Rosa Markham Papers (hereafter Markham), File 24/4: Letter from Sydney Walton to Miss Markham (13 February 1918); *Dictionary of National Biography*.
[65] Barnett, *British Food Policy*, p. 154.
[66] Markham 24/4: Letter from Sydney Walton to Violet Markham, n.d.
[67] Barnett, *British Food Policy*, p. 156.

concerning food control having been made before the Council sat for the first time, it nevertheless produced a flurry of decisions and recommendations that recognised the consumer as the focal point for long-term economic and political change. It is in the minute details of food controls that a consumer philosophy of the Council can be seen to have emerged. For instance, with regard to milk, the Council urged the state purchase of milk wholesalers in order to combat the influence of private producers, whose pricing policies were to be 'regarded as one of the worst forms of profiteering, injurious not only to the present but to coming generations'.[68] Accordingly, they advocated not only regulated prices, but the supply of subsidised milk to all nursing mothers, invalids and children under five.[69] As for milk, so with a whole range of other basic commodities: subsidies, further price controls, measures to combat profiteers, and state intervention were all proposed for goods as diverse as coal and fish. More generally, it bemoaned the lack of consideration given to the consumer in transport policy and the absence of any representation in the 1919 Bill for Agricultural Councils. It managed to prevent the exclusion of working women and adolescent girls from supplementary meat rations in certain industries. It always put purity before adulteration and it developed an international outlook in its calls for a food aid programme in 1919 to alleviate a potential famine in Central and Eastern Europe.[70] But in an indication of the limitations placed on the Council's influence, many of its resolutions were often ignored. Rhondda established a number of Fair Trading Councils, consisting of voluntary representatives of trade and retail organisations, to advise him on prices and distribution issues of specific goods. The Consumers' Council was not invited to sit on these committees and, despite a formal protest, the Food Controller made no changes to this policy which the Council feared offered no check to or criticism of 'any steps the traders may take in their own interest'.[71] Whereas progress was made in securing greater consumer representation on local Food Committees, the Council complained bitterly from 1919 that its objections to the de-control of jam and meat had been ignored, while orders relating to net weight standard of quality had been revoked, the bread subsidy had terminated and the Ministry had not listened to the demands for the state regulation of the milk industry.[72]

[68] CC CP 94/3: pp. 7–8.   [69] CC CP 94/3: p. 18.

[70] *Ibid.*; CC CP 289: *Report on the Work of the Consumers' Council, statement on agricultural position* (14 July 1920).

[71] CC CP 292: H. S. Syrett, *Report on the Work of the Consumers' Council* (5 November 1920), p. 2; CC CP 290: *Summary for Report on Work of Consumers' Council*, p. 2; CC CP 289: *Draft Report*, pp. 5–7.

[72] CC CP 289, p. 5; CC CP 292: p. 2; CC CP 289: *Statement on bread subsidy* (10 March 1920, 5 May 1920, 27 July 1920, 24 August 1920).

The Council clearly committed itself to many initiatives whose popularity in wartime hid the radical socialist agenda that often inspired
its resolutions. For instance, in the period of voluntary food controls
women of the bourgeois philanthropic tradition joined forces with activists such as Marion Phillips and Mary MacArthur in the promotion
of National, or Public, Kitchens. The first of these to be state-run was
opened on the 21 May 1917; various titled ladies were seen to be helping
out while even the Queen ladled out rice pudding at one kitchen.[73] Later,
the Consumers' Council eagerly seized on the initiative and supported
their continuation beyond the war as a counterbalance to the perceived
profiteering in private restaurants.[74] The kitchens, however, proved insufficiently popular, workers preferring to eat at home and the communal
aspects being too strongly reminiscent of the old soup kitchen and the
demeaning aspects of reliance on the charitable endeavour of the wives of
the local elite.[75] If the Council's enthusiasm for such initiatives was not
always met with popular demand, this did little to quell its radical agenda.
From the end of 1918, while various interests favoured the removal of all
wartime controls, the Council made more explicit its socialist leanings as
it defensively proposed a number of measures which it hoped would be
made permanent amidst the general pressure for de-control.

Not only did the Council oppose de-control, it instead suggested a
massively expanded role for the state. Arguing that world trade instability necessitated the continuance of controls, Ministry officials such
as Beveridge recognised that many Council members had ulterior mo-
tives, believing that 'state control or ownership of food was in itself a
good thing, for peace as well as war'.[76] The Reforms Sub-Committee
set about developing a broader consumer policy in the face of pressures
for the end of wartime conditions. It proposed a monopoly of state purchase of imported foodstuffs in order to control supplies and prices and
to make permanent the Ministry of Food which would oversee all of these
activities. It proposed the introduction of rationing whenever price rises
threatened the interests of 'the mass of the people' and it insisted that
the consumer be given the full rights of citizenship within the apparatus
of the state: 'it is absolutely necessary that no question of general policy
should be decided upon [by the Ministry of Food], and no definite action
taken, until all relevant facts are placed before the Consumers' Council
and their views ascertained'.[77] It hoped for a comprehensive system of
international control so that 'it will be possible for every nation to regulate the price and distribution in their own countries from the time of

---

[73] Peel, *Year in Public Life*, p. 187.   [74] CC CP 94/3: p. 18.
[75] Clemesha, *Food Control*, pp. 30–1; Barnett, *British Food Policy*, p. 151.
[76] Beveridge, *British Food Control*, p. 276.   [77] CC CP 94/3: p. 10.

importation to that of sale to the retail purchaser, and it is upon this basis alone that the future can be safeguarded, and the people of all communities be protected against the evils of extreme scarcity, and an enormous increase in the cost of living'.[78]

Here the consumer interest was understood in complete contrast to the rational individualism of liberal economics. The consumer was a citizen standing in opposition to the agendas of businessmen and the vested interests found in the House of Commons. Most government departments as currently constituted could not be trusted 'to protect the consumer'. Instead a new ministry was required that would protect the people 'with regard to supply, with regard to sufficiency of produce, with regard to home production and to standard of quality, and in respect of proper weight and measures'.[79] In addition, protection ought not to be limited only to food, but should cover all the necessaries of life: clothing, fuel, transport and shelter. The Council's Parthian shot in January 1921 was to urge all organisations 'representing Labour, Co-operators and other Working-Class Bodies' to campaign for a department of state 'concerned primarily with the protection of the consumer as distinct from the trader'.[80] The consumer needed to be incorporated into the machinery of government:

Are consumers content that through their apathy Traders and Trusts should triumph over them once again: that their representatives on the Consumers' Council should be ignored: and that the Ministry of Food with its powers to protect the Consumers' interests should be stamped out? If not, now and now only is the time to make a stand.[81]

The Council was over-reaching itself. If at its inception it had captured a popular mood in favour of rationing and the control of consumption in accord with the egalitarian principles of the war effort, at its close it was seen by many in government to be speaking either for, above or beyond the concerns of the ordinary consumer. In any case, events were conspiring to weaken the influence of the Council. By the autumn of 1919 producers were once again dominating food control, as their lobbyists fought for their interests in the Board of Trade and the Treasury. Increasingly, the Council found its resolutions dismissed and unheard,

---

[78] CC CP 94/3: Appendix C: *Report of the Sub-Committee on Reforms* (28 May 1919), p. 29.
[79] CC CP 94/3: Appendix D: *Report of the Sub-Committee on Reforms* (9 April 1919), p. 31; PRO MAF 60/150: Consumers' Council: Sale of Food, 1918–1922: *Memorandum from the Reforms Sub-Committee for the Information of Organised Bodies of Consumers* (21 April 1920).
[80] CC CP 315: Consumers' Council, *Resolution to be submitted for consideration by the Joint Conference of Constituent Organisations* (4 January 1921).
[81] CC CP 292: p. 2.

it was kept in ignorance about crucial decisions affecting consumers until the measures had been put in place and, if it wished to protest, the Prime Minister refused to meet its deputations.[82] Clynes, who had replaced Rhondda briefly as Food Controller but had returned to the back benches by 1920, sought to champion the Council's cause in the Commons, only to find that the low attendance in the debate did not reflect the same concern for prices as shared by 8 million newly enfranchised women voters.[83] Similarly, another Labour MP, Jack Jones, commented on the indifference of politicians to consumer issues: 'We know of laughs that have gone up in the House of Commons when we have put questions as to prices. Any question of limiting the power of profiteers is looked upon as outside the domain of politics'.[84] In the face of this lack of widespread support in Parliament from politicians of all parties and the dismissal of its resolutions in Whitehall, the Consumers' Council saw no choice but to resign.[85] Believing strongly that during the war the trading community had entrenched itself within government and that it acted against 'the well-being of the people', the Council nevertheless saw no role for itself in a government committed to abolishing all controls as well as the Ministry of Food.[86] The Council thus came to an end in January 1921 and the Ministry followed in September 1922.

The Council may well have advocated a democratic notion of consumerism that quelled the potential for food riots throughout the provincial cities, but its focus on the consumer came up against the interests of business and the related indifference of Conservative politicians in Parliament. To suggest that consumer issues were readily dismissed as trivial by other groups outside of Parliament is however to misunderstand the widespread critique of profiteering that occurred at the end of the war. On this issue, the concerns of the Consumers' Council, the Co-operative movement, the Labour Party and the trade unions neatly coalesced. Just as today protests against globalisation bring together first world consumers and third world producers, so too did an anti-trust movement unite trade unionist and co-operator, worker and consumer, husband and wife. Bernard Waites has commented that the productivist or economistic approaches of both Marx and Lenin have blinded scholars to 'the fundamental shift in ideology that took place during the war'.[87]

---

[82] CC CP 290: pp. 1–3.   [83] *H. C. Deb.*, 128 (6 May 1920), cols. 2296, 2318.
[84] CC CP 126/2: *Consumers' Council Conference, 19th February, 1920: Report of the Proceedings*, p. 20.
[85] MAF 60/150: Minutes of the meeting of the Consumers' Council (14 December 1920).
[86] CC CP 316/1: Consumers' Council, *Statement on their Resignation from Ministry of Food*, pp. 1–2.
[87] B. Waites, *A Class Society at War: England 1914–1918* (Leamington Spa, 1987), p. 221.

The critique of profiteering strengthened the socialist cause by combining class-based politics with wider 'them' and 'us' oppositions invoked in demands for 'fairness' and 'fair play'. As the anger in the queues heightened in 1917 and the WEC forefronted consumer issues, labour groups formed local Food Vigilance Committees and short strikes occurred throughout the country. The issue of profiteering fed directly into the campaigns of the Consumers' Council, especially since demonstrations were being held against the unequal distribution policies set out by local Food Committees just as the Council was first meeting.[88] It pointed out any example of profiteering it found relating to a particular commodity, though it felt the problem ran much deeper than this and ran to the heart of government: in December 1919 the Council believed 'a vehement and organised agitation was being carried on against the Ministry of Food by profiteers of great financial and political influence to put an end to the Ministry altogether'.[89]

Profiteering, socialism and co-operation

The government response to the agitation was the appointment of the Committee on Trusts in February 1918. From the start, this was a measure intended to defuse labour unrest, 'not to respond to it in any positive way'.[90] Its recommendations led to the Profiteering Act which enabled the Board of Trade to investigate any monopoly, combination or agreement where there was *prima facie* evidence that the public 'interest' was adversely affected.[91] Strongly objecting to the measures proposed by the Committee a Minority Report was written by the four radical members: the economist, J. A. Hobson, Ernest Bevin of the Labour Party, Sidney Webb and the co-operator and Consumers' Council representative, W. H. Watkins. They believed that the powers of investigation of the Board of Trade needed much strengthening and that the best protection of 'the public of consumers' lay in the promotion of Co-operative stores, the continued state control of certain industries and the forced regulation of prices. Reflecting the collectivist concerns of Bevin, the mixed economy arguments of Hobson and the co-operative principles of Watkins, the document advocated an economic system similar to that promoted by Webb

---

[88] Waites refers to a demonstration against a Food Committee held by up to 10,000 munitions workers in Bedford: Waites, *Class Society*, p. 230.

[89] CC CP 94/3: p. 17.

[90] H. Mercer, *Constructing a Competitive Order: the Hidden History of British Anti-Trust Policy* (Cambridge, 1995), p. 44.

[91] Ministry of Reconstruction, *Report of the Committee on Trusts*, Cd. 9236 (London, 1919), p. 12.

in his *Constitution for the Socialist Commonwealth of Great Britain*. Private enterprise was accepted (Hobson), but where elements of combination and monopoly control began to appear in an industry then its functions ought to be assumed by either the 'Co-operative Movement', 'Municipal Enterprise' or 'State Ownership'.[92] Their opinions were of little influence and the resulting Act was deliberately anodyne in character, with officials such as Beveridge admitting it was a mere instance of 'window-dressing' since the legislation was in any case 'wholly unnecesary'.[93] When investigations did begin to be made by the Standing Committee on Trusts, Watkins felt that business interests were influencing the tenor of reports and Webb soon resigned in October 1920 as he disagreed with most of the conclusions. Helen Mercer has concluded that 'both the intention and effect of the Profiteering Acts were to check social criticism of private enterprise, educate the public and especially the working classes in the inevitability and rightness of trusts, high prices and profits, while giving businessmen a court for their grievances against competitors'.[94] It was a belief certainly shared by the Consumers' Council who predicted its complete ineffectiveness: 'The consumer would be well advised not to rely upon the high sounding terms of the Act or its advertisement by its sponsors, but rather to bathe in the waters of Jordan and join his local co-operative store.'[95]

Though it only existed for three years, there is in the First World War Consumers' Council the culmination of a developing consumer consciousness. The protests over prices and shortages were channelled first through labour and co-operative organisations and ultimately through the Council itself. This enabled a grass-roots anger to combine with democratic, socialist, radical and co-operative ideas articulated by the likes of Webb and Hyndman in the WEC and then Hyndman and his colleagues on the Consumers' Council. Here, the consumer was largely imagined as working class and poor and was more often than not gendered in the sense that the grievances of the housewife (the presumed family provisioner and therefore consumer) became both a persistent political concern and a recognised partner in the labour movement. Consumerism was frequently equated with citizenship as the interests of the former were posited as the fulcrum around which the economy and often politics ought to be organised. Yet, some qualifications to these assertions are necessary. Firstly, it has to be reiterated that the formation of the Consumers' Council was a deliberate act of political containment. Secondly, such a street-based consumer consciousness and its more abstract

[92] *Ibid.*, Addendum, pp. 13–14.   [93] Beveridge, *British Food Control*, p. 289.
[94] Mercer, *Constructing a Competitive Order*, p. 46.
[95] CC CP 31/2/5: Notes by Mr Uthwatt, *Profiteering Act* (3 November 1919), p. 2.

articulation at state level could only occur in the special circumstances of the war, as attested by the campaigns by retailers, manufacturers and Liberal and Conservative politicians to disband the Ministry of Food and the systems of control as soon as the war was over. But, thirdly, there is a great danger in ascribing a coherent vision to the consumerist concerns of the Council. By 1920, it may well have advocated a consumerism closely aligned to state socialism (thus differing from the middle path chosen by countless other consumer activists during the twentieth century), but this could only be done by fracturing organisations of consumers themselves, principally in the classic British political divide: Free Trade versus Protection.

Frank Trentmann has highlighted this division in the consumer interest, pointing out how many in the Co-operative Wholesale Society (CWS) rejected the Council's advocacy of a strong state and instead embraced de-control in the immediate years after the war.[96] Not willing to support measures which might limit its own expansion, the confident CWS with its 9 per cent of retail sales, saw trusts and combines as much less of a threat than 'state trading'. This was a long-standing split within working-class consumerism, reflecting very different conceptions of the relationship between the state, the market and the individual. And it was a split taken advantage of by both Labour and Conservative politicians. Even Clynes, eager to promote the consumer cause, was able to use the Council's co-operative members' prior dislike for state subsidies to reject the Council's call for an extension of its grant.[97] The divisions came to a head at a conference of the constituent organisations of the Council in February 1920. Attended by all members of the Council and with strong attendance from the Labour Party Executive, the WEC, all branches of the Co-operative movement and prominent women activists (Bondfield, Macarthur and Lawrence), the conference opened with a strong statement by Hyndman on the need for state control of supply purchasing and the setting of maximum prices. He listed what he saw as some of the great achievements of the Council (for example, milk distribution, National Restaurants), before urging a resolution for a permanently constituted Ministry of Food to defend especially the interests of 'the people', 'the working classes' and 'consumers generally'.[98] Hyndman was supported by his colleagues on the Council such as Phillips and Sexton who urged

[96] CC CP 83/1: H. S. Syrett, *Memorandum as to the Position of the Ministry of Food and the Consumers' Council* (5 January 1920); Trentmann, 'Bread, milk and democracy', pp. 149–52.

[97] Coller, *State Trading Adventure*, p. 184.

[98] CC CP 126/2: Consumers' Council, *Conference with Representatives of Constituent Organisations* (19 February 1920), pp. 3–6.

the Ministry of Food to be extended to defend the consumer with regard to all necessities. Opposition was led by the Co-operative Council member, Gallacher, who, in a defence of the CWS's Free Trade principles, gave countless examples of the inefficiency of state interference to which a permanent consumer body could only add.

The conference ended bitterly, with Labour and trade union representatives accusing the CWS of allying itself to the Federation of British Industry in its support for de-control, employing workers at low rates of pay and thinking only of itself as a retail enterprise rather than a consumers' organisation.[99] In its rejection of the Council's resolution, the Co-operative movement highlighted many of its difficulties since the Women's Co-operative Guild refused to join the CWS and the Parliamentary Committee of the Co-operative Congress. It also isolated itself from the labour movement's new consumer consciousness, heightening the distance between the two that had already occurred when co-operative representatives resigned from the WEC. Yet it also demonstrated the well-known difficulties the movement faced in negotiating its relationship with the state. On the one hand, the CWS certainly did not wish to associate its activities with a 'capitalistic Government' and believed its real power lay in its continued growth as a retail organisation: once a socialist government came into being, the CWS, so it claimed, would happily 'merge our movement into the hands of the Government'.[100] Yet by keeping its distance from the state, the movement also separated itself from the increasingly protectionist stance of the labour movement's attitude to the market and consumer protection. And it also opened itself up to being eclipsed by more government-friendly manufacturing and retail interests. Indeed, it was the experience of the First World War, when the government imposed the Excess Profits Duty on the co-operative 'surplus' in the same way as on the profits of a capitalist concern, that forced the Co-operative movement to form its own political party to defend its interests in Parliament.[101]

Despite these divisions – typical of all movements which try to unite the entire populace behind one identity or consciousness – the importance of the First World War in crystallising a consumerism or consumer politics should not be underplayed. Kenneth O. Morgan has suggested

[99] *Ibid.*, pp. 17–18.   [100] *Ibid.*, p. 11
[101] Gurney, *Co-operative Culture*, pp. 210–15; S. Pollard, 'The foundation of the Co-operative Party', in Briggs and Saville (eds.), *Labour History*, pp. 185–210; P. Maguire, 'Co-operation and crisis: government, co-operation and politics, 1917–1922', in S. Yeo (ed.), *New Views on Co-operation* (London, 1988), pp. 187–206; T. F. Carbery, *Consumers in Politics: A History and General Review of the Co-operative Party* (Manchester, 1969).

one result of the war was discernible in Christopher Addison's Ministry of Reconstruction which by the summer of 1918 had 'sketched out a totally new social agenda, a socialism for consumers if not yet for producers'.[102] Programmes and policies had been developed for housing and slum clearance, land settlement for demobilised soldiers, medical care and insurance (there was to be a new Ministry of Health), improved education and the scrapping of the Poor Law. Within the consumer policies of working-class organisations, important precedents had also been set. Even those sceptical of the usefulness of the Consumers' Council attested to its legacy, leading directly as it did to the establishment of the Royal Commission on Food Prices in 1925.[103] Immediately after it was announced in Parliament that the Council was to be abolished, questions were asked as to how the consumer was to be protected in the future. The Labour Party, the Co-operative movement and the trade unions all began to focus increasingly on consumer issues throughout the inter-war period, with the cost-of-living index becoming a particular rallying point for both workers and consumers united in a joint political project. As will be seen in the following chapter, the principle of consumer representation was also established by the Consumers' Council, provoking many subsequent calls for its revival. Finally, in assessing the legacy of the war, the activities of the Council and the WEC legitimated various forms of state intervention in the marketplace and in the lives of shoppers which would see the greater regulation of the prices of staples and the end of the principle of laissez-faire in many sectors.

[102] K. O. Morgan, *Consensus and Disunity: The Lloyd George Coalition Government, 1918–1922* (Oxford, 1979), p. 24.
[103] Beveridge, *British Food Control*, p. 309; Coller, *State Trading Adventure*, p. 329.

3   The right to live: consumer 'ideology' in inter-war Britain

In 1928, the historian of the Co-operative movement, Percy Redfern, was invited by the publisher, Ernest Benn, to collect together a series of essays on 'social and economic problems from the hitherto neglected point of view of the consumer'.[1] Dominated by co-operative thinkers and activists such as Beatrice Webb and A. V. Alexander, the twenty-four pamphlets attest to the richness and variety of consumer 'ideology' in the inter-war period. Co-operation and socialism were broadened to include a notion of the consumer as citizen, standing hand-in-hand with the worker in the struggle for the 'co-operative commonwealth'. Prominent figures of the Left such as Harold Laski, Philip Snowden, Leonard Woolf, Walter Citrine and Margaret Bondfield wrote of consumerism as a new force in society acting for 'the people' and social justice. The influence of the *Self and Society* series was limited, in terms of its impact upon mainstream party politics, and it is difficult to argue that a unified consumer philosophy emerged. But to apply a test of theoretical precision to abstract 'consumerism' is to miss the diversity and contradictions that have ever dominated the politics of the Left, never mind any specific definitions of 'socialism' or 'trade union consciousness'. What the *Self and Society* series highlights is the flourishing of consumerist thought during the 1920s and 1930s which would see the Ruskinian and Morrisian tradition revived through the works of J. A. Hobson, the development of the concept of the 'living wage' by the Independent Labour Party (ILP), the progression of co-operative thought and propaganda and the promotion of new ideas and strategies as diverse as Major Douglas' thoughts on social credit, G. D. H. Cole's advocacy of guild socialism and the focus on research, evidence and forecasting by Political and Economic Planning (PEP). In all of these ideas and institutions, the consumer assumed a prominence and a centrality that has been overlooked in histories of alternative political formations in this period.

---

[1] P. Redfern (ed.), *Self and Society: Social and Economic Problems from the Hitherto Neglected Point of View of the Consumer*, 2 vols. (London, 1930).

Following – and often inspired by – the work of the First World War Consumers' Council, the inter-war decades witnessed a burgeoning set of ideas about consumers, consumption and citizenship. The concern was primarily with issues of basic provisioning and how to incorporate the consumer interest into food and agricultural policy, but important critiques began to appear that would feed through into the consumer politics of affluence associated with the 1950s. While the co-operative ideologues and ILP policy framers expanded consumerism into notions of citizenship, in the sense that access to necessitous goods was formulated as a social right, bodies such as PEP extended these rights to apply to durables as well as perishables. The comparative testing organisations which would come to the fore in affluent Britain – but already existing in the United States – were researched and analysed for their effectiveness in championing the consumer cause. Here, the critique of profiteering merged with the exploration of social democratic ideals as various forms of 'third way' politics were advocated to escape the perceived powerful bind of the corrupt organised interests of the corporate state. Consumers, just as they would in the late twentieth century, were positioned as political entities who would free the state from the limited visions of either trade unions or employers. Such liberation was possible, it was argued, because the consumer was everybody and as such could not be reduced to a specific interest group. But, as will be seen in chapter 4, this optimism and universalism had the potential for division and containment by other interests as well, particularly when the theory of consumerism was adapted to suit specific policy proposals.

The Co-operative movement

It is in co-operative thought that consumerism as a political and economic concept truly came to prominence. In the inter-war period, a number of European thinkers were translated into English and became important reference points for British co-operators. They attempted to raise the profile of co-operation from a practical system of distribution to an abstract system of political economy. In France, Charles Gide believed the consumers' co-operation of the Rochdale Pioneers to be a formula for not only abolishing the profit motive but for achieving moral and social progress as well. While the dividend provided an immediate purpose of economic improvement for the individual member, the mutual aid principles of the organic and familial institution of the co-operative society would establish a 'reign of truth and justice'.[2] Although Gide

---

[2] A. Bonner, *British Co-operation: The History, Principles and Organisation of the British Co-operative Movement* (Manchester, 1961), pp. 203, 293.

rose to prominence in the decades around the turn of the twentieth century, his branch of political economy did not find an institutional setting until he obtained a Chair in Co-operation at the Collège de France in 1921 and after he had set up the International Institute for the Study of Co-operation in 1931, just before he died.[3] Consumers' co-operation, according to Gide, led to reductions in the cost of living and the abolition of such fraudulent business practices as adulteration, as well as the removal of 'all forms of commercial falsehood and trickery, thus raising the ethical standard of business life'.[4] Co-operation was a perfectly workable system in and of itself that could expand incrementally into areas such as clothing, furnishing, housing, entertainment, the media, education and philanthropy, to the extent that the capitalist state would be rendered redundant. Instead of profit, business would be run on the principles of the 'fair price', where the sole aim of economic activity would become that of satisfying consumer needs; there would be no place for 'advertisement, lying, cheating, and inducements to extravagance'.[5] He distanced himself from both the collectivist socialists who saw in co-operation a means to strengthen the proletariat in the class war and from the 'bourgeois' sympathisers who saw the dividend as a badge of thrift, sobriety, saving and individual social advancement.[6] Instead, he agreed with Alfred Marshall's address to the 1889 Co-operative Congress that 'What distinguishes co-operation from every other movement is that it is at once a strong and calm and wise business, and a strong and fervent proselytising faith.'[7] Reversing the scorn thrown at his 'Nîmes School' of political economy by mainstream economists, Gide embraced the 'mystics' who saw in co-operation a 'living organism' 'in conformity with justice and social benefit' which would spontaneously realise 'the best of all possible worlds'.[8] Unlike Beatrice Webb, who sought to incorporate co-operation into a state socialist system, Gide aimed to expand the co-operative store into a 'Social Democracy' as it gradually eclipsed all other forms of economic and political life. His vision was shared by contemporaries and collaborators such as Ernest Poisson whose work, *The Co-operative Republic*, was translated into English in 1925. In Sweden, Anders Örne, though not utopian in his outlook, was nevertheless committed to the Rochdale principles, a democratic system which he felt in *Co-operative*

---

[3] *Dictionnaire de Biographie Française* (Paris-VI, 1980), col. 1479; K. Walter (ed.), *Co-operation and Charles Gide* (London, 1933); R. H. Williams, *Dream Worlds: Mass Consumption in Late Nineteenth-Century France* (1982; Los Angeles, 1991), pp. 276–321.
[4] C. Gide, *Principles of Political Economy* (London, 1903), p. 680.
[5] C. Gide, *Consumers' Co-operative Societies* (1913; Manchester, 1921), p. 8.
[6] C. Rist, 'Charles Gide: his life and teaching', in Walter (ed.), *Co-operation*, pp. 19–30.
[7] Gide, *Consumers' Co-operative Societies*, p. 10.
[8] *Ibid.*, p. 11; B. Lavergne, 'Charles Gide, founder of the doctrine of consumers' co-operation', in Walter (ed.), *Co-operation*, pp. 45–62.

Ideals and Principles (English translation, 1926) to be the antithesis of capitalism as well as a viable alternative to state absolutism.[9]

In Britain, the main theorists of co-operation included such figures as Leonard Woolf, who saw in co-operation a rational system for the control of industry, and A. M. Carr-Saunders, P. Sargant Florence and Robert Peers, whose collective investigation of 1938 found that consumers' co-operation represented the necessary middle way between laissez-faire liberalism and rigid state planning. The problem, they wrote, was that the Co-operative movement had failed to clarify its aims and objectives, which had resulted in an uneasy alliance with the trade unions and the Labour Party. If the movement did not define its view of the Co-operative Commonwealth with any precision, then the natural tensions that existed within the Left between a society of consumers and an organisation of producers (whether employers or workers) would always remain.[10] In any case, they argued, British socialists for too long had maintained a productivist mentality, unable to think beyond the role of profit in economic theory and the centrality of production to economic organisation. This was so much the case that even the Webbs, whose investigations had made them extremely favourable to the Co-operative movement, could not imagine consumers' co-operation as the sole basis of a new society, but as merely the distributive wing of a centrally organised state socialist system, within which the trade unions would maintain greater power in the control of production.[11]

In many respects, the Webbs' proposed constitution for a socialist state of workers, consumers and citizens was a compromise between the allegiances made to consumerist and productivist politics by numerous committed co-operative and trade union activists, though they perhaps also saw in consumerism an opportunity to instil democracy within their otherwise centrist and state-oriented Fabianism.[12] On the co-operative side, Percy Redfern emerged as a leading advocate of consumer socialism, seeing consumption on its own – with or without the assistance of the trade unions – as the key to transforming industry. In 1920, he argued that divisions between workers and employers could only ever be based on sectional interests, whereas the 'consumers' interest in an abundant world is the great, common human interest'.[13] Although vague on the

[9] Bonner, *British Co-operation*, pp. 204–5, 293, 494.

[10] A. M. Carr-Saunders, P. S. Florence and R. Peers, *Consumers' Co-operation in Great Britain: An Examination of the British Co-operative Movement* (London, 1938).

[11] K. Walter, 'Introduction', in Walter (ed.), *Co-operation*, p. 8; B. Webb and S. Webb, *A Constitution for the Socialist Commonwealth of Great Britain* (London, 1920).

[12] M. Bevir, 'Sidney Webb: utilitarianism, positivism and social democracy', *Journal of Modern History*, 74 (2002), 217–52.

[13] P. Redfern, *The Consumer's Place in Society* (Manchester, 1920), p. 10.

details, Redfern was in no doubt as to the potential of his 'new social order', mixing nineteenth-century idealism with evangelical missionary fervour: 'The consumer is the full human being in relation to all the uses of life. A social philosophy, a human ideal and a new economic method are all to be found in consumers' service.'[14] Redfern hoped to mobilise a 'consumer consciousness' to eradicate poverty and to instil a 'religious sense of the meaning of life' so that consumers would take care to ensure equitable systems of production all around the world, the end of adulteration and the promotion of fair and honest service.[15] Co-operation was the means by which a politics of the factory was to be replaced by a politics of the shop:

We – the mass of common men and women in all countries – also compose the world's market. To sell to us is the ultimate aim of the world's business. Hence it is ourselves as consumers who stand in central relation to all the economics of the world, like a king in his kingdom. As producers we go each unto a particular factory, farm or mine, but as consumers we are set by nature thus to give leadership, aim and purpose to the whole economic world. That we are not kings, but serfs in the mass, is due to our failure to think and act together as consumers and so realise our true position and power.[16]

As with all optimistic socialists, education was the key to the raising of the new consciousness. The nation's youth was to be educated about the 'voluntary socialism' of co-operation and of 'true and free citizenship'.[17] As other co-operators put it, there was a whole 'mob' of sheep-like consumers just waiting for a shepherd to guide them to this 'new economy of human living'.[18]

Redfern's 1928–30 collection of twenty-four leading co-operative thinkers was predicated on a particular defence of the Co-operative movement, but they also called for a general morality of consumption to lift the economic act of purchasing to the level, even, of a religious duty.[19] The trade unionist Margaret Bondfield asserted that all systems of trading ultimately disintegrated unless founded on a general set of moral values. Her views here were supported by the academic historian, A. Elizabeth Levett, who adopted a typical romanticised medievalism to uphold the notion of the 'just price' said to predominate in peasant societies.[20] Similarly, the definition of consumption was inverted so that it no longer

[14] *Ibid.*, pp. 16–17. [15] *Ibid.*, p. 56. [16] *Ibid.*, p. 12.
[17] P. Redfern, *Twenty Faces of the World* (London, 1929), pp. 17–22.
[18] L. P. Jacks, *The Road to Enjoyment* (London, 1928), p. 18; F. Henderson, *Capitalism and the Consumer* (London, 1936), p. 111.
[19] H. Johnson, *Religion Interferes* (London, 1928); H. Clay, *Co-operation and Private Enterprise* (London, 1928).
[20] M. Bondfield, *The Meaning of Trade* (London, 1928), p. 29; A. E. Levett, *The Consumer in History* (London, 1929).

connoted the shabbiness of the mass, so common in discourses of luxury, but encapsulated the potential for art and literature, through the collective consumption of state-promoted opera, theatre and libraries, to reach everybody.[21] Perhaps the most utopian argument of all came from Leonard Woolf who suggested that while consumption based on laissez-faire principles led to war and conflict, consumption based on the mutual aid principles of co-operation would ultimately, if expanded to an international system, result in world peace.[22] Finally, the feminist consumer politics of Teresa Billington Greig were revived by several authors, reflecting a turn to demand and consumption by a number of women academics within the social sciences.[23] Bondfield asserted the duties of women as shoppers to bring 'joy and beauty into life' while the Dean of Manchester, Hewlett Johnson, celebrated the enfranchisement of the housewife: 'a great thing for industry when the hand that rocks the cradle shares in controlling the policy of the business world'.[24] But Evelyn Sharp was most explicit about the potential role of women believing the housewife to be the ultimate controller of trade since she was the 'queen of consumers' as the family buyer. Particularly for the co-operative housewife, already engaged in a radical enterprise, she was 'the New Woman of the masses'.[25]

Beatrice Webb refused to think of consumption purely as purchasing, explaining that the history of all hitherto existing associations were either of producers (guilds, trade unions, employers' federations, professional bodies) or of consumers (the Co-op, the Friendly Society and the Building Society). Even the state, through its collective provision of essential services ranging from transport to health, to art and entertainment, had become an 'Association of Consumers'.[26] This was not so much a clever twist of theoretical perspective but a serious call for a shift in the mentality of working-class radicals, to understand that fundamental economic and political change did not always have to begin with the wage. However, if she here appeared to follow Gide and J. T. W. Mitchell, her reservations respecting the radicalism or politicisation of the vast majority of

---

[21] I. Brown, *Art and Everyman* (London, 1929).

[22] L. S. Woolf, *The Way of Peace* (London, 1928).

[23] E. Gilboy, 'The cost of living and real wages in eighteenth-century England', *Review of Economics and Statistics*, 18:3 (1936), 134–43; E. Gilboy, 'Demand as a factor in the industrial revolution' (1934), in R. M. Hartwell (ed.), *The Causes of the Industrial Revolution in England* (London, 1967), pp. 121–38.

[24] Bondfield, *Meaning of Trade*, p. 27; Johnson, *Religion Interferes*, p. 14.

[25] E. Sharp, *Daily Bread* (London, 1928), pp. 10–11. See also J. Stephen, *Flapdoodle about "Flappers"* (London, 1918); E. Barton, *Women: In the Home, the Store and the State* (Manchester, c.1928).

[26] B. Webb, *The Discovery of the Consumer* (London, 1928), pp. 4–5.

co-operative members (the mere dividend hunters) perhaps also encouraged her to identify a number of limits to co-operation. She doubted whether co-operation would spread to all public services and believed that because some had to be provided free of charge and to all, they necessarily involved non-optional compulsory levies – i.e. taxation – and required associations of citizens (municipal government or the central state) rather than consumers. Consumerism could only ever form one plank of the socialist project and she therefore returned to a statement as to the idealised constitution as she had set out earlier with Sidney: consumers, producers and citizens, through co-operatives, trade unions and government, were to exist in 'organic unity', their roles clearly defined and their position to one another clearly respected.[27]

Other contributors realised that this relationship between the producer and the consumer, this conflict between higher wages and cheaper goods, required further elaboration. Beyond the naive assertions made by some that since we are all both producers and consumers in our everyday lives it is illogical that there could ever be a conflict between the two, attempts were made to set out the relationship between the co-operative and the trade union.[28] The general secretary of the TUC, Walter Citrine, called for unity between consumers and workers in the opposition to monopoly capitalism. Close collaboration, such as through the Labour Party's proposed Consumers' Council (see chapter 4), could result in the regulation of industry to the extent that both higher wages and lower prices were achieved at the expense of dividend payments. Citrine had little to say about areas of the market not subject to market abuse, though he felt that all problems of worker and consumer exploitation would ultimately be solved through the massive expansion of trade union and co-operative control of industry.[29] Writing in a volume not part of the Benn series, but published at the same time, Margaret Digby saw in the Co-operative Wholesale Society (CWS) an institution which could cater to the interests of societies of consumers, associations of workers and collectives of farmers. The CWS would be able to negotiate, without the need for the assistance of the state at either national or international level, the requirements of producer organisations to sell and distribute their produce and the requirements of co-operative consumers for goods manufactured for use.[30] For others, though, the state was seen as the final negotiator for the different aspects of citizenship. The Labour Chancellor, Philip Snowden, invoked a notion of democracy which involved the

---

[27] *Ibid.*, p. 32. [28] G. W. Daniels, *Capital, Labour and the Consumer* (London, 1929).
[29] W. M. Citrine, *Labour and the Community* (London, 1928).
[30] M. Digby, *Producers and Consumers: A Study in Co-operative Relations* (1928; London, 1938).

active participation of all the wings of the mutual aid movement within the apparatus of the state. Schemes for insurance, welfare and the supply of necessities could be handed over to the friendly societies, trade unions and co-operatives as workers and consumers sought the greater participatory citizenship of voluntary democratic association.[31] Harold Laski celebrated the Ruskinian consumer as one who purchased goods to develop both individual personality and collective social responsibility.[32] The capitalist system would triumph so long as wants remained 'atomic in character' so the state should therefore assist consumers by promoting those systems of distribution which ensured that items of the 'common stock' reached all those who shared the 'equal right to self-realisation'.[33] To assist in this new form of citizenship, science and statistics were to be enrolled in the collection of information about the consumer as much as the producer.[34] And, finally, although in 1928 he focussed on international developments in co-operation, Leonard Woolf reiterated his arguments for the consumer control of industry. Once citizens had accepted 'a totally different psychology' based around consumption instead of production, they would seek to control industry by use, or real consumer demand, which in turn would limit consumption as they – again mixing the agrarian idealism of Morris with the utopian asceticism of the Webbs – would seek more leisure and less work.[35] Woolf did not, however, share the view of the Webbs as to the limitations of co-operation. In an argument with the Webbs at a Fabian summer school in 1913, while they put forward their ideas as to the relationship between co-operators and trade unionists in the 'socialist commonwealth', Woolf advocated instead the universal extension of co-operation to create a 'democracy of consumers' and, reflecting his life-long commitment to world peace, an international co-operative trading network.[36]

The Benn series of essays may have failed to outline a specific programme for the implementation of a consumer's democracy, but it marked a high point of labour concerns with consumerism. The need for unity between trade unionists and co-operators was also a mainstay of Co-operative Union propaganda in the inter-war period, particularly in *Advance Democracy*, a 1938 film made by four metropolitan co-operative societies, in which a trade unionist husband and co-operative wife unite

---

[31] P. Snowden, *The Faith of a Democrat* (London, 1928).
[32] H. Laski, *The Recovery of Citizenship* (London, 1928).   [33] *Ibid.*, pp. 10–12.
[34] J. W. F. Rowe, *Everyman's Statistics* (London, 1929). See also G. W. Monier-Williams, *Food and the Consumer* (London, 1935).
[35] Woolf, *Way of Peace*; L. S. Woolf, *The Control of Industry by the People* (London, 1915); L. S. Woolf, *Socialism and Co-operation* (London, 1921).
[36] Woolf, *Socialism and Co-operation*, p. 107; L. S. Woolf, *Co-operation and the Future of Industry* (London, 1918).

as worker and shopper in a May Day parade against fascism and for democracy.[37] The co-operative message was also promoted through the Co-operative Party, set up in 1917 to represent the movement's interests in Parliament. However, despite the symbolic appointment of A. V. Alexander as parliamentary secretary to the Board of Trade in the Labour Government of 1924, the agenda of the Co-operative Party remained largely subservient to the direction of Labour, and no systematic practical exploration of the relationship between the consumer and producer was ever worked out along the lines proposed by Bondfield, Woolf, Laski and Citrine.[38] In any case, despite Redfern's optimism in attempting to mobilise the universal interest of consumerism, divisions remained between the authors. As in many other periods, this was a consumerism which drew both its combinatory strengths and its fragmentary weaknesses from its potential universality. All the pamphleteers may have been in favour of a focus on the consumer, but Woolf's single-minded championing of the consumer would be bound to clash with Citrine and Bondfield's concerns for the trade unionist if ever the ideas in the series were to be formulated into policy. Also, problems could arise in a series which brought together the concerns of committed atheists within the labour movement and the overtly religious consumerism of Johnson. The problem of consumerism being used to support other interests is seen most clearly in Ernest Benn's own contribution. He advocated a balance between the interests of producers and consumers, insisting that this could only come through economic liberty, in a marketplace not dominated by the vested interests of trade unions, employers or the state.[39] Benn was a self-professed 'individualist', his other writings suggesting an advocacy of laissez-faire liberalism indistinguishable from a right-wing libertarianism.[40] Yet he could use the anti-statist and pro-consumer message of the Co-operative movement as a vehicle for his own stance against bureaucracy, collectivism and the trade unions. This malleability of the definition of the consumer interest would prove a recurring theme of consumerism's interaction with the state, both in the inter-war period and beyond.

[37] *Advance Democracy* (1938), on *The People's Cinema: The Films of the Co-operative Movement* (National Co-operative Film Archive); A. Burton, *The People's Cinema* (London, 1994).
[38] T. F. Carbery, *Consumers in Politics: A History and General Review of the Co-operative Party* (Manchester, 1969); P. Gurney, *Co-operative Culture and the Politics of Consumption in England, 1870–1930* (Manchester, 1996), p. 221; J. Birchall, *Co-op: The People's Business* (Manchester, 1994), pp. 113–16; G. Scott, *Feminism and the Politics of Working Women: The Women's Co-operative Guild, 1880s to the Second World War* (London, 1998), p. 231.
[39] E. Benn, *Producer vs. Consumer: Thoughts on Difficulties* (London, 1928).
[40] E. Benn, 'The curse of collectivism', *National Review*, 118 (1942), 359–63; *Dictionary of National Biography*.

The Independent Labour Party and the 'living wage'

If the Labour Party had an institutional link with the Co-operative move-ment and a range of ideas that encouraged a focus on the consumer rather than the worker as the basis of social and political change, so too were economists in its ranks concentrating on consumption as the starting point for the more equal distribution of wealth. J. A. Hobson picked up on the Morrisian and Ruskinian legacy to argue that consumption was an agent of 'aesthetic and moral advance' and that care ought to be taken to avoid the 'ostentatious leisure' and 'conspicuous waste' of the unpro-ductive consumption of the rich.[41] He took it as a natural law that the satisfaction of a physical effort is only realised by the effort put in, so the rich, despite their vast luxury, never spent all their incomes on consump-tion. Instead they saved, much more so than families who might put some money aside for future use, and thus their 'underconsumption' reduced the impetus given to the economy. Were incomes to be redistributed to the poor, then consumption would increase: 'No class of men whose "savings" are made out of their hard-won earnings is likely to oversave, for each unit of "capital" will represent a real want, a piece of legitimate consumption deferred.'[42] The freeing up of working-class incomes would lead to not only enlarged consumption but more individualised consump-tion as the working classes would seek greater self-realisation through con-sumption, leading to the encouragement of non-mass-producing crafts workshops so beloved by William Morris. Expanded consumption would prevent the existence of 'unemployed producing power' and would ul-timately prevent Imperialism: 'If the consuming public in this country raised its standard of consumption to keep pace with every rise of pro-ductive powers, there could be no excess of goods or capital clamorous to use Imperialism in order to find markets.'[43] The economic policy impli-cation of Hobson's theory of underconsumption was the redistribution of income from the non-spending rich to the non-saving poor.[44] Here, Hobson followed much left-wing thought in believing that the capital-ists used their excess savings for investment, resulting in over-production and a glut of goods that the remaining income could not absorb at prices

---

[41] J. A. Hobson, 'The General Election: a sociological interpretation', *Sociological Review*, 3 (1910), 113; N. Thompson, 'Hobson and the Fabians: two roads to socialism in the 1920s', *History of Political Economy*, 26:2 (1994), 203–20; J. Townshend, *J. A. Hobson* (Manchester, 1990).

[42] J. A. Hobson, *The Problem of the Unemployed* (1896) and *Imperialism: A Study* (1902), in M. Freeden (ed.), *J. A. Hobson: A Reader* (London, 1988), pp. 110, 165.

[43] Freeden (ed.), *Reader*, pp. 116, 161.

[44] H. F. Bleaney, *Under-Consumption Theories: A Historical and Critical Analysis* (London, 1976).

sufficient to recover the investment. But whereas other socialists thought over-saving a permanent cause of poverty, Hobson argued it to be only the cause of periodical economic breakdowns, a trade cycle which could then be avoided through the careful redistribution of income away from the savings of the rich and to the pockets of the poor, either through increased wages or as social benefits.[45] Hobson then followed through the logic of his economic theory to question the nature of political participation. Since organisations of producers would pay insufficient attention to the nature of effective demand required to lift an economy out of slump, 'citizen-consumers' were to be given an active role in the management of the economy, the better to ensure that production would be oriented to those types of good consumed by poor consumers who did not contribute to economic downturns through oversaving.[46]

The main policy outlet for Hobson's theories was in the campaign for the 'living wage' run by the Independent Labour Party (ILP) in the 1920s. Along with Henry Noel Brailsford, A. Creech Jones and E. F. Wise, Hobson set out the principal elements of the living wage in 1926, though the main ideas were also outlined in the more famous ILP publications of that year: Brailsford's *Socialism For Today* and F. W. Jowett's *Socialism in Our Time*.[47] Just as Lawrence Glickman has argued of US labour history, the living wage was a constant source of reference in all trade disputes and wage negotiations. Whereas Glickman has demonstrated that the living wage made sense to Americans as a minimum standard necessary for workers and their families to participate as consumers in the economy, British historians have overlooked the consumerist elements of the phrase.[48] In fact, as Hobson *et al.* pointed out in 1926, although the living wage as a principle was 'more generally accepted throughout the Labour Movement' than any other, 'no positive use' was made of it.[49] A 'living income' was both an ethical and an economic issue: ethical, because it was

---

[45] Warwick Modern Records Centre, Trade Union Archive (hereafter MRC) MSS292/117/8: Living Wage Committee: J. A. Hobson, *Memorandum on the policy of high consumption* (24 November 1927), p. 5; R. Skidelsky, *Politicians and the Slump: The Labour Government of 1929–1931* (London, 1967), p. 31; N. Thompson, *Political Economy and the Labour Party: The Economics of Democratic Socialism, 1884–1995* (London, 1996), pp. 36–7.

[46] F. Trentmann, 'Civil society, commerce and the "citizen-consumer": popular meanings of Free Trade in modern Britain', in F. Trentmann (ed.), *Paradoxes of Civil Society: New Perspectives on Modern German and British History* (Oxford, 2000), p. 323.

[47] H. N. Brailsford, *Socialism for Today* (London, 1926); F. W. Jowett, *Socialism in Our Time* (London, 1926).

[48] L. B. Glickman, *A Living Wage: American Workers and the Making of Consumer Society* (Ithaca, 1997).

[49] H. N. Brailsford, J. A. Hobson, A. Creech Jones and E. F. Wise, *The Living Wage* (London, 1926), p. 2.

the duty of society to ensure that every citizen could reach 'the full stature of humanity'; and economic, because too few of the profits of capital had gone into wages to create a market for the products of new investments, resulting in recession. From this classic under-consumptionist position, Hobson's answer was to expand credit and currency to keep pace with the growth in output (while maintaining more rigid checks on finance, prices and distribution) at the same time as creating a more equal spread of purchasing power. Workers were to receive not a standardised national minimum wage, but a living wage paid 'to each according to his need'. This would be set firstly according to the needs of 'a man and his wife' supplemented through a family allowance as advocated by Eleanor Rathbone (financed by the state through direct taxation and paid directly to the mother through the Post Office). The living wage itself was to be set through an official enquiry that would take into account medical assessments of nutrition, housewives' descriptions of budgets, experts' assessments of housing and education needs and general estimates of funds needed to participate in 'cultural life'. In any future pay negotiations workers would be able to plea for a share in any new prosperity enjoyed by an industry as well as being able to point to a moral benchmark of 'the requirements of civilisation' embodied in the officially determined level of the living wage.[50]

The living wage proposals, submitted to the National Administrative Council of the ILP and accepted as official policy, embraced the consumer as much as the worker interest. Brailsford was able to use both a productivist and consumerist rhetoric in his standard critique of trusts and combines, suggesting price fixing, cartels, conspiracies and 'tied' systems served to 'loot' the consumer as well as 'harming the worker's wage'.[51] Rich consumers, however, were engaging in an orgy of luxury dependent on 'such gross inequality that the rich can enjoy their superfluities only if the poor dispense with necessities. The total national income is not high enough to justify indulgence in any class. If some wear fur coats, others must be content with rags. If some dine at the Ritz, others must go hungry.'[52] This older critique of luxury was used by all the living wage advocates to condemn the rich for their offences 'against social morals' while the poor were inscribed with a set of consumer entitlements to those goods determined as central to the calculation of the living wage. Indeed, the consumption of the poor, according to Hobson's underconsumption theory, was 'productive' in the classic liberal dichotomy use by Mill, since it would lead to increased national wealth and an expanded economy.

---

[50] Ibid., pp. 20–34.   [51] Brailsford, Socialism for Today, pp. 22–5.   [52] Ibid., p. 39.

Care must be taken not to exaggerate the extent of the ILP's consumerist mentality. Brailsford himself maintained a fundamental belief in the dignity of labour. While he bemoaned the lack of freedom given to the consumer in the market, he also thought it a 'poor thing that we should have the choice of buying some of our goods at competitive prices to-day from Mr. Selfridge and tomorrow from Mr. Whiteley, if self determination is denied to us in our active life as producers. It is this life which absorbs most of our energies; here, if anywhere, we create; here we ought to realise ourselves.'[53] Yet others were aware of the danger of focussing too much on the wage and trade union interests. F. W. Jowett, Chairman of the ILP, urged the labour movement to extend its battle front beyond Keir Hardie's call for the 'Right to Work' and fight instead for the 'Right to Live': 'the right of every worker to live in a decent and well-equipped house, the right of every worker to be well clad and to have good food, the right of every worker to have the means and facilities for education and leisure . . . No one can claim the right to enjoy luxury until everyone has the right to enjoy comfort.'[54] Accordingly, the consumer was to form a central pillar of the socialist state. Within any scheme of nationalisation, statutory national and regional Consumers' Councils were to be set up, consumers having full access to all the papers and accounts of the industries concerned. Either nominees of the Councils or else full-time salaried consumer representatives were to sit in on the Boards of Industry to act as constant critics and advisors.[55]

The ILP embarked on a propaganda drive to have the living wage proposals accepted within the rest of the labour movement. However, the trade unions disliked the ILP's interference in matters of wages policy and they were unwilling to accept a system of wage control that reduced their own power in negotiations. The Parliamentary Labour Party also rejected the proposals, Ramsay MacDonald being personally antagonistic to Brailsford and disliking programmes which seemed to bind the Party to particular policies.[56] In any case, the Labour Party was far more influenced by the Webbs and the Fabians, whose gradualist plans for their version of state socialism clashed with the ILP's relegation of nationalisation to secondary importance behind increased purchasing power. And Hobson's faith in the capacity of consumers to act rationally was not matched by the Fabians who feared the 'anarchic irresponsibility' of the shopper and saw only irrationality in the private market, preferring instead, in *Labour and the Nation* (1928), the scientific rationality of control

---

[53] *Ibid.*, p. 33.
[54] Jowett, *Socialism in Our Time*, p. 5.   [55] Brailsford, *Socialism for Today*, p. 87.
[56] R. D. Rowse, *Left in the Centre: The Independent Labour Party, 1893–1940* (London, 1966), pp. 130–6.

by an efficient managerial elite.[57] At the 1927 Labour Party conference, the ILP living wage proposals were effectively killed off, condemned by MacDonald as a collection of 'flashy futilities'.[58] A Joint TUC General Council and Labour Party Executive Committee was set up to investigate the living wage, but this was merely a tactic to ignore the issue and the Committee reported in 1929 that it was unable to make any definite recommendations.[59] The ILP then drifted away from the Labour Party, disaffiliating in 1932, and the living wage proposals, together with Hobson's liberal-socialist political economy, were eclipsed by other nationalising agendas within Labour. Only the maternity benefits remained as a distinct policy, and while disputes arose as to how this should be provided, it was at least debated seriously in trade union and Labour Party circles.[60]

The Labour Party made it clear that the consumer-oriented living wage proposals were not to become policy when MacDonald created an Economic Advisory Council in 1930 to draw on talents outside of Parliament. It included such trade union figures as Ernest Bevin and Walter Citrine, as well as the worker-oriented views of G. D. H. Cole and the ascetic principles of R. H. Tawney. Hobson was not included but, in a portent for the future, John Maynard Keynes was. If trade-union interests dominated within a self-denying Fabian-inspired Labour Party, it was unlikely that a politics of consumption would be developed which skilfully negotiated the boundaries between luxury and necessity. Instead, all but the most basic goods could be dealt with comfortably if the Party was not to accept Hobson's more pro-market policies. And the Council's hostile view of the market meant they ruled out pricing and distributive mechanisms as instruments of economic policy which could have served to increase purchasing power and provide a more effective policy for the Labour Government in dealing with the economic crises at the beginning of the 1930s. Consumption, it seemed, was to play no significant role in macroeconomic policy, at least in the sense envisaged by Hobson and the ILP, and the Council was to produce only one report, through its Committee on Economic Information, which dealt specifically with

[57] Thompson, 'Hobson and the Fabians', p. 205; Thompson, *Political Economy*, p. 73.
[58] Skidelsky, *Politicians and the Slump*, p. 50.
[59] MRC MSS292/117/8: Living Wage Committee, 1928: Joint Committee on the Living Wage (26 November 1929). The Committee was chaired by Margaret Bondfield and also included Walter Citrine, who had also contributed to the Benn consumer pamphlet series. Their comments in that series need to be read in the light of their dismissal of the living wage and a consumption-directed policy in this Committee.
[60] MRC MSS292/117/8: Joint Committee on the Living Wage, *Interim Report on Family Allowances and Child Welfare* (London, 1928); A. Marwick, 'The Independent Labour Party in the 1920s', *Bulletin of the Institute of Historical Research* 35:91 (1962), 62–74.

consumption. Even then, this was to urge consumers to engage in 'wise spending' in 1932, directed to the concerns of trade and industry and thus confirming the self-denying traditions of Labour's long-standing unease with consumption and mass culture.[61]

The problem of consumption was instead avoided through the adoption of Keynesianism, although his economic theories would not become central to the Party's policies for some time. Keynes avoided any discussion of consumption and hence any awkward moral and ethical dilemmas over the place of material abundance within a productivist politics. Keynes held that consumption was determined by a series of objective and subjective factors. Objective factors included such determinants as wages, the difference between income and net income, fiscal policy and windfalls, while subjective factors included a number of incentives (enjoyment, shortsightedness, generosity, miscalculation, ostentation and extravagance) and disincentives (precaution, foresight, calculation, improvement, independence, enterprise, pride and avarice). Significantly, Keynes regarded subjective factors as based upon the entrenched habits and customs of a community, and therefore extremely unlikely to change in the short term. Accordingly, only the objective factors were of interest to the economist, and even these resulted in a fairly stable 'propensity to consume'. However, the propensity to consume was crucial to the calculation of the multiplier, the factor at the heart of Keynes' theory, since it was the definite ratio between income and investment and to total employment directly employed on investment. In the demand management of employment and the economy, then, consumption played an abstract and relatively straightforward role. Once the marginal propensity to consume had been calculated (and this was usually around 80 per cent of any increase in the wage unit), the multiplier could be calculated and thus the impact on employment of any change in investment.[62]

Keynes positioned himself against the classical economic orthodoxy that supply creates its own demand and he therefore potentially positioned consumption as an area of economics worthy of much greater exploration than in mainstream liberalism. Yet, in a sense, he made consumption an even more abstract economic term than it had ever been in the nineteenth century: even Mill, in his focus on productive and unproductive, had at least implicitly enabled questions of individual morality to relate to wealth creation and, if he did not do so himself, he at least

[61] S. Howson and D. Winch, *The Economic Advisory Council, 1930–1939: A Study in Economic Advice During Depression and Recovery* (Cambridge, 1977), p. 287; C. Waters, *British Socialists and the Politics of Popular Culture, 1884–1914* (Manchester, 1990).

[62] J. M. Keynes, *The General Theory of Employment, Interest and Money* (1936; London, 1964), chaps. 8–10.

opened the door for critics such as Ruskin to moralise the liberal marketplace. But for Keynes, 'virtue and vice play no part'.[63] He removed the beauty, the ethics and the politics from consumption, reducing it to a concept of little interest to the economy, other than the overall propensity to consume which even he dismissed as requiring little exploration due to its rather fixed and traditional nature. This might seem little more than a minor theoretical point, except that we can see in Keynes' approach to consumption a potential appeal to the Labour Party. While an economic theory which focussed on full employment was of obvious interest to the trade unions, Keynes's system avoided all discussion of individual consumption, ethics, morality and the politics of purchasing. Whereas the implication of the Hobsonian approach would have been a foregrounding of all these non-economic factors in the discussion leading to the determination of the living wage, now such topics as the appropriate level of personal consumption were taken off the agenda. For a political party imbued with the ascetic inheritance of Tawney and the Webbs, that was content to discuss necessity, yet perpetually ill at ease in any debate about the relevance of privately provided material abundance in working-class life, Keynes' 'general theory' was the perfect means of diverting the issue. As soon as the Labour Party adopted demand management as a fundamental economic tool, the liberal socialist attitudes to the market of Ruskin, Morris and Hobson were of no consequence. Disputes would continue over specific products, but the living wage was to become an irrelevance within the Keynesian framework.

Guild socialism and social credit

Hobsonian theories of underconsumption and ILP campaigns for the living wage suggested a third way in British politics where economic decisions were not determined according to the vested interests of either the trade unions or employers. G. D. H. Cole had earlier suggested a prominent role for the consumer in his version of guild socialism. Although the guild socialism advocated by the likes of A. J. Penty and S. G. Hobson in A. R. Orage's *New Age* was firmly rooted in a system of worker and trade union control, Cole attempted to re-write the consumer back into the guild socialist 'commune'.[64] He recognised one of the central problems of any political system based upon the consumer: that is, 'Who is the "consumer"? Some say he is Mr. Everybody, and therefore entitled

---

[63] Keynes, *General Theory*, p. 110.
[64] Thompson, *Political Economy*, pp. 25–9; A. W. Wright, *G. D. H. Cole and Socialist Democracy* (Oxford, 1979).

to all power and consideration. Others say that, being Mr. Everybody, he is also Mr. Nobody, and can be safely let out of account.'[65] He worried that the consumer was essentially a 'mirage' since no coherent set of interests could be ascribed to him over all aspects of his purchasing life. But Cole aimed not to place control entirely in the hands of the workers through producer co-operation or of consumers through a system of state sovereignty which made decisions for the collective mass of consumers, but to base his system on a division between four types of consumption, thus recognising administratively four types of worker and of consumer. In *Self-Government in Industry* (1917) he proposed distinguishing between, firstly, personal needs, serviced by housing guilds and guilds of small producers, in which the consumer was to be represented by the Co-operative movement. Secondly, local needs were to be serviced by industrial guilds for public amenities and civil and entertainment guilds for health and pleasure in which the consumer cause would be represented by locally elected neighbourhood bodies. Thirdly, national needs were to be met by the great guilds of the railways, the Post Office and so on, with consumer bodies nominating officials to National Congresses of public education, public utilities and public health and housing. Finally, guilds were to be established for workers in areas such as international transport and communication in which consumers' international interests were to be articulated again by National Congresses or 'functional parliaments'.[66] In *Guild Socialism Restated*, published three years later, Cole simplified his system to create a straightforward division between personal and domestic consumption where individual preference was important, and collective consumption, where the product was undifferentiated and supplied in the mass (public utilities). The consumer interest was to be defended for the former through the Co-operative movement and for the latter through Collective Utility Councils, meeting at local, regional and national levels. Reinforcing his earlier disavowal of state socialism, Cole argued that disputes between producers in guilds and organised consumers were not to be resolved by the arbitrary action of the state, but through special tribunals which formed the basis of the Commune which brought together the four pillars of society: the producers' guilds, the consumer organisations, the civic guilds and the citizen organisations of the cultural and health guilds.

   Despite his usual support for the worker, Cole's notion of guild socialism seemed to give equal power to both the consumer and the producer. Yet certain flaws in the system perhaps prevented other socialists from

[65] G. D. H. Cole, *Guild Socialism Restated* (1920; London, 1980), p. 78.
[66] G. D. H. Cole, *Self-Government in Industry* (1917; London, 1919), pp. 12–19.

taking up the consumer cause and, certainly, the consumer machinery eventually placed within the post-1945 nationalised industries was very distant from Cole's original formulation. In the commune, there was nothing to stop any dispute going to tribunal, the danger being that a huge bureaucracy would rapidly develop to cope with the actions, appeals and counter-appeals that could see the most minor local dispute in wage-price bargaining reach every level of the guild and consumer apparatus. Furthermore, Cole claimed that the producer would be prevented from exploiting the consumer by a system of national taxation which meant any arbitrary price rise and hence worker productivity in relation to profit would mean the guild paid a higher rent to the state. Such a blunt tool, together with the inherent conservatism often ascribed to protected industries, would not act as a disincentive to innovation, Cole claimed, since the guild system would inculcate a 'philosophy of active citizenship' in which guild workers would become naturally more progressive and dynamic.[67] Cole himself later moved away from guild socialism and such a focus on the balancing power of consumers has otherwise been lost in producer-oriented socialist systems, though his recognition that citizenship, and hence the political system more generally, had to take into account men and women's dual roles as producers and consumers was taken up by other left-leaning groups outside of the mainstream Labour Party.

In one of the few, if only, serious assessments in recent years of social credit, Hutchinson and Burkitt have argued that guild socialism provided an important forerunner for a system that aimed to control, rather than be controlled by, the capitalist system of finance. They claim that all the main political parties avoided 'a body of theory capable of producing a socially equitable and ecologically sustainable economy'.[68] Social credit was a complicated mathematical theory of finance but was essentially based on the premise that the costs of production were passed on to consumers at a later date. There was always a gap between production and consumption since the value of national wealth distributed in wages never equalled the price demanded for goods by producers. Prices always reflected past costs and purchasing power was never able to keep up with prices. Both producers and consumers always had to resort to credit either to make purchases or remain in business with unused output. Yet credit was provided by an international finance system interested only in profits so its loans further raised costs, stimulating yet further price rises or else international competition (and ultimately war) as manufacturers

---

[67] Cole, *Guild Socialism Restated*, p. 255.
[68] F. Hutchinson and B. Burkitt, *The Political Economy of Social Credit and Guild Socialism* (London, 1997), p. 3.

attempted to offload surplus produce on external markets. Social credit, instead, offered a system of 'real credit' and the 'fair price'. Real credit would be distributed on the potential supply of goods and the needs of the community through a National Dividend and a fair price set on the mean rates of consumption and production, rather than just past costs. Through precise calculations of real costs, the dividend could be distributed by a central financial agency to every household in order to remove the gap between production and consumption. While orthodox economics would describe this as inflationary, advocates of social credit saw it as a means to solve all the attendant social evils associated with a profit-oriented finance system. Ultimately, 'social credits' distributed as the national dividend would replace the past-cost based wage as the main form of income for all citizens.[69]

According to Hutchinson and Burkitt, social credit emerged from the radical traditions of Ruskin and Morris, syndicalism and political pluralism, G. D. H. Cole and guild socialism, and even the underconsumption ideas of Hobson and Prince Peter Kropotkin. The main ideas were first outlined by Orage, the guild socialist, and Major Clifford Hugh Douglas, an engineer turned monetary reformer with whom social credit is usually associated. While hardly a form of consumerism in the same sense as that found in the Co-operative movement, social credit nevertheless chose the consumer as the basis of the distribution of income rather than the worker. In its early years, it received a number of adherents. The Social Credit Secretariat, a loose group formed as early as 1921, had as many as thirty-four study groups within just one year. It appealed to a large section of the disaffected working class, was debated seriously by most leading academic economists of the day, and in Alberta, Canada, resulted in a political party and provincial government.[70] Yet its appeal was limited for a number of reasons. Firstly, the complex financial formula which lay at the heart of the calculation of the national dividend was never made more digestible to potential supporters by Douglas' tortuous writing style. Secondly, he himself provided no fulcrum to the movement. He disliked party politics, was no leader of men and, when he did involve himself more closely with the Social Credit Secretariat, he produced huge internal splits and irreconcilable differences between members. Thirdly,

---

[69] *Ibid.*; C. H. Douglas, *Economic Democracy* (London, 1920); C. H. Douglas, *Social Credit* (London, 1924); M. Mertens, 'Early twentieth-century youth movements: nature and community in Britain and Germany', Ph.D. thesis, University of Birmingham (2000), p. 95; J. Hargrave, 'The case for social credit', *Cavalcade* (8 May 1948); B. Jordan and M. Drakeford, 'Major Douglas, money and the new technology', *New Society* (24 January 1980), 167–9; MRC MSS 292/560.1/22: Social Credit Party, 1931–1958: 'That Douglas Social Credit Scheme!', *Labour Bulletin* (April 1932), 372–8.

[70] Hutchinson and Burkitt, *Political Economy*, pp. 79, 142, 160.

while a less informed media might dismiss Douglas' National Dividend as 'funny money', serious writers also cast doubt on the practicability of his schemes: Cole later dismissed social credit as flawed; Keynes thought it contained 'much mere mystification' and was 'hopelessly confused'; and D. H. Robertson thought it 'a fallacy so crude that it is almost impossible to believe that it can really have been put forward'.[71] Fourthly, as with the 'living wage', the Labour Party and the trade unions dismissed Douglas and social credit. In a 1922 report, leading figures of the Left (including Sidney Webb, Hobson, Arthur Greenwood, Tawney, Cole, and Hugh Dalton) found social credit to be fundamentally opposed to the nationalisation and Fabian principles of the Labour Party.[72] Similar conclusions were reached in 1935, prompting Hutchinson and Burkitt to argue that 'the labour movement joined forces with capitalism in endorsing the legitimacy of financial mechanisms which were essential to capitalist growth economics'.[73] Yet the reactions of labour were understandable, especially when Douglas was proposing to cut all wage rates by 25 per cent and to exclude from the national dividend all those unions who violated a wage agreement.[74] Finally, social credit has never been able to cast off its associations with fascism. Douglas' dislike of formal politics and his talk of a conspiracy of financial elites produced certain parallels with the anti-Semitic rhetoric of fascism, but the adoption of social credit by John Hargrave's Green Shirts only served to compound this view.[75] Hargrave, cast out of the Boy Scout Association for his 'over-zealous Red-Indianism', set up the Kibbo Kift Kindred (KKK) in August 1920, a movement which advocated a world brotherhood of medieval guilds. Once converted to Douglas' ideas, the KKK became the Green Shirts or the Social Credit Party of Great Britain in 1927 and Hargrave embarked upon a series of stage-managed political meetings which resembled the efforts of Oswald Mosley and continental extremists. The links with fascism were only exacerbated by the Green Shirts' military style insignia and Douglas' attempts to court the Nazis when he sent his ideas to Goering's Four Year Plan Office.[76] Against all these obstacles it

---

[71] Keynes, *General Theory*, p. 371; Hutchinson and Burkitt, *Political Economy*, p. 23; MRC MSS 292/560.1/22: G. Biddulph, *The Major Douglas Delusions* (15 March 1951).

[72] Labour Party, *The Labour Party and Social Credit: A Report on the Proposals of Major Douglas and the 'New Age'* (London, 1922).

[73] Hutchinson and Burkitt, *Political Economy*, p. 111; Labour Party, *Socialism and Social Credit* (London, 1935).

[74] MRC MSS 292/560.1/22: Social Credit Party of Great Britain (19 January 1938).

[75] MRC MSS 292/560.1/22: Note on Social Credit Party (19 March 1945).

[76] Mertens, 'Youth movements', pp. 91–9. The link between consumer politics and youth movements was not restricted to the Kibbo Kift and social credit. The Woodcraft Folk, formed in 1924, had strong links with co-operation through the organisational affinities with the British Federation of Co-operative Youth: Mertens, pp. 106–7.

is clear why social credit failed to gain wider acceptance, an important social, political and intellectual context largely forgotten in Hutchinson and Burkitt's recent attempt to celebrate the ideal.

Political and Economic Planning

Far more influential, in terms of placing the consumer at the heart of a new political economy, were the policy documents published by Political and Economic Planning (PEP). PEP was set up in 1931 by a group of journalists, civil servants, economists, businessmen and academics including Julian Huxley, Noel Hall, J. C. Pritchard, Oliver Roskill, Lawrence Neal, Israel Sieff, Kenneth Lindsay and Max Nicholson. It represented part of a wider movement in 1930s Britain dedicated to planning as a means of solving the nation's social and economic problems and which witnessed the emergence of the centrist Next Five Years Group of J. A. Hobson, H. G. Wells, Siegfried Sassoon and Seebohm Rowntree and the capitalist Industrial Reorganisation League associated with Lloyd George.[77] Funded during the first few years by Dorothy and Leonard Elmhirst of Dartington Hall, and moulded around the ideas set out in Nicholson's *A National Plan for Britain*, PEP was committed to long-term research into political and economic affairs, so that problems would be anticipated and alternative solutions offered. Ultimately, many members hoped a capitalist plan of national reconstruction would emerge to solve the problems arising from the onset of economic depression, to be propagated through a 'Planning Party' committed to the 'planned society'.[78] PEP organised itself around a number of working groups (e.g., on industry, land planning, distribution, social structure and the early radical grouping, Technique of Planning or TEC PLAN, led by Nicholson's 'Young Prometheans') which held discussions at the lunchtime PEP Club and produced internal reports which were then published in the organisation's soon-to-be influential monthly 'broadsheet', *Planning*.[79] Largely non-political, unattached to any other body and independent in spirit,

---

[77] D. Ritschel, *The Politics of Planning: The Debate on Economic Planning in Britain in the 1930s* (Oxford, 1997); J. Stevenson, *Social History of Britain* (1984; Harmondsworth, 1990), pp. 323–5; A. Marwick, 'Middle opinion in the thirties: planning, progress and political "agreement" ', *English Historical Review*, 79 (1964), 285–98.

[78] British Library of Political and Economic Science, Political and Economic Planning Archive (hereafter PEP), 12/164: Leonard K. Elmhirst Papers: *Consumer Research*; PEP UP 10/3: Unprinted Papers: *PEP History: The Thirties*; C. Beauchamp, 'Consumer interest and public interest', M.Phil. thesis, University of Cambridge (2000), p. 6; Ritschel, *Politics of Planning*, p. 145.

[79] K. Lindsay, 'PEP through the 1930s: organisation, structure, people', in J. Pinder (ed.), *Fifty Years of Political and Economic Planning: Looking Forward, 1931–1981* (London, 1981), pp. 9–31.

PEP saw itself as an association of the classic public sphere: 'in between the social and economic organism, on the one hand, and Parliament or the press on the other'.[80] Dissatisfied with the frustrations facing policy workers through the 'absence of large-scale and long-term planning on behalf of the community as a whole', the members of PEP, imbued with the professional ethos which would come to the fore in the construction of Britain's welfare state, were 'interested in furthering the social and economic reconstruction of this country upon lines of common sense by means of fact finding and agreement rather than through compulsion of any kind'.[81]

In serving this entire community, PEP had to find a basis of citizenship not already tied to an existing organisation or interest associated with what it saw as an out-of-date political and economic system. Often, then, the consumer was invoked as the person for whom planning initiatives ought to be made. The consumer represented a new type of citizen, universal in nature and representative of the entire community whom politicians, trade unions, businessmen, academics and the media ought to be made to serve. For instance, in its plans for reform of the electricity industry, PEP urged the creation of consumers' consultative councils 'as a means of maintaining contact and confidence' with its customer base.[82] Whenever roads, railways and transport were discussed, PEP would ask, 'what about the consumer?'[83] A general discussion of the problems of the entire nation's distribution problems was approached by the question of 'what the consumer wants'.[84] Government was to be organised 'from the consumer end' in order to 'throw off old prejudices' and avoid the collapse of democracy.[85] Authoritarian government was a producer-dominated system: 'democracy alone is government from the consumer end'; 'the State must be consumer-minded rather than producer-minded'.[86] To achieve this, ministries, departments, public committees and Parliament were to be subjected more rigorously to public scrutiny through a system of 'watchdogs' and public knowledge and facts were to be collated and analysed with the consumer in mind.[87] PEP admired the consumer-oriented

---

[80] M. Nicholson, 'PEP through the 1930s: growth, thinking performance', in Pinder (ed.), *Fifty Years*, p. 47.
[81] *Planning*, 6 (4 July 1933), 14–15; *Planning*, 1 (1933), 1–3.
[82] 'The public concern', *Planning*, 5 (1933), 7.
[83] 'Some problems of transport', *Planning*, 21 (1934), 6.
[84] 'What the consumer wants', *Planning*, 7 (1933), 3.
[85] 'Government from the consumer end', *Planning*, 10 (1933), 1–3.
[86] 'The person, the group and the state', *Planning*, 23 (1934), 4; 'What planning means', *Planning*, 35 (1934), 9.
[87] 'Government public relations', *Planning*, 14 (1933), 11; 'Knowledge from the consumer end', *Planning*, 17 (1934), 3.

reforms of Roosevelt's New Deal and its own planned 'consumer's economy' insisted it would 'take its order from the consumer'.[88]

Of great influence in the consumer-oriented approach was the Research
Working Group which first met on 21 July 1933, a time by when the businessmen of PEP had purged the organisation of some of the communistic
tendencies of TEC PLAN.[89] It was concerned that 'research had been
undertaken hitherto mainly in the interests of the producer'.[90] According
to the Research Group secretary, F. R. Cowell, 'the consumer, rather like
that side of the moon unseen by human sight, has existed in political economy on presumptive rather than on empirical evidence'.[91] If the situation
was not reversed, producer interests would predominate and consumers
were unlikely to have their needs met. While many of the retail interests
within PEP felt that consumers were in a situation far from crisis, it was
recognised that more could be done on their behalf. A definition of the
consumer interest was adopted to include not only the satisfaction of
needs through the marketplace by fairly priced, safe and well-made commodities, but also the consumer's general welfare. The Research Group
even went so far as to use working definitions of 'consumer research'
and 'research from the consumer angle' as 'ultimate human ends'.[92] The
initial reason for PEP's concern with consumers arose out of the scant
regard given to them under food distribution policies and especially the
Agricultural Marketing Acts where the consumer committees were held
to be practically ineffective. Given the absence of consumer research at
the time, PEP looked favourably on those emerging organisations, such as
the Good Housekeeping Institute and the Ideal Home Exhibition which
set consumer standards. Throughout 1934, the Research Group discussed the creation of a government-financed Consumer Research Council to set minimum standards and encourage higher quality manufacture
through product testing in collaboration with the British Standards Institution (BSI) and the Department of Scientific and Industrial Research
(DSIR).[93] PEP wanted a central source of consumer information and a
body to act as a clearing house for complaints, though they shied away
from recommending that the government should establish preferences

---

[88] 'Planning for liberty', *Planning*, 9 (1933), 9; 'The American New Deal', *Planning*, 54
(1935), 4–15; *Planning*, 33 (1934), 8.
[89] Ritschel, *Politics of Planning*, p. 174; PEP 12/153: Research Group, *Minutes* (21 July
1933).
[90] PEP 12/154: Research Group, *Minutes* (22 February 1934).
[91] PEP 12/154: F. R. Cowell, *Memorandum on 'Research for consumers'* (20 September 1934),
p. 2.
[92] PEP 12/154: Research Group, *Note on work up to date* (22 February 1934).
[93] PEP 12/154: Research Group, *Minutes* (22 May 1934); *Minutes* (8 June 1934).

between competing products.[94] Instead, the Research Group looked increasingly towards the US private consumer body, Consumers Research, as a potential solution, though not without the aggressive reservations of retailers such as John Rodgers, Secretary to the Distribution Group, who felt it 'apt to be an irritant to producers' tending 'to lump together ethical and unethical manufacturers'.[95]

In September 1934, Cowell distributed a memorandum on research for consumers. It came out in favour of the expansion of market research by private firms into consumer needs and preferences, either by private firms or associations of producers, such as the Building Centre or the Radio Centre. State protection was looked upon favourably, particularly in the fields of adulteration, nutritional expertise provided by the Medical Research Council, Parliamentary scrutiny of particular market abuses, the research undertaken by the DSIR and the Food Investigators Board and the whole field of prices where the British Food Council was acknowledged to be ineffective, especially in comparison to such interventionist and far more powerful bodies as the US Federal Trade Commission. PEP saw much potential in the expansion of the BSI into setting standards for consumer as well as industrial goods, but it was particularly impressed with the activities of Consumers' Research which had seen its membership reach 45,000 in just five years.[96] PEP felt that a consumers' organisation could improve the efficiency of firms, raise the quality of goods and possibly lift the economy out of depression, though it deliberated as to whether this would be best achieved by a voluntary body of professional businessmen, the state bureaucracy or consumers themselves. Yet from this consultation document emerged PEP's first important statement on consumer research. *What Consumers Need*, published in October 1934 and largely written by Robert Spicer of the Retail Distributors Association, reflected the attitude of figures such as the Vice-Chairman of Marks & Spencer and prominent member of the Industry Work Group, Israel Sieff, who preached the need for responsiveness from manufacturers to consumer choice.[97] They believed the consumer required greater information on, for example, housing and nutrition, and some state action on noise, accidents and pollution, but they avoided any truly radical solutions.[98] The document argued that most respectable manufacturers gave

[94] PEP 12/154: Research Group, *Minutes* (8 June 1934).
[95] PEP 12/154: Research Group, *Minutes* (1 August 1934).
[96] PEP 12/154: Cowell, *Memorandum*, p. 14.
[97] 'What consumers need', *Planning*, 36 (1934), 1–13; O. Roskill, 'PEP through the 1930s: the Industries Group', in Pinder (ed.), *Fifty Years*, p. 68; Beauchamp, 'Consumer interest', p. 7.
[98] *Planning*, 36 (1934), 4.

the consumer a fair deal, that some consumers had only themselves to blame (especially those who continued to purchase poor quality food from the same places) and it preferred the implementation of voluntary standards only, wishing to avoid all methods of compulsion save in the reform of the libel law which as it stood appeared to prevent the public assessment of commodities for fear of actions against the defamation of goods. PEP hoped that through education, the enlightened views of every producer and every consumer would create an idealised vision of non-exploitative trading and political relations.

What Consumers Need was only a preliminary investigation, provoking much more substantial research by PEP. Although the Research Group continued to lead the investigations, the Distribution Group (if not also the Industries Group) arrived at similar conclusions, though the focus of its work was on the basic necessities of life such as milk and those food items covered by the Agricultural Marketing Acts.[99] Whether discussing a government board of regulation or a private customer, the continued lack of attention given to the consumer was construed as a potentially disastrous problem. Thus for PEP, consumerism was not simply about either luxury or necessity; it embraced a politics of consumption that spoke of minimum living standards as well as the value for money of more durable items.[100] There was believed to be a new political agenda that presented new opportunities for a unity of interests between producers and consumers to be built. Producer interests had directed policy towards protection and away from the consumer's old philosophy of Free Trade liberalism which provided free imports and imposed a 'divide and rule' policy upon manufacturers and farmers. Consumers, too, must now be protected in the new economic environment, though the controls to ensure improvements in both quantity and quality ought never to conflict with the aims of manufacturers.[101] While the Distribution Group focussed on consumer issues in food policy, the Research Group invited comments on its consumer broadsheet. In late 1935 a special Consumer Research Group was established consisting of Cowell and some prominent PEP members such as Nicholson.[102] It developed a notion of the consumer interest that matched the concerns of many consumer activists in the post-Second World War period in that it sought to improve rational buying by countering the effects of mass suggestion and ignorance of

---

[99] 'Consumer research', *Planning*, 28 (1934), 14.

[100] 'The measurement of needs', *Planning*, 29 (1934), 2.

[101] PEP WG 6/3: Distribution Group: *First draft for broadsheet, 'Distribution and Marketing Boards'* (17 July 1935).

[102] PEP WG 6/2: Distribution Group: *Memorandum on Consumers' Committees* (14 April 1934); PEP 12/164: Consumer Research Group: *Minutes* (19 October 1935).

alternative possibilities. Once consumers' true needs were then realised, business and industry could only improve through being better able to satisfy their customers.[103]

Increasingly, the Consumer Research Group identified the need for an organisation, similar to the US Consumers' Research, to empower the consumer. PEP recognised the difficulties involved in creating such a body. Firstly, they had to contend with the apathy of the shopper who was happy at times to be 'diddled'. Of those who were concerned, there was a fear that any such organisation would appeal only to a 'high brow minority' and PEP aimed to ensure that it drew its strength 'not only from the public spirited, but also from the habitués of the multiple shop and the Bargain Basement'.[104] Secondly, PEP realised that certain vested interests would have to be overcome, especially from the big advertisers who might use the press to attack the new organisation. And, finally, there were the legal issues resulting from the ease with which manufacturers would be able to sue for 'slander of goods'. PEP felt that the association would have to be registered as a limited company in order to protect consumer-subscribers and a large fighting fund would have to be set up in order to pay for any legal battles. The resulting broadsheet, *The Outlook for Consumers*, published in December 1935 nevertheless favoured a comparative testing body since they doubted the ability of the state to stamp out all negative forms of trading through its actions alone.[105]

Significantly, PEP's advocacy of a comparative-testing consumer organisation was never meant as a solely economic body that would improve the value-for-money of members' purchases. A British version of Consumers Research was always considered a social organisation as well. In a speech made by C. J. Bartlett, Managing Director of Vauxhall Motors, to the PEP Club in November 1936, he argued that the aim of such a body might well be to increase the number of things available and at a cheaper price, but this, at a time of depression and widespread poverty and unemployment, had the strong social aim of improving the general standard of living.[106] Just one year after the publication of *The Outlook for Consumers*, PEP published *Standards for Consumers* which bemoaned the absence of any uniformity or rigour with which standards were enforced for the benefit of consumers. While farmers now received much protection, the consumer faced exploitation through varied measurements of the units of gas and electricity, the absence of seals of approval and the poor administration of the 'National Mark' for agricultural produce. It

[103] PEP 12/164: *Draft for Broadsheet on Consumer Research* (13 November 1935), p. 1.
[104] *Ibid.*, p. 3.   [105] 'The outlook for consumers', *Planning*, 63 (1935), 1–13.
[106] PEP 12/164: C. J. Bartlett, 'Where the consumer comes in' (25 November 1936), p. 6.

was expected that pressure would mount on the government to produce more regulations regarding minimum standards of service, measurement and manufacture, but PEP criticised the slow progress in the protection of the 'ordinary consumer'.[107] PEP continued to discuss consumer research throughout the 1930s and beyond, as did the Advertising Association and even the Trades Unions Congress, though the legal issues surrounding 'slander of goods' prevented PEP from providing the initiative for the creation of a consumer testing organisation.[108] It would form an important bridge to the consumerism of the latter half of the twentieth century, linking the politics of necessity to the politics of affluence, especially when Michael Young became Secretary of PEP during the Second World War, when ideas about consumer research continued to be circulated.[109] In its discussions of consumerism it experienced none of the dilemmas as those economic collectivists and moral individualists of the Left, who happily promoted the socialisation of the distribution of basic foodstuffs while treating a broad range of luxuries with condemnation, silence or denial. From the very beginnings of the Research Group's meetings, the consumer was alleged to face both economic exploitation by the large-scale manufacturer and ignorance in making everyday purchasing decisions. It did not matter whether the product was a vegetable or a vacuum cleaner, to PEP no distinctions were necessary.[110] The consumer needed advice and protection in the consumption of both.

As many have said of other political 'third ways', the precise direction of policy formulas can seem a little hazy. Certainly, PEP's apparent radicalism was open to interpretation by other groups. At times its consumerism seemed a committed attempt to forge a new basis of political progression, but it was also a comfortable rhetoric for many businessmen, enlightened or otherwise. Indeed, even in PEP it was invariably the large-scale retailer who spoke for the consumer, and mainly those with links to the Retail Distributors Association and later the Retail Trading Standards Association, organisations which encouraged consumer protection through codes of practice which had the added bonus of making smaller competitors appear less reputable. Stripped of any support for state measures, PEP's consumerism consisted of voluntary measures of the kind favoured by business from the 1950s when a different political climate

---

[107] 'Standards for consumers', *Planning*, 89 (1936).
[108] PEP 12/164: World's Press News, 'AA to probe consumers' movement' (3 February 1938); MRC MSS.292/660.77/1: Scheme for a Consumers' Advisory Council (20 December 1937).
[109] M. Young, 'The Second World War', in Pinder (ed.), *Fifty Years*, p. 93. Private correspondence between Michael Young and author.
[110] PEP 12/154: Cowell, *Memorandum*, p. 3.

encouraged an expansion of legislation to protect the consumer. But this openness to translation was common to other consumer politics of the inter-war period. Percy Redfern's utopian urges suffered from a universalist consumerism that too readily glossed over the important differences that could exist between various groups of consumer. Even in his edited collection, *Self and Society*, not all authors agreed on the relationship between the Co-operative movement and the state, the synonymity between the consumer and the citizen and the degree of nationalisation and collectivism within the Co-operative Commonwealth. And, within the broad spectrum of left-wing consumerism, difficulties emerged between schools of thought. While Hobson overrode traditional fears about the irrationality of the consumer in his theories of underconsumption and the living wage, others on the Left could not bring themselves to accept that economic growth could arise out of the unfettered expenditure of the undiscriminating masses. One contributor to Redfern's series, Sir George Paish, held firmly on to the self-denying traditions of Victorian liberalism. He may have followed economic orthodoxy in urging the growth of savings for more investment, but the references to will-power, thrift and restraint demonstrated also the nonconformist and individualist morality at the heart of this strand of liberalism.[111] Finally, while revisionists today point to the guild socialist roots of Major Douglas' social credit scheme, the analysis ignores the naivety with which he allowed his theory to be tarnished with fascism.

Nevertheless, all the consumer politics outlined in this chapter represented genuine attempts to provide alternative models for the role of the consumer in the market. By the inter-war period, Free Trade – traditionally seen as a bulwark against state domination, high prices and hunger – was no longer regarded as the best protection for the consumer. Economy and politics had moved into a protectionist phase and the ideas summarised above might be seen as attempts to forge a new relationship between the individual, the market and the state. Certainly, PEP regarded the Co-operative movement as increasingly irrelevant to consumer politics in 1938. Mirroring the investigation of the same year headed by Carr-Saunders (also an active member of PEP at this time), the broadsheet, *Consumers' Co-operatives Examined*, found that while it still offered an alternative to capitalism, 'without a renewed spark it may atrophy'. Without unification, centralisation, co-ordination and the education of a new generation of co-operators in more up-to-date ideals, the old-fashioned business practices and anti-state philosophy would become

---

[111] G. Paish, *Ought we to Save?* (London, 1928).

increasingly irrelevant.[112] It was the case that the divisions demonstrated at the closing conference of the First World War Consumers' Council had never been resolved, and the Co-operative movement failed to take the lead in protecting and speaking for the consumer in a new protectionist environment. But there were many other reasons too why co-operation did not feature as a central principle of inter-war government consumer policy. Producer, either employer or worker, interests predominated not only over those of the Co-operatives but over the other consumer ideologies of the period. In the next chapter, it will be seen just how few of these ideas were actually put into practice.

[112] 'Consumers co-operatives examined', *Planning*, 116 (1938), 14.

4   The price of depression: consumer politics in inter-war Britain

Just as unemployment was a cause of poverty in inter-war Britain, so too were fluctuating prices felt to add to the hardships of consumers. In the late 1930s, the Labour Party and the trade unions attempted to mobilise women in a series of cost-of-living campaigns meant to bring pressure on the government's food policy. In a 1937 pamphlet, *My Family's Food Costs More and More*, a woman is seen forlornly examining her purse. She is told that her plight mirrors that of the farmer and the worker in the food industry, all of whom have been exploited by 'big business', 'the middlemen' and 'profiteering food combines'. 'What can the housewife do about it?' asked the Labour Party:

> Nobody knows the bitter results of rising food prices better than the housewives. They know that the week's food money buys less and less solid nourishment; and they know what the effect will be sooner or later on their families.
> Nobody can do more about it than the housewives. There are millions of them. They hold together the homes of Britain. The Government dare not ignore their influence if they all protest together.[1]

The appeal to the housewife was part of a broader propaganda campaign to show that 'food policy is part of socialism'.[2] Women were to strengthen the labour movement in unity with their trade union husbands. The Labour Party Women's Section aimed to collect 1 million signatures in protest at the cost of living and ultimately to gather at the Friends' Meeting House on the Euston Road in London on 23 February 1938 to present the Prime Minister with a petition against rising prices.[3]

There is much to suggest that the actions of the Labour women had the potential for some success given the greater attention being paid to women as consumers across Europe.[4] In Britain, the enfranchisement

---

[1] Labour Party, *My Family's Food Costs More and More* (London, 1937), p. 3.

[2] *Ibid.*; Labour Party, *How the Housewife Suffers* (London, 1938).

[3] MRC MSS 292/174.91/4: Letters from Mary Sutherland, Chief Women's Officer, to Secretaries of Women's Sections (2 and 4 February 1938).

[4] B. J. Davis, *Home Fires Burning: Food, Politics, and Everyday Life in World War I Berlin* (Chapel Hill, 2000); A. Ellmeier and E. Singer-Meczes, 'Modellierung der sozialistischen

of the housewife in 1918 resulted in a new form of political rhetoric. The Labour Chancellor, Philip Snowden, proclaimed his proposed indirect tax cuts of 1924 a 'housewife's budget' and the ILP argued that 'for the cheap loaf workers must wait for Socialism'.[5] On the Right, Stanley Baldwin constantly reminded the newly enfranchised electorate that 'every housewife knows what inflation means in prices'.[6] In the move away from a Free Trade econsmic policy and the shift towards state intervention there was an opportunity for the consumer to become the new political citizen around which policy revolved. Even the Empire was to be bolstered by consumer action. The Empire Marketing Board, set up in 1926, spent over £3 million in eight years promoting Empire foodstuffs so that re-directed consumer choice would result in a self-sufficient economic unit.[7]

The absence of a dominant set of consumer political principles explains why the consumer remained a malleable being, though the entrenched interests of both employers and trade unionists within the political structure meant that consumers did not achieve greater institutional recognition. The history of consumer politics in the inter-war period is the history of an alternative relationship between the individual and the state that never came to fruition. Although for most individuals consumer politics simply meant the daily struggles to 'make ends meet', this chapter demonstrates the continued importance of issues of food, price and necessitous consumption to the labour movement, especially during periods of financial hardship when workers and consumer interests were indistinguishable. Throughout the period, the trade unions and the Labour Party assisted and promoted cost-of-living campaigns, though the consumer was never to receive the same level of recognition as had been the case in 1918. The 1925 Royal Commission on Food Prices led to the establishment of a Food Council, but producer interests ensured that this body was almost wholly ineffective. Renewed pressure by Labour resulted in greater

konsumentin. Konsumgenossenschaftliche (frauen)politik in den zwanziger jahren', *Zeitgeschichte*, 16 (1989), 410–26.
[5] P. Snowden, *The Housewife's Budget* (London, 1924); MSS 292/174.91/4: ILP Information Committee, *Weekly Notes*, 291 (5 February 1925).
[6] Cited in S. Gunn, 'The public sphere, modernity and consumption: new perspectives on the history of the English middle class', in A. Kidd and D. Nicholls (eds.), *Gender, Civic Culture and Consumerism: Middle-Class Identity in Britain, 1800–1940* (Manchester, 1999), p. 23.
[7] S. Constantine, '"Bringing the Empire alive": the Empire Marketing Board and imperial propaganda, 1926–1933', in J. M. Mackenzie (ed.), *Imperialism and Popular Culture* (Manchester, 1986), pp. 192–231; S. Constantine, *Buy and Build: The Advertising Posters of the Empire Marketing Board* (London, 1986); R. Self, 'Treasury control and the Empire Marketing Board: the rise and fall of non-tariff preference in Britain, 1924–1933', *Twentieth Century British History*, 5:2 (1994), 153–82.

consumer representation within the administration of the Agricultural Marketing Acts, but again the consumer councils were ignored. In Parliament, the Labour Party maintained the pressure for an economic policy which incorporated consumer concerns and it introduced Consumers' Council Bills in both 1929 and 1939. However, this was a consumerism produced mainly by negative considerations. It sought to fix prices, restrain the profiteer and protect the consumer of household necessities but, as the Conservatives were quick to point out, it was an ill-thought-out measure which attempted to set maximum prices without the state control of the food supply. Even if the Bills are to be regarded as a more fully developed policy, then the proposed Consumers' Council was envisaged by a trade-union dominated Labour Party as the first stage on the path to nationalisation and state socialism: it was the means rather than the end in itself. In the inter-war decades, issues of consumption continued to revitalise the Left, but the concerns of both manufacturers and workers ensured that the consumer was never to have the central position within the state and the economy that much of the apparently pro-consumer rhetoric suggested.

The cost of living

The experience of poverty between the wars meant families and especially housewives continued to negotiate the difficulties of getting and spending. A discrepancy will always exist between the abstract formulations of the consumer interest and the practical responses developed by family provisioners in combating the problems of consumption. Before any party political campaign could begin, consumer politics usually meant the more mundane aspects of maintaining a satisfactory standard of living on a limited income. And, as David Vincent has suggested, 'the poorer the household, the more sophisticated the financial wheeling and dealing'.[8] These responses were personal and private, hidden from any public sphere of politicised consumerist concerns. As Ferdynand Zweig found of affluent workers, profound inhibitions were apparent in the discussion of financial matters among the working class, even between husband and wife, whose communication on the subject might not extend beyond the tipping up of the male breadwinner's wage to the housewife at the end of the week.[9] These were inhibitions bolstered by the conventions of respectability and status consciousness found within the local community,

[8] D. Vincent, *Poor Citizens: The State and the Poor in Twentieth-Century Britain* (London, 1991), p. 92.
[9] M. Tebbut, *Making Ends Meet: Pawnbroking and Working-Class Credit* (London, 1984), p. 37.

which ensured a certain instrumentalism when poor consumers had to rely on neighbours in various mutual aid initiatives.[10] Within this context, social historians have focussed on the working-class housewife as the family strategist, an often adept and highly skilled manager of the weekly budget and an often imposing presence within the household whose domestic authority was rooted in her success or otherwise in matters of consumption.[11] If the image of 'our mam' now approaches a cliché, this is not to deny that 'her skills at mending and making do, her vigilance against all waste, and her knowledge of where and when in the neighbourhood bargains in food and clothing were to be had were crucial to the survival of the family'.[12]

The housewife's tactics ranged from the skills associated with production – sewing, mending, maintaining, cooking, cleaning – to those more obviously consumerist strategies of finding cheaper goods. Money was set aside for various holiday clubs, Christmas goose clubs, boot clubs, coal clubs, mail-order clubs and the purchase of cheques for clothing clubs.[13] For the very poor, certain forms of charity could be relied upon, especially for the young, such as the Children's Country Holiday Fund and the Ragged School Union. Housewives often managed a complex network of credit arrangements, from securing 'tick' at the local corner shop to purchasing on the 'never-never', using (and often hiding from) the tally man, buying 'provident cheques' and borrowing from a local moneylender who was often simply another woman who informally lent to friends and neighbours at nevertheless exorbitant rates.[14] Most infamously, there was the pawnshop, an institution which proliferated throughout the interwar decades and to which almost all working families turned at some point during the poverty cycle, despite the negative social connotations attached to it. Not simply a means of relieving distress, the pawnshop could be a regular feature of the week's consumption routines as best suits and jewellery were pledged and redeemed almost mechanically every Monday morning in order to raise sufficient funds for purchasing food and paying the rent. Indeed, cash was sometimes illegally excluded from this overall circulation as articles of clothing were seen to be exchanged directly for

---

[10] P. Johnson, *Saving and Spending: The Working-Class Economy in Britain, 1870–1939* (Oxford, 1985).
[11] C. Chinn, *They Worked All Their Lives: Women of the Urban Poor in England, 1880–1930* (Manchester, 1988); E. Roberts, *A Woman's Place: An Oral History of Working-Class Women* (Oxford, 1984); J. Bourke, *Working-Class Cultures in Britain, 1890–1960: Gender, Class and Ethnicity* (London, 1994).
[12] Vincent, *Poor Citizens*, p. 94.
[13] E. Martin, *The Best Street in Rochdale* (Rochdale, 1985), p. 10.
[14] Johnson, *Saving and Spending*; J. Blake, *Memories of Old Poplar* (London, 1977), p. 8.

small items of food.[15] According to Ross McKibbin, these individualist strategies ultimately impacted upon politics as the working classes were more likely to see their struggles in personal terms rather than developing a universal or structural explanation. And this politicisation was particularly gendered since 'the domesticated, money-conscious, family-managing working-class wife was much closer to the Conservative Party's ideal of the good citizen than was her husband. Equally, no doubt, the Conservative Party was closer to many working-class wives' ideal of good politics than were its opponents.'[16]

Evidence which points to the overall increases in the standard of living would seem to reinforce McKibbin's point, as working-class consumers were able to engage in the politics of consumption individually at the store rather than collectively at the ballot box. Despite the experience of hardship suffered by the unemployed and the low paid, real wages rose during the 1920s and did so again – on average by 7 per cent – during the 1930s.[17] This was the period of industrial depression, but also of the rise of mass advertising and retailing, of new developments in light manufacturing, of cheap branded goods, of rising rates of expenditure and of some cheaper, and more plentiful, food.[18] An expanding leisure industry and the proliferation of petty luxuries were seen by social observers to make life bearable, especially for those newly affluent teenagers and young wage-earners and for those inhabiting J. B. Priestley's much-quoted England of democratic consumption in which all were 'as good as one another so long as you had the necessary sixpence'.[19] Yet this overall decline in prices and emergence of 'the consumer society' hid both the practical difficulties faced by many working-class housewives and the many local level discrepancies not seen by the averages of historical revisionism. Frequently, branch trade union representatives wrote to the TUC expressing concerns about local price rises and how it was felt that these were not reflected in the government's cost-of-living index. Indeed, the index itself proved a constant source of frustration for many labour representatives, as its calculation was alleged to reflect poorly the common purchasing expectations and routines of the average working-class

---

[15] M. L. Davies, *Life as We Have Known It* (1931; London, 1990), p. 21; Tebbutt, *Making Ends Meet*, pp. 6–7.

[16] R. McKibbin, *Classes and Cultures: England 1918–1951* (Oxford, 1998), p. 204.

[17] J. Stevenson, *Social History of Britain* (1984; Harmondsworth, 1990), p. 117.

[18] J. Benson, *The Rise of Consumer Society in Britain, 1880–1980* (London, 1994); W. H. Fraser, *The Coming of the Mass Market, 1850–1914* (Basingstoke, 1981).

[19] J. B. Priestley, *English Journey* (1934; Harmondsworth, 1987), p. 6; G. Orwell, *The Road to Wigan Pier* (London, 1937); D. Fowler, *The First Teenagers: The Lifestyles of Young Wage-Earners in Interwar Britain* (London, 1995); A. Davies, *Leisure, Gender and Poverty: Working-Class Culture in Salford and Manchester, 1900–1939* (Milton Keynes, 1992).

family.[20] Eventually, trade union discussions permeated Labour Party questions in Parliament, especially in the early 1920s and the later 1930s when prices did begin to creep up again. The main point of contention was that the index figure was derived from the increases in the cost of living based on the average working-class household budget of 1904. A satisfactory standard of living was therefore implicitly assumed in the index, though it was at a pre-World War One level which had been disputed by most figures on the Left at the time and which had become increasingly anachronistic as the years and decades passed. By 1937, Labour complained bitterly that while nobody felt the current standards of living of the poor to be adequate, the cost-of-living index (based on 1904 measurements of poverty) was still being used to justify the absence of change in unemployment allowances and public assistance.[21] The poor were being denied a basic level of consumption due to the subjective assumptions about an adequate lifestyle enshrined within an institutional mathematical formula.

Often the complaints against the cost-of-living index were begun by the women's sections of the trade unions and frequently a 'much wider and more modern' interpretation of the standard of living was demanded. The index base, used purely for statistical convenience, consisted mainly of food items. Reflecting Hobson's and the ILP's notion of the living wage, activists urged an index that took better account of other items such as clothing and even forms of recreation, entertainment, holidays and education. These were goods and services not 'statistically necessary' but 'certainly necessary from the psychological point of view'.[22] When the Labour Party was in government, there were certainly opportunities to reflect these consumer concerns. Although no changes were made to the calculation of the index during Labour's first term of office, Snowden's budget introduced a number of consumer-friendly measures. Duties were reduced substantially on the basic staples of sugar, tea and coffee, as well as on the luxuries of motor cars, musical instruments, clocks and watches and films, leading him to proclaim, using an older liberal rhetoric, that 'these proposals are the greatest step ever made towards the realisation of the Radical ideal of a free breakfast table'.[23] And moves were made to launch an enquiry into food prices and the cost of living. Once Labour was ousted from office in 1924, the Conservatives proceeded with plans

---

[20] MSS 292/174.91/3: Letter from William May to General Secretary, TUC (November 1922); Letter from TUC to Shop Assistants' Union (24 November 1922).
[21] H. C. Deb., 326 (6 July 1937), cols. 241–4.
[22] MRC MSS 292/174.91/3: TUC, Cost of Living and Standard of Living (3 January 1930), p. 3.
[23] Snowden, Housewife's Budget, p. 14.

for what was to be a Royal Commission, the dangers of which the trade unions were well aware. They knew that some trade union representatives would be likely to be called to sit on the investigative committee but that this would be in far fewer numbers and at a level at which they would be guaranteed to be overshadowed by manufacturers' interests than had the Commission been appointed by Labour.[24]

The reductions in prices did ease the agitation against the cost of living in the late 1920s, but by the mid-1930s, when Walter Citrine had increased the role of the TUC in the Labour Party and in government, it had again become a central concern.[25] Part of the labour movement's problem had been that it was unwilling to launch an enquiry into the calculation of the cost of living and working-class budgets at a time of industrial depression and unstable working-class incomes. There was a fear that a new statistical budget would be devised that reflected an impoverished state of affairs rather than how they should be. In the second Labour Government of 1929, the General Council of the TUC pressed for another investigation into the cost of living and a Committee of the Economic Advisory Council produced a report calling for changes in its calculation so as to reflect the increased costs of rent in working-class budgets. The report was never published and the issue disappeared from mainstream debate after 1931, not least because of Labour's fall from office. The trade union position, too, contained a degree of ambivalence. The cost-of-living index provided a focus for protest and any increase in it gave the workers a reference point during an industrial dispute, but if ever the index fell, the position of the employers in wage negotiations would likewise be strengthened. Following the publication of a Ministry of Labour pamphlet, *The Cost of Living Index: Its Method of Compilation*, attention was again alerted to the 1904 statistical base and in 1935 the trade unions began to discuss the issue once more. Perhaps reflecting Citrine's desire to make the labour movement appear more respectable and moderate, the TUC rejected the notion that the index ought to be based on an ideal standard of life and supported instead a figure that reflected the majority of its members.[26] Nevertheless, as inflation began to rise, the cost-of-living index again became a rallying point and by July 1937 the TUC was sending deputations to the Minister of Labour urging him to adjust the Unemployment Insurance Fund in line with the increased cost of living.[27]

[24] MSS 292/174.91/3: *Cost of Living*, p. 4.
[25] N. Riddel, 'Walter Citrine and the British Labour Movement, 1925–1935', *History*, 85:278 (2000), 285–306.
[26] MSS 292/174.91/3: *Cost of Living* (October 1935).
[27] MSS 292/174.91/4: Deputation to the Minister of Labour, Ernest Brown (27 July 1937).

Although the Labour Party received support in its campaign from bodies such as the Socialist Medical Association, it was the women in the labour movement who took the initiative. Mary Sutherland, on behalf of the Standing Joint Committee (SJC) of Industrial Women's Organisations, prepared a questionnaire requesting information on the precise nature of the increased costs within working-class budgets.[28] Originating in the First World War, the SJC had provided representatives of the working-class housewife to the Consumer Council, including Marion Phillips who acted as secretary from the SJC's inception in 1915 to her death in 1932.[29] It consisted of eight delegates each from the Labour Party, the trade unions and the Co-operative movement and aimed to ensure women's interests were heard at all levels of the labour movement.[30] In terms of consumer politics, regular debates were held on the position of the housewife in relation to world food supplies and resolutions were frequently passed (and subsequently taken up at the Labour Party conference) calling for the development of co-operation at international level.[31] The housewife and the consumer were conflated as political agents in the rhetoric against profiteering and the 'useless middleman' and the SJC joined with other bodies such as the ILP in condemning the Royal Commission on Food Prices for the few working-class and women members of its investigative committee.[32] Following similar patterns within the labour movement as a whole, fewer proclamations about consumption were made by women's groups during the late 1920s, though by the early 1930s the SJC was fully supporting the Labour Party's proposals for a newly constituted Consumers' Council. It also opposed both Free Trade and the Conservatives' protectionist tariff policy in favour of public ownership and control and was being asked to represent the consumer point of view in a whole range of social settings, such as the Socialist Medical Association's investigation of the 'consumer's' (that is, the patient's) point of view within the health services.[33]

Sutherland's efforts therefore built upon persistent themes within the women's organisations, though her petition of 1937 was to amass only 70,000 signatures and the Prime Minister, Baldwin, refused to meet her

---

[28] MSS 292/174.91/4: Extracts from Minutes of National Council of Labour (23 November 1937).

[29] MSS 292/62.14/1: Standing Joint Committee of Industrial Women's Organisations (SJC), *Report* (1932), p. 1.

[30] MSS 292/62.1/1: SJC, *Constitution* (1927); SJC, *Its Aims and Its Constitution* (1926?).

[31] MSS 292/62.1/1: SJC, *Report* (1924), p. 3; MSS 292/65.2/1: National Conference of Labour Women, *First Agenda* (13–14 May 1924), p. 7.

[32] MSS 292/65.2/1: *First Agenda*, p. 10; *Final Agenda* (27–28 May 1925), p. 10.

[33] MSS 292/65.2/1: National Conference of Labour Women, *Final Agenda* (1930), p. 12; *Final Agenda* (1932), p. 13; MSS 292/62.1/1: SJC, *Report* (1931), p. 5.

deputation.[34] Undeterred, she helped organise a series of meetings on the cost of living around the country and arranged a mass meeting in London on 23 February 1938, events which had been stimulated through a special article on the cost of living in the January 1938 edition of *The Labour Woman*. After speeches by Sutherland and four 'ordinary' housewives', Susan Lawrence handed over the petition to the Labour Party leader, Clement Attlee, the moral force of the housewife thus being transferred to the politician who would then take up the woman's cause in Parliament. In this symbolic exchange, the Labour Party appeared to have demonstrated both its consumer and worker consciousness. According to Labour Party thinking on the standard of living, the housewife was 'more acutely affected by a rise in prices than anyone else in the community'.[35] Her interests in this sphere needed to be brought directly into the concerns of the labour movement since 'the question of the cost of living is the question of wages from the housewife's point of view'.[36] When women complained about price rises their views were not to be dismissed through economic ignorance, since the information provided about the cost of living was itself highly dubious. Indeed, women's experiences of daily provisioning gave them an area of expertise which meant that 'their views on national well-being are as important as the views of any section of industrialists'.[37]

In such rhetoric the Labour Party appears to have had an equal regard for prices and wages. Despite a usual focus on the incomes of trade union members, statements on the standard of living frequently mentioned that any rise must 'come mainly, or at any rate, partly, through falling prices'.[38] The Party disregarded any suggestions that the cost of living actually fell slightly during the general slump in producers' prices in the early years of the 1930s depression. It was felt that any defence of prices in 1938 on the ground that they were no higher than those of 1929 was politically wrong, since it was also to say 'that the majority of the poorer classes must never expect to share at all in the world's economic progress'.[39] Here, a politics of consumer necessity emerged based on rights to a certain standard of living. The Labour Party advocated the unrestricted supply of all essential foodstuffs and the support for uneconomic home producers through direct taxation in order to ensure the supply of basic provisions. Such a policy was entirely in accord with other socialist principles, once

---

[34] MSS 292/174.91/4: Letter by Sutherland to all Women's Sections (6 January 1938); MSS 292/62.14/1: SJC, *Report* (1937), p. 4; SJC, *Report* (1938), p. 4.
[35] MSS 292/174.91/4: *Draft Report on Socialism and the Standard of Living* (1938), p. 1.
[36] *Ibid.*   [37] *Ibid.*, p. 10.
[38] MSS 292/174.91/4: D. Jay, *Memorandum on the Rise in Food Prices and Government Food Policy* (January 1938), p. 1.
[39] *Ibid.*

it had been demonstrated that cheap prices would emerge not through the payment of low wages but through the reduction in incomes provided to 'landowners and other rich rentiers'.[40]

Caution must be expressed in this articulation of a consumer politics. More general statements on consumption did not necessarily reflect a grass-roots movement as ordinary consumers sought to overcome their economic difficulties through individual budgeting and purchasing decisions. And many of the Party's richest discussions of the cost and standard of living appeared only in speeches to the National Conference of Labour Women. In a 1938 address on *Socialism and the Standard of Living*, the Labour Party entered into a detailed and informed discussion on the use of the problematic cost-of-living index by the government and the need for the incorporation of the housewife/consumer into the protests against it. But the Party also believed that high prices were often necessary in a slump if producers were to rise out of economic depression and there was a clear faith in the trade union interest that much could be resolved simply by increasing wages. If prices were reduced through specific state controls there was also the further danger that employers would demand wage reductions. Ultimately, the concerns of the housewife/consumer had to give way to the defence of the trade unions and the Party goal of state socialism: the housewife 'can give a lead in interpreting Labour's policy in terms of her own job'.[41] Women were to use consumption to bolster existing agendas rather than having existing policies transformed through a reworking of the economy at the point of consumption and through the housewife. Labour tied itself to a trade union wage consciousness rather than a consumer consciousness that might have emerged through an expansion of the Co-operative movement. While there was room for a politics based on both price and wage to continue, a significant element of the Labour mindset ensured wage and work would always be more significant than price and consumption. In a time of economic depression and unemployment, such agendas were entirely understandable, but they call into question the consumerist rhetoric employed by Labour in the disputes over the constitution and administration of, as will be seen below, the Food Council, the Agricultural Marketing Acts and the Consumers' Councils Bills.

The Royal Commission on Food Prices and the Food Council

Immediately after the Consumers' Council of the First World War was abolished, calls were made by many on the Left for the creation of a

---

[40] *Ibid.*, p. 5.   [41] MSS 292/174.91/4: *Draft Report on Socialism*, p. 26.

replacement body. Complaints were heard in Parliament against both profiteering and the statistical base of the cost-of-living index. Although the Labour Party had considered the issue during its first Government, the Conservatives took the lead once in power and a Royal Commission on Food Prices first met on 29 November 1924. If many on the Right recognised the case for some protection of the consumer in an era that had moved beyond Free Trade, much cynicism was still expressed by those who doubted Stanley Baldwin's pro-consumer rhetoric.[42] His election promises of cheap food and slogans such as 'Return Mr. Baldwin and Food will come down' were seen as populist measures fuelled by the supportive propaganda found in Lord Rothermere's newspapers.[43] Nevertheless, in setting up the Commission, Baldwin was appealing to 'the public' and the reconciliation of interests so typical of pragmatic Conservatism in the inter-war years.[44] The aim of the Commission was to investigate the prices of food at various stages in their distribution and retail and to compare these with those paid by the final consumer.[45] Following the closure of the Ministry of Food in 1922, doubts remained as to the pricing policies of British agriculture. The Food Department at the Board of Trade continued to examine specific cases and the 1923 Linlithgow Committee on the Distribution and Prices of Agricultural Produce had investigated in considerable depth several staple food items, though from the point of view of the producer. The issue was sufficiently prominent in the concerns of public opinion to warrant further study, this time with the consumer interest made paramount.

Before the Report of the Commission had even been published, its membership, constitution and proceedings had been condemned by the Left. The principal objection was that there was a strong bias towards the producer rather than the consumer. As one Labour MP commented after examining the minutes of the Commission, 'I have come to the conclusion that the producer makes nothing, . . . that the export and transport companies are philanthropists, and are in the job for what they can give away, that the importer is a charitable institution, that the wholesaler and the retailer are on the dole, and that the only villain in the piece is the consumer, who has not been paying enough.'[46] The Commission's membership consisted of no representatives of working-class women's

---

[42] G. G. Anderson, *The Call for Protection in the Interest of the Consumer* (London, 1925).

[43] *H. C. Deb.*, 181 (4 March 1925), col. 551.

[44] P. Gurney, *Co-operative Culture and the Politics of Consumption in England, 1870–1930* (Manchester, 1996), p. 221; R. McKibbin, *The Ideologies of Class: Social Relations in Britain, 1880–1950* (Oxford, 1990), pp. 259–93.

[45] Royal Commission on Food Prices, *Volume I. First Report*, Cmd. 2390 (London, 1925), p. 1.

[46] *H. C. Deb.*, 181 (4 March 1925), col. 592.

organisations and only one each from the CWS and the trade unions. Instead, figures such as Sir Auckland Geddes were selected, a man condemned by the veteran Labour leader and founder of the *Daily Herald*, George Lansbury, for his close connections to the Federation of British Industry and the Anti-Socialist National Propaganda organisation.[47] Too many of the other Commissioners had close links with Lord Inchape, the 'business dictator of Britain', and Lansbury set out in detail their willingness to listen at length to important representatives of the 'meat trust' and 'food combines' – their cross-examination by Geddes being 'like Satan reproving sin'.[48] As the leader of the Co-operative Party in Parliament, A. V. Alexander, put it, the Royal Commission was just a means of avoiding taking any action on food policy, the selection of its members merely reinforcing the common opinion that it was a 'make-believe inquiry'.[49]

Through the selection of witnesses called to give evidence, it was more that 'the consumer' was an entity constructed by others, and especially manufacturing interests, than a citizen who spoke for him or herself. Although there were a number of individuals interviewed who could be expected to provide an alternative politics of consumption such as Alexander, a few other co-operators and Hobson's colleague, E. F. Wise of the ILP, their numbers were eclipsed by the nearly eighty representatives who could be seen as having a far greater concern with the affairs of the producer over the consumer. Even the handful of witnesses selected from voluntary associations came from the less radical groups such as the National Citizens' League and the National Council of Women rather than the Women's Co-operative Guild or the trade unions, though this was part of a more general trend of middle-class women's groups becoming the spokesbodies for the housewife during the inter-war period.[50] The problem was exacerbated by their subsequent treatment: while labour leaders' claims would be subject to further scrutiny, those of retailers were treated as fact. Geddes was said to 'sneer' at, 'belittle' and bully working-class housewives when they appeared before the Commission, his own wealth determining that he had no empathetic knowledge of the importance of what seemed to him minor increases in price. According to Fred Jowett, Geddes' behaviour was 'scandalous' while Ellen Wilkinson claimed he 'acted as counsel for the defence in the case of profiteers who came before him, and towards Labour representatives as though they were prisoners in the dock'.[51]

---

[47] *Ibid.*, cols. 552–3, 591.   [48] *Ibid.*, col. 554.   [49] *Ibid.*, col. 580.
[50] Royal Commission on Food Prices, *Report*, pp. 169–72. On the changing class and gender of the consumer, see M. Hilton, 'The female consumer and the politics of consumption in twentieth-century Britain', *The Historical Journal*, 45:1 (2002), 103–28.
[51] *H. C. Deb.*, 181 (4 March 1925), col. 575; Gurney, *Co-operative Culture*, p. 224.

Because the Commission was regarded by the Left as a purely cosmetic measure to cover up a growing number of press complaints, Lansbury and the Co-operative MP, George Barnes, moved to pre-empt the final report with a vote of no confidence and a statement supporting instead further legislation against profiteering.[52] When the report was published, it adopted a moderate tone throughout, it did not dispute the calculation of the cost-of-living index, it regarded competition as the norm and the natural order of things, it implied price increases were due to the excessive wage demands of labour and it gave far more space to the arguments against state trading in food than those for. Yet it did propose the creation of a Food Council, an organ of state designed to 'watch over the supply of wheat, flour, bread and meat to the people of this country'.[53] It was to act not as an advocate, but as a 'mediator' between producer and consumer, fostering 'an atmosphere of mutual respect and understanding': indeed, for 'all honest traders' it was 'to be a friend and advisor'.[54] Its twelve members were to be appointed by the President of the Board of Trade, with just one man and one woman from each of the trade unions and consumers' organisation (though it was also recommended that one member of the CWS be appointed). It was not to be allowed to publish details about any businesses investigated, it was to have only a small staff, voluntary measures or the threat of adverse publicity were to be sought at all times and the Commission shied away from any discussion of the earlier profiteering legislation or recommendations as to how they should be replaced. But it did accept that if all methods of persuasion failed to prevent a dishonest or unfair method of trading, some form of compulsion ought to be instituted through statutory powers. It was this point that prompted the reservations of one Commissioner, Thomas Howard Ryland, President of the National Farmers' Union, who saw in the Food Council the disastrous first step on 'the slippery slope of Socialism'.[55]

Ryland's fears were unjustified, as he might easily have reflected that the recommendations of the Commission were just another form of political containment, as had occurred with the earlier weak profiteering legislation, or with the business 'capture' of anti-adulteration measures. Certainly, the provisions for a Food Council were moderate in comparison to some of the demands of the Commission's witnesses. The former Free Trader, Chiozza Money, proposed an imperial purchasing scheme with domestic controls to limit the price of bread.[56] E. F. Wise and the ILP had recommended the state control of the import of wheat and flour,

---

[52] *H. C. Deb.*, 181 (4 March 1925), col. 549.
[53] Royal Commission on Food Prices, *Report*, p. 3.   [54] *Ibid.*, p. 140.   [55] *Ibid.*, p. 173.
[56] Royal Commission on Food Prices, *Volume III. Statements of Evidence*, Cmd. 2390 (London, 1925), p. 65.

the encouragement of Dominion trade and the removal through bulk purchasing of various middlemen who only served to increase the final price of the loaf.[57] Alexander defended the system of co-operation against other witnesses' calls for the taxation of the CWS's surplus.[58] The TUC called for the creation of a powerful International Economic Commission as a permanent branch of the League of Nations to regulate the international food supply and it followed the Labour Party in advocating a Food Consumers' Council to limit the powers of trusts and combines.[59] None of these expected the proposed Food Council to wield any effective power, especially with its proposed tiny staff and limited budget. But MPs were not given the opportunity to debate the report of the Commission and the Prime Minister refused to hear a deputation of organised consumers led by Alexander.[60] The Food Council was mocked as 'Baldwin's balsam' and even the government's own Food Department chief at the Board of Trade resigned and refused to become the chairman of the proposed new body on the grounds that it was not given statutory powers.[61] Christopher Addison, former Liberal (and first) Minister for Health, but now a Labour convert, subjected the report's 'futile recommendations' to a lengthier critique.[62] In *Why Food is Dear*, he both equated consumerism with socialism and sought to repeat much of the evidence presented to the Commission which attacked middlemen's activities and suggested instead the extension of state trading and 'bulk purchasing on national account'.[63]

The reactions to the report by Addison, the Labour Party and the trade union and Co-operative movements was of little effect. The Food Council, as constituted, was to have even fewer powers than the Commission had recommended, though its principal handicap was to be the absence of any powers of compulsion in the obtaining of price and profit data from any company being investigated. Lord Bradbury, a former Treasury official, was selected as chairman and, although business interests were not as prominent as on the Commission, it was nevertheless dominated by public officials and civil servants connected to the Board of Trade. In clear denial of the Commission's recommendations, only one trade

[57] Royal Commission on Food Prices, *Statements*, p. 120. Royal Commission on Food Prices, *Volume 2. Minutes of Evidence*, Cmd. 2390 (London, 1925), pp. 240–54.

[58] Royal Commission on Food Prices, *Minutes*, p. 184; Royal Commission on Food Prices, *Statements*, pp. 94–9.

[59] Royal Commission on Food Prices, *Report*, p. 132; Royal Commission on Food Prices, *Statements*, pp. 179–82; MSS 292/181/2: TUC and Labour Party, *Memorandum of Evidence* (February 1925).

[60] *H. C. Deb.*, 184 (11 June 1925), col. 2220; 186 (6 July 1925), col. 190.

[61] *H. C. Deb.*, 184 (10 June 1925), col. 1985; 184 (11 June 1925), col. 2220.

[62] C. Addison, *Why Food is Dear* (London, 1925), p. 3.   [63] *Ibid.*, p. 19.

unionist was selected, and he, F. W. Birchenough, was a right-winger connected to the General Federation of Trades Unions rather than the TUC. W. E. Dudley, the CWS Commission member, maintained his position, but he was not joined by any other representatives of organised consumerism.[64] While one working-class housewife was on the Council, she headed no women's body and had little experience in public affairs, though given the constitution of the Council it is unlikely that any greater incorporation of organised working-class consumers would have made much difference. However, the Council might have drawn on the expertise of the WCG or even less feminist and less radical groups such as the Women's Institutes and Townswomen's Guilds which were increasingly involved in consumer issues such as housing and domestic economy in the 1920s. The government's attitude to the Food Council was made obvious in its very first meeting. Sir Philip Cunliffe-Lister, President of the Board of Trade, stated the importance of maintaining the 'fullest co-operation' with business and the chair admitted to knowing 'nothing about the subject'.[65] He advised his colleagues of the dangers of trying to 'perform impossibilities' and he limited the Council's work to obtaining and disseminating information about prices. The purpose of this was not to empower the consumer but to have 'the effect of allaying apprehension where this was unfounded'.[66]

The work of the Food Council confirmed the fears of its critics. As a non-statutory body it existed quietly for its first few years, producing only sixteen reports by the end of 1930. In 1925 it investigated the prices of bread and was able to encourage London bakers to observe a scale of prices for the 4lb. loaf, but it scored few other public successes.[67] Throughout the late 1920s it was dismissed as 'absolutely ineffective' and a 'farce' as a consumer advocate. It formed few subcommittees and did little to extend its work with even Cunliffe-Lister admitting its achievements were 'not spectacular'.[68] The most persistent problem was the Council's inability to compel traders to provide it with facts and statistics, a disadvantage which had become painfully apparent by 1928 when both the London Millers' Association and the Amalgamated Master Dairymen refused to co-operate.[69] The Council, fearing

[64] *H. C. Deb.*, 187 (28 July 1925), cols. 224–5.   [65] Gurney, *Co-operative Culture*, p. 225.
[66] PRO MAF 69/6: Food Council, *Minutes* (31 July 1925).
[67] MAF 69/6: *Minutes*, 1925–30; POWE 26/203: Consumers' Council Bill: Appointment of a Consumers' Council, *Brief for Second Reading* (30 March 1931), p. 6.
[68] *H. C. Deb.*, 191 (2 February 1926), cols. 29–30; 191 (15 February 1926), col. 1531; 199 (10 November 1926), col. 1073; 227 (6 May 1929), col. 1977.
[69] MAF 69/12: Royal Commission on Food Prices and Food Council: Report by the Food Council to the President of the Board of Trade, *Powers to Obtain Information* (17 May 1928), pp. 4–6.

the consequences of such defiance, privately appealed to the Board of Trade for an extension of its powers so it could force traders to comply and Baldwin, demonstrating a passive integrity, responded with a placatory speech in Parliament insisting that compulsory powers would be granted should the need arise.[70] Compulsory powers were, however, never introduced and the Food Council was increasingly humiliated, especially when the London bakers increased their prices in 1930, a decision taken, according to the Council, as an act of open 'defiance', performed 'with the object of rendering the Food Council impotent in the future'.[71]

By this stage, a new Labour government, frustrated at the Council's inability to limit bread and milk prices, had moved to introduce a far more effective Consumers' Council. The delays which occurred in the attempts to introduce this legislation further undermined the Food Council as its position remained uncertain. From 1930 the Council began to meet irregularly and attendance was sparse, limiting its discussions only to questions of 'exceptional importance'.[72] Even after the moves to create a Consumers' Council had been withdrawn, the Food Council was left permanently scarred. In 1931, the Conservative government asked the Council to investigate once more London bread prices. Taking over a year to report, all bakers were cleared of any charges of profiteering and the Council continued to slumber.[73] It failed to meet at all from December 1932 to December 1933 since the new chair felt that 'nothing had occurred in the earlier part of the year to necessitate a meeting'.[74] The total running costs amounted to only £945 for the year up to March 1933, spent mainly on the travel expenses of just a few members.[75] The government, however, refused to disband it. Although it did observe something of a revival in its fortunes with the establishment of the consumer councils in 1933 under the Agricultural Marketing Acts (see below), it merely spluttered on throughout the 1930s and MPs were occasionally surprised to learn that it still existed.[76] With the outbreak of war in 1939, the Council agreed to its own suspension, though the anger of the then Chairman, Geoffrey Peto, at its treatment, perhaps reflects most suitably

[70] Baldwin stated that compulsion would be granted once the Food Council itself requested such an extension of its powers. When they did in May 1928 this was not granted: *Ibid.*; *H. C. Deb.*, 222 (12 November 1938), col. 501.
[71] MAF 69/6: *Minutes of 28th Meeting* (11 April 1930).
[72] MAF 69/6: *Minutes of 30th Meeting* (18 December 1930).
[73] MAF 69/6: *Minutes of 32nd Meeting* (10 December 1931); *Minutes of 35th Meeting* (19 December 1932).
[74] MAF 69/6: *Minutes of 36th Meeting* (15 December 1933).
[75] *H. C. Deb.*, 283 (28 November 1933), cols. 673–4.
[76] *H. C. Deb.*, 328 (26 October 1937), col. 77; 329 (23 November 1937), col. 1039; 338 (11 July 1938), col. 1084.

what had been the underlying attitude of the government to the Council all along. In the secret plans for the creation of the new wartime Food Ministry which were implemented immediately, no mention was made at all of the experience of the Council and none of the apparent expertise it had developed over fourteen years was to be drawn upon in the new food controls.[77] The Food Council had been an irrelevance to government and its constitutional weaknesses so crippling that it had never become a focus of consumer concerns for the either the Left or the populace as a whole. Its establishment owed more to the cynical populist measures of Baldwin's electioneering and its survival to his party's subsequent need to appear to be doing something about prices when complaints in the press and through public opinion became too vociferous. It represented no force for consumer activism and attempts to incorporate the consumer into state affairs came through the initiatives for new organisations rather than through an organisation from which consumers had been excluded from the beginning.

The Consumers' Council Bills

Frustration over the weakness of the Food Council and the absence of working-class consumer representation at state level encouraged the Labour Party to introduce a Consumers' Council Bill during its second period in office in 1929. The previous Conservative government had threatened to make the Food Council a Tribunal of Inquiry in 1928, but even as the milk distributors continued to refuse to listen to Council directives, Baldwin never took up his promise. In its election manifesto, *Labour and the Nation*, the Labour Party outlined its consumer policy which was to focus on both the encouragement of co-operative trading and 'the stringent control over monopolies and combines, by enlarging the powers of the Food Council'.[78] Once in power, the continued underlying weaknesses of the Council convinced the Party to develop an entirely new consumer body that proposed to go well beyond acts of persuasion and introduce instead measures for the rigid control of prices in sectors where profiteers were seen to offend repeatedly.

Alexander, who was to be in charge of the Bill in its passage through Parliament, had since 1925 been advocating the creation of a Consumers' Council to revive the politics of its First World War predecessor and

---

[77] MAF 69/9: Letter from Geoffrey Peto to D. F. Eades (8 October 1939); Peto to William Brown, Board of Trade (21 October 1939); Oliver Stanley to Peto (25 October 1939); Peto to Stanley (27 Octboer 1939).

[78] PRO T 161/299: CP 278(29): Memorandum by the President of the Board of Trade, *Food Policy and the Protection of Consumers: Trusts and Combines* (17 October 1929), p. 2.

ensure the articulation of the consumer voice at state level.[79] This suggests the persistent advocacy of a consumerist politics at the pinnacle of the labour movement, but the Bill never represented a finely tuned economic programme as its opponents in various Standing Committees were quick to point out. It does, however, demonstrate the importance of consumer concerns to the ranks of the labour movement and it is an area which has been almost entirely overlooked in existing social and political histories.[80] Issues surrounding the economic depression and the pressing question of unemployment certainly dominated politics at the time, as well as subsequent accounts, but for many within the Labour Party, and particularly those sponsored by the Co-operative movement, the Consumers' Council Bill was inseparable from the range of other measures adopted to alleviate the plight of the poor. In assessing the performance of the Labour government of 1929–31, Robert Skidelsky has provided the harshest and most lasting interpretation. Divided between a utopian socialism and a commitment to constitutionalism, the Party failed to develop a social democratic or gradualist programme of reform. 'It thought in terms of total solution to the problem of poverty, when what it was offered was the limited opportunity to cure unemployment. It was a parliamentary party with a utopian ethic. It was not fit for the kind of power it was called upon to exercise.'[81] It is an analysis that might be applied to its consumer policy as well. On the one hand, the proposed Consumers' Council was a pragmatic solution and outlet for the difficulties faced in day-to-day getting and spending, while on the other it offered measures only really workable in a wholesale state socialist system. The Bill appeared to enshrine this inconsistency, contributing to its demise.

The Consumers' Council Bill 1930 aimed to establish a body similar in principle to that of the Food Council. It was to consist of seven people including a chairman and deputy chairman selected for their general administrative experience, an economist, an accountant, a representative from the labour movement and a middle- and a working-class housewife.[82] In addition to these changes in membership the proposed organisation was to differ from the Food Council in terms of its powers. It would be able to compel businesses to hand over for scrutiny any documents it wished to examine, its remit was not restricted to any particular

[79] J. M. Wood, *Protecting the Consumer* (London, 1963), p. 17.
[80] R. A. Bayliss, 'The Consumers' Councils Bills 1929–1939', *Journal of Consumer Studies and Home Economics*, 4 (1980), 115–23.
[81] R. Skidelsky, *Politicians and the Slump: The Labour Government of 1929–1931* (London, 1967), p. xii.
[82] POWE 26/183: Consumers' Council Bill Papers, *Notes on Clauses and Amendments* (May 1930).

commodities and, most crucially, it was to submit recommendations to the Board of Trade as to the appropriate price to be set in an industry which could then be followed up with a Departmental Order fixing the price for named classes of trader who would be subjected to fines and imprisonment for non-compliance.[83] It was estimated that the total cost of the Council would amount to £20,000 per annum.[84] Although there was much agreement within the Labour Party over the need for such powers of investigation, the President of the Board of Trade, William Graham, had misgivings over the price fixing clauses. Experience from the First World War suggested that any maximum price set by the state had a tendency to become the minimum price and he recognised that any system of price control would be ineffective unless state control of supply was introduced as well. This was clearly the aim of the state socialist project, but broader nationalisation of distribution measures were recognised as 'impractical for the moment'.[85] Even after the decision to press ahead with the Bill had been approved by Cabinet, Graham still worried over its inconsistencies. On the one hand he was pledged to support a seemingly arbitrary price-fixing institution which he felt unworkable within a capitalist marketplace. On the other, the provisions for the Council avoided any direct socialisation of the food industry which, although believed to be the ideal solution, he knew also the Labour Party 'had no mandate to establish in the present Parliament'.[86]

The passage of the Bill through Parliament reflects both the hostility towards it by the Conservative Party and the ambiguities in the Labour position to necessitous consumerism. The Bill received its First Reading on 30 April 1930 and provoked a heated debate upon its Second in May. Graham attempted to present the Consumers' Council as the logical development for a society concerned with prices. Since the First World War there had been sixty reports on prices by various Committees, from the twenty-eight issued under the Profiteering Acts, to the five investigations of agricultural produce by the Linlithgow Committee and the sixteen reports of the Food Council.[87] Even the Conservatives had pledged themselves to certain forms of price control such as when Baldwin apparently committed his government in May 1928 to the extension of the powers of investigation of the Food Council.[88] But Graham

[83] P. P., *Consumers' Council Bill*, Bill 177 (London, 30 April 1930).

[84] PRO T 163/61/8: Consumers' Council Bill, Session 1930–1.

[85] T 161/299: *Food Policy and the Protection of Consumers*, p. 6.

[86] *Ibid.*, p. 8; *Memorandum by the President of the Board of Trade* (25 October 1929); *Cabinet memo* (2 April 1930); *Cabinet memo* (15 April 1930).

[87] POWE 26/203: Consumers' Council Bill, *Brief for Second Reading* (30 March 1931), p. 4.

[88] *H. C. Deb.*, 217 (17 May 1928), col. 1221.

also tied the Bill to the specific concerns of the depression, suggesting that as close attention to purchasing power as to wages and incomes was the best means of alleviating the pressures on the authorities caused by poverty.[89] These were arguments acceptable to the Conservatives who were prepared to extend the powers of the Food Council but who were incensed at the price-fixing measures – 'the apotheosis of bureaucracy' – especially coming from a President of the Board of Trade whom they had previously imagined as 'the keeper of the Ark of the Free Trade Covenant'.[90] It was legislation seen as an 'orgy of price-fixing' by the farmers, a 'disastrous half measure' by Beveridge, a 'supreme dictatorship' by Lord Balniel, and a Bill to 'cripple industry' by Salmon, an MP with important retail connections.[91] And despite general agreement on the futility of the Food Council, some even defended this body as an appropriate individualist measure: if the 'stupid' housewife could not then live within her budget, then she herself was to blame.[92] Yet it was able to pass through Parliament at this stage because of the deal made with the Liberals who surprised the Conservatives by coming out in favour of this protectionist measure.[93] Within the Labour Party it received its most enthusiastic support from those consumer-oriented groups who wished to enhance the political power of 'the woman with the basket' and of the position of consumption more generally, such as E. F. Wise in his commitment to Hobsonian economics.[94]

After passing its Second Reading, the Bill was referred to Standing Committee where it fell foul of Conservative MPs' delaying tactics who attacked what they saw as a product of the 'miscegenation' of anti-trust sentiments and 'full-blooded Socialism'.[95] Reintroduced in November 1930 with some minor amendments over price-fixing Orders to further placate the Liberals, Graham's 'abortion' was again attacked for creating an 'administrative outrage' not 'committed since Caligula made his horse a consul'.[96] The Labour Party, it was claimed, had had its hand forced by the Co-operators, who had designed the Bill purely to attack the small shopkeeper.[97] Yet poignant divisions emerged on the Left too as the self-interested questioning shopworker trade unionists, concerned for the livelihoods of those who worked in a condemned store, ensured fractures occurred in the consumerist alliance.[98] Once in Standing Committee

[89] *H. C. Deb.*, 238 (8 May 1930), col. 1178.   [90] *Ibid.*, col. 1181.
[91] *Ibid.*, cols. 1188–9, 1192, 1214, 1224.   [92] *Ibid.*, cols. 1245–6.
[93] *Ibid.*, col. 1204.   [94] *Ibid.*, cols. 1220; 1195–6.
[95] POWE 26/184: Consumers' Council Bill, *Notes on Clauses and Amendments;* Standing Committee D, Consumers' Council Bill, *Fifth Day's Proceedings* (26 June 1930), col. 164; P. P., *Report and Special Report from Standing Committee D on the Consumers' Council Bill with the Proceedings of the Committee*, 144 (London, 1930).
[96] *H. C. Deb.*, 250 (30 March 1931), cols. 791, 819.   [97] *Ibid.*, col. 871.
[98] *Ibid.*, col. 813.

again, the Conservative Majors Colfox and Tryon introduced a series of delays which saw the first four days devoted to a series of quibbles over the Bill's first four lines.[99] Speeches were delivered at a 'tortoise pace' (apparently Colfox even made his supporters 'squirm'), ridiculous motions to adjourn were introduced at regular intervals and 'humiliating' and irrelevant debates took place such as on the functions of ministers of religion in public life.[100] Alexander was forced to ask for 'kangaroo' powers to dismiss many of the proposed amendments but an 'emasculated' version of the Bill emerged from Committee which limited the ability of the Board of Trade to fix maximum prices only where the free play of competition was restricted.[101] In any case, the Bill had progressed too slow and the proposed Third Reading for 20 October meant the intervening May Report on Britain's financial crisis had brought down the Labour government.

While Skidelsky calls into question the competence of a Labour government committed to the socialist goal but unaware of how to reach it through a parliamentary system, the Party's faith in 'consumerism' must also be doubted. It was certainly not a policy development that co-ordinated with other attempts to deal with poverty. Insufficient attention was given to the precise divide between persuasion and coercion in the Council's activities and the implications of fixed prices were insufficiently thought through. Furthermore, the delays suffered and the timing of the initial introduction of the Bill just before the end of a parliamentary session calls into question the Party's commitment to the consumer interest. Trade union concerns for the plight of shopworkers suggest one such division, to the extent that the Bill's opponents questioned Labour's strength of purpose. Baldwin even accused the government itself of using delaying tactics, citing as evidence the lengthy gaps between Readings and Committee stages. He suspected the Labour Party attached too little importance to a Bill that rushed towards socialism with inadequate forethought.[102]

Nevertheless, consumer concerns persisted within the Parliamentary Labour Party, though not to the extent that a consumer campaign captured the full imagination of the leadership. At the end of 1938, Rev George Woods, backed by Alexander and several backbench Labour MPs, introduced another Consumers' Council Bill virtually the same

---

[99] P. P., *Report and Standing Committee C on the Consumers' Council Bill with the Proceedings of the Committee*, 141 (London, 1931).
[100] *H. C. Deb.*, 253 (19 June 1931), cols. 2105–7, 2115.
[101] *Ibid.*, cols. 2167–8; P. P., *Consumers' Council Bill (as amended by Standing Committee C)*, Bill 222 (London, 1931); POWE 26/203: *Brief for Second Reading*, pp. 37–8.
[102] *H. C. Deb.*, 253 (19 June 1931), col. 2109.

to that of 1930.[103] The Bill was soundly defeated, the Conservatives objecting to it on similar grounds as before. They supported an individualist approach to the market, this time celebrating the capabilities of the housewife shopper and suggesting that the 'ridiculous' clauses of the Bill were included so as to induce such a confusion in the conditions of commerce 'that people will feel that the only solution is to be found in State Socialism'.[104] The political climate had swung firmly in favour of business. The Council was alleged to be both prosecutor and judge, a situation which would inevitably destroy the goodwill that had supposedly emerged – if only through passivity – between the Food Council and the retail trade. The Government opposed the Bill not only because of its price fixing measures but also for its powers of compulsion in the collection of evidence, a point which the Conservatives had been willing to concede in 1930.[105] Instead, governments would always be able to appeal to the 'public spirit' of powerful corporations to provide the necessary co-operation.[106] Finally, reference was made to the consumer safeguards within existing legislation such as the Agricultural Marketing Acts. These, it was suggested, provided adequate space for the concerns of consumers about the supply and prices of food staples.[107] But, as will be seen below, the provisions for the consumer in these agricultural schemes were deeply flawed. That the Conservatives were able to refer to them suggests the perennial significance of smokescreen institutions and containment measures to many officials within the governments of the inter-war period.

Agricultural Marketing Acts and Boards

The Labour Party's other means for protecting the consumer was through the Consumers' Committees set out in the Agricultural Marketing Act 1931. In an industry dominated by rings, combines and large-scale producers it had long been felt that the interplay of supply and demand was serving neither the interests of the farmer, the agricultural labourer nor the consumer. The proposed Agricultural Marketing Boards were designed to protect British farming through their control of purchasing and distribution, both raising the price paid to the producer and lowering that paid by the consumer. The Act, and others which followed up

[103] P. P., *Consumers' Council Bill*, Bill 20 (London, 1938); BT 63/25/1: Consumers' Council Bill 1939: *Yorkshire Post* (24 December 1938).
[104] *H. C. Deb.*, 343 (10 February 1939), col. 1266.
[105] BT 63/25/1: *Note for Second Reading of CC Bill (10 February 1939)* (20 January 1939), p. 5.
[106] BT 63/25/1: CC Bill, *Note by General Department* (20 January 1939).
[107] BT 63/25/1: CC Bill, *Consumer safeguards under existing legislation* (February 1939).

to 1935, applied to certain named products, such as hops, wool, cereals, cheese, livestock, potatoes and milk.[108] It was a clear shift away from Free Trade policy and served as a measure of protection for the farmer against foreign competition. But by abolishing a system within which the consumer could no longer bargain, the state was 'under a logical obligation to substitute some other method of price regulation'.[109] For this reason, a Consumers' Committee, effectively a single body with various sub-committees for each of the listed goods, was to be attached to the Boards to ensure that consumer interests were not entirely unheeded.

Support for consumer representation was only ever lukewarm. In the first Marketing Bill of February 1931 no provision was even made for the consumer.[110] If the Conservatives' affinities were to lie with the farmer, the Labour Party at this stage felt more concern for the agricultural labourer. In any case, Graham's Board of Trade Consumers' Council Bill dealt far more effectively with the interests of the consumer and those who drafted the Agricultural Marketing Bill recognised 'the undesirability of putting in too many safeguards for consumers, otherwise farmers would be apprehensive and disinclined to favour schemes'.[111] Realising later, however, that some provision was needed for the airing of consumer views, the Committee was set up specifically 'to act as a focussing point for the complaints of the unorganised mass of consumers'.[112] Here, though, influence was to be limited. The Marketing Boards, which had the real power in drawing up the schemes, saw the Committee's complaints work as a useful means of diverting away from themselves such tasks which 'would hamper its consideration of more important matters', though they reserved the right to sit in on any Committee meeting which discussed a complaint.[113] Once constituted and having met for the first time in December 1933, the Committee was hampered by its lack of independence, representation and its membership. Explained as a purely 'administrative convenience', but reflecting also an absence of commitment to consumerism, the Food Council was merely reconstituted as the Consumers' Committee and was therefore open to the same criticisms as to its membership. Its permanent staff consisted only of a seconded secretary from the Ministry of Agriculture, together with the existing secretary

---

[108] Skidelsky, *Politicians and the Slump*, p. 257; C. Beauchamp, 'Consumer interest and public interest', M.Phil. thesis, University of Cambridge (2000), p. 10; MAF 34/719: Agricultural Marketing Acts, 1931–1933, *Consumer Committee Reports*.

[109] MAF 69/8: Letter from Hugh Molston to Sir Geoffrey L. Corbett (12 August 1934).

[110] MAF 194/815: Consumers Committees, *History And Development Out Of Pre-War Food Council*.

[111] *Ibid.*, p. 1.   [112] *Ibid.*, p. 2.

[113] MAF 34/28: Agricultural Marketing (Consumers' Committee) Regulations, *Agricultural Marketing* (26 August 1932).

of the Food Council, though it was able to draw on the expertise of other government departments as and when required. Prior to the outbreak of the Second World War, the Committee only wrote ten reports, seven of which were published. In a government review some thirty years later, the Committee was concluded to have possibly been 'something of a nuisance' to the Marketing Boards in the sense that its critical comments were often picked up by the press. But it was more likely the case that the Committee's reports received little attention from the Boards and governments did not 'appear to have felt it necessary to take much heed of what the Council said'.[114]

The establishment of the Consumers' Committee did, however, revive the fortunes of the Food Council which had remained entirely silent during Labour's plans for a Consumers' Council. It began to take the initiative on a number of issues, even capturing the public imagination to a limited extent. In 1935 it investigated the possibility of broadcasting food prices over the radio after having studied the daily announcement of the best prices and bargains for common household goods made by New York City's Consumer Service Division on eleven radio stations.[115] Some precedents already existed, despite the complaints of manufacturers against the publication of prices: prior to 1930 the Ministry of Agriculture and Fisheries had a twenty-minute radio slot commenting on current plentiful foodstuffs; from April 1928 to February 1930 the Empire Marketing Board provided information to the BBC on 'Empire foodstuffs now in season' which was then broadcast on a Friday evening following a housewives' talk; and a series of 'Housewives' News Bulletins' ran from January 1931 to August 1932, broadcast on Tuesday mornings, again bringing attention to seasonal goods, recipes and occasionally prices.[116] The Food Council became involved in extensive negotiations with the BBC and a special conference was held on 24 April 1936 with representatives from 'practically every woman's organisation' in the country attending.[117] At the conference there was a tendency for the middle-class housewife to assume greater importance, Eleanor Barton of the Women's Co-operative Guild complaining that the cookery stall 'did not

---

[114] MAF 194/815: Consumers' Committees, p. 4; MAF 69/8: Note on the Food Council and the Consumers' Committee (20 July 1934).
[115] MAF 69/10: Ethel M. Wood, *Consumer Interest in the USA* (27 June 1935); *Minutes of Food Council*, (11 October 1935); F. F. Gannon and W. F. Morgan, *The Consumers' Service Division: Its Organisation and Work* (n.d.).
[116] MAF 69/10: *Memorandum as to the collaboration of MAF in the broadcasting of market information of interest to the housewife* (23 October 1935).
[117] MAF 69/10: Note by Mr. Mackinney on broadcasting of information about food, February 1936; BBC Conference, 'Questions for discussion' (24 April 1936); *The Times*, 25 April 1936.

understand the practical exigencies of the working class home' and that a 'rather sniffy' tone had been adopted.[118] Yet much agreement did at least exist on the need for some sort of consumer information service, whether about price or, less controversially, the practical skills of housewifery. The BBC continued to air programmes which discussed issues of concern to the housewife-consumer, though no extensive and regular broadcast was made of the availability of fresh produce and current market rates.[119]

In 1936, the Food Council began publishing its own *Annual Reports* directly for the Board of Trade. It reported as the Food Council, recognising that its remit was much wider than that of the specific goods they were entitled to examine when its members sat as the Consumers' Committee.[120] Here, it was able to set out more clearly its approach to the problems of consumers. Although generally pro-market and pro-competition, the Council saw its function as that of a vigilant watchdog of any price increase which seemed 'unjust to the consumer', of any 'abuse of power' by producers or distributors and of any feature of an existing system of distribution which pointed to inefficiency and extravagance.[121] Within this brief period of revival, the Council/Committee appeared a more useful consumer protection body to certain branches of the labour movement and the trade unions attempted to become more involved just when labour women embarked on the cost-of-living campaign. Pointing to the original recommendations of the Royal Commission, the TUC urged the President of the Board of Trade to nominate two members of the trade union movement.[122] At first, the request was refused, but following a deputation led by Walter Citrine, the Board of Trade acceded to the demand and eventually, though the date by this time was June 1939, two nominees were accepted.[123]

If the Food Council had developed into a slightly more effective body by the late 1930s, the influence of the consumer upon government affairs was not necessarily altered. When the Council members served in their dual role as the Consumers' Committee to the Agricultural Marketing Boards, they particularly felt their lack of power. By 1938, they were in 'near revolt', frustrated and angered by the lack of consideration given to their proposals by the Marketing Boards and the government.[124] The most

---

[118] MAF 69/10: J. R. Willis, note on BBC conference (24 April 1936).
[119] MAF 69/10: BBC memorandum, *Information as to Broadcasts on Foodstuffs* (n.d.).
[120] Food Council, *Annual Report* (London, 1937).
[121] Food Council, *Annual Report* (London, 1938), p. 2.
[122] MSS 292/174.91/8: TUC, *Cost of Living and the Food Council* (3 February 1939).
[123] MSS 292/174.91/8: Letter from I. Beer, Board of Trade, to TUC General Council (7 March 1939); TUC Economic Committee, *Cost of Living and the Food Council* (4 April 1939); Letter from General Secretary to Oliver Stanley (29 June 1939).
[124] MAF 194/815: *Consumers' Committees for Great Britain*, p. 4.

sustained criticism of this situation came from PEP who first examined the functioning as the Consumers' Committee in 1934 as part of its general investigation of the position of the consumer in modern economic and political life.[125] PEP recognised that in the retreat from Free Trade, the farmer's interest had been secured through the 'coherent marketing policy' set out by the Agricultural Marketing Act, though little power was now given to the consumer.[126] It sought instead a new structure for the distribution of food between producer protectionism and Free Trade, a structure which recognised the unity of interests between farmers and consumers.[127] Planning for food therefore had to take into account such wider social factors as the scientific assessment of nutrition levels, the measurement of the level of poverty and the need for a national food policy if the nation's standing in the world and the quality of its citizens were not to decline in tandem.[128] Food policy, for PEP, was a consumer policy and a matter of economic and national emergency: 'It has to be recognised as a first-rate national interest that more milk, butter, eggs, vegetables, and so forth, of good quality, shall be available not only to those who can afford to pay for the wastes of an inefficient productive and distributive system, but to everyone.'[129]

What PEP found instead, however, was a form of consumer consultation which could only be described as 'absurd' and 'unsatisfactory', particularly the lack of administrative distinction between the Food Council and the Consumers' Committee.[130] While these perceived inadequacies encouraged PEP to investigate other forms of consumer organisation, especially those in the United States, it continued to list its criticisms of the marketing schemes. The Consumers' Committee was not representative, since the individuals selected spoke authoritatively for no group of consumer. It had employed no staff, even though it had been granted powers to do so. It had no effective power in its advisory power so the consumer was effectively 'forgotten'. And, even if the original Act had been well intentioned, the subsequent development of agricultural policy meant that the Marketing Boards were ruled by 'vested interests', postponements and 'inevitable compromises' which resulted in no investigation

[125] PEP WG 6/2: Max Nicholson, *Points referred to Distribution Group by Research Group* (19 March 1934); WG 6/1: Distribution Group, *Notes of a Joint Meeting on National Food Policy* (17 December 1934).
[126] PEP WG 6/3: Distribution Group, *First draft for broadsheet, 'Distribution and marketing boards'* (17 July 1935).
[127] PEP WG 6/1: John Ryan, *Distribution* (6 December 1934).
[128] *Planning*, 25 (1934), 7; 'The measurement of needs', *Planning*, 29 (1934), 1–13; PEP WG 6/1: PEP, *Distribution Group* (2 February 1935).
[129] 'What sort of plenty?', *Planning*, 44 (1935), 11.
[130] PEP WG2: *Memorandum on Consumers' Committees* (14 April 1934).

of what the consumer actually wanted.[131] Focussing on specific products such as milk, PEP found that the product did not reach those consumers who needed it the most, such as school children, and proposed instead more effective research institutions which would examine better forms of transport and distribution, so that both consumption and production might be increased.[132] Food policy was therefore to be dictated not by the clash of interests, with the power of the Board substantially greater than that of the Consumers' Committee, but through separate research departments for each point along the food chain. The findings of each committee, whether concerned with farmers, distributors or consumers, would then reach the Board in order that the most rational overall policy be adopted.[133]

PEP's alternative food policy was, however, never implemented in the 1930s. The careful selection of those chosen to represent the consumer, the relationships constituted with other more important bodies and the resources made available to them ensured that the Food Council and the Consumers' Committee of the Agricultural Marketing Boards remained extremely weak voices of consumer discontent. All this ensured that many of the ideas articulated for a consumer politics and the general concern with price by many sections of the labour movement never reached an institutional or even corporate setting. This is a situation very different from that argued to have existed in the United States where consumerism is held to have been equated with citizenship in the New Deal era. Political discourse repeated that being a good American was being a good consumer and the public was urged to buy its way out of depression. This championing of the consumer was translated into political rights, the differences between votes in the marketplace and choices made in political allegiance becoming blurred. Within Roosevelt's reforms, 'citizen consumers' were incorporated as the voice of the public within New Deal agencies where the consumer was to play a central role in the nation's recovery programme.[134] Although further research may well suggest that

---

[131] Ibid.; 'Marketing Board and distribution', Planning, 56 (1935), 1; 'The output of knowledge', Planning, 17 (1934), 7.

[132] 'Milk for those who need it', Planning, 62 (1935); 'How milk is distributed', Planning, 93 (1937); 'Agriculture's part – II', 98 (1937); 'Milk distribution proposals', Planning, 106 (1937).

[133] PEP WG2: Memorandum on Consumers' Committees (14 April 1934).

[134] C. McGovern, 'Consumption and citizenship in the United States, 1900–1940' and L. Cohen, 'The New Deal state and the making of citizen consumers', in S. Strasser, C. McGovern and M. Judt (eds.), Getting and Spending: European and American Consumer Societies in the Twentieth Century (Cambridge, 1998), pp. 37–58, 111–25; L. Cohen, 'Citizens and consumers in the century of mass consumption' and M. Jacobs, 'The politics of plenty in the twentieth-century United States', in M. Daunton and M. Hilton (eds.), Politics of Consumption: Material Culture and Citizenship in Europe and America (Oxford, 2001), pp. 203–21, 223–39.

this incorporation of the consumer within the institutions of the US state was by no means as complete as it first appears, the references to consumer citizenship do suggest important differences with Britain. For in Britain it would be difficult to argue that the consumer was confused with the citizen within institutions such as the Food Council. Powerful interests ensured that the consumer was largely seen as a rational individual unit whose sphere of activity belonged purely within the economic confines of the market. This was so much the case that even the traditional respect accorded to the working-class housewife and family provisioner could be quickly forgotten if she chose to translate her expertise beyond the marketplace.

All this is, perhaps, of little surprise, given the evidence of existing accounts of business influence in anti-profiteering and adulteration legislation. But the history of consumer politics cannot solely be explained through the operation of private vested interests on the side of the mass manufacturer. The labour movement too had its private interests in the form of the trade unions, though older discourses about consumption and consumers remained prominent too. The price and wage consciousness seen in the campaigns against the cost of living and the appeals of popular politics does not mean consumer issues were treated with the same urgency as questions of unemployment and income by the labour hierarchy. Understandably in a period of acute economic depression, policies dealing with the immediate relief of distress and poverty assumed a greater urgency than rises in the price level. But trade union desires to protect workers and wages above wives and prices meant less attention was given to consumer affairs. While this helps explain the success of Fabian policies over more consumer-oriented politics, as seen in chapter 3, it also meant that the Food Council, the cost-of-living index, the Consumers' Council Bill and the consumer provisions within the Agricultural Marketing Acts were never at the very top of the Labour agenda. Sometimes, this meant campaigns were led to increase trade union representation on these committees rather than co-operative representation or even that of the Women's Co-operative Guild. Trade unionists could be famously hostile to their allies in the CWS: when fighting to have two trade union representatives on the Food Council they argued to the President of the Board of Trade that they would make far better working-class representatives since the Co-operative movement itself was actually an employer. At other times, it meant Labour Party consumer policy was either forgotten or confused. Labour Party criticism of the Food Council could have been far more vociferous and even if the Consumers' Council Bill was not an attempt to introduce nationalisation of the food supply by the back door as Tory opponents suggested, it was at least a naïve policy which had not fully calculated the implications of a price-fixing régime. Lurking in the background of all these events, though, remained the traditional labour movement's theoretical distaste for luxury and its concomitant embrace of the ascetic life. Necessitous and luxury consumption are normally easy to differentiate, as seen in the rich politics of necessitous consumption developed in the inter-war period, but feelings of guilt, triviality and irrationality lay around the corner of any discussion of consumption should it veer from needs to wants. At times this was a fine distinction and, as will be seen in the next chapter, had the potential to restrict the Left's thinking and actions on the consumer and the marketplace.

5 Austerity to affluence: the twilight of the politics of necessity

Luxury and necessity, vice and virtue, use and abuse, productive and unproductive – these traditional dichotomies all continued to inform debates about consumption throughout the twentieth century, particularly those of the British Left. While necessity implied a set of rights to a basic standard of living around which citizenship and socialism could be built, luxury remained more problematic. It could either represent, in the classical sense, the vampirism of the aristocracy and futile status seeking of the bourgeoisie, else it connoted the dehumanising standardisation and compensatory pleasures of the mass market 'culture industry'. If the former moulded political prejudices, the latter, for many left-wing intellectuals at least, only weakened the class struggle through distraction and false consciousness. Yet throughout the 1940s the politics of consumption underwent a number of important changes, where such polarised divisions lost their social validity. Firstly, wartime controls saw unprecedented state intervention in supply, distribution and consumption, stretching the sphere of government activity well beyond the usual boundaries of bread and milk. Secondly, if this really was a 'people's war', then the consuming desires of these people had to be considered. Even before the spread of affluence in the 1950s, politicians had to address the issue of wants not needs, and of the rights of consumers to the cheap luxuries, conveniences, customs and simple pleasures of the mass market which they had enjoyed for at least half a century. Within this context, distinctions between luxury and necessity, or between a life of ostentation and asceticism, were of little use in a world which accepted the right of the masses to some degree of material abundance and participation in consumer society.

Certain figures adopted a pragmatic attitude to the new consumer environment. If they never demonstrated a settled comfort with consumption beyond the ordinary, they at least acknowledged its importance or harmlessness within working-class culture. For those who had grown up with the new mass market, consumption, whether luxurious or necessitous, was a fact of life, to be negotiated with, rejected, but also, at times, embraced. It was recognised by 1947 that only a relatively small proportion of the incomes of the poor was taken up with the biological necessities of food, clothing and shelter, the rest being spent on goods important to identity formation or to provide 'psychological satisfaction'.[1] J. B. Priestley was perhaps the foremost chronicler of this spirit. At times, he shared wholeheartedly that distrust of luxury, whether shabby or genteel, which he would later condemn as the 'Admass' society.[2] He shared also the productivist ethic which celebrated work above all forms of consumption, as witnessed in his mournful hymn to the collapse of 'real men's work' found in the shipyards, the coal mines and the workshops: 'For all that, a chap' at's learnt his trade an' can use his hand – he isn't a machine an' he isn't a flippin' monkey – he's a man lad, wages or no wages, a *man*.'[3] Yet when he wrote that modern England was 'Blackpooling itself' he knew also that there was much in the marketplace that might even warrant celebration. The poor and the ordinary had just as much of a right to leisure and sport, pleasure and waste, luxury and enjoyment. In collections such as *Delight*, Priestley often set out in loving detail his favourite commodities, enabling the working-class smoker, for example, to cherish and eulogise his favourite tobacco in the same glowing terms as the most celebrated connoisseur of London's clubland.[4] Richard Hoggart, too, maintained a healthy ambiguity towards consumption. His *The Uses of Literacy* appears to be a critique of the new mass culture, but it was also a testament of faith in the ability of the working classes either to resist or to negotiate with commercialism and Americanisation.[5] Indeed, for much of the sixties and seventies, Hoggart's Birmingham Centre for Contemporary Cultural Studies served as an institutional embodiment of this approach.

But for most of the leading intellectuals of the British Left, mass market consumerism remained a topic to be avoided, some looking with unrestrained glee to its destruction within a socialist society. What did not occur was a debate as to the role of material abundance in modern life such as there was within many of the Scandinavian labour and trade union movements. Nor was consumption associated with the national way of life as it had been for several decades in the United States, even within the minds of workers' leaders. Instead, the image of the dour socialist ascetic of the mid-twentieth century still resonates and the contention

[1] E. A. Laver, *Advertising and Economic Theory* (Oxford, 1947), pp. 14–15.

[2] J. B. Priestley and J. Hawkes, *Journey Down a Rainbow* (London, 1957), p. 43.

[3] J. B. Priestley, *The Good Companions* (1929; London, 1950), p. 637; J. Baxendale, ' "I had seen a lot of England's": J. B. Priestley, Englishness and the people', *History Workshop Journal*, 51 (2001), 87–111.

[4] J. B. Priestley, *Delight* (London, 1949), pp. 26–7; J. B. Priestley, 'A new tobacco', *Saturday Review*, 144 (1927), 216–17.

[5] R. Hoggart, *The Uses of Literacy* (1957; Harmondsworth, 1973).

that the Labour Party never resolved its relationship with the consumer until 1997 still has some justification. However, throughout the 1940s, new forms of consumerism did emerge and it can be seen that the Labour Party provided some stimulating ideas which stretched its older politics of necessity to new classes of service and commodity. Recent scholarship has focussed on the failure of the Labour Party to arrive at a positive attitude to private goods after the Second World War, resulting in its electoral defeat of 1951. The first section of this chapter will re-examine some of these debates assessing the forms of consumer control during the war and their legacy for the Left in the late 1940s. Austerity measures were not the sole politics of Labour, a party which oversaw the celebrations of modernity found in the Festival of Britain and the Britain Can Make It Exhibition of 1946. But in the practical outcome of many of its policies, Labour's productivist bias asserted itself: a second section of this chapter will focus on the sidelining of the consumer interest within the bureaucracy of the newly nationalised industries. Labour's consumer advocates had to look elsewhere and rallied around the 1949 election manifesto promise committing the government to a wholesale re-assessment of its 'fair shares' and consumer policies. Harold Wilson's Board of Trade launched a broadsweeping investigation into consumer affairs which offered the potential for an empowered and state-sponsored consumerism that encapsulated a whole range of goods beyond the merely necessary. Eventually, questions of finance, electioneering and the comparative importance of the government's other agendas prevented Labour's Consumers' Charter being developed beyond a departmental investigation, but this provides a more complicated narrative than found in the assumption that consumption did not feature in Labour's policy agenda. The Labour Party's plans for a Consumer Advice Centre, with an annual budget of £1 million, could have, electorally, been extremely successful. It was on the verge of developing a consumerism that bridged the gap between necessity and affluence and which sought to place the consumer at the heart of both economic and political affairs. In this sense, then, there was a missed opportunity by the traditional Left to lead the way in the new consumerism of the 1950s to be discussed in the second section of this book.

Rationing and the Second World War

The system of food control and rationing introduced during the Second World War has been most comprehensively summarised by Ina Zweiniger-Bargielowska. Following the successful rationing schemes of the First World War, the Board of Trade (Defence Plans) Department had set out a commodity control policy during the 1930s which was quickly put into effect at the outbreak of war. Flat-rate individual rations were set for all, in order to ensure 'fair shares', though a 'buffer zone' of non-rationed bread, potatoes and restaurant meals was set up to meet different energy requirements. The whole scheme was overseen by the state's complete control of supplies and by an administration which incorporated business expertise and the public through 1,400 local food control committees. With the further introduction of a points system of rationing in December 1941 (enabling consumers to choose freely within a given range of weekly points), and the partial alleviation of shortage for some through a black market, public support for control remained strong. Although meals became more dull, calorie-intake differentials between income groups were narrowed as were the different rates of consumption of essential vitamins and proteins, making for a healthier diet for many working-class families. 'Fair shares' was also seen to work in the extension of control to non-food items, with restrictions on the production of jewellery, clothing, toys, ornaments, fancy goods and gadgets removing the luxurious indicators of the rich and the privileged.[6]

Zweiniger-Bargielowska seeks to destroy the myth of a Blitz-spirited nation contentedly grasping its ration cards and thinking only of the higher purpose above individual grievance. Instead, 'grumbling' was a persistent and serious indicator of low home morale, especially for those women who bore the brunt of the queues and the shortages. And universal sacrifice and egalitarianism become more complex when measured against the tales of luxury feeding, the illicit trade in commodities and fresh produce, the uneven distribution of non-rationed goods and the complaints of certain classes of heavy manual worker against flat-rate rationing.[7] However, in comparison to the First World War, the frustration was never so embittered and no Consumers' Council had to be created to contain the anger of working-class anti-profiteers. Instead, ordinary citizens from across the social hierarchy were enrolled into the state apparatus. On one level, the CWS, largely excluded from the administration of government control schemes from 1914 to 1918, was given a much greater role, though with 8.5 million members, 350,000 employees, nine Co-operative MPs and 11 per cent of the total retail trade its economic significance was much more difficult to ignore.[8] But on another level, so too were middle-class, 'non-feminist' women's organisations such as the Women's Institute, the

[6] I. Zweiniger-Bargielowska, *Austerity in Britain: Rationing, Controls and Consumption 1939–1955* (Oxford, 2000), pp. 9–59; BT 131/33: Ministry of Supply, *Control over the Manufacture and Supply of Miscellaneous Consumer Goods*: chapter of Board of Trade War histories.
[7] Zweiniger-Bargielowska, *Austerity in Britain*, pp. 79, 96.
[8] J. Birchall, *Co-op: The People's Business* (Manchester, 1994), p. 136.

Townswomen's Guild and the National Council of Women incorporated into the state apparatus.[9] These had all played an important role over the previous twenty years in politicising domestic issues and to some extent had eclipsed the role of working-class organisations in speaking for the ordinary consumer on issues such as housing and social welfare. The Women's Voluntary Service recruited one million members and maintained a strong middle-class presence in those philanthropic activities increasingly supervised by the state.[10] While Zweiniger-Bargielowska claims that middle-class and working women had an increasing amount in common as the number of servants drastically declined, what is clear is that the working-class housewife no longer occupied such a position of moral and political legitimacy as she had in the First World War and the consumer had come to be more typically equated with a classless domestic feminine ideal.

That the working-class consumer did not have to be specifically represented in a separate body was largely due to the intensive investigations of consumer demands and grievances conducted by 'the shopper's friend', the Consumer Needs Section (CNS) set up in 1941.[11] It was used as a 'sort of watchdog' to check continuously the effects of control schemes and to defend the consumers against manufacturers' and distributors' interests within the Board of Trade.[12] It claimed to be 'on the side of the consumers', attempting to ensure if not always 'fair shares' then at least 'fair chances', though recognising that the consumer's interest also lay in the efficient use of 'labour and materials needed to win the war'.[13] The CNS collected data through statistical surveys conducted by Mass-Observation, Gallup and British Market Research, through information gathered from expert sources such as commercial travellers and department store buyers and from 3,000 housewives who every month recounted their difficulties in obtaining thirty selected necessary items. At the same time, 12,000 consumers made a record of the clothes coupons they had spent, and 'wardrobe checks' were made of the clothes owned by 'typical' families. Stock counts were taken of local shops and measured against consumers' expressed desires so that production targets could be

[9] C. Beaumont, 'Women and citizenship. a study of non-feminist women's societies and the women's movement in England, 1928–1950', Ph.D. thesis, University of Warwick (1996).

[10] J. Hinton, 'Voluntarism and the welfare/warfare state: Women's Voluntary Services in the 1940s', *Twentieth Century British History*, 9 (1998), 274–305.

[11] BT 64/1976: Consumer Needs Department, *Note in Evening Standard* (11 October 1941).

[12] MRC MSS 292/660.77/1: Board of Trade, *Consumer Needs in the Board of Trade* (1946), p. 1.

[13] BT 64/1977: F. Meynell, *On Looking While You Leap*, p. 3.

better managed. Thirty-seven staff were employed as Area Distribution Officers to monitor and 'iron out' regional distribution problems as well as dealing with various crises such as the difficulties caused by bombing raids.[14] In the attempt to put forward the consumer viewpoint to the Board of Trade, the level of detail could be extraordinary, one survey assessing attitudes to buttonless, round-necked vests.[15] The CNS was extremely different from the socialist First World War Consumers' Council, which the wartime government had, in any case, no desire to recreate. It operated purely as a hyper-efficient marketing organisation rather than as the forum for political statements about future food policy. But the CNS did play an effective role in dealing with both real and potential consumer grievances such that the radicalism which flourished in the Council was never allowed to become so institutionally focused in the Second World War.

For many on the Left wartime controls represented concrete examples of a socialist politics of consumption in action. They met many of the demands and desires of earlier radical consumerists and the Left continued to support such measures as the communal feeding halls of British Restaurants long after most consumers showed their desire to return to traditional eating patterns after 1945.[16] Similarly, large sections of the labour movement were pleased with the moralities of consumption enshrined in the Utility schemes and the Purchase Tax. With declining turnover and shortages in raw materials and labour, manufacturers tended to concentrate on higher quality goods with greater profit margins. This created shortages in cheaper goods, especially clothing for children and working-class families, prompting the government to direct the Essential Clothing Programme in July 1941, quickly replacing it with a longer-term Utility scheme in September. During the course of the war, furniture and various household textiles were all brought into the schemes, meaning their manufacture had to conform to strict guidelines in order to qualify for the 'Utility mark' and had to be sold at prices within certain defined limits. This was done not so much to provide value for money for working-class consumers, but to 'make the most economic use of the limited supplies of labour and raw materials available'.[17] Nevertheless, the Utility schemes were popular with many labour leaders and

[14] *Ibid.*, p. 2; M. Ogilvy-Webb, *The Government Explains: A Report of the Royal Institute of Public Administration* (London, 1965), p. 61; Zweiniger-Bargielowska, *Austerity in Britain*, p. 120.
[15] MSS 292/660.77/1: *Consumer Needs*, p. 2.
[16] Zweiniger-Bargielowska, *Austerity in Britain*, p. 33; S. Fielding, P. Thompson and N. Tiratsoo, *"England Arise!" The Labour Party and Popular Politics in 1940s Britain* (Manchester, 1995), pp. 108–10.
[17] P. P., *Report of the Purchase Tax/Utility Committee*, Cmd., 8452 (London, 1952), p. 5.

many consumers too. Utility goods literally fitted the utilitarian moral and economic categories of consumption, so common to non-hedonistic Victorian liberalism. They could readily be defined, in Mill's classification (but also Morris'), as productive rather than unproductive, and made for real use rather than for false pleasure. Yet within the main schemes, for clothing and furniture, some artistic licence was still available. The manufacture of cloth was subject to strict regulation but there was greater freedom in the actual design of the finished products and many of the items of furniture bearing the Utility mark were said to express an aesthetic of 'wholesome simplicity'.[18] According to the Board of Trade, the word 'utility' had become a 'noble title', though in reality the value for money signified could vary greatly from one commodity type to another, and was often below that of goods outside the Utility schemes but which had still had their manufacture standardised.[19]

The dictates of economic efficiency converged with moral distinctions between luxury and necessity when Utility goods were exempted from the Purchase Tax. The stated reason for this fiscal measure was to keep the price of essential goods as low as possible 'so as to offset rises in the cost of living from other causes'.[20] After the war, pressure to restrict imports and the desire to remove inconsistencies with materially similar non-Utility goods (subject to the Purchase Tax) resulted in the Utility schemes being extended further.[21] Conservative Party de-control rhetoric stressed the essential drabness of Utility goods and certainly large numbers of affluent consumers felt this to be the case, though many working-class organisations continued to praise the schemes. In its evidence to the Douglas Committee in 1951, the TUC claimed to have opposed the Purchase Tax when it was first proposed in 1940 on the grounds that all indirect taxes were, by their very nature, regressive. But once Utility goods were exempted, creating a fiscal distinction which mirrored the moral distinction between luxury and necessity, the trade unions offered their support. The TUC saw many advantages in the tax – provided 'normal working-class expenditure were exempt' – which gained in appeal when it was 'regarded as a tax on luxuries, the production and importation of which must be discouraged'.[22] Utility schemes combined with the Purchase Tax

---

[18] C. Sladen, *The Conscription of Fashion: Utility Cloth, Clothing and Footwear, 1941–1952* (Aldershot, 1995); H. Dover, *Home Front Furniture: British Utility Design, 1941–1951* (Aldershot, 1991); J. Attfield (ed.), *Utility Reassessed: The Role of Ethics in the Practice of Design* (Manchester, 1999).
[19] BT 131/33: *Consumer Goods*, pp. 15–19.   [20] P. P., *Report of Purchase Tax*, p. 5.
[21] BT 258/352: Consumer Protection Policy, *Utility Schemes: Factual Summary as at 30 April 1950*.
[22] MSS 292/183.4/9: TUC, *The Purchase Tax/Utility Committee Draft Statement* (14 November 1951), p. 2.

therefore offered a system of regulated consumption, previously seen only with regard to specific commodities or at times of particular social and political upheaval. It offered an inverted rationale to that found in sumptuary legislation, having the potential to create an egalitarian economic democracy instead of a rigid social hierarchy.

The moralisation of consumption found within the tax structure was only part of the Labour Party's broader commitment to the 'fair shares' of commodity and price control.[23] This, although said to be ultimately unpopular with the electorate, had the strong support of most branches of the labour movement, especially the women's sections.[24] It formed just one pillar of Labour's post-war reforms which strove 'to the greater end of the full and free development of every individual person'.[25] Yet, undoubtedly, it appealed to the older critiques of luxury which still witnessed Orwell's embrace of the possibility of fewer goods during the first few years of the socialist state. While Churchill's accusation that Labour had made a 'fad' out of austerity was putting it a little too strongly, Attlee was clearly keen to revive an older consumerist discourse when he pitted 'the people's needs' against 'mink coats'.[26] G. D. H. Cole even seemed to take a Bunyan-esque pleasure in recognising that the economic situation was such that 'continued austerity is forced upon us as a condition of future prosperity'.[27] These sentiments would stand in opposition to the termination of the Utility schemes, despite growing evidence that in peacetime the schemes no longer guaranteed the best value for money and the imposition of the Purchase Tax contradicted Britain's signature to international trading agreements.[28] As part of a wider system of rationing and commodity control, the Utility schemes represented a genuine commitment to the egalitarian principles of 'fair shares' and an attempt to continue the precedents set in war into peacetime. On their own, however, Utility schemes and the Purchase Tax represented a controversial paternalist consumer politics in which questions of the moral value of individual commodities were answered not by, but on behalf of, consumers. In the 1940s, such value judgements were reinforced by the power of the state and backed up by a wartime bureaucracy able to supervise unprecedented levels of government intervention in the private sphere of consumption. The real test as to whether the Utility schemes

[23] Labour Party, *Let Us Face the Future* (London, 1945), p. 2.
[24] MSS 292/62.14/1: Standing Joint Committee of Industrial Women's Organisations, *Report* (1947); MSS 292/65.2/2: Labour Women's Conference, *Agenda* (15–17 October 1946).
[25] Labour Party, *Let Us Win Through Together* (London, 1950), p. 1.
[26] C. Attlee, *Labour Keeps Its Word* (London, 1946), p. 10.
[27] G. D. H. Cole, *Labour's Second Term* (London, 1949), p. 3.
[28] P. P., *Report of Purchase Tax*, pp. 21–2; MSS 292/183.4/9: Purchase Tax/Utility Committee, comments from Mr Heywood (14 November 1951).

and the Purchase Tax formed a consumer politics that genuinely represented the different interests of consumers would come when consumers were given a chance to speak for themselves. As will be seen in the next section, government and the Labour Party were far more willing to impose a consumer politics than they were to have consumer representatives formulate their own.

Consumer representation and the nationalised industries

In the immediate post-Second World War years, there was much that suggested the consumer might become the focus for both economic reconstruction and the bureaucracy of the welfare state. A new consumer orientation could be said to have existed in the creation of the Council for Industrial Design (CID) in 1944 and the Britain Can Make It Exhibition of 1946.[29] The CID's campaigns to improve the aesthetic judgements of young consumers fed into the projections of the future promoted at the Festival of Britain in 1951, when the consuming public was shown a 'modern and scientifically assisted version' of Britain just around the corner.[30] And in the wider processes of nationalisation and socialisation, Herbert Morrison was able to proclaim that the consumer would escape the exploitation that had occurred under private monopoly.[31] Here, consumerism reflected what Galbraith would later call a countervailing power, Morrison's rhetoric suggesting that consumers would form an important power bloc within the public corporation.[32] The attention paid to the consumer built on the concerns of the Webbs and guild socialists such as Cole in the inter-war period who had recognised the need for consumer participation in any form of socialised industry in order to protect the interests of the public as a whole.[33] Consumers were known

[29] P. Maguire and J. M. Woodham (eds.), *Design and Cultural Politics in Postwar Britain: The Britain Can Make It Exhibition of 1946* (London, 1997).

[30] B. Conekin, ' "Here is the modern world itself": The Festival of Britain's representations of the future', in B. Conekin, F. Mort and C. Waters (eds), *Moments of Modernity: Reconstructing Britain, 1945–1964* (London, 1999), p. 245; R. Hewison, *Culture and Consensus: England, Art and Politics Since 1940* (London, 1995); J. M. Woodham, 'Managing British design reform II: The film *Deadly Nightshade* – an ill-fated episode in the politics of "good taste" ', *Journal of Design History*, 9:2 (1996), 101–15.

[31] MSS 292/660.77/1: H. Morrison, *The Consumer in Relation to Non-Competitive Industry*, Oxford Management Conference (16 October 1948), p. 3.

[32] J. K. Galbraith, *American Capitalism: The Concept of Countervailing Power* (1952; Harmondsworth, 1967); C. Beauchamp, 'Consumer interest and public interest', MPhil thesis, University of Cambridge (2000), p. 15.

[33] J. Tomlinson, *Government and Enterprise since 1900: The Changing Problem of Efficiency* (Oxford, 1994); R. Millward and J. Singleton (eds.), *The Political Economy of Nationalisation in Britain, 1920–1950* (Cambridge, 1995); D. N. Chester, *The Nationalisation of British Industry, 1945–1951* (London, 1975).

to be passive, even in public utility services set up for them, where often 'the citizen as consumer tends to wait with his mouth open to catch what he is given'.[34] For this reason, early discussion of different forms of nationalisation highlighted the importance of setting out the precise institutional relationship between producers and consumers so that the interests of one never trampled over the other.

Despite Morrison's professed regard for the consumer, this did not translate into policy. Within Labour Party thinking, there was an 'implicit belief that nationalisation itself would ensure a fair deal for the consumer' since the Boards of the nationalised industries would 'hold the balance fairly between consumer and worker'.[35] There was therefore no need to establish a consumer committee as a regulatory body, acting as a powerful check on the policies of the Boards because, as Emanuel Shinwell, Minister of Fuel and Power, put it, there would be 'no inducement on the part of those administering the industry to take advantage of the consumer'.[36] Even then Shinwell emphasised that the consumer 'is not organised, and is never likely to be' and cited the practical difficulties arising from this as an excuse for doing little about the problem. Dismissing both suggestions that the National Coal Board should implement structures to maintain close contact with consumers and that consumers should have recourse to an official tribunal to deal with their complaints, he proposed instead a consultative body to advise the Minister on, rather vaguely, 'matters such as price levels'.[37] Complaints were raised that such a body would have neither authority nor dignity, but Shinwell, in conspiratorial fashion, believed that 'though such a [Consumers'] Council might prove abortive it would be a body which would appear to be useful, and that was an important factor'.[38] Later, Morrison would place the emphasis on the consumer as individual to reform the system, rather than establishing a structure in which consumers were heard at all levels. The implemented consumer councils were not to deal with individual complaints, the most likely reason a consumer would respond directly to an industry, but nor were consumer representatives to exert influence in Parliament or through specific government departments dealing with each industry. Consumers were to take responsibility themselves as the

---

[34] C. D. Burns, 'The appropriate types of authority for the operation of publicly owned utility services, and the powers which they should have: the consumer and public utility services', *Public Administration*, 4:4 (1926), 325.

[35] PRO POWE 17/82: Ministry of Fuel and Power, *Departmental Working Party on Consumers' Councils* (21 January 1953); MSS 292/660.77/1: Morrison, *The Consumer*, p. 7.

[36] POWE 17/82: *Working Party*.

[37] POWE 28/26: Minister for Fuel and Power, *Memorandum* (October 1945).

[38] *Ibid.*; *Note on Consumers' Councils* (1 November 1945).

watchdogs of state enterprises. In 1950 Morrison argued that 'consumers only have themselves to blame if the Consumers' Councils do not take up grumbles of which the grumblers have never told them'.[39] Not only did such a public announcement belittle the nature of consumer dissatisfaction, it belied the national industries' attitude to consumers which was reflected in the institutional support offered to consumers from the very beginning.

The actual Consumers' Councils were established at the same time as the nationalised industry Boards. The first to come into existence was through the Coal Industry Nationalisation Act of 1946. This legislated for an Industrial Coal Consumers' Council consisting of representatives of industrial purchasers and members of the National Coal Board, and a Domestic Coal Consumers' Council (DCCC), consisting of coal merchants, and representatives of local authorities and consumers' groups. The latter were usually taken from women's organisations, who were more often than not individual amateurs who were liable to be overwhelmed by the industrial expertise of the majority trade representatives. Reporting to the DCCC were twelve regional panels, with similar memberships to the national body. Equivalent structures were adopted for the other nationalised industries. The Electricity Act 1947 created fourteen Electricity Consultative Councils, one for each of the regional electricity Boards, and the Gas Act 1948 established twelve Consultative Councils for its Boards. The Transport Act 1947 created a Central Transport Consultative Committee which oversaw eleven area Transport Users' Consultative Committees.[40] In addition, a Consumers' Council was set up for the oil industry and the Consumers' Committees of the Agricultural Marketing Boards were still in nominal existence.[41] The purpose of all these committees was purely advisory. They were to inform the Boards of consumer needs and dissatisfactions but were not to act as a counterbalance to the authority of the Boards. The Boards were to have primary responsibility in all matters, including satisfying consumers, and the Consumers' Councils were almost relegated to the role of explaining Board decisions and policy to the public at large.

The Consumers' Councils were criticised from the very beginning. Against the power of the Boards, the influence of consumers was insignificant. The role given to the consumer was even less than that given to the worker. If it was the case that 'Labour had not thought closely enough

[39] CAB 124/5: H. Morrison, *Address to the Oxford University Labour Club* (22 April 1950), p. 4.
[40] Consumer Council, *Consumer Consultative Machinery in the Nationalised Industries* (London, 1968), pp. 80–5.
[41] MSS 292/660.77/1: *List of Consumers' Committees* (April 1949).

about the worker's place in a nationalised concern and did not really care about participation', then the attitude to consumers was worse still.[42] The major issue facing the consumer was invariably one of price, yet, apart from the transport industry which had a price tribunal, the Councils had very little say and their retrospective complaints against price changes often went unheard. As early as the fuel crisis of the winter of 1947, the Councils were seen to be powerless as champions of the consuming public. They were regarded as failures from all sides of the political divide. Conservatives complained more generally about the 'great betrayal' of nationalisation which had arguably resulted in high prices and poor quality while the Fabians found that unlike in the French nationalised industries where Boards were constitutionally obliged to select nominated consumer representatives, the British system merely perpetuated the dominance of the producer over the consumer as was found in private industry.[43] The activities of the Councils were hampered by the lack of specialist knowledge among their members. For instance, of the twenty-five members of the DCCC in 1950, only twelve had some professional expertise in solid fuel. Amidst this amateur spirit then sat representatives of the Boards, often the Chairman and his secretary, who brought with them a power and authority exacerbated by the practice of holding Council meetings in Board offices and using Board staff and secretarial support. Mirroring the problems of the Agricultural Marketing Acts, the agendas of the Board often dictated Council discussions, Councils often found themselves under pressure to support the Boards in other policy and institutional arenas and their infrequent meetings prevented any sustained unity emerging between members. Furthermore, all Councils were accused of having little contact with ordinary consumers and few members of the public were aware of their existence or how to contact them. From June 1947 to February 1949, the DCCC received only seventy complaints, a situation the Council was unwilling to alter through greater publicity since it was aware of its own inability to affect policy. The Minister and the Board were under no obligation to follow Council recommendations whose annual reports were described as 'limp and platitudinous documents, which do little more than apologise for the inability of the Council to do anything for the consumer in the present circumstances'.[44]

---

[42] Fielding, et al., "England Arise", p. 117.

[43] J. J. R. Richardson, The Great Betrayal: The Impact of Nationalisation on the Worker, the Trade Union, Local Authorities, the Consumer, Management and the Taxpayer Since 1946 (London, 1950); L. Freedman and G. Hemingway, Nationalisation and the Consumer (London, 1950).

[44] Freedman and Hemingway, Nationalisation, p. 13; M. Stewart, Consumers' Councils (London, 1953); POWE 17/82: Public Criticism of Consumers' and Consultative Councils (n.d.).

Despite the flood of criticisms of the Consumers' Councils which occurred towards the end of the 1945 Labour government, no plans were discussed for reform. Once in power, the Conservatives were also unwilling to make any changes and even considered increasing Board representation in order 'to make available to the Council industrialists of standing and personality'.[45] Labour leaders did not see a need for a professional form of effective consumer representation. Hugh Gaitskell, in a foreword to a pamphlet that was severely critical of the Consumers' Councils sought only to rationalise the existing system, reminding readers that the Councils were to act as 'advisory partners' to the Board and not as 'professional critics'. In writing that 'the success or failure of the Councils will probably turn more on the personalities and abilities of those appointed to them than upon anything else', Gaitskell placed more emphasis on individual character than on informed opinion, critical expertise or specialist knowledge.[46] Here, he returned to older Fabian doubts about the irrationality of the consumer and the lack of trust to be placed in him or her as a force for change or active citizenship. Their minimal role therefore persisted under both Conservative and Labour governments throughout the 1950s and 1960s. The Councils remained distant and little known to the mass consuming public, while Ministers persisted in ignoring organised consumer groups and selected instead 'public-spirited individuals' from women's groups who had no 'particular background knowledge of the market or of consumers' affairs': 'they are in no position to challenge the Boards' experts; they can only represent a layman's view'.[47] Without statutory provisions and direct access to independent expertise the Councils were doomed to remain ineffective and irrelevant. They had never become, and were never likely to be, powerful fora for an officially sanctioned consumerism, such as had been the case in the consumer provisions of the US New Deal state. There was no incorporation of the consumer interest into this sphere of state activity, despite the Left's older politics of necessitous consumption which had advocated an equal role for workers and consumers in the administration of socialist economic organisations. Instead, the Councils represented the weakness of the ordinary consumer in the face of state bureaucracy and here the Labour Party, in establishing these consumer bodies during its nationalisation plans, merely replicated the structural weakness that it had found, and aggressively criticised, in earlier state consumer bodies.

[45] POWE 17/82: *Note on membership of Consultative Councils* (12 January 1953).
[46] Stewart, *Consumers' Councils*, p. 1.
[47] L. Tivey, *Nationalisation in British Industry* (London, 1973), pp. 153–5; Consumer Council, *Consumer Consultative Machinery*, pp. 65–9.

The Consumer Advice Centre

For the long-term consumer advocate Michael Young, working in the Research Department during the first post-war Labour government, the Consumers' Councils would be typical of the disregard given to the ordinary individual during the rationalist planning of Labour's welfare state and its reconstruction policy. The weaknesses of the Consumers' Councils, apparent to all from their implementation, ensured that neither Young nor any other consumer advocate would see in the nationalised industries the opportunity for the incorporation of consumers into public life. For that to occur, very different forms of institutionalised consumerism would need to be put in place. In recognising these problems, Young committed the Labour Party in its 1949 election manifesto to a thorough investigation of the consumer problem and to the possibility of the creation of a wide-ranging, well-funded, representative and powerful Consumers' Advice Centre. This would represent both the culmination of a half century of left-wing consumer politics and the first indicator of the role to be played by the state in the post-Second World War period of affluent consumption. The subsequent Board of Trade review was an important link between a politics of consumption based on poverty and one based on comfort. Topics discussed included the by now traditional consumer concerns such as the regulation of monopolies and restrictive practices, the desirability of fixed pricing, especially through local price committees, and the abuses of the market caused by misleading advertising and product misrepresentation. Added to this were reviews of the 1940s austerity measures such as the Utility schemes, new developments in the scientific management of the home and methods of social survey data collection. But, prefiguring the dominant form of late twentieth-century consumerism, an investigation was even launched into the efficacy of state involvement in the comparative testing of a broad range of consumer durables.

The Labour Party was not the first organisation to explore the applicability of US *Consumer Reports* to the British context. Political and Economic Planning had done so in the 1930s, and in late 1937 the TUC stated that most consumers were unable 'to assess the intrinsic value of most commodities'.[48] It suggested that some comparative testing organisation was required, though, unlike in the US model, care would be taken not to antagonise any reputable businesses and the goods of accredited firms would even be promoted. Although many consumers 'chose

[48] MSS 292/660.77/1: Letter from G. Woodcock to W. Citrine (27 January 1938); Letter from A. E. Blake to W. Citrine (13 December 1937).

to be ignorant', an organisation catering to just a few hundred thousand families would be able to raise standards, promote reputable firms, cut down waste in distribution and reduce exaggerated, false, emotional and irrelevant forms of sales promotion. The proposed organisation would consist of a testing laboratory, research staff, a panel of judges, a publishing branch, an association of consumers and an advisory bureau, all financed through the revenues from advertisements of approved goods. As a bulwark against the state direction of consumption, no US-style 'best buys' or 'not acceptable' labels were to be awarded and the consumer would ultimately 'have to use his own judgement'.[49] Ultimately, the TUC was persuaded by bodies such as the Retail Trading Standards Association (RTSA: see chapter 6) that the British law of libel would make it difficult to criticise the goods of individual manufacturers. The RTSA also argued that a consumers' organisation would meet with resistance from business and advertisers which 'would combine to negative any action taken by the Consumers' Council', though the TUC was less concerned by this warning than by the large costs imagined to be involved in creating such a body and its own specific concerns which observed that organised consumerism would offer little to lower paid workers.[50] The conclusions reached reflected the trade unionists' concerns with the consuming habits of their worker members, though traditional unease about the political legitimacy and rationality of the consumer, not all of whom were working class, meant the TUC shied away from the advocacy of a new consumer body.[51] Instead, and citing the reasons of finance and the law (problems which never actually materialised in later organisations), the TUC rejected the scheme and continued its support for the Co-operative movement with the assumption that 'with every extension of this predominantly working-class organisation the need for other organisations to protect the consumer against the evils inherent in private enterprise will diminish'.[52]

The immediate predecessor to the Labour government's investigation of the consumer problem therefore came not from the trade unions, but from PEP. During the 1940s, ideas for a consumers' organisation were still being discussed within PEP circles and Michael Young took these with him to the Labour Party when he joined its Research Department in 1945.[53] At first, Young largely followed Labour Party thinking on fair

[49] MSS 292/660.77/1: A. E. Blake, *Shopping Reports* (13 December 1937), p. 4.
[50] MSS 292/660.77/1: Memorandum of interview with J. M. Paynton of RTSA, 21 December 1937; TUC General Council Research Department, *Scheme for a Consumers' Advisory Council* (20 December 1937).
[51] MSS 292/660.77/1: Letter from W. Citrine to A. E. Blake (11 February 1938).
[52] MSS 292/660.77/1: *Scheme*, p. 6.
[53] Private correspondence between author and Michael Young.

shares, nationalisation and the role of the state, but increasingly he began to pay attention to the role of the 'small man' within the machinery of the modern state.[54] His ideas led directly to the consumer clauses of the 1949 election manifesto which promised a 'square deal for consumers'.[55] According to the mythology surrounding Young, the idea was 'completely his own' and had just been 'slipped into' the Party's election pledge, without either the press or the National Executive even noticing.[56] A Gallup Poll then subsequently conducted in 1950 found that the general public identified the 'square deal' as its most favourite item in the Manifesto and the Labour Party was obliged to investigate the matter further once re-elected. But this rather ingenuous account is to miss the widespread concern with difficulties faced by the consumer at this time. Organisations such as the British Housewives' League mobilised opinion against controls and the National Council of Women approached the British Standards Institution to introduce standards on consumer goods.[57] But a cross-section of the Left also demonstrated the general desire for greater government intervention in consumer affairs. The Association of Scientific Workers put forward a unanimously accepted resolution at the Trades Union Congress of 1945 calling for a 'Council for Consumer Research' to engage in the comparative testing of 'advertised consumption goods' and to determine the quantity, type and standard of commodities demanded by the public.[58] Others had demanded the retention of the Consumer Needs Section into peacetime and the general maintenance of supply and price controls.[59] The Co-operative movement and the Women's Co-operative Guild came especially out in favour of maintaining subsidies and price controls.[60] And as early as 1946 Percy Daines had asked the

[54] M. Young, *Labour's Plan for Plenty* (London, 1947).
[55] Labour Party, *Labour Believes in Britain* (London, 1949), p. 17; Labour Party, *Let Us Win Through Together* (London, 1950).
[56] N. Sargant, 'Consumer power as a pillar of democracy', in G. Dench, T. Flower and K. Gavron (eds.), *Young at Eighty: The Prolific Public Life of Michael Young* (Manchester, 1995), pp. 187–97; A. Briggs, *Michael Young: Social Entrepreneur* (Basingstoke, 2001), p. 96.
[57] J. Hinton, 'Militant housewives: the British Housewives' League and the Attlee government', *History Workshop Journal*, 38 (1994), 129–56.
[58] MSS 292/660.77/1: *Congress Resolution 1945*; Association of Scientific Workers, *Spotlight on Shopping: Consumer Research* (London, 1951).
[59] MSS 292/660.77/1: Economic Committee, *Blackpool 1945 Congress Resolutions* (14 November 1945); Ministry of Food Public Relations Division Information Branch, *Protection of the Consumer as to the Quality, Labelling and Advertising of Foods* (December 1947); MSS 292/174.91/6: various correspondence between TUC and L. St. Clare Grondona (1947–55).
[60] F. Trentmann, 'Bread, milk and democracy: consumption and citizenship in Britain, c.1903–51', in M. Daunton and M. Hilton (eds.), *The Politics of Consumption: Material Culture and Citizenship in Europe and America* (Oxford, 2001), pp. 156–9.

government in the House of Commons whether it intended to set up a Consumer Research Council.[61] These organisation's and individual's concerns reflected the continued emphasis placed on the consumer by several government departments after the war. The Ministry of Food had published a series of *Food Facts* on a weekly basis and the Citizens' Advice Bureau and Social Survey had become increasingly involved in consumer affairs. From 1947 the Women's Organisations Committee of the Treasury's Economic Information Unit assisted the government in publicising economic issues to housewives and the Information Unit continued to publish monthly *Talking Points* and *Reports to Women* until 1952.[62] As an article in the *Observer* put it in 1946, 'housewives are on the move', forming leagues and demanding the creation of a 'National Consumer Council'. This was a trend to be celebrated since British manufacturing would only improve if the consumer was 'no sheep-like purchaser but a discriminating and exacting patron of the domestic arts'.[63] The range of concerns was diverse and conflicting as some consumers demanded more choice not continued controls, or a focus solely on quality rather than price and supply. Yet all were agreed on the need for the government to pay greater attention to the consumer. Zweiniger-Bargielowska's equation of consumerism with the Conservatives' policy of market liberalisation therefore forms just one part of the interests of an electorate of disgruntled shoppers. The Labour Party's advocacy of a state-funded consumer body examining necessities and mass-produced 'luxury' items was just as popular with voters and may go some way to explaining the extension of the vote in the 1951 election.

In response to these varied calls for a consumer service and in recognition of what the Labour Party perceived to be the importance attached to consumer affairs by the public, the government launched its wide-ranging overview of consumer affairs immediately following the February 1950 election. Attempts were made at capturing the agenda by various interested groups. For instance, the RTSA wrote to every newspaper listing all the 'unfair and misleading' practices engaged in by the 'spiv' type of trader, making it clear that the best means by which housewives could avoid being 'caught for suckers' would be to shop at RTSA-listed stores.[64] But what is most remarkable is the different process of consultation adopted by the Board of Trade in comparison to the investigations of

---

[61] MSS 292/660.77/1: Letter from TUC to P. Daines, MP (19 March 1946).
[62] Beauchamp, 'Consumer interest', p. 31. The Chair of the Women's Organisations Committee was Eirlys Roberts who was to become first editor of *Which?* magazine.
[63] MSS 292/660.77/1: *Observer* (17 February 1946).
[64] BT 258/355: Consumer Protection Policy: Letter from R. Diplock, RTSA, 'for the attention of news editors and women's page editors' (6 March 1950).

the consumer interest undertaken earlier by the 1925 Royal Commission on Food Prices and later by the Molony Committee on Consumer Protection. Although business and trade groups were interviewed, the majority of institutions advising the investigation consisted of academics, government departments, political and voluntary organisations and women's and consumer groups.[65] And, in principle at least, the Board of Trade officials initially excluded no field of consumer affairs and sought not to restrict their field of enquiry. The investigation covered resale price maintenance and competition policy as well as consumer advice and protection, all issues to be potentially included within a comprehensive Consumers' Charter and Consumer Protection Bill.[66] Consumerism was an area that could only be understood in conjunction with the growth of employers' organisations, government intervention in the marketplace and the adoption of full employment as a major plank of economic policy. It was not, in terms of the initial remit of the Board of Trade's study, a matter of sole interest to the housewife and the day-to-day problems encountered in the marketplace.

There is much to suggest that the Labour Party, or at least sections of it, maintained a genuine commitment to consumerism as the new basis of political action. The President of the Board of Trade, Harold Wilson, believed low prices, high quality and optimum service to the consumer were central to economic policy. Private industry was to be subjected to public, or consumer, accountability through Consumers' Consultative Committees in order to raise standards and efficiency and boost the export drive and a Consumers' Charter was to create the Advice Centre, regulate hire purchase, misleading advertising and resale price maintenance, and 'make permanent the quality standards implicit in the utility schemes'.[67] In discussing the relationship between government and private industry, Wilson was attempting to fill 'a vacuum in Socialist thought' as little attention had been given to 'the role of the private sector in a Socialist economy'.[68] He accepted that not all consumers were convinced of the efficacy of the nationalised industry Consumers' Councils, but he also observed a broad desire to establish permanent regulation of private enterprise, a system which would represent a middle path between wartime control and unfettered free market liberalism. The Cabinet came out in favour of a mixed economy, acknowledging that if it was to win the next

[65] BT 258/355: List of organisations from whom information was requested (1950).
[66] BT 258/353: Consumer Protection Policy: Attached note on consumer protection (n.d.).
[67] PREM 8/1183: Prime Minister's Office, 1945–1951: Memorandum on the Relations between Government and Industry: H. Wilson, *The State and Privatised Industry* (4 May 1950), p. 15.
[68] PREM 8/1183: H. Wilson, personal covering note to *Memorandum on the Government and Private Industry*, p. 2.

election it must, according to Christopher Mayhew, show itself to be 'representative of the consumer': 'The party has been built up as a party of producers, but the last Election showed that the electorate was tending to vote more as consumers.'[69] Wilson was impressed by Mayhew's point and reiterated it to his Cabinet colleagues. While he remained convinced that 'full employment and all that goes with it' must remain Labour's principal policy objective, if it was to tackle the Conservatives' populist pro-choice consumerism at the next election, then 'by being vigorous in protecting the consumer, both against public and private industry, we can help to redress this electoral imbalance'.[70] The mixed economy message was designed to appeal to both workers and consumers, though it was to be a consumerism of protection, control and guidance rather than one of simply greater individual choice.

The potential range of this new state-sponsored consumerism can be seen in the discussions over the extent and scope of the Consumers' Charter. Wilson proposed the enrolment of consumers into local and central price committees to monitor the Utility schemes which would themselves be extended, not as rigid criteria for production, but as marks or certifications of minimum standards which would then act as a type of guarantee as to the product's value for money.[71] In tying the consumer discussion to competition more generally, trade associations and restrictive trading agreements were to be registered, resale price maintenance (both collective and individual) was to be scrapped and the workings of the newly appointed Monopolies Commission (created by the 1948 Monopolies and Restrictive Practices Act) were to be speeded up.[72] The Merchandise Marks Acts were to be extended to apply to false descriptions in advertising as well as direct labelling, and to oral as well as written deceptive trade practices.[73] Likewise, the Hire Purchase Act 1938 was to be reworked to insist on a minimum deposit of 12 per cent in order to protect consumers both from their own impecunious spending and from 'touts using high-pressure salesmanship'.[74] The consultative machinery within the nationalised industries was to be reformed so that it 'is not only

[69] PREM 8/1183: Note of a meeting held on 17 May 1950 to discuss the memorandum on the state and private industry, p. 4.
[70] PREM 8/1183: H. Wilson, personal covering note to *Memorandum on the Government and Private Industry*, Second draft.
[71] BT 258/352: *Consumer Protection: Value for Money: Part III. Long Term Measures for Improving Quality;* Minute from H. W. [Wilson] (3 March 1950).
[72] BT 258/352: Meeting in President's room (24 May 1950); *Consumer Protection: Registration of Trade Associations;* H. Mercer, *Constructing a Competitive Order: The Hidden History of British Anti-Trust Policy* (Cambridge, 1995); B. S. Yamey, *Resale Price Maintenance and Shoppers' Choice* (London, 1960).
[73] BT 258/352: *Consumer Protection: False Description.*
[74] Cited in Beauchamp, 'Consumer interest', p. 30.

effective, but is seen to be effective' and better points of contact with consumers were considered.[75] The National Institute of Houseworkers, an organisation set up in 1946 by the Ministry of Labour, and the Women's Group on Public Welfare's Sub-Committee on Scientific Management in the Home was to provide information on the fitness for purpose of various domestic goods and home designs.[76] Along with these and other interested bodies, the government was to engage in market research to understand better consumer demand and their complaints.[77] Various types of past and existing consumerism were also investigated, whether in the form of a review of the Labour Party's plans for a Consumers' Council in the 1930s, PEP's broadsheets on consumer needs from 1934–6, or the practices of 'consumer' organisations such as the RTSA and the Good Housekeeping Institute.[78] And a detailed report was provided on the Consumers' Union, setting out its methods of comparative testing, its membership and the attitudes of various business and media groups towards it.[79]

The outcome of these overviews was a series of 'Con P' papers falling under three headings. Firstly, three papers on quality, false description and hire purchase were aimed at possible government action directed at manufacturers and distributors. Secondly, a paper on a Consumer Advice Centre made up the main possible action directed at consumers. And, thirdly, two papers on resale price maintenance and the registration of trade associations constituted the possible action to control widely prevalent restrictive practices.[80] The main recommendations of all these consisted of working with the BSI to develop voluntary minimum standards of quality, strengthening the Merchandise Marks legislation, extending the scope of the Hire Purchase Act, prohibiting all forms of resale price maintenance, and deferring action against trade associations. It had been envisaged that a Consumer Advice Centre would engage in comparative testing, operating on a budget of £1 million per year and a staff of approximately 100, but it was felt that this would not represent 'value for money'. A Centre would only be able to test branded goods, the demand for which many consumers determined through subjective preferences:

[75] BT 258/352: G. Parkes, *Consumers' Consultative Machinery* (20 March 1950).
[76] BT 258/355: National Institute of Houseworkers, *Note* (12 June 1950); Sub-Committee on Scientific Management in the Home, *Report on Research in Progress or Carried out Since 1945*.
[77] BT 258/355: L. Moss (The Social Survey), *Consumers' Advisory Centres* (31 May 1950).
[78] BT 258/355: Good Housekeeping Institute, *Note* (1950); *Consumers' Council Bill* (6 November 1950); Letter from R. J. Goodman, Director of PEP (18 April 1950).
[79] BT 258/352: *Consumer Protection: A Consumer Advice Centre*, Appendix; BT 258/355: Note on *Consumer Testing* (22 May 1950).
[80] BT 258/353: *Consumer Protection*.

when it came to a choice between Whitbreads and Watneys, or Players and Gold Flake, 'we all like to "suck 'em and see" '.[81] Furthermore, officials continued to worry about the 'slander of goods' under British libel law and believed the tests would only benefit an affluent minority, having little impact on the mass of consumers.[82] What was actually proposed, then, was a Centre to provide consumers with 'general advice' and education to encourage 'efficient purchasing' through such materials as pamphlets on consumer law, other information sources, fact sheets on generic characteristics of goods, and guides to wise shopping. It was intended the Centre be regarded as a 'Consumer's Friend': 'the professional secretariat of the consuming public'.[83] It was to engage in research and testing only to identify particular 'bad buys', warn of particular 'black spots' and 'disadvertising', launch specific prosecutions and advise government on consumer problems. Ideally, the Centre would provide an opportunity for 'consumer pressures becoming focussed in a coherent and articulate way and so having in our economic life an influence commensurate with that of employer and employee pressure groups'.[84]

Following an inter-departmental consultation process, leading to further questioning of the state's involvement in comparative testing, Wilson still aimed to introduce a wide-ranging Consumer Protection Bill to respond to the various election manifesto pledges.[85] But in late 1950, the Bill was held up in Cabinet as it was thought better to proceed with the various clauses separately because of the complexity of the different legal implications.[86] In December, the Cabinet's Distribution and Marketing Committee, chaired by Hugh Dalton, reiterated the opposition to a costly testing service but suggested further investigation into a Consumer Advice Centre on the assumption that it would be set up in one form or another.[87] This departmental committee was to be made up of six civil servants, a member of the RTSA, a trade unionist, an economist, a Co-operator and, again in contrast to previous and future consumer committees, just one manufacturer or retailer.[88] Plans for proceeding were

[81] BT 258/352: *Consumer Protection: A Consumer Advice Centre*, p. 1.
[82] *Ibid.*, pp. 2–10.   [83] *Ibid.*, p. 13.   [84] *Ibid.*, p. 14.
[85] BT 258/354: Letter sent to various government departments on consumer protection (August 1950); CAB 124/2749: Letter from H. Wilson to H. Morrison (13 October 1950).
[86] BT 258/352: *Consumer Protection Bill* (8 September 1950); CAB 124/2749: Minutes of a meeting held on 8 September 1950 at the Board of Trade; PREM 11/1542: D.M.(50) 29: Memorandum by the President of the Board of Trade (20 October 1950).
[87] CAB 124/2749: Letter from D. H. F. Rickett to J. D. Jones (20 December 1950); PREM 11/1542: Memo from H. Dalton to Prime Minister (19 December 1950).
[88] BT 258/354: Cabinet Committee on Distribution and Marketing, *Minute 10:2* (13 December 1950); *Terms of Reference and Membership of a Departmental Committee to Consider the Scope of a Consumer Advisory Service* (n.d.).

delayed due to the political problems facing the government in 1951 and the need to switch funds from civil expenditure to a war economy.[89] The Consumer Advice Centre was a luxury that nobody was prepared to support at a time when budgets were reflecting a rearmament programme and 'the retreat from Jerusalem'. And, once Wilson had followed Aneurin Bevan in resigning from government in April 1951, the plans for a state-sponsored consumerism were shelved if not forgotten and the Board of Trade study was not mentioned again in Cabinet during Labour's period of crisis management until its defeat in October.[90]

Undoubtedly, as in 1931, the immediate explanation for the failure of state-sponsored consumerism lay in the practical financial considerations of the last months of government. It was unlikely that the Centre would find any champions at a time when most advocates of social welfare were busy supporting Bevan's defence of the National Health Service. Yet the failure of the proposals to reach even a departmental committee stage cannot solely be explained by economic factors. It might even be doubted whether a strong government consumer body would have been created even had Labour enjoyed another term of office and witnessed an economic recovery. There is some substance to Michael Young's claim that he surreptitiously inserted the consumer commitments into the manifesto when one considers the general air of scepticism towards the consumer and consumer protection held both by many senior Labour leaders and top civil servants. It is difficult to assess Wilson's overall attitude to consumerism and his commitment to it beyond the professional thoroughness with which he launched the investigation though Young felt strongly that Wilson had been opposed from the very beginning to the insertion of the consumerist clauses in the manifesto.[91] But it is also certain that many of Wilson's colleagues were having difficulty translating their attitudes to luxury and necessity to a broad middle range of consumer durables. Philip Chantler, Minister of Fuel and Power, for instance, beyond a pro-consumer rhetoric, believed his own department 'insufficiently concerned to require any formal consultation' in the matter, despite his responsibility for 'citizen-consumers' of the gas, coal and electricity Consumers' Councils.[92] In Cabinet, scepticism was common and a certain ignorance of the issues suggested that not all Ministers had given the topic much thought and, indeed, were even irritated by the

---

[89] BT 258/354: Distribution and Marketing Committee, *Memorandum by President of the Board of Trade* (February or March 1951).

[90] K. O. Morgan, *Labour in Power, 1945–1951* (Oxford, 1986), pp. 453–4.

[91] J. Epstein, *The Early Days of Consumers' Association: Interviews with CA's Founders and Those Who Carried on Their Work* (London, 1989), p. 21 (Michael Young).

[92] BT 258/354: Note from President's Office (1 January 1951).

discovery that the manifesto had committed the Party to such a venture. Herbert Morrison thought the scheme 'half-baked', Hugh Gaitskell was quick to point out the financial costs and Hugh Dalton admitted that he had 'never much believed in this particular item in the programme'.[93] Morrison and Gaitskell were the chief advocates of referring the study to a private departmental research committee. They knew they had to be seen acting upon their electoral pledge, but they aimed to ensure that the government could not be embarrassed by any proposal an open Committee of Inquiry might make which could then force the direction of policy against the Government's wishes.[94]

This general atmosphere of doubt was exacerbated by the tone adopted by senior civil servants in writing the 'Con P' papers. There was an apparent reluctance by the administration to develop a consumer policy and it is not unlikely that civil servants' attitudes affected the outcome of the consumer proposals, perhaps establishing a lack of enthusiasm which none of Wilson's Ministerial colleagues wished to overturn. The principal investigator, Geoffrey Parker, later Under-Secretary of the Board of Trade, chose to preface his report on quality control by asserting that consumer protection 'must always be subsidiary to' the main purpose of maintaining the economy, since the best form of protection lay in 'unlimited competition . . . under a free enterprise economy': protection measures could only introduce artificially what competition brought 'automatically'.[95] Furthermore, responsibility for protection ultimately lay with the individual consumer and it was the role of government 'to ensure that the pursuit of political, social or other non-economic objectives is not carried out in such a way as to preclude the operation of free competition over the major part of the field of consumer goods'.[96] When Jack Rennie, of the Commercial Department of the British Embassy in Washington was asked to list the pros and cons of the US Consumers' Union, his language gained an extra flourish when detailing the complaints made against that organisation. The media, he claimed, opposed consumer activists as 'a pitiful collection' of the sort who voted for Henry Wallace (the unsuccessful Progressive Party candidate in the 1948 election). They were the 'sort of people who would sit up half the night counting the number of sheets of toilet paper to see whether somebody was cheating them': 'Perhaps, like most crusaders, they are unable to

---

[93] CAB 124/2749: Letter from H. Morrison to H. Dalton (1 November 1950); Note from H. Gaitskell to the Prime Minister (8 January 1951); Letter from Dalton to Gaitskell (22 January 1951).
[94] CAB 124/2749: Letter from D. Le B. Jones to J. J. Shaw (10 January 1951).
[95] BT 258/352: *Quality Control as a Measure of Consumer Protection* (4 April 1950).
[96] *Ibid.*

afford the luxury of a sense of humour and though they undoubtedly resist swallowing any camels they devote a somewhat disproportionate amount of their time to straining at gnats.'[97] One could only conclude from his report that consumerism was made up of cranks and fanatics.

It is difficult to tell whether such sentiments influenced the government's thinking or whether, from a different perspective, Ministers were content for such a biased assessment to emerge as it fitted their own reluctance to develop a consumer policy. The intentions of the civil servants are also not so clear, though it is apparent that they may have been more prepared to exercise their will over a young President of the Board of Trade than they would have with a more senior Minister. When deciding upon the membership of the departmental committee, officials not only made recommendations to Wilson but enthused over those they felt might prove a more reliable consumer spokesperson. Consequently, Roger Diplock was initially preferred as the RTSA representative since he was unlikely to hold 'a starry-eyed pro-consumer anti-trader approach'.[98] Wilson was able to keep his own counsel and preferred another candidate in this instance, but the behaviour of civil servants was beginning to be picked up on in the press. Even the *Ironmonger's Weekly* gossiped about the government's plans for a Consumer Advice Centre, claiming that the civil servants were 'in some sense reluctant about carrying it forward'.[99] Such influences upon policy can never of course be determined precisely, but the language used by Ministers and civil servants does reflect the broader scepticism towards state-sponsored consumerism shared by many. On the one hand, civil servants seemed to dislike the potential encroachment of the state into an arena of life seen as the last bastion of individual liberty in a world of creeping, nanny-state welfarism. On the other, Labour leaders were uncomfortable with a consumerism that extended beyond necessities and involved a substantial financial outlay for the assessment of goods just beyond the reach of their traditional working-class supporters. Had the Consumer Advice Centre proposed analysing only those goods classified more readily as necessities, the attitude of Ministers may well have been different.

The Office of Price Administration maintained a similarly effective system of rationing and price controls in the US as occurred in Britain. Its success has been held to have encouraged the sense of the right of all to a high standard of living in the post-war years.[100] Similarly in Britain,

---

[97] BT 258/355: *Consumer Testing* (22 May 1950).
[98] BT 258/354: Minutes of meetings on Consumer Advisory Centre (19 December 1950).
[99] BT 258/354: *Ironmonger's Weekly* (10 August 1950).
[100] M. Jacobs, ' "How about some meat?": the Office of Price Administration, consumption politics, and state building from the bottom up, 1941–1946', *Journal of American History*, 84:3 (1997), 910–41.

wartime measures and a rhetoric of 'fair shares' set precedents in the relationship between the state and the consumer and raised demands for the participation of 'the people' in a reconstructed consumer economy. While austerity therefore provides the economic context for the 1940s, the politics around its attendant privations were based on an expected future affluence. The Conservative Party in particular has been singled out for its success in presenting an image of future material abundance based on de-control, choice and the liberalisation of the market. At the 1950 election, Charles Hill, 'the Radio Doctor', serving as the Conservatives' Priestley-esque, middle-brow man of the people, complained of the 'queuetopia' he alleged Labour had put into place.[101] This was followed, in 1951, by Churchill's Manifesto promise to make 'freedom and abundance' his aims.[102] By way of contrast, Labour and Co-operative appeals to the housewife often urged thrift, restraint and wise spending, a rhetoric which Zweiniger-Bargielowska contends resulted in Labour's electoral defeat in 1951.[103] As one housewife put it in 1951, 'the last election was lost mainly in the queue at the butcher's or the grocer's'.[104] But there is much else that needs explaining in what is inevitably a more complex picture. Firstly, other historians have pointed to the continued acceptance of austerity measures by 1950 and the limited influence of choice-oriented pressure groups such as the British Housewives' League whose influence at the ballot box was 'remarkably constrained' despite contemporary beliefs to the contrary.[105] Secondly, though, it would be incorrect to present Labour as the Party without a consumer policy. Its commitment to a Consumer Advice Centre at the 1950 election may even have kept the Party in power for another year and Wilson was keenly aware of the need to protect and cater to the consumer interest. If plans for the Centre and Labour's Consumers' Charter had had time to come to fruition, there is much to suggest that a mixed economy, providing consumers with choice but also guidance, safety and protection, would have proved popular with an electorate demanding both a share in any economic recovery and a more interventionist state that shielded consumers from the excesses of monopoly capitalism, unfair distribution and high prices.

In terms of the longer history of consumerism, what is more signif-icant still is the sense of ambiguity pervading Labour circles towards

[101] Briggs, *Michael Young*, p. 97.
[102] Conservative Party, *Manifesto 1951* (London, 1951), p. 3.
[103] A. E. Oram, *Labour's Good Housekeeping* (London, 1950); I. Zweiniger-Bargielowska, 'Bread rationing in Britain, July 1946 – July 1948', *Twentieth Century British History*, 4 (1993), 57–85; I. Zweiniger-Bargielowska, 'Rationing, austerity and the Conservative Party recovery after 1945', *Historical Journal*, 37 (1994), 173–97.
[104] M. Pugh, *Women and the Women's Movement in Britain, 1914–1959* (Basingstoke, 1992), p. 291.
[105] *Ibid.*, p. 290; Hinton, 'Militant housewives', p. 150.

consumerism and consumption. While there is a case that Labour offered an alternative vision of consumerism to the electorate, it is more doubtful whether that rhetoric would have been put into practice and the Party's consumer statements need to be assessed alongside its commitments to other policies. It is interesting that in Labour Party statements of policy after 1951, though democratic attitudes to living standards were still expressed, the space reserved for consumer issues and practical solutions declined dramatically.[106] Even at the time of Young's consumer policies, other Labour pamphleteers were either calling for a more traditionally socialist policy, else giving little attention to the consumer interest.[107] But the wider absence of consumerism outside the centre-left sections of the Party cannot be explained simply by the stranglehold of the productivist interests of its trade union members. Consumption remained an ideological problem for the party, especially in this crucial period of austerity overshadowed by the expectation of affluence. Unlike social democratic organisations in other countries, which had either already committed themselves to a high consumption agenda or were beginning to debate the role of material abundance within trade union and left-wing thought, sections of the British labour movement remained shackled by the older discourse of luxury and necessity. Concerns by vast sections of the working classes over the price, supply and quality of basic household goods remained legitimate expressions of political discontent. As over the previous fifty years, Labour was willing to incorporate the demands of the housewife over necessities within its agenda. It is noteworthy that the Board of Trade's discussions about the regulation of monopolies, the control of restrictive practices and the prohibition of false description proved the least controversial in Cabinet discussions: all these issues built on established critiques of profiteering, a central plank of Labour policy for several decades. But unease crept in, and not only because of the immediate dictates of finance, when it was proposed that the state begin to advise consumers on more expensive, one-off, consumer durables. Too much of this smacked of condoning luxury, pandering to the irrational desires of consumers before the socialist infrastructure had been put in place. It satisfied individual dilemmas over commodities with no immediate corresponding benefit for the wider good. It implicated the poor

[106] See, for instance, Labour Party, *Challenge to Britain* (London, 1953).
[107] H. Morrison, *Team Work for the Nation* (London, 1947); I. Mikardo, *The Second Five Years* (London, 1949); C. Attlee, *What Labour Has Done* (London, 1946); R. Acland, D. Bruce, B. Castle, R. Crossman, H. Davies, L. Hale, T. Horabin, M. Lipton, I. Mikardo, S. Swingler, G. Wigg and T. Williams, *Keeping Left: Labour's First Five Years and the Problems Ahead* (London, 1950); D. N. Pritt, L. Solley, J. Platts-Mills and L. Hutchinson, *Crisis and Cure: The Socialist Way to Prosperity and Peace* (London, 1950); J. Strachey, *Labour's Task* (London, 1951).

in what would later be termed 'bourgeoisification', a process that could only reduce the class struggle as the masses became obsessed with the same irrational desires that had transfixed the leisured classes for centuries past. Brought up on the Webbs, Tawney and the assumptions of the Fabians about the anarchy of the market, Labour leaders supported the productive, rational, Utility-scheme purchasing consumer, but shied away from advocating the rights of the people to novelty, fashion and mass-marketed comfort. The labour movement continued to feed on the consumerist concerns of the working class, but only those that fitted the correct side of traditional moral dichotomies about consumption were allowed to spearhead the policies of the labour movement.

There were important implications in this termination of Labour's plans to develop a consumer policy around a Consumers' Charter and a Consumer Advice Centre, together with it being out of office for the next thirteen years. In various European contexts, post-Second World War consumerism has developed in distinctive ways. In France, for instance, the Left has continued to have a say in consumer issues and its organisations have been officially recognised by state institutions concerned with the consumer. French consumerism has long been seen as the product of a three-pronged defence of the consumer interest by, firstly, commodity testing organisations, secondly, family-oriented organisations and, thirdly, a whole host of labour, co-operative, farmer and trade union based organisations which have helped maintain a stronger connection to political radicalism than is found in other countries' consumer movements.[108] Similarly in Sweden, trade union and co-operative organisations were quick to present themselves as the defenders of the consumer interest and the main countervailing force to business. A labour movement more receptive to debates on the role of material abundance in modern life and a state more willing to incorporate the concerns of consumers has ensured a more interventionist consumer policy, such that Sweden established the world's first consumer ombudsman and Market Court.[109] In Britain, the reluctance of sections of the Left to engage with a politics of affluent consumption, and the lack of opportunity for those consumer-oriented Labour politicians to put forward their ideas from 1951 to 1964 meant that consumerism in the 1950s took off outside those organisations which had traditionally been associated with the consumer interest.

[108] L. Bihl, *Consommateur: Défends-toi!* (Paris, 1976); G. Trumbull, 'Strategies of consumer-groups mobilisation: France and Germany in the 1970s', in Daunton and Hilton (eds.), *Politics of Consumption*, pp. 261–82.
[109] K. Blomqvist, 'Swedish consumer movement', in S. Brobeck, R. N. Mayer and R. O. Herrmann (eds.), *Encyclopedia of the Consumer Movement* (Santa Barbara, 1997), pp. 544–7.

Consumerism came to be dominated, in terms of protection, by the interventions of the Conservative Party and a grass-roots movement was contained within the growth of a largely middle-class Consumers' Association, independent from the state and wholly divorced from the TUC, the Co-operative movement and the Labour Party. The Consumer Advice Centre had represented the opportunity for the labour movement to provide the institutional bridge between the older politics of necessitous consumption and the emerging politics of consumer affluence to be examined in the next section of this book. That this opportunity was lost, for a variety of intellectual and practical reasons, meant that the Labour Party was not able to take the lead again in consumer affairs until the 1970s and the politics of price, poverty and profiteering were almost sidelined from the main concerns of post-war British consumerism.

Part II

Affluence

In the affluent society, no sharp distinction can be made between luxuries and necessaries.

J. K. Galbraith, *The Affluent Society* (1958; Harmondsworth, 1999), p. 228.

6   The new consumer: good housewives and enlightened businessmen

Modern, value-for-money, comparative-testing consumerism did not begin with the establishment of the Consumers' Association in 1956. In 1945, the National Council of Women (NCW) set up an Advisory Committee on Consumer Goods and approached the British Standards Institution (BSI) with a view to extending the work on standards to domestic commodities.[1] The following year, six representatives of the Advisory Committee met at the BSI for the first time 'to offer to the BSI the views of women as consumers on specifications which were in the course of preparation, concerned with household goods and similar subjects'.[2] It was a type of consumerism unrecognisable from the socialist politics of necessity espoused by many labour organisations before the Second World War. The NCW was an umbrella organisation for largely middle-class and socially and politically conservative women's organisations such as the Women's Institute (WI), the Townswomen's Guild, the National Federation of Business and Professional Women's Clubs and the Women's Voluntary Service. The Advisory Committee's terms of reference were restricted to providing the 'consumer' view on matters determined or already set in motion by the BSI. Its creation in 1946 appears to have been a purely conciliatory measure. At its first meeting, the BSI Director did not even bother to welcome them, preferring instead to send a memorandum dictating the items to be discussed (that is, the already drawn-up standards for building materials and the sizing of women's garments).[3] Acknowledging their restricted influence and recognising the limited value of their essentially amateur input into the highly technical language of standards specification, the NCW representatives quickly lost heart with the venture. The planned monthly meetings lasted only from March until June and thereafter only two women (Miss P. Garbutt

---

[1] C. D. Woodward, *BSI: The Story of Standards* (London, 1972), p. 69.
[2] British Standards Institution Library (hereafter BSIL), Minutes of Consumer Committees OC/11: NCW Advisory Committee on Consumer Goods: 2M(OC) 9056: *First meeting* (6 March 1946).
[3] *Ibid.*

of the Good Housekeeping Institute and Miss A. W. Wakefield of the NCW Executive) bothered to attend on a consistent basis, though even then only eleven meetings were held between 1946 and September 1950. However, the approach by the NCW to the BSI signified a broader shift in consumerism in which the middle-class housewife was increasingly to become the voice of the consumer interest. In response to the report of the Cunliffe Committee in 1950 which urged greater representation in the setting of standards, the BSI moved to establish a more formal relationship with the NCW.[4] In 1951, the Women's Advisory Committee (WAC) was established within the BSI, this time consisting of twenty-six women attached to the NCW and with the broader purpose of not only commenting on draft standards but also recommending areas to which standards could be extended.

The NCW–BSI alliance emerged out of the increasing attention given to the consumer and housewife in the Second World War and the recognition that improved standards in consumer durables were important both if the ordinary person was to see the benefits of economic reconstruction and if business and industry were to lead the way in the export drive. The WAC was to concern itself with those goods either too expensive, too infrequently used or too modern to be classified as traditional necessities and yet too common or everyday to be regarded as classical luxuries. These were the goods around which a new form of consumerism was emerging, begun in the efforts to establish seals of approval and marks of certified quality by organisations such as the Good Housekeeping Institute (GHI) and the Retail Trading Standards Association (RTSA). They were goods about which institutions such as Political and Economic Planning, the trade unions and the Labour Party had at times suggested an extension of an older politics of necessitous consumption into areas such as comparative testing, consumer advice and consumer education. In the post-Second World War period, these goods were to be the new, standardised, mass-produced, technical commodities increasingly available to an affluent working and middle class: refrigerators, stereos, cookers, electrical appliances and, eventually, motor cars. They were the durable household goods upon which national expenditure would shoot up from £189 million to £1,268 million in the ten years after 1945.[5]

In an earlier century such classes of good might have been termed semi-luxuries, decencies and conveniences – those goods which required

---

[4] BSIL OC/11: 3M(OC) 6746: *Tenth meeting* (19 April 1950); M. S. Thompson, *The History of the Women's Advisory Committee of the British Standards Institution* (1975), unpublished manuscript held at the BSI archive, p. 1/1.

[5] B. R. Mitchell and P. Deane, *Abstract of British Historical Statistics* (Cambridge, 1962), p. 371.

a further classification outside what were felt to be the too rigid moral implications of luxury and necessity. Today, standard economic textbooks
label them as 'normal' or 'ordinary'. The classification is apparently a
technical one, meaning the good has a positive income elasticity of demand (IED) of between zero and one: that is, we buy more of the good as
our income increases but not to the extent that our demand rises out of
proportion to our income (which would imply a positive IED of greater
than one and the classification of the good as a luxury; goods with a
negative IED are 'inferior'). But for all the bluff that economists 'cannot
make judgments about what people's goals should be', the classification
has a moral or political implication as well, equating rationality – where
the consumer 'weighs up the costs and benefits to him or her of each
additional unit of a good purchased' – with the everyday purchase of consumer durables de-politicised by their supposed ordinariness or normal-
ity.[6] While such labelling justifies the complete absence of any discussion
of consumerism within introductory economics courses,[7] it should also
raise questions about the political principles involved in the categorisation
of what is normal. This section of this book provides the history of the
politics of 'ordinary' consumption. Post-1945 consumerism has politicised consumption through the greater scrutiny and comparative testing
of common branded household commodities. It has actively promoted a
particular rationality of consumption distinct from the consumerism of
the early twentieth century. It has thereby contributed to the equation of
affluent consumption with normalcy, yet, as will be seen in later chapters,
it has also developed various consumer politics which simply cannot be
contained within the orthodox economist's view of consumer choice.

The absence of serious academic scrutiny of modern British consumerism has enabled many mythical and whiggish narratives to appear
about the movement's growth. The Consumers' Association (CA), set
up in 1956, is generally recognised as the most important moment in this
history, its predecessor being not the various organisations in Britain but
the Consumers' Union of the United States upon which CA was directly
modelled.[8] Such a narrative recognises the importance of the CA and it

---

[6] J. Sloman, *Economics*, 4th edn (London, 2000), p. 92.
[7] As well as the already cited Sloman, see also the following introductory texts used for
university teaching: D. Begg, S. Fischer and R. Dornbusch, *Economics*, 4th edn (London,
1994); M. Parkin, M. Powell and K. Matthews, *Economics*, 4th edn (London, 1998);
R. G. Lipsey and K. A. Crystal, *Positive Economics*, 8th edn (Oxford, 1995); P. A.
Samuelson and W. D. Nordhaus, *Economics*, 13th edn (London, 1989).
[8] On the development of US consumerism, see: S. Chase and F. J. Schlink, *Your Money's
Worth: A Study in the Waste of the Consumer's Dollar* (New York, 1927); C. McGovern,
'Consumption and citizenship in the United States, 1900–1940', in S. Strasser,
C. McGovern and M. Judt (eds.), *Getting and Spending: European and American Consumer*

will be analysed in appropriate depth in the next chapter, but to assume that British and, indeed, European consumerism followed and simply copied a US model ignores both the complexities of the politics of consumption in America and the important continuities in institutions, personnel, thematic priorities and definitions that occurred in Britain from the 1930s to the 1950s. What is apparent, however, is the eclipsing of older consumer voices by, first, the middle-class ladies of the NCW and, later, the consumer professionals of the CA. The Labour government's investigation of a Consumer Advice Centre in 1950–1 was an important indicator of the future direction of post-war consumerism, but it was to be the Labour Party's last opportunity to lead the discussion on the consumer interest until the 1970s. It remained committed to increasing consumer protection throughout the 1950s, as did the trade unions and the Co-operative movement who both followed the Labour Party line in this decade, but the precedents set in consumer advocacy and representation took place outside of the labour movement. As this chapter will first show, several organisations began to investigate the viability of comparative testing before the CA in the late 1940s and 1950s. But the one institution which had the resources to set up such a service – the Co-operative movement – lacked the imagination to step beyond an older politics of necessity. The new advocates of the consumer cause were instead the women of the NCW. Although the Women's Co-operative Guild was represented on the NCW executive, its voice was drowned out by the many other women's groups within the NCW and consequently the Women's Advisory Committee of the BSI. They articulated a pro-business consumerism that helped to channel an increasing number of consumer complaints away from more radical solutions. Responding to the widespread calls for consumer testing and advice, the BSI extended the activities of the WAC with the creation of the Consumer Advisory Council in 1955. A third section will show how just as advertising sought to create a particular idealised consumer, so too did the alliance of women's groups, journalists and business organisations seek to create a modern consumer who would see the

Societies in the Twentieth Century (Cambridge, 1998), pp. 37–58; M. Daunton and M. Hilton (eds.), *The Politics of Consumption: Material Culture and Citizenship in Europe and America* (Oxford, 2001), especially essays by Cohen, Jacobs and Cross; L. B. Glickman, 'The strike in the temple of consumption: consumer activism and twentieth-century American political culture', *Journal of American History*, 88:1 (2001), 99–128. On the US influence on Britain see C. Beauchamp, 'Getting *Your Money's Worth*: American models for the remaking of the consumer interest in Britain, 1930s–1960s', in M. Bevir and F. Trentmann (eds.), *Critiques of Capital in Modern Britain and America: Transatlantic Exchanges 1800 to the Present Day* (London, 2002), pp. 127–50; M. Hilton, 'Americanisation and consumerism: the Consumers' Association and the International Organisation of Consumers Unions', in M. Kipping and N. Tiratsoo, *Americanisation in 20th Century Europe: Business, Culture, Politics* (Lille, 2002), pp. 25–40.

solution to his or her problems in more information, further education and advice and trust in the responsible activities of British businessmen. Although this consumerism was to be criticised for its close associations with industry, the activities of the Consumer Advisory Council, through its complaints service, its testing magazine, *Shopper's Guide*, and its general commitment to the consumer cause suggest that it was not so different from the CA and was certainly more effective and radical than the Consumer Council of the 1960s, a decade which saw the expansion of state involvement in consumer protection. What is perhaps most remarkable about the CA, therefore, is not that it gave rise to modern organised consumerism in Britain, but that it was able to become the leading consumer advocate in the face of so much competition to represent the consumer interest.

Comparative testing before the Consumers' Association

Chapters 4 and 5 have already shown how the Food Council, Political and Economic Planning and the TUC considered the possibility of setting up a comparative testing consumer organisation. All aimed to provide objective information to consumers in the light of the inflated 'puffery' of advertising, a problem which had long been associated with patent medicines and which had resulted in earlier calls for specific testing.[9] Problems associated with legal costs and potential membership diluted the advocacy of this form of consumerism, though the TUC would continue to support throughout the 1950s a publicly funded testing agency, along the lines of the original proposals considered by the Labour government.[10] Amidst this inability to extend more socialist-inclined types of consumerism to the range of affluent goods with which many middle- and working-class consumers were now concerned, several pro-business organisations attempted to make themselves the champion of the consumer interest. There were long traditions of re-defining 'the consumer' away from her associations with either market irrationality or empowered working-class housewife co-operation. As well as speaking for the consumer in government and other institutional frameworks, new marketing initiatives, such as mail order, suggested that here was a novel venture to create a unison between manufacturer and consumer. Since the 'English consumer is a force to be reckoned with', a mail order initiative argued in 1934, manufacturers must respond to 'our criticisms and complaints' which amounted to a 'movement to bring to our homes those necessities

---

[9] British Medical Association, *Secret Remedies: What They Cost and What They Contain* (London, 1906).
[10] PRO BT 258/880: Committee on Consumer Protection: CCP 28: *Submission by TUC*.

and luxuries to which we are justly entitled'.[11] At the turn of the century there had been efforts to unite the more pro-market shopper with the retailer against the growing power of both monopoly manufacturers and co-operators.[12] Later, others attempted to bring into the market the more haughty discourses of connoisseurship, equating the right of the consumer to enjoy fine food and wine with the rights of 'Britons' to eat and drink what and how they pleased. The short-lived National League of Consumers of 1930–1 promoted a form of market libertarianism that betrayed the close connections of its magazine's editor, W. Vance Packman, with the drink trade.[13]

But more serious and lasting forms of consumer advocacy were also begun in the inter-war period, in part due to the emergence of market research as a discipline which stressed the importance of knowing and responding to consumer demand. In 1924, the Good Housekeeping Institute was started as an offshoot of *Good Housekeeping* magazine. It tested food and household products and awarded a 'Seal of Guarantee' to those items felt to match a set of minimum standards.[14] Although a later investigation found the Institute not to be acting solely for private profit, the use of the seal was clearly designed to promote the interests of its associates as much as consumers as a whole.[15] The Institute's view of consumerism was one of protecting the consumer from the exploitation of unscrupulous manufacturers while at the same time promoting a free market ethic. The consumer needed guidance, not protection, the Institute argued, its Seal of Guarantee providing a service which gave 'him all the protection which he could possibly require'.[16] The standards for such seals were not too onerous upon business, and the Institute was strongly criticised in 1962 for the various shortcomings in setting its minimum standards. These included its lack of independence from manufacturers who regarded the lax assessment criteria as an aid to obtaining the seal for advertising purposes rather than a rigorous or independent defence

---

[11] *Direct Buying Magazine* (March 1934), 3. Originally subtitled, *The Consumer's Magazine*, *Direct Buying* was first published in October 1933 until it became in April 1934, the *Mail Order Magazine*, adopting a format someplace in between a modern catalogue and *Reader's Digest*.

[12] See, for instance, the propaganda found in the *Trader and Consumer*, first published in August 1902, and which served as the public organ of the National Trader's Defence Association.

[13] *The Consumer: A Quarterly Review of Fine Foods, Wines, Spirits, Beers, Liqueurs, etc*, (Winter 1930–1), 1, 22. After Packman's death in early 1932, the editorship was taken over by nutritionist G. Doré-Boize, and thereafter *The Consumer* became increasingly concerned with health, diet, naturism, vegetarianism and pure air.

[14] J. Aspinall, 'Glossary of organisations active in consumer affairs', in J. Mitchell (ed.), *Marketing and the Consumer Movement* (London, 1978), p. 270.

[15] Committee on Consumer Protection [Molony Committee], *Final Report*, Cmnd. 1781 (London, 1962), p. 112.

[16] PRO BT 258/879: CCP 14: *Submission by the Good Housekeeping Institute*.

of the consumer interest.[17] By the time the Molony Committee's investigation into consumer protection commenced in 1959, the extent of the popularity of this form of consumerism was apparent. The Institute's seal had been joined by the BSI's Kitemark, the Harris Tweed Association's 'Orb' decree and the Ministry of Health's NH monogram for spectacle frames, as well as less reputable certifications issued by the Coal Utilisation Council, the Gas Council, the Quality Certification Bureau, the Lux Washability Bureau and the marks which proclaimed 'Courtaulds Tested Quality', 'Tebilised Double Tested' and 'Dylan Shrink Resist'.[18] Such guarantees issued by private associations of businesses would become one of the principal concerns of the newly organised consumer movement in the 1960s.

But this move to speak for the consumer, rather than letting the consumer speak for him or herself, was perhaps an inevitable outcome of the move to association that has come to dominate twentieth-century business life, as firms have attached greater importance to national lobby groups instead of local Chambers of Commerce. While manufacturers grouped around the Federation of British Industries (FBI), retailers flocked to various commodity and sector specific organisations to protect the position of distribution in an age of mass advertising, production, branding and pre-packaging.[19] More general bodies, such as the Retail Distributors' Association, would attempt to speak for the consumer in the usual manner of emphasising that 'the customer's best protection is to deal with a reputable retailer'.[20] But the consumer came to be an entity whose protection served the dual purpose of promoting the interests of one sector of commerce over another. One organisation which sought to speak for consumers in this way but which also extended the boundaries of consumer advocacy was the Retail Trading Standards Association (RTSA). Inaugurated in March 1935, the RTSA was dominated by the large department stores and multiple chains. Although it claimed to represent 'large and small businesses' from every town of over 50,000 inhabitants, it was nevertheless run by the likes of Selfridges, Harrods, John Lewis and a number of larger provincial stores.[21] Indeed, its aim could

[17] Committee on Consumer Protection, *Final Report*, pp. 111–12.
[18] PRO BT 258/880: CCP 68: *Certification Trade Marks – Note by the Board of Trade*.
[19] H. Levy, *Retail Trade Associations: A New Form of Monopolist Organisation in Britain* (London, 1942); M. Winstanley, *The Shopkeepers' World* (Manchester, 1983); H. Levy, *The Shops of Britain: A Study of Retail Distribution* (London, 1947); M. Hilton, 'Retailing history as economic and cultural history: strategies of survival by specialist tobacconists in the mass market', *Business History*, 40:4 (1998), 115–37.
[20] PRO BT 258/880: CCP 74: *Submission by Retail Distributors' Association*.
[21] 'Summary of progress', *Bulletin of the RTSA*, 1 (1935), 1; 'Officers and committees', 2 (1936), 2; Warwick Modern Records Centre (MRC) MSS 292/660.77/1: TUC General Council Research Department, *Scheme for a Consumers' Advisory Council* (20 December 1937), p. 1.

**MEMBERS OF THE
RETAIL TRADING STANDARDS ASSN**

Figure 3   Insignia of the Retail Trading Standards Association.

be regarded as specifically against the small trader since it sought to promote 'the wide adoption of uniform and accurate descriptions relating
to merchandise' which only the larger stores could hope to meet.[22] The
RTSA set out detailed standards of retail practice which all members had
to follow, enabling them to display the official insignia of the organisation (see Figure 3) as an advertisement for the quality of their service.[23]
But if the standards were not met, members could be brought before
the RTSA Tribunal, something of a kangaroo court, in which the five
judges sat also as prosecutors and jury.[24] The willingness of the RTSA
to act upon itself was severely restricted. As well as few smaller retailers actually joining the organisation, it also failed to attract the support
of the Co-operative movement. No real efforts were made to solicit the
opinions of the public and around 80 per cent of the complaints made
by consumers to the Tribunal were dismissed as 'frivolous'. Members
brought before the Tribunal went unpunished, either because the case
was dismissed or because they promised to abide by the standard in the
future. A more rigorous approach was only taken when it took up prosecutions under the Merchandise Marks Acts against non-members, an
action allowed through the RTSA's official recognition under the Board
of Trade's Charter of Incorporation.[25]

---

[22] RTSA, *To the Thoughtful Retailer* . . . (London, 193?), p. 4.
[23] RTSA, *Standards of Retail Practice* (London, 1935).
[24] 'Tribunal and machinery for dealing with alleged breaches of the standards', *Bulletin of
the RTSA*, 1 (1935), 3.
[25] MSS 292/660.77/1: TUC, *Consumers' Advisory Council*, pp. 2–3; *Bulletin of the RTSA*, 1
(1935), 3; 3 (1936), 3, 9; 7 (1938), 3.

In this sense, then, consumer protection legislation was being used, as it had in adulteration regulations, weights and measures guidelines and sales of goods legislation, as a means of promoting the interests of one business group over another. Yet the RTSA did also make more credible efforts to support the consumer. In 1937, it set up its own Testing House, together with its own 'Emblem' which approved manufacturers were allowed to use in their advertising.[26] Serious issues of independence were overlooked as the Testing House Board and facilities were made up of those companies who would themselves be applying to use the Emblem, but the service suggested to a wider public that the RTSA was an emerging advocate of the consumer interest. It developed close links to Political and Economic Planning, the RTSA member Robert Spicer becoming one of the principal architects of PEP consumer goods policy in the 1930s, and even the TUC was prepared to conclude, after a meeting in December 1937, that the RTSA was 'making a sincere attempt to prevent mal-practices in the retail trade'.[27] By the time of the Molony Committee, the RTSA had positioned itself as one of the most prominent bodies concerned with consumer protection. The gregarious character of its then chief spokesman, Roger Diplock, came in for particular praise by the Committee's secretary and he and the RTSA were given a comfortable cross-examination by Molony's colleagues when providing evidence.[28] This is a significant detail, since the RTSA reflected a broader respect accorded to businessmen speaking for consumers rather than consumers speaking for themselves. Also, the RTSA promoted a type of consumerism distinct from the organisations which represented the working-class consumer. As well as opposing forms of state consumer advocacy such as Labour's Consumer Advice Centre, the RTSA propounded the virtues of 'commonsense' purchasing and consumer education. It was actively involved in the process of creating the subject of the consumer. Dismissing the complaints of consumers themselves as 'grumbling' or the exceptional circumstances propounded by 'the eloquence of certain professional broadcasters and women journalists, as well as similar self-styled representatives of the housewife', the RTSA promoted instead an individualist mentality within consumer affairs.[29] The onus was not to be on the producer to trade fairly, though the RTSA positioned itself as the

---

[26] 'Testing House', *Bulletin of the RTSA*, 4 (1937), 3–6.

[27] MSS 292/660.77/1: TUC, *Memorandum of interview* (21 December 1937); O. Roskill, 'PEP through the 1930s: the Industries Group', in J. Pinder (ed.), *Fifty Years of Political and Economic Planning: Looking Forward, 1931–1981* (London, 1981), p. 68.

[28] PRO BT 258/879: CCP 9: *Proposed Submission by the Retail Trading Standards Association*, note by Mitchelmore [Secretary]. One Molony Committee member, Ramage, was even a member of the Council of the RTSA.

[29] PRO BT 258/879: CCP 9: *Proposed Submission by the RTSA.*

watchdog of certain abuses, but on the consumer to get 'your money's worth', a process which involved shopping around and not state interference.[30] Problems could be overcome by an education programme of the sort that appeared in the RTSA's *The Intelligent Woman's Guide to Shopping* (1935). This positioned the retailer as the friend of the consumer and laid out the RTSA Standards in plain non-technical knowledge. 'Armed' with such information, 'the woman shopper will find herself on a better and more confident footing with the salesman'.[31] Women were therefore to demand through individual empowerment the relationship they all held with the shopkeepers they already trusted who 'will put them right'.[32] An open letter, written by the pseudonymous 'John Draper', explained in startlingly simple terms to the 'intelligent woman' that problems of mis-description were not the fault of the tradesman and that if only the shopper allowed the retailer to take care of standards (or the 'Shopper's Magna Carta') then her problems would be solved. Even prosecutions for infringements of the laws of consumer protection were to be left to the vigilance of the RTSA Tribunal rather than any state or municipal-sponsored weights and measures or trading standards agency.[33]

Amidst the emergence of business spokesmen for the shopper, it is appropriate to ask how the Co-operative movement reacted to the eclipsing of its role as the foremost consumer advocate. Co-operation, however, struggled to take the lead in the politics of consumer affluence, and provided few dynamic responses to consumer interests until, possibly, the 1990s with the development of its ethical trading initiatives. In 1938, the situation had been made clear to the Co-operative movement. A. M. Carr-Saunders, P. Sargant Florence and Robert Peers, in their comprehensive overview of British co-operation, stated that co-operative consumers already demonstrated a keen interest in food values and the properties of objects of common consumption. If the Co-operative movement was to survive it needed to extend this interest to more affluent goods and engage in the type of testing and standards work associated with the Good Housekeeping Institute. Carr-Saunders and his colleagues urged the Co-operative movement to embark on consumer education, teaching discrimination, aesthetic considerations and value-for-money criteria. Only then would co-operation become more inventive in the supply of goods, catering to the tastes and desires of its members. Better channels of communication needed to be set up between co-operative officers and customers in order to give consumers what they wanted and free the movement of its associations with drabness and poor taste. Essentially, the authors were urging an extension of the co-operative politics of consumption from one

[30] 'How to get your money's worth', *Bulletin of the RTSA*, 5 (1937), 15.
[31] RTSA, *The Intelligent Woman's Guide to Shopping* (London, 1935), p. 4.
[32] *Ibid.*, p. 4.   [33] *Ibid.*, pp. 10–22.

based on necessities to one that embraced more expensive household durables as well. The Co-operative movement had been urged in 1938 to engage in the forms of market research, comparative testing, consumer education and advice with which late twentieth-century consumerism would become associated.[34]

The Co-operative movement failed to heed the warning. In *Cartel*, the journal of the International Co-operative Alliance, which acted as a 'Review of Monopoly Developments and Consumer Protection', it did make some headway in combining an older politics of necessity with one of affluence. Articles criticised the 'kid-gloved' powers of the Monopolies Commission (set up by the 1948 Monopolies Act), the limitations of the 1951 Board of Trade statement on resale price maintenance and the continued abuses within hire purchase, agricultural marketing and collective discrimination.[35] But an older anti-profiteering rhetoric was also positioned alongside an enthusiasm for consumer protection initiatives launched in Europe in the 1950s, such as the 1953 Norwegian Consumers' Council, and in 1955 *Cartel's* inside sleeve proclaimed the general commitment 'to protect consumers against deceptive practices and to provide them with the information they need to buy wisely and well'.[36] Furthermore, the Co-operative movement remained committed throughout the 1950s to the creation of a Ministry of Consumers' Welfare, promoting the sort of umbrella consumerism that embraced poverty and affluence as had been discussed in the final months of the post-Second World War Labour government.[37]

However, the Co-operative movement was not at the forefront of consumerism in this period, with many of its schemes following rather than leading the new consumer agendas. Thus, while it might propose such initiatives as a 'Buyer Beware!' scheme to show the abuses of certain manufacturers, it did not propose the more positive 'Best Buy' that would soon become a feature of *Which?* magazine reflecting consumers' desires to participate in, as much as critique, the modern marketplace.[38] And developments in consumerism were reported after the event, rather than

---

[34] A. M. Carr-Saunders, P. S. Florence and R. Peers, *Consumers' Co-operation in Great Britain: An Examination of the British Co-operative Movement* (London, 1938), pp. 507–8.

[35] R. Evely, 'British anti-monopoly legislation', *Cartel*, 1:1 (1950), 9–17; C. A. R. Crosland. 'The future of resale price maintenance', *Cartel*, 4:2 (1954), 42–7; G. Darling, 'Restrictive practices – the new British approach', *Cartel*, 6:2 (1956), 44–7; Committee on Resale Price Maintenance [Lloyd Jacob Committee], *Report*, Cmd. 7696 (London, 1949); Board of Trade, *A Statement on Resale Price Maintenance*, Cmd. 8274 (London, 1951).

[36] P. Söiland, 'The Consumers' Council in Norway', *Cartel*, 3:6 (1953), 210–14; K. Kuhne, 'Consumer protection: a German view', *Cartel*, 5:3 (1955), 89–95; cover notes to *Cartel*, 5 (1955).

[37] H. Campbell, *Wanting and Working* (London, 1947); G. D. N. Worswick, *The Consumer: His Place in Society* (London, 1946).

[38] Regular feature in volume 6 of *Cartel* (1955).

being anticipated. Modern consumer champions such as Colstone Warne of the US Consumers' Union were invited to contribute to *Cartel*, provoking no follow-up articles or responses, while British initiatives were viewed with suspicion.[39] For instance, the CA was felt to be just another form of market research organisation that would ultimately aid rather than hinder competition.[40] It was not really until the end of the 1950s that, in *Cartel* at least, co-operation began to realise that consumerism could not only be a negative critique of business but a positive embrace of market interventions such as the promotion of 'wise buying', a better understanding of shopping habits, the creation of local advice centres and the promotion of consumer education.[41] By this time, though, both the Consumer Advisory Council of the BSI and the CA itself were firmly established as the leading consumerist groups to the extent that co-operative policy appears as a reflection of their agendas, with just a slightly greater degree of emphasis upon state intervention being advocated. Indeed, in its evidence to the Molony Committee, much of the Co-operative Union's submission was taken up reviewing and commenting on the activities of organisations other than itself.[42] As if in recognition of its failure to marry an older consumer politics of necessity with one of semi-luxury, in 1961 *Cartel* reverted to its original focus on anti-monopoly measures, publishing instead a *Consumer Affairs Bulletin* to concentrate on issues emerging from modern comparative-testing consumerism.[43] This split, however, was not a success and in October 1964 the International Co-operative Alliance published the last issue of *Cartel*.[44] In the consumerist environment of affluent Britain, the Co-operative movement found itself marginalised, though its older ascetic politics of consumption perhaps made it unsuited to a more imaginative engagement with an expanding world of goods.

The consumer as middle-class housewife

If the traditional outlet of a consumerist politics failed to capture the spirit of post-war Britain, others were keen to posit themselves as the

[39] C. E. Warne, 'Consumer organisations – an international conference?', *Cartel*, 7:1 (1957), 2–5; C. E. Warne, 'Consumer representation in government', *Cartel*, 9:4 (1959), 112–13.
[40] J. Y. Kennish, 'Consumer research in Britain', *Cartel*, 8:2 (1958), 51–3.
[41] E. Burton, 'Aids to wise buying: the next step', *Cartel*, 8:3 (1958), 74–8; E. G. West, 'Shopping habits', *Cartel*, 8:3 (1958), 81–3; D. Lazell, 'Patterns of consumer education', *Cartel*, 10:1 (1960), 26–7; R. Calvert, 'Local consumer advice in Great Britain', *Cartel*, 10:1 (1960), 95–7.
[42] BT 258/882: CCP 9: Co-operative Union, Parliamentary Committee, *Memorandum*.
[43] 'Publisher's announcement', *Cartel*, 11:4 (1961), 109.   [44] *Cartel*, 14:4 (1964).

spokesmen and women of the consumer. The first such group to do so were the largely middle-class women of the National Council of Women. Freshly confident from the high levels of participation she had made in the war effort, the British housewife obtained a moral legitimacy which increased her importance at the ballot box. Building too on the activities of voluntary groups in social welfare reform in the inter-war period and through business-sponsored promotional ventures such as the Electrical Association for Women and the Women's Gas Federation, women from within but mainly beyond the Co-operative Guilds and the Labour Party increasingly posited themselves as the authentic voice of the nation's housewives. According to Martin Pugh, the attention given to domestic issues such as housing, the milk supply and the extension of gas and electricity by the wartime government politicised the female electorate, such that its voting patterns were less easy to predict.[45] While this has led to a historical controversy on the extent to which women influenced the outcome of the 1950 and 1951 elections, it is undeniable that the Conservative Party focus on domestic issues and the anti-austerity propaganda of women's magazines gave a greater prominence to the housewife. It was a consumerism which was 'cosy, individualist, home-owning, [and] materialist' and it offered an ideal for women which emphasised marriage and family life.[46] It has been seen as a backward step in the politics of a feminist movement, but it was certainly the crucial context with which to understand the approach of the NCW to the BSI immediately after the end of the war.

If the resultant Advisory Committee on Consumer Goods, which met for the first time in 1946, was only ever a half-hearted venture, the BSI expressed a firmer commitment to the women's groups which had 'done useful work in advising on various questions connected with Utility schemes, fuel supplies, and other matters arising out of government controls' when it established the Women's Advisory Committee (WAC) in 1951.[47] The BSI's enrolment of 'non-feminist' women's organisations supposedly gave the WAC access to 1,500,000 constituent members, or 'the views and experiences of at least one family out of eight'.[48] Unlike the original meeting of 1946, the BSI Director, H. A. R. Binney, did attend

---

[45] M. Pugh, *Women and the Women's Movement in Britain, 1914–1959* (Basingstoke, 1992), p. 290
[46] Pugh, *Women and the Women's Movement*, p. 292.
[47] Thompson, *History of the WAC*, p. 1/1.
[48] BSIL: WAC Reports: *Draft of the First Annual Report of the WAC*, 26 February 1962, p. 1; C. Beaumont, 'Women and citizenship: a study of non-feminist women's societies and the women's movement in England, 1928–1950', Ph.D. thesis, University of Warwick (1996).

the first meeting of the WAC in March 1951, where he stressed the importance of the housewife in setting standards. Reacting immediately to the employment of the term 'housewife' in the terms of reference, several representatives insisted that it was substituted with 'women' and, seizing the initiative, successfully arranged that the WAC not only considered standards but helped disseminate information about theirs and the BSI's work in a broader programme of consumer education.[49]

In its first year, the WAC advised on the testing of cookers, the lengths of sheets and blankets, textile labelling and the fire-proofed fabrics for children's clothes. It examined fourteen draft standards, demonstrated a 'continuing concern with elastic' and, indicating a 'battle' that was to last for over twenty years, the height of kitchen units which were felt to be designed with little regard for the actual user.[50] WAC representatives sat on various BSI technical committees and its Publicity Panel oversaw the arrangements for press releases, lectures, seminars, conferences, the publication of leaflets and its annual 'At Home'. In 1954, it published *Consumer Report*, a leaflet with a circulation of 26,000 which informed the WAC's constituent organisations about developments in consumer standards and regulations.[51] It advised not only the BSI but also private manufacturers who saw in the WAC a rudimentary market research organisation and it liaised with several other public and voluntary bodies concerned with promoting standards and the labelling of common household goods.[52] In 1952, when the Douglas Committee suggested that Utility goods be replaced with the adoption of minimum standards, created through collaboration between private industry and the BSI, the WAC saw a potential space for it to speak more frequently on the needs of the domestic consumer.[53] The WAC quickly stressed the importance of the BSI 'Kitemark' in making consumers 'standards conscious'. By 1954, for instance, over 300 firms had been awarded licences to Kitemark their furniture and the WAC moved to ensure the public knew of this.[54] They published a list of goods bearing the Kitemark in a *Shopping Guide* and arranged for its frequent 'Housewives' Quiz' to test general recognition of the symbol as well the overall ability of women to judge what they were buying.[55]

[49] BSIL OC/11: 3M(OC) 8749: 15 March 1951; Thompson, *History of the WAC*, p. 1/3.
[50] Thompson, *History of the WAC*, p. 1/4; BSIL: WAC Reports: *Draft of the First Annual Report*, p. 2.
[51] Woodward, *Story of Standards*, p. 71; BSI, *Look Before You Buy: Report on the Conference of Women's Organisations, Pavilion Theatre, Brighton, 9 April 1956* (London, 1956), p. 4.
[52] BSI, *Annual Report, 1954–1955* (London, 1955), p. 129.
[53] BSIL OC/11: WAC Minutes: 3M(OC) 755: 5 March 1952.
[54] Woodward, *Story of Standards*, p. 71.
[55] BSI, *Annual Report, 1954–1955*, p. 130; BSI, *Look Before You Buy*, p. 7; BSI, *Annual Report, 1955–1956*, p. 131; BSI, *Annual Report, 1957–1958*, p. 131; Thompson, *History of the WAC*, p. 2/2.

The WAC stressed the importance of standards as the best means of promoting the interests of the consumer. After all, 'the consumer is on the whole a reasonably sensible person and, except where health and safety are concerned, emphasis should be on consumer education and guidance rather than consumer protection'.[56] Such faith was predicated on a definition of the consumer as 'an intelligent sensible woman'.[57] 'Ultimate responsibility for the standard of merchandise' 'rested with shoppers who had to learn to discriminate.' In the economic environment of the 1950s this was by all means possible and the WAC saw no reason why if a woman's 'job was well done', her home should not 'reflect her careful judgement and good taste'.[58] It was ultimately an individualist mentality in which the responsibilities of the shopper were greater than those of business, a view of consumerism in which the rhetoric of identifying women as 'the purses of the nation' assumed a far less radical slant than it had in Margaret Llewelyn Davies' propaganda for the Women's Co-operative Guild.[59] As various WAC conferences put it, women were advised to 'look before you buy' and to 'buy wisely – buy well'.[60]

By the late 1950s, other consumer groups would deplore the lack of expertise of the WAC which, it was suggested, meant its representatives were out-manoeuvred on any technical committee. Indeed, its lack of impact on even standards specifications may be related to the BSI Executive's repeated stated pleasure in the work of its dedicated housewives. But the WAC members took a pride in their amateur status, rejecting payment for their services even in an era when consumerism had entered a new professionalism.[61] They saw themselves as the handmaidens of industry, often demonstrating their acceptance of the gender dimensions to a consumer–producer dichotomy, as they would hold tea receptions for the businessmen attending standardisation conferences.[62] Their public proclamations repeated their pro-business stance. It was taken as a given that British manufacturers had the consumer's best interests at heart,

---

[56] PRO BT 258/879: CCP 12: *Submission by WAC*, p. 5.
[57] BSI, *Buy for Safety: Buy for Service. Report on the Conference of Women's Organisations, Glasgow, 4 November 1959* (London, 1959).
[58] BSI, *Standards for the Shopper: Report on the Conference of Women's Organisations, Ipswich, 21 March 1960* (London, 1960).
[59] BSI, *Standards and Safety: Report on the Conference of Women's Organisations, Belfast, 25 April 1961* (London, 1961).
[60] BSI, *Look Before You Buy: Report on the Conference of Women's Organisations, Wolverhampton, 5 April 1960* (London, 1960); BSI, *Buy Wisely – Buy Well: Report on the Conference of Women's Organisations, Sunderland, 24 January 1961* (London, 1961); BSI, *Look Before You Buy: Report on the Conference of Women's Organisations, Portsmouth, 19 October 1961* (London, 1961).
[61] BSIL OC/11: M62/1593: 13 August 1962.
[62] BSI, *Annual Report, 1958–1959* (London, 1959), p. 122.

that retailers did not want to stock unreliable goods or that manufacturers would be anxious to remedy any faults discovered.[63] Tellingly, the WAC opposed the setting up of an Associates scheme as its role was not to assist the public but to aim at a 'higher level'.[64] The WAC did not aim 'to incite the public to complain all the time' and Marjorie Byrne, Chairman from 1955 to 1958 and executive of a leading London advertising agency, even called on women to tell manufacturers 'about satisfactory, fairly-priced goods in order to have positive evidence put beside complaints'.[65] Despite their own entry into the consumer-political sphere, the housewife-consumer imagined by the women of the WAC was a rather compliant being, though an active agent in the perpetuation of her status – consumer education, for many, consisted of inviting senior schoolgirls to WAC conferences.[66]

Often the WAC was indecisive and lacking in initiative. In 1959 it considered withdrawing its eight representatives on the Consumer Advisory Council (CAC) as it was felt they were 'ineffective', though for some time Byrne had become infuriated at the lack of cohesiveness in the WAC's policy decisions, so much so that she had at one point even recommended that 'it should be prepared to withdraw as a body'.[67] It was not even clear how seriously the BSI took the WAC. When, in 1951, the WAC made its first attempt to force the BSI to introduce standards on new ranges of goods – on the size, strength, absorbency and sterility of sanitary towels – manufacturers were unwilling to collaborate and the WAC's project failed after many years of pressure.[68] Often, 'negotiation' with technical committees consisted of BSI experts explaining to the frequently overawed amateur WAC representative why her proposals could not be met.[69] As the BSI moved to create the CAC in recognition of public demand for some form of consumer representation, the WAC was not even consulted. After Binney detailed the already decided plans of the BSI Executive the WAC found itself with a struggle simply to obtain a presence on the CAC, though it eventually secured eight representatives.[70]

The WAC survived into the 1960s and continued long after the BSI abolished its CAC, not least because the BSI required at least the appearance of some form of negotiation with consumers in the creation of

---

[63] BSI, *Look Before You Buy: Report on the Conference of Women's Organisations, Pavilion Theatre, Brighton, 9 April 1956* (London, 1956), p. 8.
[64] BSIL OC/11: 5M(OC) 503: 17 May 1956.
[65] BSI, *Look Before You Buy: Report on the Conference of Women's Organisations, Scarborough, 3 October 1956* (London, 1956), p. 5.
[66] BSI, *Annual Report, 1961–1962*, p. 141.
[67] BSIL OC/11: 5M(OC) 5863: 19 May 1958; 5M(OC) 7517: 26 January 1959.
[68] Thompson, *History of the WAC*, p. 1/5.   [69] *Ibid.*, p. 2/2.
[70] BSIL OC/11: 4M(OC) 6671: 3 November 1954; Thompson, *History of the WAC*, p. 2/4.

standards on domestic goods. In the 1970s, the WAC believed a new framework for consumer representation was required and its name was changed to the Consumer Standards Advisory Committee in 1971, anticipating the appointment of men to the body from March 1973. Since 1990 it has been known as the Consumer Policy Committee and it draws on the expertise of various consumer, voluntary and official bodies, whose nominees and other staff receive specialist training so that they become more effective representatives of the consumer within the BSI's various technical committees.[71] Its modern professionalism contrasts with the amateur spirit that dominated the early years of the WAC in the 1950s when it was assumed the straightforward, plain speaking of the common-sensical housewife would be enough to raise the standards of British industry such that no state involvement would be required within the field of consumer protection. The existence of the WAC may have resulted in little more than the demonstration that further consumer representation was required, but for a brief moment it made the middle-class housewife the champion of the consumer cause. Inverting the presumption of irrationality that had long been ascribed to women shopping for goods other than necessities, the implied attributes of the middle-class homemaker were celebrated by business groups to an extent that the woman consumer achieved a level of semi-official recognition far greater than anything achieved by previous working-class women's groups. The women who entered into partnership with trade in 1951 were not the socialists and radicals of the Co-operative and labour movements, but the voluntary workers who had been carefully selected by the BSI for their, at worst, acquiescence or, at best, acknowledged parity in attitude towards the state, the market and the individual. The National Council of Women effected the emergence of a newly prominent consumer voice in national life, but one which organised business was keen to contain within its construction of the consumer.

Business as the champions of the consumer

There is a book waiting to be written on the shaping of the consuming self in Britain by the professional expertise found in such marketing, advertising and business associations as the Federation of British Industry, the National Union of Manufacturers, the Association of British Chambers of Commerce, the Advertising Association and the countless trade associations connected to the distributive sector. Coupled with such

---

[71] BSI Consumer Policy Committee, *Annual Report 1999* (London, 1999); BSI, *Speaking Up for Consumers: Information about BSI and Consumer Representation* (London, 1999).

clear interests would be the tactics of persuasion found in the advertising image itself, the dominance of the model of the rational individual within orthodox economics and the equation of democracy with consumption within the popular media which, although clearly more prominent in the United States, nevertheless was not absent from the propaganda of Beaverbrook and Northcliffe's newspapers.[72] Such a project would take in the promotion of new forms of expertise for understanding the consumer and the attempts to channel his or her desires to a mass-produced chain of packaged pleasures.[73] The analysis of the influence of the 'psy' professions within commercial bodies clearly lends itself to an understanding of the nexus of 'governmentality' by which the individualistic, acquisitive, materialist self has been imagined and realised. Nikolas Rose has already begun such a project, focussing on the Tavistock Institute for Human Relations in the first two decades after the Second World War, when marketing experts and psychologists combined in a project that was 'not so much the invention and imposition of "false needs", but a delicate process of identification of the "real needs" of consumers, of affiliating these needs with particular products, and in turn of linking these with the habits of their utilisation. Making up the consumer entailed simultaneously making up the commodity and assembling the little rituals of everyday life which would give that commodity meaning and value.'[74] For Rose, constructing the consumer is part of a wider process of inventing the modern self 'and the terms that cluster around it – autonomy, identity, individuality, choice, fulfilment'.[75] The guidance of the self, no longer dependent on the authority of religion or traditional morality, 'has been allocated to "experts of subjectivity" who transfigure existential questions about the purpose of life and the meaning of suffering into technical questions of the most effective ways of managing malfunction and improving "quality of life".'[76] To the range of such experts and their institutions – schools, prisons, clinics and so on – Rose has demonstrated the importance of the 'psy' professions: it is only a matter of time before a comprehensive history emerges that adds marketing to

[72] D. L. LeMahieu, *A Culture for Democracy: Mass Communication and the Cultivated Mind in Britain Between the Wars* (Oxford, 1988); G. Cross, *Time and Money: The Making of Consumer Culture* (London, 1993).

[73] See, for instance, P. Redmayne and H. Weeks, *Market Research* (London, 1931); A. P. Braddock, *Applied Psychology for Advertisers* (London, 1933); H. W. Eley, *Advertising Media* (London, 1932).

[74] P. Miller and N. Rose, 'Mobilizing the consumer: assembling the subject of consumption', *Theory, Culture & Society*, 14:1 (1997), p. 6.

[75] N. Rose, *Inventing Our Selves: Psychology, Power and Personhood* (Cambridge, 1996), p. 1.

[76] *Ibid.*, p. 151.

this process of governance, arguing for the adjective, 'consuming', to be added to the list of the definitions of the modern self.[77]

It is a tempting analysis, not least because of its totalising nature and its ability to draw consumers themselves within its remit under a less tangible but nevertheless apparent process of self-governance. But it is also a rather positivist history of the consuming individual self which both ignores the lack of concern given to consumers by manufacturers throughout the twentieth century and the ability of consumers to provide alternative critiques of the market through such organisations as the Co-operative movement and later the Consumers' Association. The history of the twentieth century cannot simply be re-written, to put it simply, as a recasting of the individual from an idealised, outer-directed, collective-spirited, producer-oriented and politically motivated worker to a dispar-aged, inner-directed, egoistical, acquisitive and apathetic consumer. In-deed, we have to question whether the agents expected to be involved in the creation of the consuming self were ever so aware of the subjects being constructed. A complaint made by many consumer activists in the 1950s was that manufacturers simply made products and sought a market to sell them[78]: there is a world of difference between imagining a purchaser and imagining the consuming self, with all its attendant implications for politics, citizenship and socio-cultural change. British business has been charged with having a poor consumer consciousness. While economic textbooks posited a rational individual whose behaviour was reasonably predictable, early works on marketing posited an irrational individual where 'sentiment, rather than logic, is the impulse in most sales of ar-ticles to the consumer'.[79] Both views are equally crude, locating con-sumer motivation within an arbitrarily drawn distinction between either the conscious or the subconscious, though such a polarisation maps on to traditional moralities of the market contained within the luxury de-bates. What consumer activists felt business did not account for were the issues of safety, ergonomics, value for money and independent informa-tion which would become the consumer movement's own definition of the consumer interest from the late 1950s. Here, 'the consumer' was as much the creation of the social democratic impulse as it was of business or professional expertise.

---

[77] For a German comparison see E. Carter, *How German is She? Postwar West German Reconstruction and the Consuming Woman* (Ann Arbor, 1997). Related, though non-Foucauldian, approaches exist on the US: R. Marchand, *Advertising the American Dream: Making Way for Modernity, 1920–1940* (Berkeley, 1985); S. Ewen, *Captains of Conscious-ness: Advertising and the Social Roots of the Consumer Culture* (New York, 1976).

[78] Interview with Rosemary McRobert, 25 March 2002.

[79] J. L. Mahin, *Advertising: Selling the Consumer* (London, 1914), p. 19.

If, however, a history of the consuming self is to be written whereby the narrowly-defined economic purchaser becomes the equally specific 'customer-citizen' of modern liberal government, then it is in institutions such as the BSI that we can see early attempts to define the consumer and place boundaries on the politicised aspects of consumption. In some senses, the BSI makes an ideal case study, since it was a voluntary organisation of companies begun in 1901 concerned with standards in manufacturing yet also a government-funded national organisation whose General Council reflected the uncertain divide between state and industry.[80] During the Second World War, following an initiative from the RTSA, the BSI became increasingly involved in the creation of standards for distribution and consumer (especially Utility) goods, a trend which was further encouraged by the post-war Lemon and Cunliffe Committees which advocated greater user involvement in the development of standards. While the BSI had responded with the creation of the WAC, by the mid-1950s some further action was deemed necessary in order to justify the £90,000 per annum the organisation was receiving from a tax-paying general public increasingly concerned with the standards of new consumer goods.[81] According to the *Financial Times* in 1955, there was a duty upon manufacturers to respond more broadly to the consuming public, since 'The consumer today is offered so bewildering a choice of goods and so many items embodying the most advanced technical skills, that ordinary common sense and experience are of comparatively little help in distinguishing them.'[82]

In this new context of emerging consumerism, BSI recognised the inadequacy of its previous efforts at conciliation through the WAC. In August 1954, it announced its intention to set up a Consumer Advisory Council (CAC) to be a source of information and advice firstly to industry about the consumer's needs in relation to domestic and personal goods, and secondly to the public about safeguards, in the way of standards and other facilities, available to them.[83] It consisted of representatives of the WAC, individuals such as the consumer journalists, Marghanita Laski and Ruth Drew, the economist Graham Hutton, the co-operator R. Southern and, later, the social scientist Mark Abrams.[84] The BSI also included the interests of its business members and five retailers and three wholesalers were selected to put forward 'the needs and views of domestic consumers'.[85]

[80] BSI, *Fifty Years of British Standards, 1901–1951* (London, 1951).
[81] Woodward, *Story of Standards*, pp. 17, 69.   [82] *Ibid.*, p. 25.
[83] Thompson, *History of the WAC*, p. 2/3.
[84] BSI, *Annual Report, 1954–1955*, p. 174; BSI, *Annual Report, 1955–1956*, p. 181; BSI, *Annual Report, 1956–1957*, p. 192; *Shopper's Guide*, 14 (1960), 16.
[85] BSI, *Annual Report, 1954–1955*, p. 10; BSI, *Standards and the Consumer: First Annual Report of the Advisory Council on Standards for Consumer Goods, 1955–1956* (London,

At the most straightforward level of consumer representation, the WAC's view that consumers were 'the women of the country' was being replaced with a less gender-specific definition, but also one in which journalists and businessmen had become the consumer advocates instead of the Women's Institutes and the Townswomen's Guilds.[86]

The CAC continued the work of the WAC in publicising the BSI Kitemark, providing information on 'wise buying', educating the public about particular standards on consumer goods, promoting the greater use of informative labelling, advising on issues of safety and assisting members of the public in complaints procedures.[87] From January 1956, members of the public were invited to become Associates of the Council who would receive fact sheets from the CAC's Advisory Service as well as the first British comparative testing magazine, *Shopper's Guide*, published from 1957.[88] The activities of the CAC rapidly expanded on to a scale not originally envisaged by the BSI General Council. By 1960, there were over 53,000 Associates, the Advisory Service was dealing with over 10,000 letters per year and around 2,000 complaints about goods which the CAC attempted to follow up.[89] The CAC had insufficient resources to co-operate so effectively with the public and by the 1960s was increasing its subscription costs, restricting the complaints service to Associates only and urging restraint: consumers were informed that one-third of their complaints were 'unjustified' and 'frivolous' and that often it was better to pursue a complaint 'in a reasonable manner' with the shop manager.[90]

The CAC was an important agent for the extension of consumerist agendas in the 1950s. It was called upon to act as the official representative of the consumer in an expanding number of official bodies and it began to collaborate with other consumer bodies on ventures such as the 1962 BBC 'Choice' programme which featured Richard Dimbleby presenting the results of tests conducted by *Which?* and *Shopper's Guide*.[91] CAC membership also reflected the growing strength of consumer activism as it began to co-opt various important figures of the burgeoning consumer movement: the lawyer Aubrey Diamond, the future Chair of the Consumers' Association, Jennifer Jenkins (wife of Roy) and the

1956); Consumer Standards Advisory Committee [later the CAC], *An Introduction to the CSAC* (London, 1956?); CAC, *Representing the Consumer Advisory Standards Committee* (London, n.d.).

[86] BSI, *Annual Report, 1954–1955*, p. 129.
[87] BSI, *Annual Report, 1955–1956*, p. 18; BSI, *Annual Report, 1956–1957*, pp. 12, 136.
[88] BSI, *Annual Report, 1957–1958*, p. 130.   [89] BSI, *Annual Report, 1959–1960*, p. 135.
[90] *Shopper's Guide*, 27 (1962), 14–15; BSI, *Annual Report, 1960–1961*, p. 8; BSI, *Annual Report, 1961–1962*, p. 7.
[91] BSI, *Annual Report, 1961–1962*, p. 7.

multi-faceted consumer worker Rosemary McRobert.[92] Despite criticisms that the CAC was insufficiently independent of business it embarked upon campaigns such as the reform of the Weights and Measures Act, for greater information about the extent and application of the Purchase Tax and for better protection of unwary consumers in hire-purchase contracts.[93] Its agendas often mirrored the campaigns of a wider consumer movement and it welcomed the decision to establish the Molony Committee on Consumer Protection.[94] Members of the CAC had even begun to feel by 1958 that a national Consumer Council was required where there were no longer such close ties to industry and, they argued, their advocacy of this in 1958 led to the formation of the Committee in 1959.[95] In its evidence to Molony, the CAC set out its plans for an independent, government-funded Consumer Council which would involve itself in consumer education and advice, comparative testing, the policing of unfair trade practices, the promotion of standards and general research into the consumer interest. Its proposed membership was to be dominated by the current members of the CAC and it was to maintain close links with the BSI, but it reflected the CAC's admission that it needed to cut its current constitutional throat in order to respond to the demands of the consuming public which, it was felt, was demanding a central government agency, if not even a Consumers' Ministry to which one *Shopper's Guide* editorial referred.[96]

Nevertheless, the outlook of the CAC was broadly in line with that of the BSI General Council and hence of enlightened businessmen more generally. The key to consumer protection lay in the adoption of voluntary minimum standards, negotiated between industry and the consumer representatives selected by the BSI. This was predicated on the belief that the consumer was an individual and that ultimately individual choice was the most fundamental and basic consumer protection that existed. Compulsory measures had therefore only to be introduced for reasons of health and safety and other measures – that is, labelling and education – had to be both voluntary and designed to improve the individual powers of discrimination rather than the position of consumers in the aggregate. And the best means of providing this impartial advice was through the expert knowledge of the businessmen of the BSI and the consumers already sitting on its CAC.[97] The CAC made efforts to maintain friendly

[92] *Ibid.*, p. 210.
[93] *Shopper's Guide*, 15 (1960), 1; 18 (1961), 13; 19 (1961), 4–6; 24 (1962), 1; 27 (1962), 11.
[94] BSI, *Annual Report, 1958–1959*, p. 13.
[95] Woodward, *Story of Standards*, p. 73; *Shopper's Guide*, 28 (1962), 1.
[96] PRO BT 258/879: CCP 13: *Submission by the CAC of the BSI*; *Shopper's Guide*, 10 (1959), 1.
[97] PRO BT 258/879: CCP 18: *Submission by BSI*.

relations with its paymasters, the manufacturers. The work of the Advertising Association was praised for its effectiveness in correcting misleading advertisements.[98] It avoided making a strong public pronouncement on resale price maintenance, a form of business protection to which the Consumers' Association was strongly opposed.[99] And it supported further investigation, rather than outright condemnation, of the mounting evidence that advertisers were co-operating with newspapers to disguise advertisements as objective features on consumer goods.[100] The purpose of consumers, the CAC argued, was not to oppose business. Rather they were to act as 'patrons' who could 'endow industry and commerce' with the application of their 'fine discrimination'.[101] The CAC was not to 'live in an ivory tower, pronouncing judgement on this and that product and leaving the consumer and manufacturer to heed or profit if they can'.[102] Instead, the key to promoting the consumer cause was through the maintenance of 'frequent and fruitful' contact with industry.

Within such a policy, consumerism was to become more about disciplining the consumer rather than the market. Its chief publication, *Shopper's Guide*, edited by the well-established consumer journalist, Elizabeth Gundrey, was developed with the 'one aim' of promoting 'wise shopping': helping consumers to 'distinguish between the good, the not-so-good, and the frankly bad that confront you whenever you go to a shop'.[103] Consumers were respectable women, not a 'militant body', who would realise that salvation lay in the 'independent' and 'unbiased advice' of the CAC. Articles were written in a chatty, familiar and homely style, common for many women's magazines and women's pages of the period, in which products would be referred to as 'our old friend cotton' and advisors would posit themselves as a typical housewife, blessed with a little more sensible knowledge about a particular issue.[104] The lesson to be learnt was that the consumer must act and think as an individual. The shopper was taught to 'judge for herself' and 'to watch the scale' and that complaining worked because retailers preferred that 'you returned the goods and explained your complaint than told all your friends that So-and-so's store is "no good"'.[105] Judgement and discrimination came not only through the rational assessment of objective criteria but through the innate skills of the housewife and the virtues of femininity. Marghanita Laski taught that in an age of reason, 'the old techniques of feeling still have their part to play': 'our senses still have the final

[98] *Shopper's Guide*, 6 (1958), 14.
[99] *Shopper's Guide*, 18 (1961), 5.   [100] *Shopper's Guide*, 22 (1961), 1.
[101] 'Consumers as patrons', *Shopper's Guide*, 20 (1961), 1.
[102] *Shopper's Guide*, 9 (1959), 1.   [103] *Shopper's Guide*, 1 (1957), 1, 4.
[104] *Ibid.*, p. 22.   [105] *Shopper's Guide*, 3 (1957), 22; 1 (1957), 12–16; 11 (1959), 5–7.

decision'.[106] Even when comparative tests were introduced in the second edition, education about 'good homemaking' remained key.[107] Unlike *Which?*, *Shopper's Guide* featured no 'best buy', refusing to influence the market through collective advice. Testing was to provide only the facts, 'And on these facts you can come to an objective decision about what you will buy. Yours, we emphasise, is the choice – not ours.'[108] *Shopper's Guide* remained a means to create first and foremost ideal consumers; only from these would an ideal market emerge.

Perhaps because of its traditional women's magazine style and its refusal to offer clearer advice on particular goods, *Shopper's Guide* failed to attract the imagination of the new consuming public. Consumer activists of the time, and even those on the CAC, admitted it was too 'dull' and not as much 'fun' as *Which?*[109] Detailed factual statements about such goods as men's socks would be presented alongside scientific tables of the fibre content with little or no interpretation.[110] Articles on screwdrivers were unlikely to appeal to the 50,000 subscribers, many of whom were connected to the women's organisations within the NCW.[111] And front cover images reinforced gender roles which may have put off the increasing ranks of men who were content to classify themselves as consumers. In the light of the success of *Which?*, *Shopper's Guide* sought to defend its refusal to identify a 'best buy' and reproduced a satirical sketch on *Which?* from the *Guardian* which suggested that too much consumer guidance destroyed choice, extended the 'police-state tyranny', infringed the 'sacred liberty of the individual' and urged instead a 'Fair Play for Manufacturers movement' and for consumers to 'make a bad buy today!'[112] This defence of a consumerism which allied the middle-class housewife with her businessman husband failed to save the magazine. After an unsuccessful short-lived venture of the BSI to sell it to a new company, the Consumer Advisory Trust, set up by Michael Heseltine's Cornmarket Press, *Shopper's Guide* published its thirty-fourth and final issue in May 1963.[113] By this time, the position of the CAC had in any case become untenable, thanks to the creation of the state-funded Consumer Council in 1963, following the recommendations of the Molony Committee. Consumerism at the BSI was subsequently restricted to the original WAC which continued to advise on the creation of standards and its Chair

---

[106] M. Laski, 'Use your senses', *Shopper's Guide*, 4 (1958), 30.
[107] *Shopper's Guide*, 16 (1960), 1.   [108] *Shopper's Guide*, 2 (1957), 1.
[109] Interviews with Rosemary McRobert, 25 March 2002, Rachel Waterhouse, 8 March 2002; BSIL OC/11: M62/405: 26 March 1962.
[110] *Shopper's Guide*, 6 (1958), 23–5.   [111] *Ibid.*, pp. 10–11; 8 (1959), 1.
[112] *Shopper's Guide*, 27 (1962), 1, 16.
[113] *Shopper's Guide*, 29 (1962), 1; 31 (1963), 2; 34 (1963), 1.

Figure 4   The Supershopper: publicity material of the BSI, OFT, CA and Inner London Education Authority (1976).

became a member of the new Consumer Council.[114] The BSI increased its collaborative work on testing with the Consumers' Association, but for most of the 1960s and 1970s, the consumer within the BSI imagination remained the middle-class housewife. She was the sensible, traditional housewife, though she developed into a type of auntie figure publishing pamphlets with titles such as 'what every mum should know'.[115] In 1974, the WAC was literally embodied as the 'supershopper', an experienced middle-aged woman who guided, through a series of educational cartoons, the young and foolish Suzie around the pitfalls faced on the high street (see Figure 4).[116] The BSI thus persisted with an image of the consumer increasingly at odds with that found in an expanding grass-roots, professional and even masculine form of consumerism.

[114] Woodward, *Story of Standards*, p. 75; WAC, *21st Anniversary Year, 1972* (London: BSI, 1972).
[115] BSI Consumer Affairs Division, *What Every Mum Should Know About British Standards* (London, 1976); BSI Archive, leaflet on the work of Consumer Standards Advisory Committee, 1971. On the details of the work of the WAC from the early 1960s, see Thompson, *History of the WAC*, chaps. 6–9.
[116] BSI, CA, Office of Fair Trading and Inner London Education Authority, *Suzie and the Supershopper* (London, 1974).

The women and businessmen connected to the BSI, though, had played a crucial role in bridging the gap in consumerism as Britain moved from a period of austerity to a world of new goods with which both the traditional skills of the shopper and the older politics of necessitous consumption no longer seemed quite so relevant. While the women of the WAC and later the CAC could argue that they were actual representatives *of* the consumer, they also, along with an increasing number of journalists, economists, retailers and social scientists, spoke *for* the consumer, defining the consumer and his or her interest as they did so. Through careful selection of consumer advocates, the BSI went some way to creating a consumer taught to think in terms of him or herself not as an individual with the rights to protection and provision, but as an individual for whom the responsibility for one's purchases lay with oneself. Advice, information, tests and representation might be carried out on his or her behalf, but ultimately consumers had to rely on their own rationality, just as orthodox economics suggested. This type of consumerism did not go uncontested, but the dominance of the housewife-consumer model owed much to the lack of initiative taken by previous organisations of the consumer, especially the Co-operative movement. The BSI was also aided by those business organisations which had taken a more 'enlightened' approach to consumers – bodies such as the Good Housekeeping Institute and the Retail Trading Standards Association – and by the women's groups who had allied with business in consumer affairs – for example, the WI and the Electrical Association for Women and the Women's Gas Federation, both of which were automatic representatives on the WAC.[117] Their consumer advocacy both supported the normalcy ascribed to affluent goods in economic textbooks and suggested the solutions to consumer problems ought not to deviate from the normal operation of the market. Here, consumer protection first required the invention of the modern consumer, taught to respect the efforts of business and to recognise the limits within which that protection could take place.

Ultimately, however, this was a type of consumerism that failed to attract the imagination of the public or the spirit of a professional affluent age. As will be seen in the next chapter, the increased attention to consumer affairs in the national newspapers demonstrated the desire for greater guidance in a marketplace which was operated by businesses and industries which could not assume the trust of its consumers. Symbolically, consumers rejected the commonsensical motherly counsel of

---

[117] M. Andrews, *The Acceptable Face of Feminism: The Women's Institute as a Social Movement* (London, 1997); A. Glendinning, ' "Deft fingers" and "persuasive eloquence": the "lady demons" of the English gas industry, 1888–1918', *Women's History Review*, 9:3 (2000), 501–37.

Shopper's Guide and flocked instead to the seemingly professional expertise of *Which?*, with its comparatively more modern and accessible style
and its informed paternalism offered through its 'best buy'. The BSI
may have played a leading role in the development of 'the consumer' in
Britain, but its efforts were insufficient for an affluent section of the consuming public which aimed to play a far more prominent role in its own
making.

7 The professionals: the origins of the organised consumer movement

Today, the Consumers' Association (CA) is regarded as a national institution. It is celebrated for its comparative testing of the value for money of different branded goods in its *Which?* magazine and its recommendation of the 'best buy'. It is called upon by government departments to advise on all matters of consumer affairs. It lobbies Parliament and other official bodies to introduce legislation furthering the interests of the consumer. And it is the first port of call for anyone in the media wishing to obtain a consumer's perspective on any particular economic development. Since its inception in 1956 and the launch of *Which?* the following year, it has run itself as a private, though non-profit-making, company catering to the interests of its paying subscribers. Its success has been dependent on its efficient operation as a business and its efforts to market itself effectively, yet it retains as well the feel of a forward-thinking social movement which was clearly foremost in the minds of many of its founders. This idealist spirit has pervaded the CA's image of itself and, as with all social movements, certain apocryphal stories have emerged of its origins. In the CA's case, and as many of its leaders like to recount, it was an organisation that began in a garage.

Original staff and Council members of the CA like to stress the gung-ho, let's-give-it-a-go ethos of the early years. The initial idea came from Dorothy (Dorrie) Goodman, a young American graduate from the London School of Economics who married Ray Goodman, the Director of PEP, in 1953. Frustrated that there existed no objective help for young couples making their first large-scale purchases, as she had seen in *Consumer Reports* in the United States, she toyed with the idea of setting up a British equivalent of the Consumers' Union. During 1955, the Goodmans began to canvas their friends and associates over dinner and held a first meeting of interested individuals at their home in Canonbury in January 1956. Over the next few months a core emerged which included the Goodmans and their friends Michael Young, the sociologist and immediate predecessor of Ray Goodman at PEP, and John Thirlwell, an

194

academic engineer at Northampton Polytechnic. After an initial meeting of interested individuals arranged in the early summer of 1956 by the Labour MP John Edwards in a private committee room of the House of Commons, Dorothy Goodman began producing several versions of a dummy magazine until her husband obtained a job at the World Bank in Washington in August 1956 and they left for the United States.[1] Young now found himself in charge of the project and he set aside a garage at his Institute for Community Studies in Bethnal Green in which Dorrie deposited the CA 'assets': several files and a desk made from an old marble-topped washstand.[2]

Young and other 'pioneers' have enjoyed stressing the amateur nature of the CA's early history, a time when friendship and enthusiasm eclipsed the absence of funds and specialist knowledge. In the ramshackle offices, intuition was more important than informed research, staff and acquaintances became the testers of branded goods and everybody 'sort of mucked in together'.[3] But this surface amateurism masked a professional ethos which pervaded the actions and spirit of many of the consumer activists who brought to the organisation much technical and intellectual leadership. Young himself was able to use his connections in politics and the media to publicise the launch of *Which?* in October 1957, the press conference in the Waldorf Hotel attracting around 100 journalists. The consequent publicity led to the attraction of around 10,000 subscribers within the first few weeks and 23,000 by January 1958.[4] At the end its first year, the CA had received free publicity in over 300 publications and 47,000 members were paying an annual subscription of 10s.[5] Young was able to employ a Director and a new editor and in February 1958 was able to take the CA out of the Bethnal Green garage and place twelve staff into a slightly more orderly set of offices in Great James Street in Holborn.[6]

Harold Perkin has argued that the class society and entrepreneurial ideal of the nineteenth century was eventually eclipsed by the values of the 'professional society', a society based on trained expertise, selection by merit and the prominence of self-made men 'who had risen by native

---

[1] Archive of the Consumers' Association (hereafter CAA) Box 27: *European Consumer Organisations: A Digest of Their Work* (1956); J. Epstein, *The Early Days of Consumers' Association: Interviews with CA's Founders and Those Who Carried on Their Work* (London, 1989), pp. 8–9 (Dorothy Goodman); E. Roberts, *Which? 25: Consumers' Association, 1957–1982* (London, 1982), pp. 12–13.

[2] Roberts, *Which?*, p. 7; CAA 27: Epstein, *Interviews*, p. 23 (Michael Young), p. 199 (Edith Rudinger).

[3] Epstein, *Interviews*, pp. 44–5 (Eirlys Roberts), p. 122 (Jennifer Jenkins).

[4] *Ibid.*, p. 27 (Michael Young).

[5] *Which?*, 1:2 (1958), 3; CAA 30: *First Annual Report, 1957–1958*, p. 2.

[6] *Which?*, 1:3 (1958), 3.

ability'.[7] These individuals were to play a quantitatively more significant role in post-war reconstruction than they had in any other period, fulfilling Orwell's prediction that older class distinctions would gave way to 'the younger sons of the bourgeoisie' in a mild-mannered English revolution: 'Most of its directing brains will come from the new indeterminate class of skilled workers, technical experts, airmen, scientists, architects and journalists, the people who feel at home in the radio and ferro-concrete age.'[8] The members of the consumer movement were precisely such professionals. As will be seen, they shared not an ideology or a set of political convictions, but an ethos of professionalism which meant they believed that the objective and comparative assessment of branded goods would rectify the imbalances in the marketplace and enable the consumer to become the true sovereign of the economy. They were a forward-thinking group of men and women, often young and almost always university educated, who felt the consumer ought to be accorded due regard in the transition from austerity to affluence.

Little has appeared on the history of post-Second World War affluent British consumerism.[9] No one has yet written of the social, economic and cultural specificity of a generation born in the first half of the twentieth century and who looked with optimism to organisations such as the CA and the role it could play in the new affluent society. Just as Labour Party planners looked forward to the growth of the welfare state, just as Herbert Morrison aimed to create an image of a future society in the Festival of Britain in 1951 and just as urban planners set about the redevelopment of Britain's cities and new towns, so too did consumers seek a reformed marketplace in which they would not only share in the benefits of reconstruction but would dictate the direction of business according to their own interests. Of the interpretations that have been made of other consumer movements, judgements based on the reactions to the perceived materialism of the 1980s have clouded assessments of the consumerists and what they stood for at the end of the 1950s. Contrasting the comparative-testing consumerism of the late twentieth century

---

[7] H. Perkin, *The Rise of Professional Society: England since 1880* (1989; London, 1990), p. xiii.

[8] G. Orwell, *The Lion and the Unicorn* (1941; Harmondsworth, 1982), p. 113; B. Conekin, F. Mort and C. Waters (eds.), *Moments of Modernity: Reconstructing Britain, 1945–1964* (London, 1999).

[9] See, however, D. A. Aaker and G. S. Day (eds.), *Consumerism: Search for the Consumer Interest*, 3rd edn (Basingstoke, 1978); Y. Gabriel and T. Lang, *The Unmanageable Consumer: Contemporary Consumption and its Fragmentation* (London, 1995); J. Winward, 'The organised consumer and consumer information co-operatives', in R. Keat, N. Whiteley and N. Abercrombie (eds.), *The Authority of the Consumer* (London, 1994), pp. 75–90; G. Smith, *The Consumer Interest* (London, 1982).

with the radical consumerism of an earlier period, Gary Cross has written of the American Consumers' Union that it has 'tended to reinforce both the individualism and the materialism of American consumption'.[10] This is undoubtedly a valid interpretation and it is certain that for the vast majority of subscribers to *Which?*, consumerism meant only value for money for the individual. For early activists too, value-for-money was the end point of the CA, but in the context of the 1950s and 1960s, when manufacturers were perceived to care all too little for the needs of the consumer, there was an idealism in this goal. Reflecting on the history of consumerism, CA workers admit to the naivety of the view that the problems of the market could be solved solely by individual empowerment and best buy advice. But to dismiss consumerism as a reinforcement of acquisitive individualism is both to gloss over the feelings and motivations of hundreds of thousands of consumers at the time and to ignore the extension of consumerism into fields well beyond comparative testing. In what follows there will be a more sympathetic attempt to understand, firstly, the motivations behind what was largely a middle-class social movement (though the ascription of class is an inadequate categorisation here). A second section will detail the 'ethos' of the CA's version of consumerism in order to understand its members' vision of the marketplace. And, thirdly, an investigation of the appeal of consumerism will be made, by both exploring the social and cultural values of the subscribers to *Which?* and the spread of dozens of local consumer groups from the beginning of the 1960s. Certainly, early consumer activists did promote an individualism, but it was an individualism that did not see its goal as the market liberalisation reforms of the 1980s from which many analysts of consumer society have reacted.

Motives

Something of a feel for the consumers' movement can be obtained from the list of twenty-five friends and colleagues of Young and the Goodmans who had been active in creating the dummy magazine and who attended the meeting at the House of Commons in the early summer of 1956. Most belonged to the professions of Perkin's thesis: economists, solicitors, engineers, scientists, social scientists, academics, civil servants and business executives. In addition, there were thirty-three 'outside advisors' including the influential barrister, Gerald Gardiner, who advised the CA (or the British Association of Consumers as it was still called at

---

[10] G. Cross, *An All-Consuming Century: Why Commercialism Won in Modern America* (New York, 2000), p. 135.

this point) that it would be safe under the law of libel against prosecution for defamation of goods, members of the BSI's consumer bodies, consumer journalists, trade unionists, a Co-operative and Labour Party MP (Oram), Roger Diplock of the RTSA and Eirlys Roberts from the Treasury who was later to become the editor of *Which?* and the CA research director. Despite the appearance of five figures connected to the Conservative Party, the majority might be said to have been sympathetic to a centre-left agenda, though Young committed the CA at an early stage to political neutrality and he selected his Council carefully to ensure cross-party support. The original Council included James Douglas from the Conservative Research Department and later its Director.[11] When he (to later rejoin), the Goodmans and three others resigned at an early stage, they were replaced by Jennifer Jenkins, the wife of the Labour politician Roy, and Young's close friend and spokesman for the centre-left Anthony Crosland.[12] However, Young also appointed the Conservative MP, Geoffrey Rippon, never losing sight of the need to appear above the political fray and this has been a persistent policy ever since. In subsequent years, the Council has included the Conservative MPs Philip Goodhart and Douglas Hogg, acting as symbolic counterweights to what might otherwise be seen as potential left-wing bias.[13]

With such a broad body of support from a range of prominent figures and with some limited financial help from the US Consumers' Union and the Elmhirsts of Dartington (with whom Young had been closely connected since attending their school), the CA was able to start its operations with immediate success.[14] Peta Fordham was appointed as a full-time director, though she left soon afterwards as she felt the CA was taking too hostile an attitude to manufacturers and the CA felt she was insufficiently rigorous in her attitude to testing.[15] Young took over until the appointment of Caspar Brook in 1958, though at this time many of the CA Council were heavily involved in the day-to-day running of the organisation, not least through the scrutiny of all the test reports.[16] Crucially,

[11] Epstein, *Interviews*, p. 78 (James Douglas).   [12] CAA 30: *First Annual Report*, p. 3.

[13] CAA 26: *CA Newsletter*, 1 (1983), 4–5; CA, *Which? and Consumers' Association* (1965; London, 1972), pp. 58–62; Epstein, *Interviews*, p. 51 (Eirlys Roberts).

[14] A. Briggs, *Michael Young: Social Entrepreneur* (Basingstoke, 2001); CA, *Thirty Years of Which?: Consumers' Association, 1957–1987* (London, 1987), p. 6; S. Franks, 'Selling consumer protection: competitive strategies of the Consumers' Association, 1957–1990, MPhil thesis, University of Oxford (2000), p. 26; Roberts, *Which?* p. 14; Epstein, *Interviews*, p. 28 (Michael Young).

[15] Roberts, *Which?*, p. 22; CA, *Annual Report, 1957–1958*, p. 1; *Which?*, 1:1 (1957), 30; Epstein, *Interviews*, p. 42 (Eirlys Roberts); PRO BT 258/878: Minutes of Meetings of Committee on Consumer Protection (10 April 1961), Minute 33:205: Oral evidence (Fordham).

[16] Epstein, *Interviews*, p. 79 (James Douglas), p. 183 (Jeremy Mitchell).

Eirlys Roberts was also employed as editor. She had previously worked at the Information Unit at the Treasury, preparing reports on commodities while also writing articles on consumer issues for the *Observer* and maintaining strong links with the women's organisations connected to the NCW and ultimately the BSI.[17] The clarity she brought to test write-ups is often argued to be a major reason for the popularity of *Which?*

The CA brought together a diverse range of individuals united by their faith in expertise and motivated by the common feeling that the consumer was being insufficiently considered by British manufacturers who too often brought highly complex, but nevertheless poor quality, goods onto the market.[18] But beneath such reactions to the immediate issues surrounding the marketplace, the new consumer activists brought with them a range of political beliefs and individual motivations. Firstly, there were direct links with previous consumer bodies. Michael Young had continued to discuss consumer testing during his time as head of PEP.[19] Ray Goodman succeeded him and both he and Dorothy maintained regular links with PEP figures such as Israel Sieff of Marks & Spencer who had been closely involved in the PEP discussions about consumerism in the 1930s.[20] Young then went on to commit the Labour Party to an investigation of the creation of a Consumer Advice Centre in 1949 and during the 1950s he used his many contacts in politics, the voluntary sector and the universities to recruit members to the CA Council.[21] The CA was also aware of the importance of not alienating existing consumer bodies in the 1950s. Media contacts were used to create discussions between the likes of Eirlys Roberts, Rosemary McRobert, Marghanita Laski and Elizabeth Gundrey, and the women of the BSI consumer panels were invited to early CA working group meetings. In this sense, there were important continuities with both the politics of necessitous consumption and the consumer organisations who did not seek to establish a position as independent from business as the CA.

Secondly, however, many of the early members of CA were motivated by a critique of advertising which was again becoming prominent in the 1950s. Inspired by many American works, many felt the Big Brother of Orwell's *1984* was not manifesting itself in the new welfare state but in the power of large-scale corporations and the advertising industry. In 1957, Packard's immensely popular *The Hidden Persuaders* spoke of

---

[17] CAA 27: National Council of Women, *Conference on Consumer Protection* (April 1956).
[18] CAA 14: P. Fletcher, 'When we were very young', *Which? Tenth Anniversary Issue* (5 October 1967), p. 290; *Which?*, 1:1 (1957), 2; *Guardian* (22 April 1959), p. 3; E. Roberts, *Consumers* (London, 1966), pp. 78–9; Roberts, *Which?*, p. 8.
[19] Franks, 'Selling consumer protection', p. 27.
[20] Epstein, *Interviews*, p. 15 (Dorothy Goodman).   [21] *Ibid.*, p. 20.

the manipulative power of big business.[22] It built on other attempts to question the role of abundance in American life and the standardisation thought to emerge from suburban living.[23] While these critiques extended into the counter-cultural questioning of the whole purpose of consumer society in the United States, in Britain worries over the power of advertising remained an issue across the political spectrum.[24] Richard Hoggart and Raymond Williams questioned the role of culture within mass consumption and mass advertising, while populist accounts of the advertising industry continued to appear in the late 1950s and early 1960s.[25] So widespread were the criticisms voiced in the media and through the Molony Committee on Consumer Protection that the advertising profession published its own counter-arguments and the Advertising Association pre-empted any legislative interference with the creation of the Advertising Standards Authority and the publication of the first British Code of Advertising Practice in 1962.[26] The critique of advertising stretches back to William Morris' Society for Checking the Abuses of Public Advertising, the sentiments behind the creation of the National Trust and the condemnations of mass culture by Leavis and his colleagues in *Scrutiny*. But these feelings were revived in the 1950s through the creation of the Advertising Inquiry Council (AIC). Although not set up until March 1959, the AIC was to receive support from the CA, as well as other bodies such as the RTSA, the CAC, Christian groups, the medical profession and women's and citizens' organisations. Led by Elizabeth Gundrey and the two legal experts, Harvey Cole and Aubrey Diamond, the AIC aimed to protect the individual consumer from exploitative and misleading advertising and campaigned for greater independent regulation of the profession, since self-regulation was felt to have proved ineffective.[27] It

[22] V. Packard, *The Hidden Persuaders* (1957; Harmondsworth, 1960); V. Packard, *The Waste Makers* (New York, 1960).

[23] J. K. Galbraith, *American Capitalism: The Concept of Countervailing Power* (1952; Harmondsworth, 1963); J. K. Galbraith, *The Affluent Society* (Cambridge, MA, 1958); W. H. Whyte, *The Organization Man* (1956; Harmondsworth, 1960).

[24] J. Fisher, *The Plot to Make You Buy* (New York, 1968); D. Riesman, *The Lonely Crowd* (New Haven, 1950); D. Riesman, *Abundance for What* (London, 1956); H. Marcuse, *One Dimensional Man* (London, 1964); G. Cross, *Time and Money: The Making of Consumer Culture* (London, 1993), pp. 188–9.

[25] R. Hoggart, *The Uses of Literacy* (1957; Harmondsworth, 1973); R. Williams, *Communications* (Harmondsworth, 1962); R. Williams, *Culture and Society, 1780–1950* (London, 1958); J. Todd, *The Big Sell* (London, 1961); A. Wilson (ed.), *Advertising and the Community* (Manchester, 1968).

[26] R. Harris and A. Seldon, *Advertising and the Public* (London, 1962); PRO BT 258/885: CCP 167: Submission by the Advertising Association; plus various other industry submissions on advertising in CCP 354–62.

[27] PRO BT 258/878: Meeting 39 (19 June 1961), Minute 39:237: Further Submission by Advertising Inquiry Council; Minute 39:328; BT 258/885: CCP 168: *Submission by the Advertising Inquiry Council*; H. R. Cole and A. L. Diamond, *The Consumer and the Law* (London, 1960).

also acted as a watchdog on television and newspaper advertising practices and, as if to point to the longer term influences on 1950s consumerism, it called its newsletter *Scrutiny*.[28]

Tied to this were similar aesthetic considerations in design. G. M. Trevelyan had identified in the work of the self-appointed philanthropists of the National Trust a Ruskinian 'spiritual economy' which attempted to raise the level of discrimination of the masses.[29] Such an instinct could be seen too in the concerns with housing and domestic life by many women's organisations in the inter-war period. But the Council for Art and Industry (CAI), set up in 1934, best represents this early concern with improving design through consumer empowerment. Drawing on the skills of such figures as Frank Pick, the designer of the London Underground posters, and Elizabeth Denby, the housing worker, the CAI made some early attempts in the direction of discriminating consumption, putting forward an educational policy and demonstrating for themselves how the working-class home could be furnished according to rational principles of good design, utility, and decent standards of taste.[30] Although wound up with the onset of war, the CAI was replaced in 1944 with the Council for Industrial Design which again embarked upon a programme of improving consumer choice. It contributed to such events as the Britain Can Make It Exhibition of 1946 and the Festival of Britain in 1951, as well as producing a number of short films such as *Deadly Lampshade* which advised young couples on setting up a new home.[31]

However, the CA could not have emerged in the 1950s if the consumer had not also become a man. The association of consumption with women stretched back to the eighteenth century. To oversimplify, the self-denying protestant ethic saw sober and black-suited bourgeois men engage in the world of creation and production, establishing at the same time a separate spheres ideology which located women in the domestic arena concerned with the maintenance of the family's status through the outward display of material possessions.[32] Men were not trivial shoppers: instead, they were self-styled collectors, rational purchasers of goods which, ideally,

[28] Consumer Council, *Information for Consumer Education* (London, 1965), p. 42.

[29] G. M. Trevelyan, *Must England's Beauty Perish?* (London, 1929).

[30] CAI, *Education for the Consumer* (London, 1935); CAI, *The Working Class Home: Its Furnishing and Equipment* (London, 1937).

[31] J. M. Woodham, 'Managing British design reform II: The film *Deadly Nightshade* – an ill-fated episode in the politics of "good taste"', *Journal of Design History*, 9:2 (1996), 101–15; R. Stewart, *Design and British Industry* (London, 1987); P. J. Maguire and J. M. Woodham (eds.), *Design and Cultural Politics in Postwar Britain: The Britain Can Make It Exhibition of 1946* (London, 1997); N. Whiteley, *Design for Society* (London, 1993).

[32] V. de Grazia and E. Furlough (eds.), *The Sex of Things: Gender and Consumption in Historical Perspective* (London, 1996); L. Davidoff and C. Hall, *Family Fortunes: Men and Women of the English Middle Class, 1780–1850* (London, 1987); J. Tosh, *A Man's Place: Masculinity and the Middle-Class Home in Victorian England* (London, 1999).

might be displayed together in a public institution or museum. For instance, nineteenth-century pipe and cigar smokers shrouded their habit in a discourse of independence and individuality, each distinctive mixture of tobacco serving to define the bourgeois liberal self. Smoking was therefore purposeful, useful and rational, a practice far from the irrational consuming desires of the mass market.[33] The same, too, might be said of wine, tailored clothing, gambling and art, but increasingly historians have uncovered the 'hidden consumer', be it in the playgrounds of London's *fin-de-siècle* West End or in the masculine cult of motoring before the Second World War.[34] Whenever goods became more technical, men became the shoppers. In inter-war Coventry, certain affluent working-class men were considered 'gadget fiends': those who, in the canteens of Coventry's light industries, traded information about bicycles, motorbikes, cars, cameras, gramophones and radios. In works magazines, they described in loving detail the technical aspects of second-hand goods in the 'For Sale and Wanted' columns, the language of objective technical rationality learnt in production being applied to consumption.[35] Just as 'in the workplace engineers based estimations of skill and job stature on the beauty or otherwise of colleague's toolboxes,' so too were they beginning to employ a language that enabled men to become the arbiters of taste and social rank in the home and the suburb.[36]

It is likely we can apply these masculine discourses of consumption to white-collar workers as well, though this is clearly an area for much further research. If we take seriously the argument of US masculinity, that the alienation felt at work by the post-Second World War 'organisation man' encouraged a compensatory investment of time and energy in the home, the family and domestic consumption, then we can speculate that the expansion of the middle classes in Britain brought a similar focus on material culture. Perkin's professionals did not have available to them the fetishism of production found in John Stuart Mill or the reification of artisanship and the dignity of labour arguments found throughout the labour movement. And not all were business executives, admittedly no longer closely connected to the actual processes of production, but capable of making

---

[33] M. Hilton, *Smoking in British Popular Culture, 1800–2000* (Manchester, 2000).

[34] C. Breward, *The Hidden Consumer: Masculinities, Fashion and City Life, 1860–1914* (Manchester, 1999); S. O'Connell, *The Car in British Society: Class, Gender and Motoring, 1896–1939* (Manchester, 1998); M. A. Swiencicki, 'Consuming brotherhood: men's culture, style and recreation as consumer culture, 1880–1930', in L. B. Glickman (ed.), *Consumer Society in American History: A Reader* (Ithaca, 1999), pp. 207–40.

[35] L. Whitworth, 'Men, women, shops and "little, shiny homes": the consuming of Coventry, 1930–1939', Ph.D. thesis, University of Warwick (1997), pp. 191–4; L. Whitworth, 'Shop/shopfloor: men's sense of belonging in 1930s Coventry', in T. Putnam, R. Facey and V. Swales (eds.), *Making and Unmaking: Creative and Critical Practice in a Design World* (London, 2000), pp. 118–31.

[36] Whitworth, 'Men, women, shops', p. 197.

a fetish of the machinery of manufacture, creating models and reproductions of vital instruments for their offices.[37] Instead, white-collar workers began to place emotional and intellectual investment in consumption rather than production. It is no coincidence that just as men became consumers in the 1950s – or became happier to accept the description – they became involved in consumer organisations which produced testing magazines that employed a language that had been formerly associated with production. As will be seen below, *Which?* assessed goods according to supposedly rational, unemotional, utilitarian, scientific and objective criteria, denying a space for aesthetics or subjective preference. Man's involvement in the CA changed the sex of the consumer, and so too did it transform the language of consumption.

This increasing attention to commodities, by both men and women, was reflected in the expansion of consumer journalism from the 1940s. Most importantly, John Hilton, a former critic of the 1919 Profiteering Acts, began to expose what he saw as the most prominent abuses in the marketplace, such as the credit system's exploitative 'tallyman', the sale of sub-standard goods and various other 'rackets'.[38] In the 1930s he broadcast regularly through radio series such as 'This Way Out', 'This and That' and 'On Having a Bit of Money' and he wrote frequent articles in the *News Chronicle*, acting as a social crusader for the problems faced by individuals in their everyday lives.[39] During the war, he continued to broadcast on domestic issues through 'John Hilton Talking' and, after his death in 1945, the *News of the World* named their advice bureau after him. This dealt with around 2–3,000 letters per week, mainly on issues facing the citizen as a worker and as a member of the armed forces but occasionally in regard to consumption.[40] After 1945, the John Hilton bureau dealt with issues such as housing, education, pensions, legal issues, marital difficulties, consumer problems, social welfare and employment difficulties. The attention given to the consumer gradually increased over the years. By 1950 the letters column was often devoted to topics such as the licensing laws, hospital waiting lists, the purchase tax, small debts, credit facilities, tipping, dealing with shopkeepers and hire purchase agreements.[41] Consumer advice quickly spread to appear in a range of newspapers. Marghanita Laski and Eirlys Roberts contributed to the *Observer*, Rosemary McRobert worked for *Home Economics*, 'Leslie

[37] M. Roper, *Masculinity and the British Organisation Man since 1945* (Oxford, 1994).
[38] J. Hilton, *A Study of Trade Organisations and Combinations in the UK* (London, 1919); E. Nixon, *John Hilton: The Story of His Life* (London, 1946).
[39] J. Hilton, *This and That: The Broadcast Talks of John Hilton* (London, 1938).
[40] Nixon, *John Hilton*, p. 305; J. Hilton, *Rich Man, Poor Man* (London, 1944).
[41] Column by 'The director of the John Hilton Bureau', *News of the World*, various issues, 1955. The archives of the John Hilton Bureau have been deposited at the University of Sussex, Special Collections.

Adrian' wrote in the *Guardian* and Elizabeth Gundrey in the *News Chronicle*.[42] Gundrey in particular achieved a broader popular recognition. She went on to edit *Shopper's Guide* at the BSI and in the 1960s she contributed regularly to the *Guardian* and published a number of advice manuals and exposés of high-pressure selling techniques.[43] This journalism, which saw most newspapers providing consumer columns by the end of the 1950s, built on other forms of consumer advice. Eirlys Roberts had worked with Lydia Horton at The Treasury's Economic Information Unit producing, among other things, advice literature on the economics of everyday life, and liaising with various women's groups through regular conferences on the quality of British commodities in order to account for the country's economic performance compared to its foreign rivals.[44] In 1956, a potential rival to the CA appeared briefly. Consumer Protection published just one issue of *The Consumer*, insisting that it was a non-party organisation committed to taking up consumers' issues with manufacturers. Consumer Protection could not boast the same independence as the CA and was clearly connected to several important trade interests, operating out of the same address as the Cheap Food League and the Council for the Reduction of Taxation.[45] It is doubtful whether an organisation so closely connected to commerce would have been able to speak for a body of consumers increasingly confident about putting across its own views.

Consumer advice columns further built on a broad cross-class and cross-party consensus emerging after the war calling for far greater levels of consumer protection, whether through the state or voluntary action. Although there were ideological divisions most were agreed that the consumer required further attention and consideration in a new economic climate. Conservative Party representatives called on industry to give 'supremacy to the consumer' and admitted of the need to curb areas of advertising to protect the 'ill-organised, inarticulate' consumers.[46] Trade

---

[42] Epstein, *Interviews*, p. 39 (Eirlys Roberts), p. 146 (Rosemary McRobert), p. 9 (Dorothy Goodman); Roberts, *Which?*, p. 15; Interview with Rosemary McRobert, 25 March 2002; CAA 27: E. Roberts, 'Cool customers' (9 December 1963), p. 6.

[43] E. Gundrey, 'Consumers' column', *Guardian* (4 June 1962), p. 6; (2 July 1962), p. 6; (3 December 1962), p. 6; E. Gundrey *Your Money's Worth* (Harmondsworth, 1962); E. Gundrey, At *Your Service: A Consumer's Guide to the Service Trades and Professions* (Harmondsworth, 1964); E. Gundrey, A *Foot in the Door: An Exposé of High Pressure Sales Methods* (London, 1965). E. Gundrey, *Help!* (London, 1967); Roberts, *Consumers*, p. 75.

[44] Roberts, *Consumers*, pp. 69–72; Roberts, *Which?*, pp. 9–10.

[45] Franks, 'Selling consumer protection', pp. 18–19.

[46] P. Goodhart, M. Bemrose, J. Douglas, I. MacArthur, P. McLaughlin and J. B. Wood, *Choice: A Report on Consumer Protection* (London, 1961); M. Baynes, *Advertising on Trial: The Case for the Consumer* (London, 1956); P. Goodhart, *A Nation of Consumers* (London, 1965).

unions such as the Association for Scientific Workers wanted more scientists to assist the shopper in choosing from a long list of technical, but nevertheless, shoddy goods.[47] Later, in 1957, the TUC was quick to lend its support to the CA.[48] The Fabians sought to remind politicians that 'goods are produced in order to be consumed' and that consumers required much greater 'impartial advice'.[49] Although the Co-operative movement remained suspicious of affluence in general it recognised the need for providing some guidance to the consumer in a 'complex' world.[50] For the Labour Party, it was no longer 'good enough for traders to say that housewives should find out for themselves what goods are like'.[51] And for Liberals, despite their principled objection to state interference in consumption, it was recognised that the richness and variety of material goods would only be improved through measures to encourage 'an increased ability to choose wisely'.[52] If we add to this list the consumer policies of the businessmen at the BSI discussed in chapter 6, it is clear that the CA emerged when critics from across the political spectrum were ready to defend the individual consumer at a time of increasing affluence but also confusion.

The ethic of consumerism: a movement without an ideology?

Given this context of a broad range of demands for a greater focus on the consumer, the CA followed a non-controversial form of individual empowerment to which no party or vested interest could seriously object. The CA was to operate principally as a comparative testing organisation, providing reports on the value for money of different branded goods. People were to buy *Which?* not for any political or ideological commitment to the position of the consumer in society as in an older Co-operative Union rhetoric, but 'to get accurate facts to help them make decisions about the things they buy'.[53] Indeed, accuracy and objectivity were promoted as ends in themselves, the first issue of *Which?* telling readers that

---

[47] Association of Scientific Workers, *Spotlight on Shopping: Consumer Research* (London, 1951).
[48] Warwick MRC MSS 292/660.77/1: Extracts from Minutes of Economic Committee (9 October 1957).
[49] C. D. Harbury, *Efficiency and the Consumer* (London, 1958), p. 1; J. F. Northcott, *Value for Money? The Case for a Consumers' Advice Service* (London, 1953), p. 1.
[50] Co-operative Union, *Consumers and the Community* (London, 1961); BT 258/882, 'CCP 9: Co-operative Union Memorandum for Submission'.
[51] E. Burton, *The Battle of the Consumer* (London, 1954).
[52] Liberal Party Consumer Committee, *Consumer Protection* (London, 1962); J. Grimond, *Better Buys* (London, n.d.).
[53] CA, *Which? and Consumers' Association* (1965; London, 1972), p. 13.

it existed 'solely to help YOU'.[54] At all times, the CA stressed its independence from business, refusing any sort of hospitality from companies, even lunches, and no Council members were to have any connections with business whatsoever.[55] To this end, the CA approach has been described as 'puritanical'. It did consider purchasing shares in each of the UK's fifty leading companies, in order that it could attend AGMs and influence commercial policy. It was decided instead that only rigid independence, however, would maintain its reputation for fair testing with the public. That said, the CA was not against business. It hoped that 'the good manufacturer will stand to gain by our work' and 'the shoddy' will be forced to improve. Indeed, it saw its function as 'bridging the gap between maker and user'. In 1965, the then Director of the CA, Peter Goldman, set out the most basic premise of organised consumerism which was to direct the efforts of the CA until at least 1970. The CA existed to create a more equitable marketplace, improving 'the imbalance between the strong seller and the weak buyer, since, inevitably, 'the more technologically advanced a society becomes, and the larger the cornucopia of goods and services it produces, the less able is the individual consumer to rely on his experience or his hunch'.[56]

How the CA was to achieve this was through a faith in science. Strengthening an already existing belief in the potential of the technician and the laboratory, the CA emphasised at all times the rigorous testing procedures to which it subjected its goods. Subscribers were canvassed for the goods they wished to have tested, Project Officers determined the test criteria and brands were purchased direct from the high street by a full-time paid shopper before being sent to various testing facilities and later to the CA's own laboratories in Harpenden. Test results were scrutinised first by a legal team and often by the entire Council, before final revisions were made by Roberts who ensured the technical reports were made accessible to a lay audience. In the first year, the CA undertook 180 tests on twenty different types of good.[57] Typical commodities covered in the early editions of *Which?* included pens, electric convector heaters, cotton fabrics, washing machines, hand tools, toasters, slimming cures, sunglasses, bathroom scales, hot-water bottles, children's toys, stomach powders and aspirin. Science and the scientist were put to the fore (see Figure 5). In a report on electric kettles the articles and the imagery seemed to stress both the fetishism of the commodity, the power of science and the

[54] *Which?*, 1:1 (1957), p. 3.
[55] Roberts, *Which?*, p. 19; Epstein, *Interviews*, p. 49 (Eirlys Roberts).
[56] CAA 27: P. Goldman, 'The relationship of consumer organisations to the work of standardisation organisations' (1965), p. 1.
[57] CA, *Annual Report, 1957–1958*, p. 1.

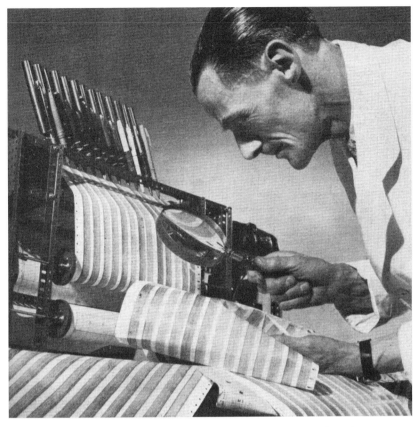

Figure 5   Scientist on the front cover of *Which?*, 1:4 (1958).

empowerment of the consumer. An array of kettles was pictured under-going a particular test in a laboratory. This was juxtaposed with a picture of a white-coated scientist performing an 'electrical leakage text'. Finally, the scientist was seen with the kettle explaining to a housewife-consumer the particular virtues of the brand being considered. She herself stands notebook in hand, firmly grasping her handbag and with a look of serious-minded critical scrutiny across her face.[58] Despite the acceptance of the de-sexing of the consumer in other CA literature, here the male scientist joins forces with the empowered housewife in a process of individual consumer empowerment.

Caspar Brook, the first paid Director of the CA, laid great emphasis on the scientific basis of *Which?* He introduced a system of checkers, verifiers

[58] *Which?*, 1:1 (1957), 4–5.

and data-checking sheets for the *Which?* reports.[59] But it was he who also did much to outline a vision of consumerism which the CA was steadily constructing, a movement based entirely on 'impartial information' of the kind which could only ever be produced by 'consumer-controlled scientific research' entirely independent of trade interests.[60] In contradistinction to earlier consumer movements, Brook argued that the 'underlying philosophy' of *Which?* was 'to strengthen the individual consumer, rather than all consumers in the aggregate'.[61] While increased membership of the CA testified to the existence of an 'army' of shoppers, ultimately each was to act alone as a 'discriminating consumer'.[62] Shoppers, he argued, wanted to make purchases on 'rational grounds, i.e. having compared the offers before them'.[63] *Which?* enabled consumers to take control of their decisions to the same extent as an industrial purchasing officer. All they needed was more factual information in order to improve their powers of individual discrimination. For Brook, the identification of a 'best buy' was something of a danger for *Which?* readers since blind acceptance of the rating would mean the CA had 'failed in [its] aim to help them become more discriminating consumers'.[64]

The hope remained, though, that science, independence, research and testing would show the consumer the virtues of rationality to which the professional experts had already committed themselves. According to Eirlys Roberts, while many of the CA's founders might be divided by a whole range of belief systems, they all shared a commitment to rationality:

All the group, whatever their politics or disciplines, were what would usually be called intellectual – that is to say, they felt at home only in a world in which they (and the people around them) at least believed that most of their decisions were rational. They found it uncomfortable that they (and other people) should be living blindly and irrationally in an important respect (buying goods and services) and that in this practical sphere they should be guided almost exclusively by appeals to their emotions (advertising). There are – they felt – spheres in which it is proper that emotion, and not reason, should operate – such as love and aesthetics – but that buying a refrigerator is not one of them. They felt they were in a confused and messy situation and the idea that it should be clarified, mapped and put in order by the presentation of facts about goods and services, appealed to them strongly.[65]

[59] Roberts, *Which?*, p. 31.
[60] CAA 27: C. Brook, 'Research by consumers', Paper for British Association for the Advancement of Science (31 August 1961), p. 16; *Sunday Citizen* (23 June 1963), p. 15.
[61] CAA 27: C. Brook, 'Research by consumers', p. 5.
[62] CAA 27: C. Brook, 'Fresh deal for shoppers', *Observer* (11 February 1962).
[63] CAA 27: C. Brook, 'The discriminating consumer', speech given to the British Institute of Management (November 1959), p. 4.
[64] CAA 27: C. Brook, 'Research by consumers', p. 14.
[65] Roberts, *Consumers*, pp. 78–9.

Thus, in a report on contraception, Roman Catholic CA staff set aside their religious principles to the greater god of objectivity. In a symbolic gesture, issues of nostalgia, tradition and politics were dismissed as an early *Which?* report criticised heavily the quality of a kettle manufactured by the Co-operative Wholesale Society.[66] If a foreign product was better than a British good, then it was up to the manufacturers to respond rather than to expect the consumer to put patriotism before reason. Questions of aesthetics, subjective preference, taste and enjoyment had to give way to the precise technical language of scientific scrutiny: 'the more blobs the better', as one later critic would put it.[67]

It is in this focus on individual discrimination that scholars have seen in consumerism an important bulwark for the politics and economics of the free market. An emphasis on rationality seemed a deliberate celebration of classical orthodox economics and consumerism could be interpreted as an attempt to create perfect competition from the consumer end. But one has to put these retrospective considerations aside if one wants to understand better the aims of the early consumer activists. For these people, scientific research, factual information, independent testing and rational assessment provided their own ethic. So long as people could be presented with objective information, free from any commercial bias, it was believed most of the problems affecting the economy could be rectified. The consumer him- or herself would improve the marketplace and create a more justified society. This sense of optimism still comes through when interviewing those involved with organised consumerism in the 1950s and 1960s. Early CA staff shared a 'belief' in the work of the organisation. It was not necessarily a political movement, but it was 'an idea for its time' and which some even 'believed . . . would change the world'.[68] They now admit to a certain naivety in their expectations, but their faith in comparative testing reflects the employment of an idealistic if not utopian language that was utilised in a wider discussion of consumerism at the time. Colin Harbury had earlier urged a society in which 'embarrassing ignorance', 'inability', 'short-sightedness' and 'wasteful, irrational' expenditure would be eradicated such that the consumer no longer acted as an 'Amazonian boy' suddenly dropped on the streets of London.[69] There is no need to tease out the wider discourses of the modern-day noble savage to which his rhetoric referred: he spoke clearly of the need for 'rational efficiency' and he was joined by others such as

[66] *Which?*, 1:1 (1957), 4.
[67] A. Aldridge, 'The construction of rational consumption in *Which?* Magazine: the more blobs the better', *Sociology*, 28:4 (1994), 899–912.
[68] Interviews with Maurice Healy and Alastair Macgeorge, 26 March 2002.
[69] Harbury, *Efficiency*, pp. 2–5.

PEP which explicitly stated consumerism to be an 'enlightenment' project in which science and technology were to play a leading role in the goal of progress.[70] Later, the *Daily Express* journalist, Robert Millar, worried especially about the 'affluent sheep' whose every movements were directed by the manufacturers who, rather spectacularly, were able to control the individual's subconscious desires (over which consumers themselves had 'little or no control'): 'They are like sheep being joggled by sheepdogs. They run hither and thither, not knowing why and totally unaware of where they are going.'[71] He asked 'Who will be the shepherds?' and saw in consumerism the opportunity to create a new world. He imagined 'two nations' of consumer emerging: on the one hand the 'efficient', 'rational', 'scientific', 'objective', 'informed' and 'discriminating', motivated purely by a desire to obtain value for money; on the other, the 'fickle', 'ignorant', 'deluded' and 'illogical'.[72] Consumerism offered a vision for the future for many activists, a vision in which the professional experts of the CA were to play just as important a role in building as business executives and trade unionists.

The appeal

It is clear that the CA's ethic of consumerism appealed to an expanding sector of the population. This was either because they wished to become Brook's empowered consumers or because of the effortless attractions of the apparently objective 'best buy' (however, a 1979 survey which found that many readers literally did simply count the number of 'blobs' to make a judgement suggests the latter).[73] The 47,000 members who had begun subscribing to *Which?* in the CA's first year were quickly joined by a further 70,000 in the second. By the beginning of 1961 there were a quarter of a million members and growth continued throughout the 1960s. By 1968 there were half a million subscribers and thereafter the rate levelled off at around 6–700,000 throughout the 1970s. However, the economic boom of the mid-1980s brought about a further surge in subscription rates and membership of the CA reached the 1 million mark in 1987. Despite this appearance of the emergence of a popular movement, the CA shied away from adopting a democratic structure. Criticised as a 'self-perpetuating oligarchy' by the Molony Committee, the CA had avoided open elections to its Council in order to maintain a direction

---

[70] PEP, 'Consumer protection and enlightenment', *Planning*, 441 (1960).
[71] R. Millar, *The Affluent Sheep: A Profile of the British Consumer* (London, 1963), p. 3.
[72] *Ibid.*, p. 196.
[73] CAA 14: Communication Research, *Report on a Qualitative Study of Subscribers' Attitudes* (London, 1978), para. 2.13.

and momentum necessary to a voluntary body and for fear of infiltration by manufacturing or other interests.[74] The Molony accusation resonated with many CA members and shortly afterwards an element of democracy was introduced with the creation of 'ordinary' members who were given voting rights at the AGM. The CA was also pushed into reflecting the Council's new national status and pressure mounted for the nomination of Scottish, Welsh and provincial consumers: for instance, Rachel Waterhouse was pressed by her colleagues in 1963 to stand as an ordinary consumer from outside of London and she was subsequently labelled, tongue-in-cheek, a 'little Birmingham housewife'.[75]

In the first few months, Young worried about the resources available to the CA for it to become a properly professional testing organisation. With this in mind he corresponded with the TUC about offering bulk subscription rates at reduced prices and in November 1957 he responded to the Consumer Advisory Council's suggestion of a merger.[76] The talks did not progress very far, and were never likely to given the CA's commitment to absolute independence from all commercial interests, a position the CAC was constitutionally incapable of meeting through its position within the BSI.[77] The CA's growth, therefore, was to come through the service it provided for its members and for much of the 1960s its staff and Council were committed to running itself as an efficient business and developing its products. Bringing in marketing experts such as Bruce McConnach from *Reader's Digest* enabled the CA to target more effectively potential subscribers and develop new lines of consumer service.[78] As early as 1959, *Which?* changed from being a quarterly publication to a monthly one. In 1962, it introduced a quarterly car supplement as an optional extra, an innovation which was to develop into a separate publication, *Motoring Which?*, from 1965. This was followed in 1968 with *Money Which?*, in 1971 with *Handyman Which?* and in 1974 with *Holiday Which?*[79] By 1979, while *Which?* itself had 654,000 subscribers, there were 575,000 separate (but undoubtedly duplicate) subscriptions to *Money Which?*, 531,000 to *Handyman Which?*, 460,000 to *Motoring Which?* and 325,000 to *Holiday Which?*.[80] In addition, the CA also began

[74] Epstein, *Interviews*, p. 33 (Michael Young), p. 15 (Dorothy Goodman), p. 123 (Jennifer Jenkins).
[75] Interview with Len Tivey, 7 March 2002, Rachel Waterhouse, 8 March 2002.
[76] MSS 292/66.77/1: Letters from Michael Young to Ted Fletcher (26 September 1957), (1 November 1957), (21 January 1958) and Vincent Tewson (5 October 1957).
[77] Franks, 'Selling consumer protection', pp. 32–7; Epstein, *Interviews*, pp. 36–7 (Michael Young).
[78] Epstein, *Interviews*, p. 56 (Eirlys Roberts).
[79] CA, *Which? and Consumers' Association*, pp. 21–7.
[80] CA, *Annual Report, 1978–1979*, p. 8.

publishing a collection of paperbacks on topics such as consumer law, health products, house purchasing, funerals, pregnancy, insurance and advice for buying secondhand goods.[81] In collaboration with particular professions, the CA published the *Drug and Therapeutics Bulletin* from 1962, the first edition of *Contraceptives: A Which Supplement* from 1963 and, in the same year, *The Good Food Guide* first appeared under CA auspices after having been purchased from Raymond Postgate.[82] Consequently, the CA's staff of five which had been based in the Bethnal Green garage had increased to 312 by 1972, divided between its administrative headquarters in London, its subscription department in Hertford and its testing facilities and research laboratories in Harpenden.[83]

The type of person who purchased all these publications has remained relatively constant since 1957. 'An analysis of the first 10,000 members showed that most were middle class, professional people, many of them men, and with a high proportion of doctors, dentists, engineers, university and technical college lecturers, and so on.'[84] Members tended to be readers of *The Times, Daily Telegraph, Manchester Guardian, Observer, Daily Mail, Spectator* and *Economist*; by contrast, reports on the activities of CA in the pages of the *Daily Mirror* brought few, if any, new members. More than half were men, most were well educated and there was a 'strong component of the technically interested'.[85] According to a 1960 survey, 49 per cent of members were 'professional' (doctors, lawyers, university lecturers, journalists, higher level managers, etc., with annual incomes of over £1,000), 40 per cent were 'lower professional' or junior managerial (e.g., teachers, clerks, nurses), leaving just 7 per cent from the skilled or semi-skilled working class.[86] In 1962 it was noted that membership was concentrated on the upper one-fourth of the population where an estimated 10 per cent were or had been members. In contrast, membership rates among the rest of the population were thought to be one in every hundred.[87] It further recruited well from those in the age range 35–54 and membership rates increased dramatically moving down from

---

[81] D. Tench, *The Law for Consumers* (London, 1962); CA, *The Law for Motorists* (London, 1962); CA, *The Travelling Consumer* (London, 1964); CA, *The Legal Side of Buying a House* (London, 1965); CA, *Radiation: Part of Life* (London, 1965); CA, *Ailments and Remedies* (London, 1965); CA, *Buying Secondhand* (London, 1966); CA, *What to do when Someone Dies* (London, 1967); CA, *Insurance and the Consumer* (London, 1968); CA, *Pregnancy Month by Month* (London, 1968).

[82] CA, *Which? and Consumers' Association*, pp. 21, 39–40.   [83] *Ibid.*, p. 5.

[84] CAA 27: E. Roberts, 'Consumer protection in foodstuffs', 1 May 1959; *Which?*, 1:2 (1958), 3.

[85] Roberts, *Consumers*, p. 81.

[86] The remaining 4% were categorised as 'other'. See CAA 27: *Who reads 'Which?'*, article for *New Society* (26 October 1962).

[87] CAA 14: Social Surveys (Gallup Poll) Ltd., *Which? Final Report* (London, 1962), p. 9.

Scotland and the north towards the capital and the home counties. Despite occasional efforts to reach consumers on lower incomes over successive decades, the membership has remained stubbornly middle class: an October 2000 study still found that '*Which?* subscribers are not representative of the population generally', being 'more likely to be older, on higher incomes and in social grades AB'.[88]

The expressed attitudes of *Which?* subscribers do not provide evidence of a wide-ranging and profound commitment to consumerism as either a social movement or a political interest. On party political issues, such as resale price maintenance in the early 1960s, members were often split and a 1962 Gallup Poll found little evidence of an abstract view of consumerism, a desire for political reform, or 'any ideology among the members'.[89] There has always been a high turnover of *Which?* subscribers. By 1962, 8 million people had looked at a copy of *Which?* yet they brought to the magazine limited expectations, seeking to use the magazine only at particular moments in the life cycle. Most subscribers were short term because they were 'primarily concerned with discovering the best way to spend their money'.[90] People felt that *Which?* was extremely useful in avoiding purchasing poor quality goods, but extremely few expressed an opinion as to the CA's role as a counterweight to industry or as representative of the consumer in a wider political arena.[91] In 1962, an article in the *Guardian* by Mary Crozier which disparaged those consumers who dared not 'trust their own judgment about buying, say, lavatory paper' provoked a storm of protest by consumers who desired both greater information and the guidance of the 'best buy'.[92] Yet this does not mean that the demand they had for help as individuals can be converted into a set of beliefs or principles which they shared as a collective whole. 'Individualism' was 'strong as an ideology' among *Which?* readers and many divisions have been noted among the membership. While some 'purists' were 'ascetic and puritanical' seeking only 'total utility' in the goods they bought, others felt themselves 'unworthy' of the scientific spirit of *Which?*[93] *Which?* could mean many things to many people and it was just as likely to attract the 'magazine buyer' type as the 'committed consumerist'.[94] Here, there are important parallels with the Co-operative

---

[88] Consumer Intelligence Unit (CIU), *Profile of Subscribers*, October 2000, internal CA document.
[89] CAA 14: Gallup, *Which? Final Report*, p. 1.   [90] *Ibid.*, p. 2.
[91] CAA 14: Social Surveys (Gallup Poll), *Enquiry into Which? A National Survey* (London: 1962).
[92] M. Crozier, 'Women talking', *Guardian* (26 February 1962), p. 2 and letters in reply (9 March 1962), p. 8.
[93] CAA 14: Communication Research, *Consumers' Association*, paras. 2.8, 2.11.
[94] CAA 14: S. Gebbet, A. Heylin and E. Soames, *Preparing for the 1980s: A Public Relations Report on the Consumers' Association* (London, 1979), p. 45.

movement and the similarly noted distinction between those consumers who merely wished to collect the 'divi' and the possibly tiny minority dedicated to the pursuit of the Co-operative Commonwealth. The majority of CA members thought of themselves purely as *Which?* readers and many remained resistant to the CA's later expansion into political campaigning. However, surveys also found that 'informants liked to regard themselves as 'concerned, enlightened, cynical and intellectually able people' and there is much evidence, from the 1960s at least, that the commitment to consumerism as a social movement stretched into the tens of thousands, in terms of participation rates, as dozens of local consumer groups emerged throughout the country.[95]

In 1961, the CA realised that it was difficult 'to get hold of the consumer voice'.[96] It disliked what it saw as the government's equation of the consumer with the housewife, yet it found it difficult to present another, more modern type of consumer. Accordingly, the CA arranged a meeting with 'ordinary' consumers – that is, invited readers of *Which?* – in Aylesbury in October, which over 500 attended. Within ten days, the first local consumer group had been set up in Oxford which, twelve weeks later, was publishing the *Oxford Consumer*, a magazine dedicated to local consumer issues and surveys of local prices, goods and services.[97] Other groups soon appeared, giving 'expression to a genuine grassroots consumer feeling' which thought that 'local volunteer consumerism provided an effective complement to the full-time professionalism of CA'.[98] The membership was usually made up of 'lively young people' who reflected the broader socio-economic characteristics of *Which?* subscribers. For instance, in 1963, the CA noted that the Chairmen of groups included 'a housewife, a BOAC pilot, a serving soldier, two University dons, a GP, a medical consultant, an industrial designer, an architect and a quality control engineer'.[99] Although part of the CA's involvement in the consumer groups was due to a desire to control a potentially business-infiltrated wing of the movement, it nevertheless thought they showed a 'hearty vitality' and were useful in helping local members of the CA know where to buy the goods recommended by *Which?* They also performed the surveys of such local services as window-cleaning, driving schools and bakeries as well as Sunday trading hours which the CA could never hope to perform as a national organisation. By March 1963 there were fifty consumer groups in existence, with a total of 5,000 members all joined to

[95] CAA 14: Communication Research, *Consumers' Association*, para. 2.17.
[96] CAA 27: D. H. Gorse, 'The growth of consumer groups', *New Outlook* (21 July 1963), p. 19.
[97] *Ibid.*, p. 20.
[98] H. Curtis and M. Sanderson, *A Review of the National Federation of Consumer Groups* (London, 1992), p. 4.
[99] CA, *Annual Report, 1962–1963*, p. 11.

the National Federation of Consumer Groups (NFCG).[100] By 1967 there were 100 groups with a total membership of 18,000 consumers.[101]

Local consumer organisation strongly followed the ethic of consumerism found in *Which?* Titles of magazines reflected the outlook of the members. The Basildon group published the *Buyer's Broadsheet*, the Sutton Group the *Vigilant*, Durham *Pick and Choose*, Derby *Choice* and Bromley's *Watchdog*.[102] To take just one example, the Birmingham Consumer Group thrived in the 1960s. Drawing its support from the relatively affluent southern areas of the city, the Group consisted of around 250 listed subscribers (though this included husbands and wives as just one entry).[103] It was to become one of the most important groups in the country, not least because of the range of talent it drew upon from what was self-deprecatingly termed the 'Birmingham University Consumer Group'.[104] One of its founders and early chairman had been Colin Harbury, a lecturer in economics at the University in 1963. He was soon joined by Leonard Tivey, then also a lecturer in political science and a former PEP worker where he had met Michael Young when the latter was originally trying to set up the CA. By the end of the 1960s, within the ranks of the Birmingham Group could be found Rachel Waterhouse, a recent Ph.D. graduate from the University's History Department and a future chair of the CA Council, Gordon Borrie, a senior lecturer in law and future Director-General of the Office of Fair Trading and Janet Upward, secretary to the NFCG until 1982. These highly articulate and intelligent professionals involved themselves in a whole range of consumer testing activities and invited prominent consumer activists to visit and speak.[105] Operating only as amateurs, they tested various public and private services as well as commenting on broader national issues such as the purpose of various consumer councils and the role of consumer protection legislation.[106] The highlight of their year was often the Birmingham 'Consumer Week' which acted as the focal point for a number of publicity events including the construction of a stall in the Pallasades Shopping Centre or the Central Library.[107] The initiative, drive, enthusiasm and sense of purpose which obviously motivated many of these affluent consumers was an important means by which they overcame an early

---

[100] *Ibid.*   [101] G. Smith, *The Consumer Interest* (London, 1982), p. 291.
[102] *Focus*, various issues, 1966–70.
[103] Birmingham Consumer Group, *Membership List*, 1976, author's private papers. Birmingham Consumer Group, *Annual Report, 1963–1964*, p. 1; *Annual Report, 1964–1965*, p. 1; *Annual Report, 1967–1968*, p. 3
[104] Interview with Janet Upward, 3 April 2002.
[105] *Birmingham Consumer*, 1 (1963), 2, 9–10; *NFCG Newsletter*, 1 (1975), 6.
[106] *Birmingham Consumer*, various issues 1963–80. Interview with Len Tivey, 7 March 2002, Rachel Waterhouse, 8 March 2002, Janet Upward, 3 April 2002.
[107] *NFCG Newsletter*, 40 (1981), para. 650.

accusation from business that local groups would consist of 'uninitiated amateurs who are insufficiently informed to assess the standards of experienced traders and that they are run by a few carping cranks'.[108]

The NFCG remained almost entirely dependent upon funding from the CA where its headquarters was also based. In 1972, though, its offices moved to the home of Janet Upward in Birmingham (and later to Kings Heath High Street) who had become its part-time secretary at a time when the CA was wishing to increase its distance from the local groups, preferring instead to rely on its own membership lists as a means of accessing the consumer.[109] The NFCG began to organise its activities more closely, ensuring that groups were informed of the tests, activities and campaigns of others. It co-ordinated national campaigns, arranged conferences on consumer subjects and published consumer guidebooks, the most prominent of which would be its *Handbook of Consumer Law*.[110] But it was also during the 1970s that overall numbers declined and the fast turnover of members was not replaced. Some respite came in the late 1970s and early 1980s when consumers who did not live in an area served by a local group were allowed to become direct members of the NFCG. By 1982, however, there were only thirty-one operational groups remaining, and half this again ten years later.[111] Today, it lingers on as certain groups have diversified into areas of poverty and social justice, but it is very different from the optimism of the 1960s and 1970s when the CA's work on comparative testing was expanded into something of a recognisable social movement. Then, groups had been able to assert confidently that through their efforts 'it augurs well for the future of the individual consumer'. This focus on an individualist interpretation of consumerism remained central to the work of the NFCG. Consumers in the local groups tended to insist on remaining a 'pure' consumer organisation: that is, focussing on the price and quality of goods and services for the individual. They eschewed the radicalism of other consumer activists and, although they collaborated with new consumer organisations in the 1970s that had taken a more 'social' agenda, they continued to focus on the shopper's value for money.[112] Their decline from the 1970s perhaps therefore indicates the specificity of an individualist consumerism, no matter how optimistic its approach, to the period of emerging affluence in the 1950s and 1960s.

[108] *Focus,* 1:1 (1966), 6.
[109] Curtis and Sanderson, *Review of NFCG*, p. 4; Interview with Janet Upward, 3 April 2002.
[110] NFCG, *A Handbook of Consumer Law: A Practical Guide to Consumers' Problems* (London, 1982).
[111] Curtis and Sanderson, *Review of NFCG*, p. 6.   [112] Interview with Janet Upward.

In many respects, the consumers of the CA were responding to a socio-political environment dominated by the trade unions and manufacturers and which was so parodied in films such as *The Man in the White Suit* (1951) and *I'm Alright Jack* (1959): they were attempting to create a new force in British industry which would better direct economic development. In 1960, Michael Young would be most explicit about this project, arguing in *The Chipped White Cups of Dover*, that if the Labour Party failed to take account of the interests of an increasingly affluent electorate, a new Consumer Party would emerge instead.[113] Clearly, few of the ordinary subscribers to *Which?* shared this vision of the political landscape, but it would be equally mistaken to interpret their actions from the extreme opposite position – that their commitment to organised consumerism stemmed only from a selfish desire to obtain value for money in their actions of acquisitive materialism. Instead, we need to recognise the third force element to consumerism in its reactions to the power of the manufacturers and the trade unions and acknowledge the limited yet nevertheless idealist visions of its leaders and staff. To do this, the consumers of the CA cannot solely be regarded as middle class. In any discussion of middle-class consumers, accounts are tinged with either the aesthetic disdain of their perceived Pooterish absurdities or the moral condemnation of their competitive status-seeking through Veblenesque conspicuous consumption. Undoubtedly, the middle classes have used goods as an outward display of their position in the world and there is every reason to suggest that *Which?* was a useful prop in this broader social purpose. But by moving away from a purely class-based explanation for the growth of the CA, both the aesthetic and moral underpinnings of consumption debate can be avoided. The consumers of the CA belonged to a social group – or habitus in Bourdieu's formulation – defined by an ethos of professionalism and technocratic expertise and a commitment to socio-economic planning and reconstruction. It is a habitus that generally rested on higher education, salaried employment, an experience of austerity and a set of 'dispositions' which committed its members to a belief that independent information, provided to individual consumers through objective criteria, could solve many of the problems and inequities of the marketplace and lead the nation to an egalitarian participation in the affluent society.[114] Consumerists sought not to overhaul industrial relations

---

[113] M. Young, *The Chipped White Cups of Dover: A Discussion of the Possibility of a New Progressive Party* (London, 1960).

[114] The most succinct definition of habitus comes in the phrase, 'systems of durable, transposable dispositions, structured structures predisposed to function as structuring structures', found in P. Bourdieu, *The Logic of Practice* (Cambridge, 1990), p. 108. See also P. Bourdieu, *Distinction: A Social Critique of the Judgement of Taste* (London, 1986).

or radically transform the relationship between the state and the individual. They shared instead a 'feel for the game' of post-war reform in which a consensus of centrist planners believed they could create a better society through the rational direction of both production and consumption.[115]

In 1986, various internal reforms at the CA led to the sacking of Peter Goldman, its director for twenty-three years. His trouble-shooter replacement, John Beishon, saw a further spate of resignations, retirements and dismissals which, save for one or two staff, gave the clear impression that the first generation of consumer activists had finally moved on. In any case, the social and economic context of an emerging affluence had long been lost and an older ethic of consumerism was no longer relevant. Speaking to this first generation of consumers confirms the impression. In one sense, they feel as though many of the original battles of the CA – on questions of safety, labelling, standards and reliability – had been largely won by the mid to late 1980s, but they regret also the passing of a spirit of consumer activism which reified independence, rationality, objectivity and information in and for itself. Now, the CA is regarded as too much of a business, its staff consisting of efficient workers with no sense of the importance of the CA's role in transforming post-war British society, culture and politics. Certain activities, such as the creation of a CA credit card, seem to compromise the earlier faith in independence and symbolically suggest the emergence of a new consumer environment within which the older activists had little role to play. By the early 1990s, the NFCG itself was in crisis, with numbers dwindling rapidly and its membership becoming increasingly elderly. A generation of consumer activists who had come to prominence from the end of the 1950s to the early 1980s was passing into retirement. But in that period these consumers had served a particular ethos, developing the CA from a garage-based adventure to an ethos of consumerism that married an economic liberalism to a wider social movement. As Michael Young said of the CA as early as 1960 when its fortunes were seen to be secure for the first time: 'The amateurs who started the Association have given way to professionals. The professionals are running a thriving business with verve but without losing the zeal which always characterises the earnest amateur.'[116]

---

[115] P. Bourdieu, *In Other Words: Essays Towards a Reflexive Sociology* (Cambridge, 1994), p. 9.

[116] CA, *Annual Report, 1959–1960*, p. 3.

8   Individualism enshrined: the state and the consumer in the 1960s

Much of the history of the common law could be read as a history of consumer protection. Every first-year university law student is familiar with a series of landmark cases in which the consumer's rights under tort and contract have been redefined, extended and made more precise. If one wants to find a history of the changing concept of individual rationality, one could look no further than the definition of the 'reasonable man' found throughout common law judgements. In the nineteenth century, this rationality was attached to a broader 'rugged individualism', generally enforced by judges who adhered to the view enshrined in the principle of 'caveat emptor' – 'let the buyer beware' – in which it was up to the customer to protect his own interests.[1] Yet there were nevertheless important developments in consumer protection throughout the century. In *Gardiner* v. *Gray* (1815), 'caveat emptor' was held not to apply when the buyer was unable to inspect the goods prior to purchase. In *Jones* v. *Bright* (1829), the legal principle was established that goods sold for a particular purpose must be fit for that purpose. Other cases followed relating to the freedom of contract, misrepresentations, exemption clauses, negligence and the duty of care owed by sellers and manufacturers. Most famously, the case of *Carlill* v. *The Carbolic Smoke Ball Co.* (1893) established that rewards offered in advertising amounted to specific contractual offers, enabling Mrs Carlill to claim her £100 compensation for an unsuccessful influenza treatment.[2] In the twentieth century, *Donoghue* v. *Stevenson* (1932) established a contractual relationship between the customer and the manufacturer, rather than just the retailer who actually sold the goods, and *Hedley Byrne & Co. Ltd* v. *Heller & Partners Ltd* (1964) held that written testimonials generally made the signatory liable for a negligent misstatement.[3] Manufacturers, however, were often able

---

[1] G. Borrie and A. L. Diamond, *The Consumer, Society and the Law* (1964; London, 1973), p. 15.

[2] *Ibid.*, pp. 107–9

[3] G. Borrie, *The Development of Consumer Law and Policy: Bold Spirits and Timorous Souls* (London, 1984), p. 9. For general overviews of consumer law see P. S. Atiyah, *The Sale*

to appeal to notions of reasonableness to avoid liability, and extensions to common law precedents often needed the reforming spirit or sense of purpose of a Lord Denning, though lower courts too have often negotiated more 'just' settlements on a case-by-case basis.[4] In the context of the rise of the modern consumer movement, in the 1950s and 1960s, it is no surprise that consumers' legal-trained activists looked to Parliament and direct state intervention rather then the slow and incremental reforms of the common law.[5]

The purpose of this chapter is to examine developments in state interference in consumer protection, not through the gradual developments in common law, but in the series of Acts and investigations into consumer protection by government committees and in the first state-funded, peacetime Consumer Council set up to cater to the broad interests of consumers rather than just their rights in relation to a particular industry or type of commodity. However, this history of state involvement in the transactions between the buyer and the seller mirrors the common law in the incremental development of the relationship between the state, the individual and the act of consumption. Scholars have argued that in the United States of the New Deal era the consumer was accorded the full rights of citizenship through his or her representation in numerous official socio-economic institutions.[6] Similarly, post-war West Germany, although lacking as large a grass-roots consumers' movement as in the UK, witnessed a more widespread incorporation of the consumer interest into the state apparatus.[7] In Britain, it is difficult to observe the entry of consumers into the corporate state to the same extent as trade unions and employers are said to have done in early twentieth-century continental Europe.[8] But neither can one see the development of a pluralist state, the reactions by government in the 1960s hardly responding directly to the

---

of Goods (1957; London, 1990); P. J. Cooke and D. W. Oughton, *The Common Law of Obligations* (London, 1989).

[4] M. Finn, *The Character of Credit: Personal Debt in English Culture, 1740–1914* (Cambridge, 2003).

[5] Borrie and Diamond, *Consumer, Society and the Law*, p. 333; D. Tench, *The Law for Consumers* (London, 1962); R. Lowe, *Sale of Goods and Hire Purchase* (Harmondsworth, 1968); H. Street, *Freedom, the Individual and the Law* (Harmondsworth, 1963).

[6] L. Cohen, 'The New Deal state and the making of citizen consumers', in S. Strasser, C. McGovern and M. Judt (eds.), *Getting and Spending: European and American Consumer Societies in the Twentieth Century* (Cambridge, 1998), pp. 111–25; M. Jacobs, ' "How about some meat?": the Office of Price Administration, consumption politics, and state building from the bottom up, 1941–1946', *Journal of American History*, 84:3 (1997), 910–41.

[7] G. Trumbull, 'Strategies of consumer group mobilisation: France and Germany in the 1970s', in M. Daunton and M. Hilton (eds.), *The Politics of Consumption: Material Culture and Citizenship in Europe and America* (Oxford, 2001), pp. 261–82.

[8] C. Maier, *Recasting Bourgeois Europe: Stabilisation in France, Germany, and Italy in the Decade after World War I* (Princeton, 1975).

consumers' movement as a separate and independent force in society.[9] Instead, as Martin Daunton has found in his analysis of welfare and taxation, one cannot rely on an overarching explanation of the development of the state, such as the decline of voluntarism, to comprehend official involvement in consumer affairs. One must acknowledge instead a 'much more complicated process of reallocation of responsibilities'.[10] As will be seen in the analysis of, first, the Molony Committee on Consumer Protection and, second, the Consumer Council of 1963–70, business interests dominated in directing the development of state consumerism, especially in the emphasis on self-regulation and the sanctity of the market. But state consumerism was influenced too by the spread of consumer voluntary bodies, by the dictates of Treasury finance and, ultimately, by the experience of actual involvement in consumer affairs. This resulted not in the development of a new theorisation of the relationship between the state and the individual in consumer protection, but in the piecemeal extension of official intervention in the marketplace. By the time of the abolition of the Consumer Council in 1970, such interventions resulted in a tension as to the extent to which consumerism was a movement designed to assist the individual in the purchase of commodities and the extent to which it was a socio-political movement concerned with the rights and obligations of the collective mass of consumers. As will be seen in chapters 9 and 10, the incremental model of state expansion into consumer affairs provided a pragmatic politics of consumption which acted both as the main strength and weakness of the consumer policy network in subsequent decades.

The Molony Committee on Consumer Protection

Throughout the 1950s the Labour opposition had pressed for legislation on standards and for more effective enforcement of the Merchandise Marks Acts (there had been only three prosecutions from 1943 to 1954), but the Conservative government preferred instead to encourage prosecutions by the RTSA and the work of the BSI.[11] It encouraged the creation of the CAC in 1955 and later provided a grant of £10,000 to assist in

[9] L. Tivey, 'Quasi-government for consumers', in A. Barker (ed.), *Quangos in Britain: Government and the Networks of Public Policy Making* (Basingstoke, 1982), pp. 137–51; L. Tivey, 'The politics of the consumer', in R. Kimber and J. J. Richardson, *Pressure Groups in Britain: A Reader* (London, 1974), pp. 195–209.

[10] M. Daunton, 'Payment and participation: welfare and state-formation in Britain 1900–1951', *Past & Present*, 150 (1996), p. 214.

[11] PRO BT 258/353: Consumer Protection Policy, *Report on House of Commons Debate on Consumer Standards* (6 May 1954); *Note of a meeting on consumer protection* (3 August 1954).

its 'Associates' scheme, hoping to restrict the notion of consumerism to 'quality standards on consumer goods . . . rather than legislation against monopolies and arrangements for protecting the consumer against high prices of home manufactured goods'.[12] But in response to mounting pressure from many sections of the media and the consumer movement, the Molony Committee on Consumer Protection was eventually appointed in 1959.[13] This was set up specifically to review existing legislation on consumer protection and to examine other means for the 'protection of the consuming public', though in the sphere of goods only and not services.[14] It was not to be concerned with measures regulating competition policy, despite the poor regard shown to the consumer from the Profiteering Acts of 1919 to the Monopolies Act of 1948 and the Restrictive Practices Act of 1956.[15] Nor was it to examine the practice of resale price maintenance, a common complaint of early consumer activists (though resale price maintenance was dealt with separately with specific legislation in 1964).[16] What it was to cover included the largely unworkable Merchandise Marks Act, first introduced in 1862, repealed in 1887 and replaced and amended at various times from 1891 to 1953, plus legislation dealing with weights and measures and adulteration. All of these actions had been introduced to protect the apparently fair and honest trader against the unscrupulous cheat, rather than to protect the general public, although the 1878 Weights and Measures Act had important secondary consequences for consumers. More often, though, as Sidney Webb said in 1926 of the 'futile' Sale of Food and Drugs Act, legislation was introduced to be of 'assistance to industries' and not consumers, despite the provisions of this Act extending the protection against short weight to all sales of food.[17] Similar accusations had been levelled against the first comprehensive adulteration measure, the Sale of Food and Drugs Act of 1875, and the consumer was hardly the centre of concern in much of the legislation relating to credit (including various Pawnbrokers Acts, Bills of Sale Acts, Moneylenders Acts and the 1938 Hire Purchase Act

[12] PRO BT 258/353: *Note by T. H. Sinclair* (13 July 1954); C. D. Woodward, *BSI: The Story of Standards* (London, 1972), p. 73.
[13] BSIL, Minutes of Women's Advisory Committee: 5M(OC) 6166: 21 July 1948.
[14] *Final Report of the Committee on Consumer Protection*, Cmnd. 1781 (London, 1962), p. 1.
[15] Monopolies and Restrictive Practices Commission, *Collective Discrimination*, Cmd. 9504 (London, 1955); H. Mercer, *Constructing a Competitive Order: The Hidden History of British Anti-Trust Policy* (Cambridge, 1995); J. F. Wilson, *British Business History, 1720–1994* (Manchester, 1995); L. Hannah, *The Rise of the Corporate Economy* (London, 1983).
[16] Board of Trade, *Monopolies, Mergers and Restrictive Practices*, Cmd. 2299 (London, 1964).
[17] PRO BT 258/353: *Report on House of Commons Debate*, p. 28; Central Office of Information (COI), *Fair Trading and Consumer Protection in Britain* (London, 1976), p. 9.

which regulated the abuses of instalment payments for the first time) which Molony had also been requested to investigate.[18] Against such a background of competition policy it is no surprise to find that Molony did not depart from the tradition of privileging business interests and newspapers were quick to describe its findings in relation to the consumer as a 'velvet glove'.[19] Indeed, the initial membership of the Committee stood in stark contrast to the working-class representatives of the labour movement that had constituted the First World War Consumers' Council. The chair, J. T. Molony, was a barrister and, of the eleven others, two were solicitors with some experience of previous protection legislation and five were businessmen, including a member of the RTSA and Lord Geddes, former director of the Shell Group as well as several other companies. Of the consumers represented on the Committee, two were 'housewives' with no obvious experience of consumer work, one a former solicitor and women's committee worker and a Miss A. L. Richmond, a veteran trades unionist who tripled up as a working-class, women's and Scottish representative.[20] Labour Party MPs immediately voiced their complaints in Parliament about the absence of more, and easily obtainable, working-class representation, especially from the Co-operative movement which had 13 million members at this time.[21] The Conservative Patricia McLaughlin responded with a declaration of faith in the two selected housewives, though their near absence from the minutes of the proceedings of the Committee testifies to their inexperience in such work.[22] The one woman who was capable and certainly did make her presence felt, Richmond, unfortunately had to retire in May 1960 because of ill-health having only attended nine meetings.[23] Although replaced by another capable woman with a firm belief in the benefits of consumer protection, Mrs I. O. Stewart, the male members of the committee, led by Molony and Geddes, continued to dominate and were happy to impose their voice on the consumer interest despite the

[18] M. French and J. Phillips, *Cheated Not Poisoned? Food Regulation in the United Kingdom, 1875–1938* (Manchester, 2000); J. Burnett, *Plenty and Want: A Social History of Diet in England from 1815 to the Present Day* (London, 1966), pp. 72–90; J. Phillips and M. French, 'Adulteration and food law, 1899–1939', *Twentieth-Century British History*, 9:3 (1998), 350–69; M. H. Whincup, *Consumer Legislation in the United Kingdom and the Republic of Ireland* (London, 1980).
[19] *Guardian* (26 July 1962), p. 8.
[20] BT 258/879: 'CCP 6: Terms of reference and minutes of appointment'; *H. C. Deb.*, 610 (27 July 1959), col. 74.
[21] *H. C. Deb.*, 608 (9 July 1959), col. 1560; 609 (16 July 1959), cols. 571–2, *43*; 610 (27 July 1959), col. 65.
[22] *H. C. Deb.*, 610 (27 July 1959), col. 48.
[23] PRO BT 258/878: *Minutes of Meetings of Committee on Consumer Protection*: Meeting 16 (2 May 1960), minute 16:78.

underlying assumption which often surfaced that consumption lay in the realm of the woman's expertise.

The constitution and membership of the committee seemed designed to guarantee a principal finding of the Committee that there was 'no single axiomatic approach' to consumer protection.[24] Molony, in particular, revelled in his lack of expertise, arguing that it helped foster a more 'detached' analysis whereby the Committee would consider only what was 'practically possible' rather than what was 'theoretically desirable in the interests of the consumer'.[25] His language of 'common-sense', 'balanced judgement' and 'fair treatment' to industry precluded any of the radicalism that had marked earlier forms of consumerism and limited the 'first objective' of the Committee to, in the words of the secretary, 'ensure that the consumer gets goods which satisfy his requirements'.[26] Accordingly, business interests were given a far more sympathetic hearing and the vast majority of the evidence taken from 277 sources expressed the concerns of commerce, with 33 companies and 109 trade associations presenting written statements.[27] Despite the complaints which would later be made in Parliament about the predominance of manufacturers' views being represented in the evidence provided,[28] the Committee had no problems inviting companies to give oral evidence one after another. The messages that voluntary measures were better than compulsion, that competition was the best form of consumer protection, that consumers themselves were often largely to blame in issues of safety and that there was too much unnecessary 'grumbling' on the part of consumers were all actually treated with the necessary criticisms by the members of the Committee, but the constant repetition of the same messages served to eclipse any views of consumers themselves.[29] The questioning that trade representatives were subjected to was also less rigorous than that given to the CA. For instance, Roger Diplock of the RTSA was hardly expected to receive an aggressive examination from Ramage, a Committee member who was also on the RTSA Council.[30] Likewise, Attwood, President of his own market research company, was unlikely to take a belligerent stance against the many representatives of the advertising industry called in for questioning. Indeed, there existed a certain clubbishness between

---

[24] *Final Report of the Committee on Consumer Protection*, p. 91.

[25] BT 258/878: *Minutes*: Meeting 1 (31 July 1959), minute 1:5.

[26] PRO BT 258/880: 'CCP 4: Draft programme of work'.

[27] *Final Report of the Committee on Consumer Protection*, pp. 317–21.

[28] *H. C. Deb.*, 678 (20 May 1963), col. 136.

[29] BT 258/878: *Minutes*: Meeting 14 (4 April 1960), minute 14:66; Meeting 20 (4 July 1960), minute 20:116.

[30] BT 258/879: 'CCP 9: Proposed submission by the Retail Trading Standards Association'; BT 258/878: *Minutes*: Meeting 27 (9 January 1961), minute 27:167.

the Committee and industry, the secretary's notes to written dispositions often mentioning characteristics which he deemed relevant: Diplock, in particular, was said to be a 'cheerful and forceful character (once, I believe, a rugger player of some distinction)'.[31] And there was too a frequent appeal to a national identity in that 'real' British traders would never engage in practices for which consumer protection was necessary. The 'national tradition', it seemed, was firmly located on the playing fields of Eton, where the spirit of voluntarism and amateurism was espoused over compulsion and 'professionalism'.[32]

In contrast, evidence from consumers and existing consumer representatives was treated with far greater scepticism and critical scrutiny. The CAC was criticised for its largely middle-class Associates scheme and the BSI more generally for its insufficient independence from business. The CA was regarded with suspicion since it was alleged to be open to corruption in its testing procedures, its constitution was famously described as a 'self-perpetuating oligarchy' and certain Committee members found it difficult to believe that the CA founders had not formed the company for personal gain.[33] Whereas business interests were asked to state their position on the issue of consumer protection, when Michael Young and Caspar Brook gave evidence to the Committee in an interview, the onus was placed upon them to prove their innocence of such charges. Their appearance before the Committee took the form of a trial in which they were expected to defend themselves against what turned out to be a spurious charge that the CA's testing methods had unfairly treated two particular firms.[34] The research the CA presented from a survey of its own membership was dismissed for its middle-class bias, a remarkable attitude by a Committee which itself had been heavily criticised for its lack of representation of the working-class view.[35] Other consumer advocates fared worse. A Co-operative pamphlet, published especially for the Molony Committee and submitted as evidence, was merely noted in the minutes and the organisation was not called upon to give oral evidence.[36] Similar treatment was given to a PEP pamphlet and to the

---

[31] BT 258/879: 'CCP 9: Proposed submission by the Retail Trading Standards Association', note by Mitchelmore [Secretary].

[32] BT 258/878: *Minutes*: Meeting 31 (6 March 1961), minute 31:191.

[33] *Final Report of the Committee on Consumer Protection*, p. 122; BT 258/878: *Minutes*: Meeting 3 (2 November 1959), minute 3:9; Meeting 15 (11 April 1960), minute 15:77; Meeting 18 (30 May 1960), minute 18:101; BT 258/883: 'CCP 114: Submissions by S. N. Bridges & Co. Ltd. and Wolf Electrical Tools Ltd.'

[34] BT 258/878: *Minutes*: Meeting 25 (5 December 1960), minute 25:146.

[35] BT 258/878: *Minutes*: Meeting 3 (2 November 1959), minute 3:9; BT 258/880: 'CCP 20: CA Questionnaire'.

[36] BT 258/882: 'CCP 9: Co-operative Union, Memorandum for Submission to the Molony Committee on Consumer Protection'.

detailed plans for consumer protection laid out by the TUC.[37] Elaine
Burton's submission, containing as it did many statements of complaint
from actual consumers, was dismissed as 'loose thinking and loose language' which 'made no positive contribution'. The Committee agreed
'that it contained no valid evidence or worthwhile suggestion which had
not already been advanced from other quarters'. Yet Burton's submission did at least contain the direct opinions of consumers, something for
which the Committee claimed to be after, but here regarding their views
as 'the unthinking acceptance, by an ill-informed and uncritical section
of the community, of equally ill-informed statements'.[38] The Committee
also received 1,000 letters from members of the public as evidence, a
sample which it claimed was too small and which appears to have been
consequently overlooked.[39]

The short measure given to consumer groups did not result, however,
in an anti-consumer report, since there was much agreement, even by
many trade associations, on the need for some extension of consumer
protection legislation. Although differences occurred over the extent of
compulsion and persuasion, Conservatives and Co-operators alike called
for a recognition of the consumer's place in society. Similar evidence was
thus collected from the Fabians, the Association of Scientific Workers,
various women's groups, the CAC and the BSI, the Bow Group and
the Labour Party. As a consequence, the Committee would make 214
recommendations, all of which were of an extremely practical nature to
do with issues such as the desirability of informative labelling, voluntary standards on production quality and the need for stricter legislation
concerning guarantees, trade descriptions and hire purchase contracts.
Although care was taken to avoid as far as possible any statement of
general consumer 'rights',[40] the Molony Committee came to be recognised as a watershed in the history of state consumerism. As will be seen
below, it led directly to the creation of the Consumer Council and its
interim report on safety issues resulted in the Consumer Protection Act
of 1961.[41] Its tidying up of the merchandise marks legislation eventually
led to the Trade Descriptions Act of 1968 and it set precedents in state
intervention which were to prove important in the abolition of retail price

[37] BT 258/878: *Minutes*: Meeting 18 (30 May 1960), minute 18:100; BT 258/880: 'CCP
28: Submission by TUC'; BT 258/884: 'CCP 136: PEP Pamphlet, Consumer Protection
and Enlightenment'.
[38] BT 258/878: *Minutes*: Meeting 17 (16 May 1960), minute 17:90; BT 258/882: 'CCP
84: Submission by Miss Elaine Burton'.
[39] BT 258/878: *Minutes*: Meeting 45 (20 November 1961), minute 45:271.
[40] *Final Report of the Committee on Consumer Protection*, pp. 299–315.
[41] Committee on Consumer Protection, *Interim Report*, Cmnd. 1011 (London, 1960),
p. 5.

maintenance and the reform of monopolies legislation. Some of its influence can further be seen in the Crowther Committee's investigation into
consumer credit and, ultimately, in the flurry of legislation in the 1970s
that included the 1973 Fair Trading Act, the 1974 Consumer Credit Act,
the 1977 Restrictive Trade Practices Act and the 1978 Consumer Safety
Act.[42]

Nevertheless, Molony's refusal to make any generalist or philosophical
statement on the nature of consumer protection reflected both the voluntarist bias of the Committee's members and the incremental nature
of British state expansion, which could only mean that the consumer
imagined by this section of the official apparatus remained an individual with none of the attendant rights suggested earlier during a period
of the politics of necessity. The position of advertising regulation after
the Committee's report reflects both the unwillingness of Molony to become involved in coercive measures and the ability of organised business
to pre-empt any state intervention. The advertising industry was called
before the Committee on several occasions and it presented numerous
written submissions. Fearing that Molony would recommend legislation,
the Advertising Association created the Advertising Standards Authority
in 1962, a self-regulatory body designed 'to promote the high standards
of advertising in the interests of the public'.[43] The British Code of Advertising Practice, against which non-TV advertisements were judged, was
thus determined by the industry itself, though its Code of Advertising
Practice Committee has always included representatives of the consumer
movement in order to maintain an appearance of impartiality in the revision of its rules.[44] Subsequent revisions to the Code have produced a
delicate balance between satisfying the demand for commercial freedom
and offsetting the calls of consumer representatives for greater legislative
intervention.[45] But as a compromise measure which avoided the intervention of the state into the marketplace, Molony was entirely satisfied
with the industry's own form of consumer protection. The Committee
recommended that the worst abuses – that is, cases of outright fraud –
be dealt with in a revision of the Merchandise Marks Acts, but that the
industry's proposed scheme of self-discipline was sufficiently rigorous to
be given a 'fair trial'.[46] State consumerism in advertising, as in so many

---

[42] G. Borrie, *Development of Consumer Law*; G. Smith, *The Consumer Interest* (London, 1982).
[43] J. Aspinall, 'Glossary of organisations active in consumer affairs', in J. Mitchell (ed.), *Marketing and the Consumer Movement* (London, 1978), p. 256.
[44] In addition, the ASA membership itself must be made up of between one-half and two-thirds of persons unconnected with advertising: *ibid.*, p. 255.
[45] Whincup, *Consumer Legislation*, pp. 150–3; COI, *Fair Trading*, pp. 40–1.
[46] *Final Report of the Committee on Consumer Protection*, chap. 18, pp. 247–68.

other areas of consumer protection, was to consist of post-hoc interventions in specific instances only after self-regulatory schemes had broken down.

The Consumer Council, 1963–70

The Consumer Council, set up in 1963 following one of the Molony Committee's principal recommendations, embodied this non-interventionist state consumerism. It was established as an independent organisation to inform itself of the consumers' interests, to consider further actions to defend or promote those interests and to provide advice and guidance for the consumer. It was deliberately prevented from engaging in the preparation of comparative test reports, the taking up of complaints on behalf of individual consumers, and law enforcement action – three absences which led to immediate criticisms in Parliament as to its limited role.[47] These restrictions made it clear that government and Molony perceived the Council as a body which added to the information held about the market; what it was not was an organisation allowed to interfere in the actual workings of the market. To this end, the Prime Minister Harold Macmillan insisted that the selected chair of the Council should be 'someone known to be acceptable to the Conservative Party'.[48] When several suggested names refused the post, the *Daily Express* speculated that they were 'as sceptical as certain Ministers about the usefulness of such an organisation. In spite of the pride with which Mr Macmillan announced that idea last July [1962] it is no secret that some Cabinet Ministers regard such a council as a waste of time'.[49] Eventually, Baroness Elliot was chosen, a Vice-President of the CA and a prominent member of women's sections of the Conservative Party. She was joined by a handful of individuals connected to existing consumer organisations (Aubrey Diamond of the NFCG, Winifred Jenkins of the WAC and Lord Peddie of the Co-operative Party, though Michael Young of the CA was not able to take up the position[50]), though most Council members were selected because of the skills learnt through their positions in management and the distributive trades or the general skills associated with the women's voluntary sector. Indeed, the government deliberately refused

---

[47] PRO AJ 2/1: CC(63)1: *Terms of Reference*; CC(63)2: *Scope of the Council's Remit and Action*; H. C. Deb., 674 (26 March 1963), col. 138; 676 (23 April 1963), col. 9; 677 (15 May 1963), col. 173; 678 (20 May 1963), cols. 33–160.

[48] PREM 11/4527: Letter from Prime Minister to Board of Trade (16 November 1962).

[49] BT 258/1494: *Daily Express* (19 February 1963).

[50] BT 258/1492: *Proposed Consumer Council: Policy Questions Arising from Establishment*: Membership of the Council (2 April 1963).

to appoint certain individuals tainted with the experience of consumer activism, including Caspar Brook of the CA, Elizabeth Gundrey of the CAC and Jean Robertson, a *Daily Telegraph* journalist and writer of the 'Leslie Adrian' consumer column in the *Spectator*.[51] Likewise, a businessman such as R. Craig Wood was approached despite his earlier public claims rejecting the whole idea of a Consumer Council. The Council's Director, however, was the capable and respected Elizabeth Ackroyd, a career civil servant who had formerly served with the Independent Television Authority's Advertising Advisory Committee.[52]

The main activities of the Council's thirty staff were centred around research, representation and information. Firstly, research into the consumer interest was necessary because the twelve members of the Council recognised they did not represent all consumers, and even accepted to a degree the criticism by Max Wood of the Co-operative Union that they were 'a bunch of middle-class intellectuals'. They therefore commissioned research through the Research Institute for Consumer Affairs, the University of Keele and the NFCG, conducted investigations with the Council's own research staff (which never numbered more than ten) and liaised with other government departments and with organisations such as the CA and the Citizens' Advice Bureau (CAB) which had greater access to the 'consumer voice' and which had been given £27,000 for this purpose as directed by Molony. Relations with the CAB were never satisfactory, since most CAB staff were unwilling to concentrate on consumer issues amidst a range of seemingly more pressing concerns affecting citizens and the vast majority of consumers were wholly unaware of the consumer advice services of the CAB.[53] Several meetings between the Council and the CAB failed to rectify the situation and the Council turned instead to such bodies as the John Hilton Bureau and the local consumer protection departments which had emerged from older municipal weights and measures inspectorates.[54] The Council recognised that if its opinions as the consumer voice were to hold any authority, it needed to engage continuously in its research activities to make informed policy decisions.[55] In

[51] *Ibid.*; BT 258/1494: Consumer Council: *Selection of Chairman*.
[52] CC, *Annual Report, 1963–1964* (London, 1964), pp. 19–20. See Appendix for full details of Council members.
[53] AJ 2/6: CC(65)24: The Council's relationship with the Citizens' Advice Bureaux; AJ 1/3: 5th meeting (27 May 1965), 5:2; *Focus*: 2:4 (1967), 6–7; AJ 2/19: CC(67)25: *Relationship between the Consumer Council and the National Citizens' Advice Bureaux Council. Report of the working party*; AJ 8/11: CC, Field Survey Reports: *A report on the research carried out on behalf of the Consumer Council during the period October 1967–October 1969*, p. 45; AJ 8/3: CC, Field Survey Reports: *Public Awareness of the Citizens' Advice Bureau*; AJ 8/4: CC, Field Survey Reports: *Knowledge of consultative organisations*.
[54] AJ 1/4: 2nd meeting (24 February 1966), 2:2; CC, *Annual Report, 1966–1967*, p. 22.
[55] AJ 1/4: 1st meeting (27 May 1966), 1:5.

a typical year, 1968–9 for example, the Council commissioned and conducted investigations into the prices of household commodities, carpets,
bank hours, insurance, electricity charges and shopping habits.[56]

Research, then, fed into the Council's second main area of activity, representation, and here the Council did begin to make its presence felt. In its
Annual Report of 1965–6, the Council was able to claim that it had helped
put consumerism firmly within the day-to-day discussion of Parliament.
It had encouraged more MPs to support consumer protection measures
and had contributed itself to initiating legislation such as the Trade Descriptions Bill, the Estate Agents Bills, the Doorstep Selling Bill and the
Hearing Aids Bill. It had encouraged more stringent voluntary measures,
had suppressed – through publicity – various sales abuses, and had spread
a greater consumer consciousness among businessmen and shoppers.[57]
While all of these 'achievements' might be attributed to a more general
politicisation of consumption in the 1960s, the Council did at least ensure the consumer voice was heard more regularly in government bodies.
It sent representatives to around thirty other committees, dealing with
matters as diverse as air safety and decimalisation, and it presented evidence to such important investigations as the Russell Committee on Adult
Education and the Crowther Committee on Consumer Credit.[58] Although it did not sit on the nationalised industries' consultative councils,
the 'Little Neddies' (Economic Development Councils), or any of the
higher level economic committees of the Board of Trade, the Council did
hold regular discussions with the main political parties, the Conservatives
and Labour both forming Parliamentary consumer groups.[59] By 1968,
the Council acknowledged the growing importance of legislative efforts
in its work, Elliot herself stating that 'the most important thing we have
done is to make our legislators consumer conscious'.[60] Furthermore, it
attempted to act as the co-ordinating body for the entire consumer movement (defined by the Council as mainly the CA and NFCG, rather than
the Co-operative Union). Though tensions and professional jealousies often arose here, many within the consumer movement felt that the Council
had assumed a central and established role by 1970.

Finally, the main work of the Council was directed at improving the
amount of information available to consumers, and its work here ranged

---

[56] CC, *Annual Report, 1968–1969*, p. 39.   [57] CC, *Annual Report, 1965–1966*, p. 7.

[58] AJ 10/60: CC Submissions: *Memorandum to the Crowther Committee on Consumer Credit*;
AJ 10/72 CC Submissions: *Evidence to the Russell Committee on Adult Education*; *Focus*,
4:1 (1969), 1–5, 20–1.

[59] AJ 10/34: CC Submissions: *Liaison between the Labour Party Consumer Protection Group
and the CC*; AJ 10/39: CC Submissions: *Liaison between the Conservative Party in Parliament and the CC*.

[60] CC, *Annual Report, 1967–1968*, p. 1.

from promoting consumer education in schools to publishing pamphlets on specific issues, the distribution of which ranged from over 2 million copies of *Making a Nightdress* to 100,000 copies of an 'About Buying' series. The Council later published its own consumer magazine, *Focus*, and it constantly fought for more funds to expand its individual consumer advice line though this work was regarded as 'soul destroying' since the terms of reference prevented an extension of this work into consumer advocacy. One significant positive venture was the introduction of its own labelling scheme, Teltag, designed to provide information (rather than an approved standard of quality) to the consumer on the product, at the point of sale. Based on the Swedish VKN labelling system, Teltag was intended to appear on a range of products such as domestic electrical appliances, textiles, household goods, photographic equipment, hardware and sports and leisure goods, presenting data on such areas as construction, weight, electrical rating, safety requirements, and the performance of the article when tested under standard conditions. Here, the Council liaised with other groups such as the CA, the Electrical Association for Women, the NFCG and the WAC of the BSI to develop standard criteria against which the goods could be tested.[61] The scheme, however, was extremely slow to take off from its launch in late 1965. Manufacturers were unwilling to commit themselves to a scheme unless it could be proved that there was a genuine consumer demand for it, while the Council could not force other manufacturers to make a trial start.[62] Within a few years, the Teltag label was being applied only to tufted carpeting and attempts to extend the scheme to various domestic electrical appliances largely failed due to the absence of industry support and co-operation.[63] But the problems over setting a performance standard, matching these with BSI standards, the lack of commercial incentive to manufacturers and the open hostility of some traders meant that the Council's main attempt to provide concrete raw data to consumers was unsuccessful.[64] In any case, many members of the Council shied away from such measures which smacked too much of direct market intervention.

Instead, the focus of the Council was to remain with more indirect methods of empowering the consumer. This was consistent within an in-stitutional framework that sought to build on existing post-war consumer initiatives and strengthen the lone customer. It aimed 'to help solve the problems of the British buying public, to help them learn to discriminate,

---

[61] CC, *Annual Report, 1964–1965*, p. 10.
[62] AJ 1/7: *The Consumer Council: A Review*, p. 8.
[63] CC, *Annual Report, 1967–1968*, p. 25.
[64] AJ 2/22: CC, *Papers*: CC(68)14: The Teltag Scheme, note by the staff; CC, *Annual Report, 1967–1968*, p. 28.

to know their rights, and to know how to go about securing them'. These rights roughly equated with those articulated by President Kennedy in 1962 and other consumer groups around the world, in that they emphasised the right to 'full information', the right to choice, to safety, to redress and to 'protection from unfair pressures'.[65] The key point of emphasis was the empowered individual, a picture of Elliot as the intelligent housewife shopper which appeared in the first *Annual Report* clearly providing a link in the notion of the consumer that had appeared in the rhetoric of the WAC and CAC (see Figure 6). However, while other consumer groups in the 1960s moved away from such a strongly gendered consumerism, the Council continued to stress that its activities would transform the women's 'ineffectiveness' and 'pathetic state of confusion' into 'bullish awareness' in the supermarket.[66] Elliot later made explicit the aims of the Council, the first being to obtain 'better self-protection by consumers through education and information'.[67] Only if this failed to remedy the situation would the Council then aim to create better voluntary codes of practice and, should this fail, legislation. At no point was it ever suggested that there was a fundamental problem with the market and competition was always regarded as a virtue. The Council sought only to 'strengthen the bargaining position of consumers in the market'.[68]

Most members of the Council remained opposed to setting out any general principles of consumerism. Many argued that they should only deal with specific issues as and when they arose and should not adopt a policy of 'a priori reasoning' – of setting out general principles in advance of a problem.[69] If an abstract politics of consumption did emerge it was more through negative considerations of its role and the rejection of formal consumerist frameworks such as that enshrined in the Federal Trade Commission of the United States. When Peddie desired to instil Morrisian notions of good craftsmanship into modern consumerism, arguing that the Council should support the Crafts Centre as 'standards of craftsmanship', it was decided that the matter was too trivial to be of interest to the Council.[70] The issue of cigarette advertising was held to be beyond the remit of the Council, as were general discussions of poverty, the moral or aesthetic content of television documentaries, the activities of 'Little Neddies', the patriotic concerns expressed in the 'Buy British' campaign

---

[65] CC, *Annual Report, 1963–1964*, p. 3.   [66] *Focus*, 1:2 (1966), 24.
[67] CC, *Annual Report, 1964–1965*, p. 5.   [68] CC, *Annual Report, 1967–1968*, p. 10.
[69] AJ 2/11: CC, *Papers*: CC(66)1: Variety in packaging, note by Mr. W. G. McClelland; CC(66)7: The operating philosophy of the Consumer Council, note by Mr. A. F. Earle; CC(66)8: The operating philosophy of the Consumer Council, note by Mr. T. W. Cynog-Jones.
[70] AJ 1/1: 6th meeting (18 December 1963), 6:2.

Figure 6   Baroness Elliot, Consumer Council, *Annual Report, 1963–1964.*

of 1968 and the targeting of children by advertisers.[71] Elsewhere, limitations on financial resources restricted a widening of the 'consumer interest'. The Council wished to conduct and co-ordinate local price surveys, but did not have the facilities necessary for such a large-scale bureaucratic enterprise and was in any case worried that such a degree of involvement in the market would bring it into a whole range of economic issues such as tariff protection about which it felt it should not be involved.[72] Official consumerism in the 1960s was therefore significantly divorced from the politics of necessitous consumption and demands for a type of consumer-citizenship which had marked earlier calls for consumer councils were dismissed. As the Council announced in 1968: 'The Consumer Council is interested in a person in his capacity as a "consumer" and not in his capacity as a voter or a citizen. If this distinction

[71] AJ 1/2: CC, *Minutes, 1964*: 1st meeting (23 January 1964), 1:4; AJ 1/3: CC, *Minutes, 1965*: 1st meeting (28 January 1965), 1:2; AJ 1/5: 2nd meeting (23 February 1967), 2:8; 4th meeting (27 April 1967), 4:4; AJ 1/6: 1st meeting (25 January 1968), 1:2; AJ 1/7: 2nd meeting (27 February 1969), 2:2.

[72] AJ 1/3: 7th meeting (22 July 1965), 7:2; 8th meeting (23 September 1965), 8:2; AJ 1/6: 2nd meeting (22 February 1968), 2:2; AJ 2/6: CC(65)9: Prices, note by the Director; AJ 2/7: CC(66)12: Prices, note by Mr. Bonner Gash.

is not made then no limitation would be placed on the Council's work. Clearly, therefore, the term "Consumer" means something different from and less than the terms voter or citizen.'[73]

Again, the voluntarist tendencies of this official form of consumerism can be seen in its approach to advertising, though practical experience was to lead to a change in Council policy. On the one hand, where the Council followed the criticisms of the Advertising Standards Authority (ASA) by the Advertising Inquiry Council (AIC), it built on an established tradition which stretched back to William Morris' Society for Checking the Abuses of Public Advertising. But it also maintained that the British Code of Advertising Practice was generally 'satisfactory' and, in the pages of its magazine, *Focus*, the Council even provided much space for Lord Robens, President of the Advertising Association, to explain at length the arguments in favour of voluntary self-regulation.[74] Increasingly, however, the experience of observing a high number of uninvestigated infringements of the Code led the Council to lose faith in the 'unsatisfactory' ASA.[75] In Parliament, the Labour MP George Darling led the attack on the voluntary system, and the Reith Commission on Advertising recommended in 1966 the creation of a National Consumer Board to judge the misleading content of advertisements.[76] The Consumer Council followed their lead and provided its support to this policy, though it worried about its own role should a new and possibly more effective consumer body be created.[77] The apparent indifference of the Board of Trade, however, or at least its greater concern for the lobbying efforts of the advertising industry, meant that the Council's arguments often went unheard and at times were even rejected for their alleged lack of objectivity.[78] The Government claimed it could not afford to implement the Reith proposals and instead retained its faith in its proposed amendments to the Merchandise Marks Acts contained in what would become the Trade Descriptions Act 1968, many of whose proposals did actually deal with some of the complaints of Reith. The Council, too, supported the progress of what was first called the Consumer Protection Bill, when it began life as a Private Members' Bill in the 1964–6 Parliament and was

---

[73] AJ 2/23: CC, *Papers*: CC(68)21: Patterns of family expenditure and the work of the Council, note by the staff, pp. 6–7.
[74] CC, *Annual Report, 1964–1965*, p. 17; *Focus*, 1:12 (1967), 9–11.
[75] AJ 10/15: CC Submissions, *Survey of press advertisement: Advertising Standards Authority*.
[76] BT 258/2103: Board of Trade Registered Files, *Consumer Protection: Policy on Advertising*: press release, 21 December 1964; AJ 1/4: 8th meeting (22 September 1966), 8:4.
[77] AJ 2/13: CC, *Papers*: CC(66)34: Reith Report on Advertising, note by the Director.
[78] BT 258/2103: Note on a discussion with the Minister of State (23 December 1964); Draft minute from the President to the Prime Minister: policy on advertising (21 January 1965); Advertising Standards Authority (16 July 1965).

introduced into the Lords by Baroness Elliot herself.[79] During the Bill's slow progress the Council tried to introduce an amendment providing the consumer with a civil remedy for damages suffered as a consequence of a false trade description, but it was unsuccessful in its efforts.[80] And it was also disappointed over the lack of a 'blanket clause which would have outlawed all statements that could have a misleading effect on the "reasonable man" '.[81] The Council continued to make these criticisms in the months following the passage of the Act, but it was content also to be highly satisfied with the immense media attention given to this aspect of consumer protection. The 40,000 complaints received (of which 25,000 were regarded as justified) in the first eighteen months of the existence of the Trade Descriptions Act ensured the Council referred to it as 'the housewife's Magna Carta', though other consumer groups still remained dissatisfied.[82]

The other main sphere of the Council's activities, education, most deliberately promoted the particular consumer philosophy of empowered individualism in which consumers were directly taught to think of themselves as purely economic purchasers or simply customers. Education was to imply the reform of the individual consumer, not the reform of the system within which the consumer operated. Education policy would lead to a perfection of the marketplace, not a rejection of it. It sought to improve competition, rather than reduce it. And, for the Council, it was the ultimate aim of consumer protection, the creation of 'the most telling pressure of all, the pressure of the informed and competent shopper'.[83] Educational policy took the form of issuing pamphlets on shopping advice, on consumer rights and issues based on the Council's research, and of distributing these leaflets through the CAB, women's organisations, local consumer groups and local authority advice centres. Publications such as *Information for Consumer Education* provided teachers and lecturers with a comprehensive list of sources of information on where the consumer should turn to in government departments, the laws that protected the consumer, the various private and voluntary consumer organisations, other bodies such as BSI, CAB and the Weights and Measures Inspectorate that had an interest in consumer affairs, and trading and industry organisations that also might help.[84] Adults were targeted through the Consumer Education Panel of the National Institution of Adult Education which devised consumer education classes with the NFCG

---

[79] CC, *Annual Report, 1965–1966*, p. 5.   [80] CC, *Annual Report, 1967–1968*, p. 3.
[81] CC, *Annual Report, 1968–1969*, p. 3; *Focus*, 2:3 (1968), 9–16.
[82] *Focus*, 5:6 (1970), 14.   [83] AJ 1/7: *Consumer Council: A Review*, p. 5.
[84] CC, *Information for Consumer Education* (London, 1965).

and the CA, through the extramural departments of provincial universities, through 'shoppers' conferences' and through the quizzes and publicity materials of the 'Wise Consumer Campaign' organised with the Electrical Association for Women.[85] In March 1965, the Council appointed its first full-time Education Officer to co-ordinate all its activities in this field.[86]

However, the most important area in consumer education for the Council was the school: 'Long term, the schools are the best breeding ground for the expert consumer of the future.'[87] The Council's bulletin, *Consumer Education*, detailed the changes in education policy, from an initial aim to introduce a separate course into the curriculum to the creation of various teaching packs that could be integrated across the disciplines. Typical courses consisted of informing students about the local shopping environment, the things to think about before making a purchase, the means and methods of payment, how to assess the good design and quality of particular products, and how to seek redress if the consumer is dissatisifed.[88] Classes were always conducted in a setting that allowed students to make associations with their own lives and often involved 'shopping projects' where students left the classroom and entered the high streets to make wise and informed choices.[89] The subject was grounded in common sense, reason, sobriety and 'wise' behaviour, though the gendered assumptions about the traditional consumer were reinforced by the Council as it assumed from the beginning that the topic would be of 'less appeal' to boys.[90] The consumer was not being taught to think about wider social issues, about the national or international economic aspects of their purchasing decisions or even about whether it is better not to consume in certain situations. Consumption was solely about choice and the methods to enhance individual agency towards such an end. If a wider social goal was invoked, it was only to make the market more decent: 'There is no doubt that a critical and responsible consuming public can obtain better personal satisfaction and influence standards of design and efficiency in everything they buy. Standards of honesty, efficiency and effectiveness that could be debased by an uncaring consuming public, rise to meet the quality of the consumer.'[91] And, at times, notions of citizenship were equated with consumerism – 'good citizenship involves wise decision making, especially those decisions which determine how each individual spends his money'[92] – but this often harked back to

---

[85] CC, *Annual Report, 1968–1969*, p. 30; AJ 2/23: CC(68)18: Consumer Education, note by the staff; AJ 2/25: CC(69)5: Consumer education: progress report, not by the staff.
[86] CC, *Annual Report, 1964–1965*, p. 9.   [87] AJ 1/7: *Consumer Council: A Review*, p. 6.
[88] AJ 2/25: CC(69)5: Consumer education: progress report, not by the staff.
[89] *Focus*, 1:9 (1966), 4.   [90] AJ 1/6: 4th meeting (25 April 1968), 4:8.   [91] *Ibid.*, p. 5.
[92] AJ 7/6: CC, Publications, *Various*: item 31: *Consumer Education*, 2 (1968/9).

nineteenth-century self-help traditions as the 'study of the improvident' and foolish consumer was also encouraged to overcome the supposed causes of social deprivation.[93] Whatever the intention, such educational packs certainly proved popular by 1970, to the extent that in Scotland a one-hour compulsory examination on consumer education had been introduced for the Higher Grade certificate in home economics.[94]

But if voluntary measures and reform of the individual were the cornerstones of consumer protection for many of the Consumer Council members, the realities of consumer politics had convinced many of the Council staff that less individualist solutions were required. In an important qualification to the individualist thesis, and following developments occurring across the consumer policy network, experienced consumer workers began to acknowledge that market disequilibrium could not be rectified by a focus on the individual alone. In its magazine, *Focus*, the Council gave voice to another type of consumer, that of the increasingly professional public sector worker concerned with reforming government in the consumer and public interest. With a limited circulation of 3,000 copies (estimated to be 13–14,000 readers), *Focus* gradually directed its articles to professional groups, such as teachers, businessmen, weights and measures inspectors, scientists and engineers, and brought to committed consumers a more general critique of state activity in the consumer interest.[95] It mixed articles on specific issues, such as medical advertising, the cost of eggs to poorer consumers, or the poor conditions of football stadia,[96] with general discussions of the problems of existing weights and measures legislation, the advantages of a US-style Better Business Bureau and the need for more local authority consumer protection officers.[97] It attempted to present itself as the spearhead of the entire consumer movement in the UK through, for example, providing an outlet for news of all the local consumer groups that proliferated in the 1960s. Other articles discussed consumerism in terms of wider social issues, one feature for instance on bank credit rating highlighting the discriminatory policies against otherwise financially-independent women.[98] *Focus* provided optimistic assessments of new consumer ventures, such as the Consumers' Association's establishment of an advice centre in Kentish Town, and it celebrated prominent consumer activists such as Ralph Nader, heralded as the 'world's greatest consumer', an 'advocate, muckraker and crusader'

---

[93] *Ibid.*, item 32: *Consumer Education*, 3 and 4 (1970).
[94] CC, *Final Annual Report, April–December 1970* (London, 1971), p. 21.
[95] AJ 1/3: 1st meeting (28 January 1965), 1:3; AJ 1/7: *Consumer Council: A Review*, p. 7; AJ 1/3: 8th meeting (23 September 1965), 8:4; AJ/4/47: Note of two-part meeting; *Focus*, 1:1 (1966), 1.
[96] *Focus*, 1:1 (1966), 13–16; 1:4 (1966), 10–11; 1:10 (1966), 2.
[97] *Focus*, 1:1 (1966), 9–12; 1:2 (1966), 14; 1:4 (1966), 18.   [98] *Focus*, 1:6 (1966), 8.

and a 'peaceful revolutionary'.[99] And it allowed a regular outlet for the Council's campaigning voice, such as in the series of articles which called for an overhaul of the legal system or, in particular, the creation of small claims courts that would enable consumers to seek redress over minor problems without incurring the considerable expenses usually associated with the recourse to law.[100]

It is in such instances – in the calls for the reform of hire purchase legislation, in the demands for an extension of legal aid, in the campaign for the tightening up of the legislation on guarantees and in the criticisms of the actions of 'Little Neddies' – that *Focus* occasionally adopted a line more radical than that of the Council members. Despite the non-populist style of writing and its failure 'to break out of a middle-class market and reach the mass of people beyond',[101] *Focus* provided a forum for Council staff to develop their expertise in consumer affairs and reflect a growing professionalism in consumer protection that meant advocates turned more to the state rather than the individual to improve the position of the consumer in the marketplace. This itself reflected a wider outlook on consumerism being developed by those in the Council who were keen to attach the organisation to international developments. Every *Annual Report* summarised the activities of the Bureau Européen des Unions de Consommateurs (BEUC) and the International Organisation of Consumers' Unions (IOCU) as well as the growth of consumer organisation in other countries.[102] Increasingly, the Council itself began to acknowledge that the individual consumer would never be able to achieve a 'fair deal' on his or her own. When Lord Donaldson took over the chair from Elliot, he was keen to extend the resources of the Council so that it could involve itself in a range of wider policy issues.[103] Donaldson remained committed to the notion that individual action within a competitive system was the ultimate protector of the consumer but he also acknowledged that consumers 'do not have this single-minded attention to consumer needs to match single-minded business or professional men . . . Time and again we have seen that the lone, unorganised consumer cannot by merely removing his custom affect the pursuit of policies that put the interests of the business or working community before the interest of the customer.'[104] And he closed with an acknowledgement that the focus on the individual consumer had proved insufficient for the operating philosophy of the Council. It had been forced to move from 'neat aphorisms about value

[99] *Focus*, 5:9 (1970), 6–7; 5:2 (1970), 9–12.
[100] *Focus*, 2:12 (1968), 2–5; 4:10 (1969), 1; 5:4 (1970), 19–22; 5:8 (1970), 2–5.
[101] *Focus*, 1:2 (1966), 1.
[102] AJ 2/17: CC(67)6: International consumer organisations, note by the staff.
[103] *Focus*, 3:3 (1968), 6.   [104] CC, *Final Annual Report, April–December 1970*, p. 1.

for money, cautionary warnings about safety and an obsession with high street shopping problems', turning its attention instead to such areas as small claims courts, the nationalised industries and decimalisation.[105] He ended with a prediction, accepting that the funding and ideology of the Consumer Council had been insufficient for what he saw as an expanding movement: 'Someday someone will have to invent a new, publicly financed body to promote and protect the consumer interest. And when they do I suspect it will cost more than the modest 1d per year per head of the population which the Council has cost the country.'[106]

Donaldson's prediction was entirely correct, though it necessitated the closure of his own Council before changes could take place. In 1970 the Conservative government abolished the Council, an act understandably felt to be a 'brutal murder' by Ackroyd and which was committed as part of a series of cutbacks within which Edward Heath failed to predict the public backlash that would meet his decision.[107] The *Guardian* labelled Heath's action an anti-democratic and 'niggardly' measure while George Smith later suggested that the Council 'received more coverage in its death throes than it had ever been given during the eight years of its existence' and Michael Whincup claims that the consequent outcry 'led to a much more fundamental shift . . . than if the axe had been spared'.[108] A different explanation for the decision to cut an institution which had always been seriously underfunded (£225,000 per annum by 1970) was that Heath was not prepared to accept Ackroyd's successor, the outspoken Des Wilson of the homeless charity, Shelter.[109] Wilson might have taken the Council into the areas suggested by the Chair, Donaldson, thus dragging it away from the cosy world of product labelling and education packs and into the more genuine consumer public sphere of social and economic policy. If this is to be believed, then it casts more light on the attitude of governments to consumer policy, at least in the 1960s, as the final achievements of the Council were limited. Although the Council was an important landmark in the history of the official recognition of the consumer interest, its restricted funds, together with the ideological outlook of many of the Council's initial members, meant it did not truly reflect the development of a popular consumer consciousness which would be more directly incorporated into the state bureaucracy in the 1970s.

---

[105] *Ibid*, p. 2.   [106] *Ibid*.   [107] *Focus*, 5:11 (1970), 1.
[108] *Guardian* (22 October 1970), p. 12; (31 October 1970), p. 10; (23 December 1970), p. 10; Smith, *Consumer Interest*, p. 1; Whincup, *Consumer Legislation*, p. 7.
[109] J. Mitchell, 'A triptych of organisations: CA, SSRC, NCC', in G. Dench, T. Flower and K. Gavron (eds.), *Young at Eighty: The Prolific Public Life of Michael Young* (Manchester, 1995), p. 13; interview with Rosemary McRobert, 25 March 2002.

The Council could not afford the publicity to ensure that it was a sufficiently well known organisation among the mass of consumers and neither could it handle complaints sufficiently well to gain the confidence and respect of the public.[110] Without a truly mass following behind it, other government departments were not obliged to listen to its demands. The Council recognised that it had very little influence on the Board of Trade's legislative programme and the Labour President, George Darling, formerly committed to consumer protection when in opposition, saw no need for much legislation beyond that of the Trade Descriptions Bill which made slow progress through Parliament.[111] It was also questionable to what extent Council representatives and other consumer advocates on various government committees made any effective contribution. A representative on the Economic Development Committee for the Distributive Trades felt herself 'outgunned' and soon resigned her position, arguing that 'a consumer representative was not appropriate on a body concerned with the general economic condition of the country'.[112] Council members often promoted the virtues of the great British 'amateur', along the lines of the women involved in the BSI, and they were reluctant to combine with traditional consumer groups such as the Co-operative movement, a body which Ackroyd thought ought to concentrate its activities on the promotion of 'a wide range of good quality products, good servicing facilities'.[113] Instead, the Council attempted to foster relations with business and industry, adopting a line so conciliatory that it frequently surprised other branches of the consumers' movement. Elliot sought to placate manufacturers by asserting that 'many complaints about suppliers are not justified' and at all times business was praised for the efforts made on behalf of consumers.[114] When such rhetoric is added to the attempts by the Council to limit consumer affairs, especially in the arena of broader government economic policy, it is clear that the assumptions about the consumer limited the development of state consumerism as much as questions of resources and restricted terms of reference.

The 1960s have been interpreted largely for the impact of the so-called 'cultural revolution', with a recent scholarship arguing that the focus on the exploration of the self and the search for novelty and new experiences was ultimately best catered for by the proliferation of new commodities in the affluent society. In an analytical leap, the 1960s are claimed to have led directly to an ideology at ease with the neo-liberalism of Thatcher

---

[110] AJ 1/2: 10th meeting (22 October 1964), 10:2.
[111] AJ 1/2: 12th meeting (17 December 1964), 12:2; *Focus*, 2:1 (1967), 2.
[112] AJ 1/7: 1st meeting (23 January 1969), 1:2.
[113] AJ 1/7: 8th meeting (25 September 1969), 8:2.
[114] CC, *Annual Report, 1965–1966*, pp. 5–6.

and Reagan and Thomas Frank has recently demonstrated the extent to which many former counterculturalists have embraced the 'new economy' as emphatically as many more obviously pro-market politicians.[115] It is tempting to see in cultural change the roots of later economic developments, but it is quite clear in this case that an individualist model of consumerism was being promoted by the state throughout the 1960s. The Molony Committee and then the Consumer Council encouraged – through its leaflets, its policy advice and particularly its educational work – consumers to think of themselves first and foremost as individuals and that the 'consumer interest' consisted of obtaining greater value for money rather than taking into consideration the range of social issues that had dominated early-twentieth century consumerism and which would again become prominent in the 1970s. The state therefore incorporated a particular vision of the consumer that would not be at odds with that found at the heart of the market reforms of the 1980s. But, again, it is too easy to impose more presentist concerns on any analysis of consumer society, in all its manifestations, cultural or political. The abolition of the Consumer Council also demonstrated the range of consumer politics which had proliferated through the 1960s and to which the main political parties would respond in various ways in the 1970s. As will be seen in the following chapters, the Council staff's belief that far more extensive measures were needed to protect the consumer was shared by a whole range of organisations concerned with the consumer cause. In 1973 the Conservatives established the Office of Fair Trading and, by 1975, the Labour government had instituted the National Consumer Council, two organisations which together extended consumerism into arenas the 1960s Consumer Council could hardly have imagined.

---

[115] C. Campbell, *The Romantic Ethic and the Spirit of Modern Consumerism* (Oxford, 1987); T. Frank, *One Market Under God: Extreme Capitalism, Market Populism, and the End of Economic Democracy* (London, 2001); A. Marwick, *The Sixties* (Oxford, 1998).

9   The right to shop: consumerism and the economy

In a speech at an international consumer conference in 1964, Michael Young, the founder of the Consumers' Association, questioned the focus his own organisation had placed on rational, individualist, affluent, value-for-money, choice-based consumerism. Reflecting the social democratic concerns that inflected the type of consumerism to be explored in chapter 10, Young highlighted three dilemmas that the consumer movement faced: (i) the needs of the poor versus the needs of the rich; (ii) the claims of commercial products versus public services; and (iii) the standard of living versus the quality of life. His answer was to urge for a broader consumer movement, one that showed that consumers, as Henry Epstein of the Australian Consumers' Association had put it in an earlier speech, 'don't intend to march around in a circle to a tune played with one finger on a cash register'.[1] Of the first dilemma, Young argued that consumerism must acknowledge that many consumers in the developing world had no choice at all and he advocated that western consumers donate 1 per cent of their annual incomes to development projects directed by the International Organisation of Consumers' Unions. Of the second, he argued that consumerism should now turn its attention to public services, consumers using their collective voice to get not just more efficient public services, but more of them in total. Of the third, Young recognised some of the limitations of comparative testing consumerism and asked to what purpose consumerism was directed: 'So that kitchens can be packed tighter, ever tighter with labour saving equipment which sometimes belies its name? Are we in the consumers' organisations no more than servants of the washing machine? A sort of human appendage to the machine age? Is our ideal, our picture of Utopia, a housewife in a great suburban house fitted from one end to the other with humming machinery, rushing frantically from one gadget to another, re-arranging the piles of treasured consumer reports from one table to another?'[2]

[1] IOCU, *Consumers on the March: Proceedings of the Third Biennial Conference*, 22–24 June 1964 (London, 1964), p. 130.
[2] *Ibid.*, p. 136

Instead, he argued in Ruskinian or Morrisian terms, consumerism needed to move beyond asking about individual products and teach consumers how to use their time wisely, how to make things for themselves, how to use leisure for individual fulfilment, 'not just what to buy, but how to make delight in all the costless pleasures of life: the open air, the trees, the sky. And perhaps the time will come when people will choose not to buy: choose themselves, as their own individual use of freedom, to limit their acquisition of property in the interest of a fuller life, which may for some people also be a simpler life.'[3]

In this essentially Promethean analysis of the consumer movement he had played such a large role in creating, he was to cast doubt on the professional ethic's stress on comparative testing as a cure to the problems of affluent Britain. Chapter 7 has demonstrated that the technocrats were not just the professional elite of post-war planning. They represented a social movement, one centred around the CA's *Which?* magazine but with the potential to be influenced and directed by a grass-roots movement of thousands of members of local consumer groups. CA success with these people has been principally due to the help and advice it provided consumers with as individuals, catering to consumers' economic activities as shoppers. Yet, from this individualist base, *Which?* has raised a further set of questions as more political remedies have been sought to deal with faulty goods and the CA has had to decide whether it represents only its individual members or is the self-elected spokesbody for consumers in the aggregate. This has provoked a series of debates within the CA, which are the focus of the first half of this chapter, pushing consumerism beyond the bounds of advice on shopping. Throughout the 1960s the CA was able to maintain a fine balance between its economic function of comparative testing and its broader consumerist agendas invoked when it has intervened in political debates. The existence of the Consumer Council from 1963 was of much help as this body was able to speak for all consumers across the country and act as the focal point for any pressure to reform the state in the interests of the consumer. The closure of the Council in 1970, however, provoked a period of self-assessment for the CA as it necessitated a greater campaigning and political role as it found itself the country's principal consumer organisation. Here, the growth of the CA mirrors the history of the Co-operative movement in that its popularity was based on an uneasy mix of an appeal to the individual pocket and an adoption of a political outlook favoured only by a minority of its members. That it was to maintain such a successful balancing act between testing and campaigning was due to the

---

[3] *Ibid.*

pragmatic approaches fronted by the Director, Peter Goldman, who always emphasised the CA's primary duty to its *Which?* subscribers while placing secondary emphasis on political reform and action.

This distinction, between speaking for shoppers as individuals within the marketplace and speaking for consumers as a whole and as interested citizens within society and the state, has found institutional expression in Britain. Chapter 10 will explore the work of the National Consumer Council, but here the Office of Fair Trading (OFT) will be examined as a narrower version of consumerism. Set up in 1973 by the Conservative government, the OFT has been celebrated by many within the consumer movement for its successful actions against business malpractice and in its work to improve trading standards as a whole through the creation of voluntary codes of practice. Yet, an effect of the OFT has been to limit consumerism to just the economic sphere, to rectifying abuses within the market and to the assumption that competition was the ultimate guarantor of the consumers' interests. It is an economic version of consumerism which sees consumer choice as a range of options provided by the free market to be selected by individuals acting solely out of self-interest. It is not a consumerism which sees choice as a decision to opt, say, for private or public provision or which creates effective channels of communication for the consumer-citizen to participate to the same extent in government activity as commerce or the trade unions. It is a consumerism which, as in many earlier instances, can appear to offer so much in practical interventions in the marketplace but which also opens itself up to infinite malleability. If consumers are constructed as individual purchasers of goods and services, the range of interests motivating their decisions is obviously limitless. This enables those seeking to speak for consumers to offer a powerful rhetoric of inclusion and universalism while at the same time avoiding those issues which specific collective groups of consumers might be most concerned. Finally, it is a type of consumerism that slotted neatly alongside the privatisation measures and market reforms of the 1980s as competition, choice and freedom offered the potential liberation of the consumer from the vested interests of both monopoly capitalism and public enterprises. Specific economic gains were traded off against broader social objectives, while at the same time the consumer was reified to the extent that he or she appeared as an individual at the heart of government concern.

Citizens or shoppers: the Consumers' Association

In 1967, to mark the tenth anniversary of the CA, a 'Consumer Assembly' was held at Church House, Westminster, on 3 November. Drawing on all branches of consumerism, from the CA to local groups, to the Consumer Council, to Anthony Crosland (CA Council member and President of the Board of Trade) and even Aubrey Jones, Chairman of the National Board for Prices and Incomes, the Assembly reflected the confidence of an economic and social phenomenon that had made considerable gains within just one decade. On one level much harmony existed between the various speakers, each attesting to the excellent relations between the CA, government, the Consumer Council and 'fair-minded suppliers'.[4] There were also few real tensions between the consumerists, the Assembly demonstrating unity and harmony rather than any underlying discord. Yet, it is also apparent that there existed a fundamental division as to how speakers defined consumerism or the consumer interest. On the one hand, certain figures clearly linked the movement to wider notions of citizenship, spoke of the responsibilities of consumers to their wider communities and emphasised the campaigning nature of consumer action. Crosland invited the CA to continue 'nagging' the government and his own Board of Trade, and Young pointed to the 'collective needs of consumers', suggesting that consumerism ought to embrace all aspects of economic debate, contributing to discussions of issues such as inflation and creating 'a politics of prices to set against the politics of wages'.[5] Tony Benn wanted information for consumers on environmental issues, Alan Day called for a 'collective complaints' service, and a range of interventions from the floor demanded an extension of consumerism into public services.[6] Yet other consumers present emphasised instead the need to restrict consumerism to the economic sphere, equating the consumer purely with the point-of-sale purchaser, and they urged the CA to concentrate on its chief task of providing comparative testing information to individual subscribers. Manufacturers and retailers attempted to co-opt the consumer cause to their own agendas, and 'private consumers' expressed their discontent at the CA's political activities. Some thought there no need for a 'futile' Consumer Council and criticised the 'highly inbred clique of charming social scientists and intellectuals' such as Young for their 'smugness' in dealing with the trade unions and other groups within government.[7] Such feelings could themselves turn into a type of petty-minded politics which stretched back to the defensiveness of the turn-of-the-century *Watch Dog*. A Mr Herne claimed positively that consumers were 'an ordinary, lower middle class lot nursing [their] hearts' and others suggested the focus should remain the problems of the pressure cooker and the washing

---

[4] CAA 67: Consumer Assembly, *Priorities, 1967–1977: Proceedings of Conference held at Church House, Westminster* (3 November 1967), p. 5.
[5] *Ibid.*, pp. 20, 24.   [6] *Ibid.*, pp. 28–9, 33, 36–7, 46.   [7] *Ibid.*, p. 32.

machine.[8] Ominously, a Desmond Fox reminded the leaders of the CA that 'This is the information that people pay for . . . The private members provide you with the finance and money to be what you are. Take them away and you are nothing.'[9]

Fox's blunt statement was at least acknowledged by the CA to be one of fact. Much of the CA's history could be written as a delicate balancing act between the two aspects of consumerism: one allied to wider political concerns over the nature of citizenship; another limited to better advice for individual purchasers of goods and possibly services. The former has always been restricted by the professional duty and economic necessity of providing the second and, as the staff of CA have come to increasingly dominate the organisation's activities, over and above the influence of the CA Council, the focus on comparative testing has predominated. During the 1960s, and as soon as the CA had become a respectable, financially secure, subscription-based institution, *Which?* became less aggressive in scope, particularly in its attitude to manufacturers and its 'knocking of dodgy goods'.[10] Growth came through a focus on research, magazine improvement and the creation of new publications, while the financial problems consequent of inflation in the early 1970s forced the CA to think of itself as a business which must succeed in the services to its members.[11] The model of comparative testing rational consumerism was therefore not so much extended but more applied to new areas. A Development Committee was set up specifically for this purpose, building on such enterprises as the funding and creation of the Institute for Consumer Ergonomics at the University of Loughborough in 1970 which complemented the CA's testing procedures by evaluating the design of goods and services from the consumer's perspective.[12] In all of this there existed an assumption that consumers ought to be addressed as individuals, especially since, as the CA put it, there was 'no strong commonality of interests among consumers'.[13]

Caspar Brook, Director of the CA from 1958 until 1964, was an important influence in this direction. In a 'cogitation paper' presented to the CA Council in January 1959, Brook concluded that he saw the future

[8] *Ibid.* pp. 32–3.   [9] *Ibid.*, p. 34.
[10] D. Grose, 'The Consumers' Association and *Which?*', in J. Mitchell (ed.), *Marketing and the Consumer Movement* (London, 1978), p. 15.
[11] CA, *Annual Report, 1969–1970*, p. 8; CA, *Annual Report, 1971–1972*, p. 7.
[12] CA, *Annual Report, 1972–1973*, p. 11; J. Aspinall, 'Glossary of organisations active in consumer affairs', in Mitchell (ed.), *Marketing*, p. 243; M. H. Whincup, *Consumer Legislation in the United Kingdom and the Republic of Ireland* (London, 1980), p. 138; CA, *Annual Report, 1969–1970*, p. 5; CA, *Annual Report, 1970–1971*, p. 7; CAA 27: Institute for Consumer Ergonomics, *List of Reports and Publications* (1980).
[13] Cited in G. Smith, *The Consumer Interest* (London, 1982), p. 159.

of the CA as a 'first class research organisation and publishing house'.[14] Following a survey of members conducted by the future author of *The Affluent Sheep*, Robert Millar, Brook argued that 'it seems to me that the majority wants us to continue to do nothing but test goods, investigate services and report the results more or less dead-pan'.[15] He advised against extending CA's activities into the 'tougher approach' of political campaigning and, although he advocated an Institute for Consumer Affairs (which was to become RICA: see below), chapter 7 has already shown his commitment to an individualist consumerism, creating what he termed 'more discriminating' shoppers. He shared little of the social-democratic idealism of the consumer pioneers of the CA Council, nor any nostalgia for previous consumer activism as he urged the Co-operative Wholesale Society to become a purely commercial organisation.[16] Consumerism, for Brook, was to be centred around *Which?* reports and run by an efficient and effective private enterprise.

Brook's interpretation of consumerism as an information guide for individuals was advocated by other prominent consumerists. Jeremy Mitchell, Director of Information at the CA before becoming, among other things, Director of Consumer Affairs at the OFT and later Director of the National Consumer Council, collaborated with John Methven, Director-General of the Confederation of British Industry, to suggest that there was never 'any real conflict of interests between suppliers and consumers'.[17] For Mitchell the moderate, 'only the market place can provide the answer'.[18] Although a forceful consumer advocate, he was proud to announce that the consumer movement was 'untainted by ideology', its basis for political action being only the desire to provide information.[19] For Mitchell, the consumer was always more than an individual unit, since some political action was ultimately inevitable, but his was a consumerism deliberately differentiated from the confrontational tactics of a Ralph Nader or the all-embracing vision of Michael Young. The role of the consumer was much less than that of the citizen, and only confusion and trouble would emerge in a democracy if the two were equated.[20]

The emphasis on the market, individual choice and competition was repeated elsewhere and beyond the CA. Christina Fulop argued for the

[14] C. Brook, 'Cogitation paper', 28 January 1959, internal CA document, private possession of author.
[15] *Ibid.*, p. 3.
[16] RICA, *British Co-operatives: A Consumers' Movement?* (London, 1964), p. 31.
[17] J. Methven, 'Foreword', in Mitchell (ed.), *Marketing*, p. vii.
[18] J. Mitchell, 'Some lessons for marketing', in Mitchell (ed.), *Marketing*, p. 3.
[19] *Ibid.*, p. 8; J. Mitchell, 'Management and the consumer movement', *Journal of General Management*, 3:4 (1976), 48.
[20] Mitchell, 'Management', p. 52.

Institute of Economic Affairs that the consumer interest lay in unrestricted trade and an expansion of the free market.[21] Her neo-liberalism coalesced with empowered individualism. Peter Goldman, Director of the CA from 1964 until 1986, continued the organisation's policy to 'help people make sensible, informed choices when shopping'.[22] Although Goldman's consumerism extended beyond the point of purchase, his aim was to meet the economist's criteria of perfect competition, 'to give substance to the theory of consumer sovereignty'.[23] In practical terms it meant that by the 1980s the CA was still very much concerned with selling *Which?* and its satellite publications, extending its services into computers, hobbies, savings and investment, campaigning for the liberalisation of shop trading hours and working to ensure that its test reports achieved a wider publicity on television and in the newspapers, as well as advertising to business corporations that 'we're on your side'.[24] Here was an agenda supported by those free marketeers connected with the very organisations which many of the left-leaning original members of the CA had earlier opposed. Just as the Co-operative movement witnessed a 'middle-class embrace' in the late nineteenth century, so too did consumerism receive the patronage of committed industry-minded figures such as the Duke of Edinburgh.[25]

Not all of this should be interpreted as having a politically or economically conservative effect, since the CA's gradual reformism captured the imagination of those who had long been involved in the 'consumer revolution'. Especially in times of inflation, greater information to the individual was held to improve not only that individual's value for money, but the economy as a whole due to the assumed deflationary pressure of rational shopping.[26] And, as has already been seen in chapter 7, liberal utopian fantasies were often attached to the transformative power of objective information. In 1972, Robin Wight extended the revolutionary analogy of Robert Millar's 'affluent sheep' further still. Made aware of the 'politico-technocratic tyranny' by first Orwell, then Packard and finally Galbraith, consumers were at the gates of a new order, though it was to be a revolution with 'no marches, no manifesto, no real leaders and few formal followers'.[27] Wight's metaphors came thick and fast. The advertising

[21] C. Fulop, *Competition for Consumers: A Study of the Changing Channels of Distribution* (London, 1964), p. 297.
[22] CA, *Annual Report, 1975–1976*, p. 7.
[23] CA, *Annual Report, 1977–1978*, p. 14.   [24] CA, *Annual Report, 1982–1983*, p. 12.
[25] P. Gurney, 'The middle-class embrace: language, representation and the contest over co-operative forms in Britain, 1860–1914', *Victorian Studies*, Winter (1994), 253–86; CA, *Annual Report, 1977–1978*, p. 8.
[26] CA, *Annual Report, 1974–1975*, p. 8.
[27] R. Wight, *The Day the Pigs Refused to be Driven to Market: Advertising and the Consumer Revolution* (London, 1972), p. xii.

industry, through its own excesses, was to bring its own 'self-destruction'. The pigs (consumers) would refuse to be driven to market, launching a 'consumer holocaust' from out of the ashes of the riots of 1968, and from amidst the herd, an almost explicitly Nietszchean 'British Ralph Nader' would emerge to make sense of the chaos, create a 'new consumer' and establish a 'new coincidence of self-interest between business and the consumer'.[28] In Wight's confused hyperbole, he was to criticise the 'sedate middle-class activity' of the 'well meaning old ladies' of the CA, as well as the 'dowager duchess' (Baroness Elliot) of the Consumer Council, but his revolution was a clear development of the empowerment felt by individuals through the provision of objective comparative testing data.[29]

Few were prepared, or had the imagination, to envision the new society coming out of a specifically defined consumerism. Much more often, an economic focus resulted in a politics of pragmatism rather than an idealist's dream. Rachel Waterhouse's period in the Chair of the Council (1982–90) saw an increased commitment to practical policy objectives built on the foundations of a successful *Which?* magazine. Her public statements understandably lacked the vision of a Michael Young and concentrated instead on the solid achievements and initiatives taken by the CA.[30] The work of the CA had to reflect the members' concern to be provided with information as individuals and the organisation's campaigning work was to be presented as a list of activities or specific goals rather than part of a coherent political vision.[31] Success was to be gained 'only if we stick close to the basic truths that have always guided CA. We are a membership organisation. Our paramount mission is to give our members the help and information they want when they want it'.[32] In her one article setting out a philosophy of consumerism, she sought to impose limits to, rather than explore opportunities for, expansion. The purpose of the consumer movement was, she argued in 1988, to assist 'an individual or person in one part of their life: that is, as purchaser or user of goods or services, whether privately or publicly supplied'.[33] She happily accepted the label, 'professional consumer', taking this to mean 'a degree of preoccupation with the immediate, with what is happening in the marketplace'.[34] Everybody was a consumer but, 'thank goodness', nobody was a consumer all of the time. Consumerism had to be differentiated

---

[28] *Ibid.*, pp. xiii, 73.   [29] *Ibid.*, p. 81.   [30] CA, *Annual Report, 1981–1982*, pp. 6–7.
[31] CA, *Annual Report, 1982–1983*, pp. 8–9; CA, *Annual Report, 1983–1984*, pp. 8–9; CA, *Annual Report, 1984–1985*, p. 7; CA, *Annual Report, 1986–1987*, p. 6.
[32] CA, *Annual Report, 1984–1985*, p. 7.
[33] CAA 27: R. Waterhouse, 'New frontiers for consumerism', *RSA Journal* (June 1988), 466.
[34] *Ibid.*

from citizenship and she provided a series of examples of issues falling outside her own realm: health, education, the tax system, nuclear power, inner city regeneration, the preservation of ancient buildings and the countryside, housing tenure and environmentalism.[35]

Within this apparently apolitical consumerism, *Which?* itself was merely another commodity, one source of information among many which consumers could increasingly buy. By the end of the 1970s, the provision of comparative information had become a competitive business in itself. From an early date, the CA had attempted to publicise its testing to a wider audience. Firstly, in 1962 the BBC's 'Choice' programme publicised the findings of *Which?* and the CAC's *Shopper's Guide*, stimulating a demand for the kind of shopping advice found in Elizabeth Gundrey's publications throughout the 1960s.[36] In the 1970s her work was followed by titles such as *How to Complain, The Innocent Consumer, Consumers: Know Your Rights* and *The Consumer Jungle*, suggesting, as with the 1960s Consumer Council, that market imperfections could be rectified through the empowerment of the individual alone.[37] Rival magazines appeared offering advice on purchasing photography equipment, DIY products, hi-fi, financial services and food: by 1985, there were twenty-five titles devoted solely to motor cars.[38] Almost all newspapers now ran consumer advice columns and sensationalist TV programming became popular, exposing the manipulators of innocent shoppers, most famously in 'the queen of the media's consumer protectors', Esther Rantzen's 'That's Life' and Roger Cook's original radio series, 'Checkpoint'.[39] Add to this independent television's 'Money-go-round' and Nationwide's 'Consumer Unit' in the 1970s and the trend was set for 'Watchdog'.[40] This programme started in the early 1980s as a local news broadcast, now has eighty permanent staff dealing with 7,000 queries every week and has resulted in a plethora of spin-offs and cheap prime time derivatives.[41] Perhaps the only perfect form of competition that consumerism has brought about is that for information-based consumerism itself. To maintain its market

---

[35] *Ibid.*, p. 467.

[36] *Guardian* (17 February 1962), p. 3; CA, *Annual Report, 1962–1963*, p. 7.

[37] C. Wright, *Better Buying* (London, 1967); C. Ward, *How to Complain* (London, 1974); M. Giordan, *How to be Exploited (And How to Avoid It)* (London, 1978); S. Margelius, *The Innocent Consumer* (London, 1967); J. V. Harries, *Consumers: Know Your Rights* (London, 1978); M. Giordan, *The Consumer Jungle* (London, 1974); A. Stannesby, *Consumer Rights Handbook* (London, 1986).

[38] S. Franks, 'Selling consumer protection: competitive strategies of the Consumers' Association, 1957–1990', MPhil thesis, University of Oxford (2000), p. 98.

[39] Smith, *Consumer Interest*, p. 1.   [40] CA, *Annual Report, 1975–1976*, p. 9.

[41] A. Burgess, 'Flattering consumption: creating a Europe of the consumer', *Journal of Consumer Culture* 1:1 (2001), 94.

share, the CA has engaged in hard-sell marketing techniques (direct mail, sweepstakes, prize draws), increased its expenditure on advertising, changed its packaging, developed human interest stories and adopted the friendlier first person singular in *Which?* – that is, precisely those forms of commercial practice early consumerists claimed prevented the consumer from making an objective assessment between goods.[42] John Beishon, appointed Director of CA in 1986 following the dismissal of Goldman, oversaw many of these changes, at one and the same time creating a more market-oriented and perhaps commercially viable CA yet offending an older generation of consumer activists who, according to Waterhouse, formed a 'Cave of Adullam' in resistance to the perceived corruption of an organisation many had created as a bulwark against rampant market values.[43] Waterhouse's period as Chair throughout the 1980s therefore marked a significant change in the history of the CA, as an earlier idealism gave way to an efficient pragmatism.

In contrast to the focus on the economic life of the consumer, a competing consumerist strand within the CA has also existed, often harmoniously, though often contradictorily. From the late 1950s, various consumers connected to the CA have shown a greater eagerness to link consumerism to notions of citizenship and a clear involvement in the political process. Michael Young's democratic socialist vision will be explored in the next chapter, but others too saw the limits of a consumer movement which expected so much from the discriminating individual. Leonard Tivey, a Birmingham University political scientist and prominent member of his local consumer group, argued that a focus on individual choice was unlikely to lead to a consumer consciousness or ideology: some greater engagement with notions of consumer protection was necessary if consumers were to have as much of a say as manufacturers and trade unionists.[44] Others stressed the importance of moving away from a notion of the consumer as 'the housewife with the shopping basket' to one of 'the citizen in almost every aspect of his daily life and as a participant in local action'.[45] Eirlys Roberts, working within the CA, asked 'where does a consumer end and a citizen begin?' and maintained a critical attitude to manufacturers and their efforts to exploit the fashion system through

---

[42] Franks, 'Selling consumer protection', pp. 112–21.
[43] Interviews with Rachel Waterhouse, 8 March 2002; Rosemary McRobert, 25 March 2002; Alastair Macgeorge, 26 March 2002; unnamed current CA staff member, 21 November 2000.
[44] L. Tivey, 'The politics of the consumer', in R. Kimber and J. J. Richardson, *Pressure Groups in Britain: A Reader* (London, 1974), pp. 195–209.
[45] R. Wraith, *The Consumer Cause: A Short Account of its Organisation, Power and Importance* (London, 1976), p. 68.

planned obsolescence.[46] She clearly saw a role for consumerism much wider in scope than that offered by Waterhouse. Consumer activists were usually 'idealists, anti-materialist, the type of those who dislike inequality of any kind and attack it instinctively' and as such ought to 'think of the consumer as a consumer not merely of commercial goods and services, but of the services of the nationalised industries, of central and local government, of the law, of the environment, indeed of the whole system under which we live'.[47]

Within the day-to-day working of the CA there was little time for the development of a consumer ideology, but what is clear throughout the 1960s and beyond is the incremental development of a political and campaigning strand of consumerism, as researchers discovered the limits to approaches based on rational individual choice. Caspar Brook's proposal for a research organisation was accepted and the Research Institute for Consumer Affairs (RICA) was established as an independent charitable trust in 1963 with the aim of investigating how adequately goods and services met the needs of all consumers, but especially underprivileged users in the spheres of government services, the nationalised industries, grant-aided bodies and the professions. Research topics were commissioned by the CA but also by other organisations such as the Sports Council, the Child Poverty Action Group and government departments.[48] Examining issues normally felt to be beyond the scope of *Which?*, RICA considered the consumer interest in the aggregate rather than at the individual level, often highlighting those areas where all purchases might be regarded as bad through structural faults in the systems of provision.[49] In its monthly bulletin, *Consumer News*, it reported on such topics as consumer law, children in hospitals, fuel, shopping facilities, the press, access to Parliament, public lavatories, shop hours and leisure and the countryside. In a series of books in the 1960s it examined the car industry, estate agency, butcher's shops and children's toys. It argued that consumerism within the NHS was synonymous with citizenship since 'the adult "consumers" whom the National Health Service sustains as patients are also those who maintain it as citizens'.[50] Consumer protection legislation was reviewed and critiqued as a whole and town planning was reconfigured not as an end product which consumers had to deal with, but as a process

[46] CAA 27: E. Roberts, 'When the goods grow old' (4 September 1967); E. Roberts, 'A fair deal for the public', *RSA Journal* (April 1976), 221.
[47] Roberts, 'Fair deal', p. 222
[48] Aspinall, 'Glossary', p. 245; L. Syson, *Fair Trading* (London, 1964); CA, *Annual Report, 1962–1963*, p. 15.
[49] *Consumer News (Monthly Bulletin of RICA)*, 17 (1964), 1.
[50] RICA, *General Practice: A Consumer Commentary* (London, 1963), p. 4.

of development within which consumers in voluntary bodies should contribute and advise as much as ratepayers and voters.[51] Consumerism was applied to new groups and subjects that had previously been considered as separate issues, such as RICA's investigations into the general problems faced by elderly consumers and the problems of the poor in the developing world.[52] It urged local consumer groups to turn the tide of democratic participation and re-infuse forms of active citizenship within the municipality, encouraging collaboration with as diverse a range of pressure groups as possible, from the Association for the Improvement of Maternity Services to the Association for the Advancement of State Education: 'These movements imply a blurring of the distinction between "consumer" and "citizen", which may be conceptually untidy, but which is socially and educationally important.'[53]

RICA's apparent radicalism should not be interpreted too far. It was generally against state intervention and deliberate impositions upon industry and, following a by now regular theme, its investigation into the Co-operative movement eschewed any faith in the ideals of the Co-operative Commonwealth and it urged the CWS to become a capitalist enterprise.[54] Dismissing the International Co-operative Alliance's definition of the 'active consumer', RICA concluded that that the true test was which organisation helped the consumer obtain the best kettle: consumers 'are concerned with price and performance, not with whether it was produced under autocratic or democratic auspices'.[55] But such rhetorical strategies were designed to establish the CA as the new authority on consumer affairs. Once older groups had been dismissed RICA was able to then add to the liberal economic model of *Which?*'s rationality. Alongside value for money ought to be considerations of 'sense and sensibility', beauty and quality as well as utility, and the wider aims of improving 'industry, commerce and society'.[56] This liberal consumer, who fought not only for his or her own rights, but for others to enjoy those same rights, was far more than the 'grumbling shopper'. He or she could often be seen in local consumer groups: 'these groups have turned the rather self-regarding act of subscribing to *Which?* or, formerly, to *Shopper's Guide*, into the basis for a concern with public issues and social improvement'.[57] With some imagination and effort, education could lead

[51] Syson, *Fair Trading*; RICA, *Town Planning: The Consumer's Environment* (London, 1965).
[52] RICA, *Elderly Consumers: The Problem Assessed* (London, 1965); RICA, *New Nations: Problems for Consumers* (London, 1964).
[53] RICA, *Consumer Education: Conceptions and Resources* (London, 1964), p. 7; *Consumer News*, 11 (1964), 1, 3.
[54] *Consumers News*, 18 (1964), 4; 11 (1964), 3; RICA, *British Co-operatives*.
[55] RICA, *British Co-operatives*, p. 5.
[56] RICA, *Consumer Education*, p. 16.   [57] *Ibid.*, p. 39.

to an improved 'quality of civilisation', since this was itself 'a reflection of how we all, as consumers and citizens, think the wealth of the country should be spent'.[58]

But just as this consumer was to be transformed into a supershopper imbued with both the hyper-rationality of liberal economics and the aesthetic sense of a Ruskinian sensibility, so too was the state to be altered to protect the interests of consumers in the aggregate. From the beginning of the 1960s, the CA increasingly turned to the state rather than the individual to rectify the abuses of the market. By 1980, *The Times* was able to claim that the CA had 'filled more pages of the statute book than any other pressure group this century'.[59] Thanks to the efforts of the Legal Officer, David Tench, the CA was able to exert an important influence on government and Parliament, often far in excess of the expectations of the CA Council. It campaigned on issues of consumer representation, informative labelling, shop and licensing hours, decimalisation, the Trade Descriptions Act of 1968, the 1973 Fair Trading Act and numerous matters of product safety, with Michael Whincup suggesting the 1971 Unsolicited Goods and Services Act to have been the first Act of Parliament directly attributable to CA lobbying.[60] It advised and submitted evidence to an increasing range of official enquiries, most noticeably the Crowther Committee on Consumer Credit but including also investigations into legal services, conveyancing, privacy, the press, data protection and financial services, all of these building on its 1960 submission to the Molony Committee on Consumer Protection. Increasing rates of inflation provoked a more general political attitude in the 1970s as both consumers in general and the CA in particular were hit by what was feared to be an 'impending catastrophe of incalculable proportions'.[61] Rising prices were bad for consumers of course, but the politics of consumption mirrored general economic policy, and inflation and trade protection were alleged to create 'mistrust and insecurity in all our transactions, thus undermining the entire fabric of society'.[62] Christopher Zealley, Chair of the CA Council from 1976 to 1982, felt such economic crises warranted a widening of the definition of consumerism: 'So far the consumer movement has stood so firmly for the individual as a free agent requiring free choice that it seems alien for consumers to combine, like trade unions, and pitch their unified strength behind policy demands'.[63] Following this, politics has played a

---

[58] *Ibid.*, p. 40.   [59] Cited in CA, *Annual Report, 1979–1980*, p. 13.
[60] Whincup, *Consumer Legislation*, p. 140; CA, *Annual Report, 1962–1963*, p. 3; CAA 27: Campaigning Resource Book: *Product Safety: CA Policy Document* (1975); *The Trade Descriptions Act 1968: A Review of the Review* (1975); *Consumer Consultative Council* (1974).
[61] CA, *Annual Report, 1974–1975*, p. 5.
[62] CA, *Annual Report, 1977–1978*, p. 5.   [63] *Ibid.*, p. 6.

continuously prominent role in the CA's activities. During the 1980s, its cross-party political campaigning assessed whether market liberalisation reforms represented an improvement for the consumer, it lobbied Parliament to influence various pieces of legislation, it incorporated environmentalism within its campaigning activities, it fought and succeeded in increasing its representative role and it recorded countless minor victories in the regulation of specific goods and services. Its involvement with international organisations also became more prominent, though this had been the case for some time since Peter Goldman had been President of the International Organisation of Consumers Unions from 1970–5 and Eirlys Roberts had become Chief Executive of the Bureau Européen des Unions de Consommateurs in 1973.[64]

These separate fields within the CA organisation – between customers and citizens, between purchasing and politics, between serving the individual or the public at large – have generally existed comfortably alongside one another, creating no great factions within the staff or the Council. With the closure of the Consumer Council in 1970, the CA found itself the only sufficiently resourced consumer body in the country capable of speaking for consumers at either an individual or aggregate level and was therefore forced into adopting a more political role to put forward 'the collective view of the consuming public'.[65] Its Consumer Representation Committee, set up in 1966, was transformed into the Campaign Committee and immediately drew on the expertise of Rosemary McRobert (formerly of the Consumer Council) and the influential legal expert, Tench. The possible tensions between the CA's campaigning and information provision roles was solved through the repeated pronouncements of Goldman, the CA Director and former Director of the Conservative Party Political Centre, a 'one nation' Tory with strong liberal principles.[66] He recognised the responsibility of the CA to cater specifically to its members' interests but by 1967 was clearly in favour of 'gradually' expanding its political activities over time, as well as its field of research and its representation of the underprivileged consumer.[67] In several flamboyant interventions, his smattering of French, German and Greek adding a cosmopolitan flair to a consumerism often wrongly accused of wittering drabness, he argued that while CA's primary function would always remain its comparative testing service for its subscribers, it must also remember its secondary purpose to campaign for general changes in the

---

[64] E. Roberts, 'Consumers in the Common Market', *European Studies*, 22 (1975), 1–4.
[65] Cited in Franks, 'Selling consumer protection', p. 82.
[66] P. Goldman, *Some Principles of Conservatism* (London, 1961); *Guardian* (23 July 1964), 8.
[67] CAA 27: *Consumer Assembly* (3 November 1967): speech by P. Goldman, pp. 1–7.

law if they believed such action was in the interest of its members.[68] During the 1960s, although CA consumerism did not 'develop a body of principles' since its members were 'much too busy with the immediate',[69] its single issue campaign tactics expanded. After the events of 1970, Goldman's division of the CA's two roles became increasingly important. He was able to be triumphalist about the legislative successes for consumerism in the 1970s, while at the same time celebrating the CA's individualist position.[70]

Goldman's division of the CA's primary and secondary activities legitimated its campaigning work to its non-committal subscribers and prevented a focus purely on comparative testing which on its own would have failed to have maintained the support and dynamism of many of the organisation's early and leading staff and supporters. It also became a mantra repeated by subsequent Council Chairs and Directors, Christopher Zealley arguing that the CA promoted individualism but also collective action to ensure that such individualism could prosper.[71] In 1987, the dual role was partially institutionalised with the creation of a charitable trust, the Association for Consumer Research, to engage in similar activities to RICA, while comparative testing publishing continued as Consumers' Association Limited.[72] This was done as part of a broader series of reforms overseen by Beishon and which has slightly disillusioned an older generation of consumerists taken aback by, for example, the threats to objectivity in financial services reporting when the CA had introduced its own credit card (selected as the best buy in September 1996).[73] It is undeniable, though, that the CA's improved market position in the 1990s has also enabled it to position itself as the authority on consumer affairs and consequently participate in many further levels of the political process. This is not to say that its wider membership has not forced a certain timidity in the expansion of the CA view of the politics of consumption – the CA has clearly followed rather than led the revival of interest in ethical and green consumerism and anti-globalism – but its campaigns are sufficiently diverse to include banking, mortgages, the price of cars in

[68] CAA 27: M. Patrick, R. Chapman and R. Winsbury, 'Consumerism searches for a new direction', *Campaign* (11 December 1970), 25–9; P. Goldman, 'Competition: a consumer approach' (7 March 1973).

[69] CAA 27: P. Goldman, 'Consumerism – art or science?', *RSA Journal* (August 1969), 1–7.

[70] CAA 27: P. Goldman, 'Consumers: the new factor in economics', *Keemat Special Issue* (March–April 1976), 17–19.

[71] CA, *Annual Report, 1977–1978*, p. 6; CA, *Annual Report, 1979–1980*, p. 5.

[72] CA, *Annual Report, 1987–1988*, p. 6.

[73] Interview with Len Tivey, 7 March 2002; A. Aldridge, 'Engaging with promotional culture: organised consumerism and the personal financial services industry', *Sociology*, 31:3 (1997), 380–403.

Britain, the Food Standards Agency, GM food, freedom of information, fuel poverty, competition policy and consumers' legal rights under international e-commerce.[74] The CA's dual role has therefore provided a degree of flexibility which has enabled continued growth and success, yet it is clear that its secondary commitment to protecting individuals in the aggregate is also extremely malleable. In chapter 10, it will be seen that it could legitimate the development of a social democratic consumer politics, but as in the OFT and the market reforms of the 1980s, it could also be interpreted to limit consumer protection to simply the economic sphere.

The Office of Fair Trading

Edward Heath's abolition of the Consumer Council in 1970 only seemed to confirm a suspicion among many in the media about the Conservative Party's commitment to consumerism as well as the Board of Trade's traditional preference for 'a tête-à-tête with "the trade"' rather than the consumer. The *Guardian* in particular came out in support of Elizabeth Ackroyd and Lord Donaldson in their 'contempt' for the government's decision.[75] The subsequent public reaction to Heath's decision therefore resulted in a Conservative U-turn, so much so that 1973 was heralded as 'the year of the consumer' as the government boarded consumerism's 'vote-winning bandwagon'.[76] By this year, Geoffrey Howe was established as the Minister for Consumer Affairs (from November 1972) within the Board of Trade, responsible for overseeing the Counter-Inflation Act which set up the Price Commission, and the Fair Trading Act was passed which set up the Office of Fair Trading along with its Director-General who worked with the Consumer Protection Advisory Committee (CPAC) within the Department of Trade and Industry.[77] The establishment of the OFT complemented the work of the CA. The official consumer protection body, assisting consumers through the regulation of market abuse, took over many of the activities that the CA would have increasingly had to take upon itself had the Consumer Council never been replaced. While the CA was able to continue its focus on providing positive support for the individual consumer, the OFT focussed on the regulation of corporate structures which prevented all consumers from exercising their individual rights to choice and discrimination.

---

[74] CA, *Annual Report, 1999–2000*, pp. 6–10.
[75] *Guardian* (31 October 1970), p. 10; (23 December 1970), p. 10.
[76] Whincup, *Consumer Legislation*, p. 7.
[77] *Ibid.*, p. 10; Aspinall, 'Glossary', p. 260; D. Butler and G. Butler, *Twentieth-Century British Political Facts* (London, 2000).

The OFT was set up in the belief that 'competition was the consumer's best friend', its two main spheres of activity focussing on monopolies and mergers and restrictive practices, though a third area concentrated on consumer affairs and, after the 1974 Consumer Credit Act, a fourth saw to the regulation and licensing of credit traders.[78] It was headed by a forceful Director-General, though he was not to have the power to take up individual cases. However, he was able to advise the Secretary of State to make references to the Monopolies and Mergers Commission and was able to advise on appropriate actions against offending businesses as well as seek assurances from concerned parties and monitor subsequent agreements.[79] In 1986, Gordon Borrie, then Director-General, rejected his role as a 'watchdog' and suggested instead he was 'a *regulator* of business, a *monitor* of markets and laws, a *proposer* of policies, and *educator* of the public and a *promoter* of high trading standards.[80] He was originally assisted by a staff of 184, organised into five divisions, though this expanded to six (Consumer Affairs, Consumer Credit, Monopolies and Mergers, Restrictive Trade Practices, Legal affairs and Information) and a total of 324 staff by 1977.[81] In its monopoly work, the OFT monitored the economic performance of industries to identify those areas warranting further study, as well as considering the flow of complaints about trading practices alleged to be unfair. If a monopoly situation was discovered the Director-General was then at liberty to recommend referral to the Commission, which itself had been reformed by the 1973 Fair Trading Act following an earlier broadening of its scope in 1965.[82] Similarly, restrictive trading practices were also monitored by the OFT through an official registry of such agreements (the Director-General judging whether they accorded with existing legislation), extended in 1977 under the Restrictive Trade Practices Act.[83] The Consumer Affairs Division, first directed by Jeremy Mitchell from the CA, also contributed to the monitoring of specific trading practices, specifically those thought to harm the shopper. In many ways, it was similar to the former Consumer Council, but with greater freedom to suggest legislative remedies and with better effective

[78] Wraith, *Consumer Cause*, p. 20; OFT, *The Work of the Office of Fair Trading* (London, 1976), p. 3; Whincup, *Consumer Legislation*, pp. 106–21.

[79] Aspinall, 'Glossary', p. 264; Whincup, *Consumer Legislation*, p. 13; Director-General of the OFT, *Annual Report, 1976* (London, 1977), pp. 94–6.

[80] Director-General of the OFT, *Annual Report, 1986* (London, 1987), p. 10.

[81] Director-General of the OFT, *Annual Report, November 1973–December 1974*, p. 13; OFT, *Annual Report, 1976*, p. 6.

[82] Central Office of Information, *Fair Trading and Consumer Protection in Britain* (London, 1976), p. 49; Whincup, *Consumer Legislation*, pp. 24–8; OFT, *Annual Report, 1973–1974*, pp. 17–18; Smith, *Consumer Interest*, p. 47.

[83] Smith, *Consumer Interest*, p. 269.

monitoring procedures.[84] It also devoted much of its energies to encouraging industries to develop voluntary codes of practice and worked with the Information Division to publish consumer advice literature.[85] Where trade practices were thought to harm the consumer, the Director-General was empowered to ask the Consumer Protection Advisory Committee, a body chaired by Gordon Borrie and independent of the OFT, to investigate the matter and report to the Secretary of State.[86] All such measures proved popular with the existing consumer movement which gave the OFT its full support. The CA set up 'close links' with the OFT, and the NFCG maintained 'friendly relations', not least because of Borrie's long-term association with the Birmingham group and through the work of the NFCG in monitoring prices and testing codes of practice throughout the 1970s and into the 1980s.[87]

The OFT promoted a clear, individualist interpretation of consumerism. According to the 1973 Act the consumer interest was an individual interest to be protected through the regulation of commerce.[88] This mirrored a broader Conservative Party philosophy which emphasised individual consumer rights and 'the rights of the individual citizen': 'the preservation and enhancement of individual freedom'.[89] Everywhere in its work the OFT would focus on 'inalienable rights' rather than obligations, at once establishing principles of state protectionism while also promoting a discourse of consumerism that excluded the types of social concern of earlier politics of consumption.[90] These rights, however, were to be extended and set in concrete legal terms only as a last resort. John Methven, a former solicitor for ICI who served as first Director-General of the OFT and subsequently as the Director of the Confederation of British Industry (CBI), determined from the beginning to make few changes in the law, a remedy he felt to offer 'no automatic panacea for consumer problems'.[91] Indeed, he was prone to ask, 'Is the consumer

[84] *Ibid.*, p. 270.
[85] OFT, *Fair Deal: A Shopper's Guide* (London, 1982); J. Humble, 'A new initiative', in Mitchell (ed.), *Marketing*, p. 147. For examples of specific codes of practice see OFT, *A General Duty to Trade Fairly: A Discussion Paper* (London, 1986), pp. 59–60.
[86] OFT, *Work of OFT*, p. 5; Mitchell, 'Management and the consumer movement', p. 51; CA, *Annual Report, 1973–1974*, p. 9.
[87] CA, *Annual Report, 1974–1975*, p. 7; Whincup, *Consumer Legislation*, pp. 144–5; OFT, *Annual Report, 1976*, p. 100; Interview with Janet Upward, 3 April 2002.
[88] Whincup, *Consumer Legislation*, p. 26.
[89] Conservative Party, *Firm Action for a Fair Britain: The Conservative Manifesto 1974* (London, 1974), p. 25.
[90] OFT, *Annual Report, 1973–1974*, pp. 20–1, 78; Consumer Protection Advisory Committee (CPAC), *Rights of Consumers* (London, 1974).
[91] Whincup, *Consumer Legislation*, p. 15; OFT, *Annual Report, 1975*, p. 9; *Dictionary of National Biography*, 1971–80, p. 567.

over protected?' and positioned himself and the OFT as 'fair and square in the middle . . . with the consumer on one side and trade and industry on the other.'[92] He refused to present himself as either the 'champion of the consumer' or 'the partisan voice of [the] consumer interest', preferring instead to enrol the consumer movement as a 'positive marketing tool' for business.[93] Remedies, if not emerging through statutory law, were to come through voluntary codes of practice, persuading the essentially decent British businessman to modify his practices. Many within the consumer network supported this stance, particularly Gordon Borrie who would succeed Methven in June 1976 and who preferred the 'moderation' of British consumerism's anti-ideological and business-friendly stance.[94] Again competition, if open to public scrutiny, was the ultimate form of protection and, following from this, the activities of bodies such as the OFT and the municipal Trading Standards Officers were to give advice to the businessman, 'helping him avoid conflict with the law.'[95] Certainly, just as many of the OFT's publications were aimed at helping the manufacturer and the retailer as they were with empowering the consumer.[96]

Throughout the 1970s, the work of the OFT focussed steadily on issues relating to monopolies and mergers investigations, as well as restrictive trading practices. It also extended its work following the Supply of Goods (Implied Terms) Act of 1973 and the Consumer Credit Act of 1974 which meant the OFT had to administer a licensing scheme of 100,000 applications designed 'to weed out from the credit and hire industry those who are manifestly unfit to be in it'.[97] With regard to more specific problems, it monitored misleading guarantee claims and the practice of selling extended warranties.[98] It investigated the mail order business and the truth of bargain offer claims, it reviewed the Price Code, monitored the quantity and range of consumer complaints and it maintained regular tabs on the ASA's self-regulatory system of advertising control.[99] Indeed, on this

[92] J. Methven, *Is the Consumer Over Protected?* (Edinburgh, 1975), p. 2.
[93] OFT, *Annual Report, 1973–1974*, p. 13; OFT, *Annual Report, 1975*, p. 10.
[94] G. Borrie, *The Development of Consumer Law and Policy: Bold Spirits and Timorous Souls* (London, 1984), p. 128.
[95] OFT, *Annual Report, 1978*, p. 13; OFT, *Annual Report, 1976*, pp. 7–9.
[96] For instance, in the mid to late 1970s, the OFT published as many pamphlets explaining the legal system to traders and advisers as they did specific protection material aimed directly at consumers: OFT, *Annual Report, 1979*, p. 114.
[97] OFT, *Annual Report, 1975*, p. 15; College of Law, *Fair Trading and Consumer Protection* (London, 1973); OFT, *Annual Report, 1976*, pp. 20–4.
[98] OFT, *Consumer Guarantees: A Discussion Paper* (London, 1984).
[99] CPAC, *A Report on Practices Relating to Prepayment in Mail Order Transactions and in Shops* (London, 1976); OFT, *Annual Report, 1978*, p. 14; Department of Prices and Consumer Protection, *Review of the Price Code* (London, 1974); Director-General of Fair Trading, *Review of UK Self-Regulatory System of Advertising Control* (London, 1978); OFT, *Annual Report, 1973–1974*, pp. 45–6; OFT, *Annual Report, 1975*, pp. 55–6.

latter point, Methven, in a speech written by Mitchell, warned the ASA in 1974 that if it did not overhaul its system of self-regulation, tighter legislative control of advertising would be introduced. This soon led to the advertising industry creating ASBOF (Advertising Standards Board of Finance) which raised money for redeveloping the ASA, funded by a levy on advertising.[100] Furthermore, the Consumer Protection and Advisory Committee (CPAC) continued to investigate references made to it by the Secretary of State, such as the practice of supplying goods which purported to exclude consumers' legal rights, the advertising of VAT-exclusive prices and the practice of demanding pre-payment for mail order transactions which then arrived late.[101] CPAC's consumer protection mechanisms were inadequate, given its inability to draft appropriate statutory regulations, but at least many of its concerns were taken up by the OFT and the Department of Trade and Industry. Its measures were also bolstered by the production of numerous codes of practice by the Consumer Affairs Division (eleven had been produced by the end of 1976) and the ongoing publication of shoppers' guides and advice literature to assist the individual consumer.[102]

By the end of the 1970s the OFT's work was further re-directed with the implementation of the Conservatives' 1980 Competition Act which extended anti-trust legislation to cover the specific abuses by individual firms and brought the activities of the nationalised industries and the work of the previous Labour government's Price Commission within its remit.[103] The Act essentially set out the government's approach to consumer protection throughout the 1980s. While it seemingly extended the work of the OFT to cover a wider range of anti-competitive practices, it also overturned the assumption that certain forms of market abuse (restrictive practices, monopolies, etc.) were against the public interest. Instead, the OFT was to reject any doctrinaire approach, investigating each case on its own merits, analysing not the practice in itself but its effect on competition. In short, the Act overturned the assumption that the form of behaviour was anti-competitive until proved benign, and suggested instead the innocence of the particular trader until proven guilty. Positively, the Act allowed the OFT to give proper consideration to 'the individual circumstances of a practice', yet at the same time the case-by-case approach opened up the potential for minor abuses to go unchecked as well as enabling effective lobbying and close relations to determine

---

[100] Private correspondence between Jeremy Mitchell and author.
[101] OFT, *Annual Report, 1973–1974*, pp. 41–2; CPAC, *Rights of Consumers*; CPAC, *Disguised Business Sales* (London, 1976); CPAC, *VAT Exclusive Prices* (London, 1977).
[102] OFT, *Annual report, 1976*, p. 11.
[103] Smith, *Consumer Interest*, p. 47; Whincup, *Consumer Legislation*, pp. 36–9; OFT, *Annual Report, 1980*, p. 14.

whether the Secretary of State or Director-General referred any such case to the CPAC.[104] Although the OFT was to remain at the forefront of competition policy and consumer protection throughout the 1980s, by the end of the decade it was still the case that earlier principled forms of opposition to market structure had been abandoned. It is hard to imagine a labour activist from a previous generation issuing the following statement about consumer protection as the OFT did in 1990: 'There is no assumption that monopolies are wrong in themselves.'[105]

However, in the course of its activities the OFT began to perceive problems within its functioning. Voluntary codes of practice were identified as being potentially most ineffective. They only worked provided businesses took their obligations seriously or could see some commercial advantage in them, and only with those firms connected to the relevant trade association, thus missing traders most likely to practise poor standards. By the early 1980s, the Director-General wanted to expand the definition of 'fair trading' and hence the activities of the OFT, though he was restricted by the parliamentary restrictions on his role.[106] In response, the OFT made moves to introduce a 'general duty to trade fairly', a commitment to a broader politics of consumption that committed the OFT to a more interventionist role in all business conducted between traders and consumers.[107] In response to the growing number of complaints (668,000 received by the OFT in 1985) and the continued activities of the 'rogue trader' who refused to follow codes of practice, the OFT looked to the example of general duties existing in the US and western Europe.[108] The aim was to enact either a positive duty to trade fairly or a negative duty to prohibit specified practices. The OFT would then draw up further detailed codes of practice both vertical (by trading practice) and horizontal (by trading sector) which would be endorsed by the Secretary of State and presented to Parliament.[109] Rather than responding to market abuses as and when they arose, forcing the OFT into an essentially defensive post-hoc consumerism in which it was 'shooting at a moving target', the general duty to trade fairly would set out the relationship between the trader and the consumer and provide a benchmark for all transactions.[110] The general duty would instead freeze the entire target

104 OFT, *Anti-Competitive Practices: A Guide to the Provisions of the Competition Act, 1980* (London, 1980), p. 7.
105 OFT, *An Outline of UK Competition Policy* (London, 1990), p. 5; OFT Consumer Affairs Division, *Consumer Strategy* (London, 1991).
106 OFT, *Annual Report, 1982*, p. 9.
107 I. D. C. Ramsay, *Rationales for Intervention in the Marketplace* (London, 1984).
108 OFT, *Consumer Dissatisfaction Report* (London, 1986).
109 OFT, *General Duty to Trade Fairly*, p. 35
110 Cited in P. J. Circus, *Towards a General Duty to Trade Fairly?* (London, 1988), p. 185.

range, making it easier to pick off localised problems, as trading standards officers performed the detailed tasks of administering the codes.

That the general duty was never implemented in the 1980s is easily understood given the context of the government's attitude to the consumer and market intervention. In the 1960s, a backlash by business to consumer protection had already emerged, as industry-sponsored investigations of *Which?* concluded it was deliberately anti-capitalist.[111] By the end of the 1970s the CBI was arguing that consumer protection had reached its limits. The purpose of any such measure was 'to get the right balance between freedom and regulation', but unfortunately consumerism had reached a stage 'at which the costs outweigh the benefits, and that the resulting waste of resources is damaging to the national economy'.[112] Consumer protection had destroyed individual judgement and encouraged the rise of the 'unscrupulous' consumer who exploited the 'honest and straightforward' trader. Instead, consumer education ought to consist of a wider discussion about citizenship in which pupils were taught and made aware of 'the role and functions of industry and the constraints within which it has to operate'.[113] The Conservative Party responded to this critique of consumerism by emphasising an older, though partially eclipsed view within the consumer reforms of the early 1970s, that competition itself was the best form of consumer protection. In its 1979 election manifesto, wider social visions of consumerism were forgotten as the terms consumer, customer, choice and individual were conflated under the banners of 'freedom' and the 'property-owning democracy'.[114] The neo-liberal message became more persistent throughout the decade. By 1983, freedom was explicitly said to rest upon 'more choice to individuals and their families', and in 1987 the property-owning democracy had become the 'capital-owning democracy' as consumerism embraced not the state but business itself as individuals were at one and the same time encouraged to buy from and buy into the privatised utilities.[115]

Against such a background, and one which was only exacerbated by recession, the OFT developed an outlook increasingly in line with the government's reforms. As early as 1979, the OFT acknowledged the complaints of business and suggested interventionist consumer protection measures could damage the competitiveness of British industry.[116]

---

[111] E. Houlton, *'Which?' Put to the Test* (London, 1967).
[112] CAA 27: Confederation of British Industry, *Principles of Consumer Policy*, June 1979, p. 2.
[113] *Ibid.*, p. 4.   [114] Conservative Party, *Manifesto 1979* (London, 1979).
[115] Conservative Party, *Manifesto 1983* (London, 1983); Conservative Party, *The Next Moves Forward: Manifesto 1987* (London, 1987).
[116] OFT, *Annual Report, 1979*, p. 9.

The OFT recognised the reality of a new relationship between government and business which saw the Conservatives reject the recommendations of the 1978 Liesner Report on mergers which had proposed that such unions be accepted only if it were shown that some positive benefits would accrue.[117] The possibility of the implementation of a general duty to trade fairly therefore became increasingly unrealistic and instead Borrie was careful to play down his 'watchdog' role, focussing less on the complaints of consumers and stressing instead the information-based individualist aspects of the OFT's consumerism: 'As I have said on many occasions, it is only if consumers assert their sovereignty by exercising their rights to ask questions and to choose between one source of supply and another that manufacturers and traders are able to serve a market effectively and genuine competition is likely to exist.'[118]

Consumerism in this period came to something of a halt, in comparison to the gains of the early 1970s. From 1979 neither the government nor the Director-General made any references to the CPAC and in September 1982, Gerard Vaughan, Minister for Consumer Affairs decided not to reappoint its members.[119] Employees of the CA recall certain difficulties with working with the Conservatives in the 1980s because of their 'producer-friendly' outlook, disguised by Margaret Thatcher as her own brand of consumerism. When the CA requested that consumer affairs be restored to full cabinet status (the position of the previous Labour government's Secretary of State for Prices and Consumer Protection was wound up in May 1979 and replaced with a junior Minister for Consumer Affairs under the Department of Trade), she replied that such a measure was unnecessary since consumer affairs were 'a top priority for the government as a whole'.[120] What this meant in practice, of course, was the series of privatisation measures and neo-liberal market reforms held to promote choice for the individual consumer. In themselves, these measures were not objected to by the consumer movement, as they maintained a line that it was for governments to decide whether a service should be provided publicly or privately: the CA, the NCC and the OFT would then assess whether the method chosen served the consumer interest.[121] While the Conservatives' policies might have been inspired by ideology, the OFT maintained its commitment to the politics of pragmatism. Faith

---

[117] OFT, *Annual Report, 1980*, p. 9.
[118] OFT, *Annual Report, 1980*, p. 16; OFT, *Annual Report, 1986*, p. 10; OFT, *Annual Report, 1988*, p. 18.
[119] OFT, *Annual Report, 1984*, p. 12.
[120] CA, *Annual Report, 1983–1984*, p. 18; interview with unnamed CA worker, 21 November 2000.
[121] Interviews with Alastair Macgeorge, 26 March 2002; Maurice Healy, 26 March 2002; Rosemary McRobert, 25 March 2002.

was kept in competition, though competition policy itself could not be 'administered by reference to any rigid rules or criteria'.[122]

The OFT's alignment with Conservative Party policy therefore drew on the individualist strands of consumerism first propagated by the CAC of the BSI, the Consumer Council of the 1960s and the comparative-testing side of the CA's work. The OFT confirmed the institutionalisation of this consumer 'ideology', only for it to be further embodied in the market reforms of the 1980s producing an ethic of consumerism similar to what Lizabeth Cohen has identified as 'customer-citizenship' in the US: a politics in which consumers are imagined only as individual shoppers who have to rely on their own devices in steering their way through a market shaped by competition and a form of state control dedicated to improving choice for those who can afford it.[123] It is a consumerism stripped of the social concerns to be witnessed in the following chapter and it is a consumerism often in accord with the interests of business. Indeed, the individualist model of consumerism continued to be promoted through the 1970s and 1980s and beyond by the Consumer Standards Advisory Committee (CSAC: the successor to the WAC) at the BSI, the ASA's Code of Advertising Practice Committee which promoted voluntarism over interventionism and, until the late 1970s, in the continued work of the RTSA which advocated the services of one type of business over another. It is a consumerism which has achieved much, but as the OFT realised itself when it moved to introduce a general duty, it is a consumerism with certain limitations.

This is an age-old problem for consumerism. As the consumer is constructed as the individual shopper, consumerism itself achieves a universal remit, thereby strengthening the movement as a whole. But precisely because it becomes everybody, the consumer also loses a distinctive sectional voice. The consumer thus becomes less an entity that speaks for itself and more a rhetorical conceit about which all can speak. The danger is the consumer becomes such an abstract political entity that it becomes a site for the articulation of other political agendas and a being so amorphous that it can come to mean everything and nothing in practical policy considerations. This is seen no more clearly than in the rhetoric of present-day politics, the constant attention given to the consumer reflecting the prominence, activities and campaigns of the affluent consumers' movement from the 1950s, while at the same time highlighting many of the dangers that former consumer activists now recognise. Taking just

122 OFT, *Annual Report, 1985*, p. 11.
123 L. Cohen, 'Citizens and consumer in the century of mass consumption', in M. Daunton and M. Hilton (eds.), *The Politics of Consumption: Material Culture and Citizenship in Europe and America* (Oxford, 2001), pp. 203–21.

two examples, from both the Conservative and Labour Parties, the potential and limitations of a consumer discourse can be seen at the same time. Firstly, in John Major's *Citizen's Charter*, presented to Parliament as a White Paper in July 1991, its aim to make public services 'answer better to the wishes of their users' reflected one of the central and repeated concerns of the consumer movement from the 1960s.[124] Setting standards, delivering quality, accountability and redress – the four themes of the document – had all been organising concerns of both British and international consumerism. Consumers themselves, however, were to have few opportunities for directing reform itself, and were positioned very much as the end product of increased choice, the free market and greater options within the health system, education, transport policy, housing, the utilities and local government. Consumers were imagined solely as individuals and never as collectives of interested parties, and their role in 'shopping' was equated with citizenship, thereby excluding many of the agendas that have inspired and fuelled consumer and citizen groups. Similarly, in 1999 Tony Blair, through Stephen Byers' *Modern Markets: Confident Consumers*, promised to put 'consumers centre-stage' and 'ensure that consumers' concerns are heard in Government'.[125] Although this document is part of a still on-going process of liaison and negotiation which does provide substantial opportunities for input from the consumer movement, it nevertheless refuses to define the consumer interest at any point, threatening to both reduce consumerism to the lowest common denominator of dependence on 'wealth generated by business' and enable the consumer interest to be articulated by groups other than consumers. At times, this type of political rhetoric incorporates the consumer into the 'heart of policy-making' and citizenship, but it does so only by first equating citizenship with the market, individual choice and the interests of business.

To return to the worries of Michael Young at the beginning of this chapter, the consumer movement has played its role in promoting an economic version of consumerism in which the consumer is equated with the shopper whose interest lies in obtaining more goods at ever lower prices. In this chapter at least, the choice not to choose was not an option made available to the vast majority of British consumers. This is precisely the type of consumerism which has enabled the definition of the term to slip from meaning organised activism to something almost synonymous with acquisitive materialism. Raymond Williams complained of the application of the word consumer to what he saw as 'users' of politics, education and

---

[124] P. P., *Citizen's Charter: Raising the Standard*, Cm 1599 (London, 1991), p. 2.
[125] Department of Trade and Industry, *Modern Markets: Confident Consumers*, Cm 4410 (London, 1999), p. 6.

health.[126] Writing as early as 1961 he argued that 'use' involved active agency, while consumption inferred passive submission to an 'external and autonomous system'.[127] This interpretation has proved remarkably resilient and has its roots in the Left's traditional unease with luxury and affluence. But it has continued to colour how historians have regarded the organised consumer movement and its impact on politics and society. In this chapter, I have followed this narrative separating one strand of consumerism within the CA and its later institutionalisation within the OFT. To this extent, the history of economic consumerism would seem to confirm the pessimism of Williams and the concerns of Young. While always a keen advocate of empowered individualism, Young never sought to restrict a consideration of one's economic interests to an ignorance of the wider social aspects of consumption. In many ways, though, the consumerism developed by the CA fed into a narrow choice-based individualism that served the development of various party political interests and would suggest an impoverished citizenship. But as the next chapter will demonstrate, this focus on the economic rather than the social aspects of consumerism was for many an artificial separation and the movement has gained strength from the broader range of interests that have been constantly fed into its guiding principles.

[126] R. Williams, *Keywords* (London, 1976), p. 70.
[127] R. Williams, *The Long Revolution* (London, 1961), p. 297.

10 The duty of citizens: consumerism and society

For Michael Young, consumerism always meant something much more than the choice between competing brands. Indeed, he would have shared the sentiment of one speaker at the third Conference of the International Organisation of Consumers' Unions in 1964 who quoted the German phrase, '*die Wahl wird zur Qual*' [The choice becomes torment], to highlight the problems facing the affluent shopper.[1] The situation has become an increasingly familiar one, whether it be the sense of mental paralysis felt when confronted by a multitude of identical brands in the supermarket or the more deeper 'tyranny of choice' said to emerge from the sense of alienation and ineptness associated with the consuming self in the branded world.[2] But these feelings, according to a long tradition of doubting consumers, are the result, not of a limited choice, but of a limited notion of choice. Should choice be restricted to selecting between goods, or about choosing the ways in which goods are supplied? Is consumerism concerned only with protecting the rights of the individual or does it imply a social duty among empowered consumers to ensure that other individuals share those rights? Is choice concerned solely with the economic act of purchasing or the whole range of social decisions that can go into an individual or group's selection of commodities and services? Where, indeed, is the ideological heart of consumerism: neo-liberal economics or the goals of social democracy and democratic socialism?

Equating the consumer interest with the customer interest severely limits consumerism yet places manageable boundaries around it and legitimates those forms of state, voluntary and private activity concerned with consumer protection. Expanding the consumer interest to incorporate an infinite variety of socio-political concerns broadens the definition such that the concerns of consumerism equate with those of citizenship, yet at the same time provides the potential for consumerism's fragmentation

---

[1] IOCU, *Consumers on the March: Proceedings of the Third Biennial Conference* (London, 1964), p. 132.

[2] S. Waldman, 'The tyranny of choice' (1992), reprinted in L. B. Glickman (ed.), *Consumer Society in American History: A Reader* (Ithaca, 1999), pp. 359–66.

and collapse. It is the latter, social-democratic vision of consumerism, however, that Michael Young held through the post-Second World War period and which motivated his many prominent interventions in the politics of consumption. His view of the consumer was not just that of the empowered shopper, but the centre of a political movement which would enable the concerns of ordinary people to filter through into political expression. In part, such a focus was a result of his disillusionment with what he saw as the centrist, faceless bureaucracy of the Labour Party's brand of state socialist planning. Although he had contributed to the writing of the famous 1945 election manifesto and followed the party faith in the state and nationalisation in *Labour's Plan for Plenty* in 1947, Young went on to write a series of articles and pamphlets from the late 1940s expressing his empathy for the ordinary individual within the large-scale private and public corporation.[3] In his 1949 pamphlet, *Small Man: Big World*, he outlined what he saw as 'the great dilemma of modern society': 'Democracy . . . seems to require smallness. But efficiency, promoted by the growth of science, often requires bigness.'[4] Asking 'how can the individual be made to matter more?', Young claimed that Labour's task for the next five years was 'for the people to run the new and old institutions of our society, participating at all levels as active members – workers, consumers, citizens – of an active democracy'.[5] Although later in this pamphlet Young would emphasise his belief that the family and neighbourhood, assisted by the researches of social science, would form the basis of a compromise between Fabian efficiency and Morrisian or Owenite idealism, he had already made reference to the consumer and the role that he or she could play in revitalising national life.

By the late 1950s, the consumerism associated with Young had begun to focus on the modern commodities of the affluent society. But the sentiment behind Young's consumerism borrowed from the older politics of consumption that posited the consumer as an active agent in society, bringing the problems of ordinary life experienced outside of the workplace into the political arena. Usually, the translation of everyday life into consumerist action is only associated with particular cohorts of the population, such as in Britain's immigrant community and the development of Jamaican 'pardner' and Trinidadian 'sou-sou' mortgage clubs.[6] But this chapter will uncover the social democratic principles of modern

---

[3] M. Young, *Labour's Plan for Plenty* (London, 1947); A. Briggs, *Michael Young: Social Entrepreneur* (Basingstoke, 2001), pp. 85–93.
[4] M. Young, *Small Man: Big World: A Discussion of Socialist Democracy* (London, 1949), p. 3.
[5] *Ibid.*, p. 4.
[6] A. Sivanandan, *A Different Hunger: Writings on Black Resistance* (London, 1982), p. 6.

consumerism in relation to (in theory at least) all goods and services and all sectors of the community, demonstrating the extent to which the consumer movement has been constantly revitalised and redirected according to both the everyday concerns of ordinary consumers and the idealistic visions of some of its early leaders. In the first half, attention will be given to the CA and its attempts in the 1960s to spread its model of consumerism to groups beyond the professional classes. The second half will focus on the institutionalisation of this social consumerism. Just as the Conservative Party responded to the electorate's demands for greater consumer protection with the creation of the Office of Fair Trading, so too did the Labour Party support another politics of consumption through the National Consumer Council (NCC), established in 1975. The NCC provided a forum for the articulation and implementation of Young's ideas, its agendas seemingly attempting to develop a middle way in politics. Indeed, there are strong continuities in this history of consumer politics. The Co-operative movement offered a third force in British politics and Young would later return to some of its mutual aid principles. His own involvement with Political and Economic Planning brought him into contact with that organisation's third way focus on the consumer, and his association with the centre-right wing of the Labour Party saw Young become a founding member of the Social Democratic Party. Finally, much of the rhetoric of the social consumerism to be outlined here predates the ideas found in the most recent *Third Way* of Anthony Giddens and Tony Blair. The potentially liberating and innovative, but at the same time vague and indeterminate, politics of New Labour's professed ideology ultimately mirror many of the strengths and weaknesses of the social democratic tendencies of affluent consumerism.

Consumerism, the CA and social democracy

Despite the CA's deliberate distancing of itself from allegiance to any one political party, the growth of organised consumerism from the 1950s cannot be understood without reference to the social democratic wing of the Labour Party. This was not only because of Michael Young's personal contacts when he established the CA, but because of the wider commitment to centrist policies favoured by many of the professionals who saw in consumerism a means of transforming society according to the dictates of rational, scientific planning rather than the concerns of vested production-based interests. The principal advocate of a new form of politics, based less on class and more on lifestyles and consumption was Young's close friend, Anthony Crosland, who in 1960, in the same year that Young was to call for a Consumers' Party, suggested that Labour might be more appealing to the modern electorate if it was termed the

Social Democratic Party (SDP). According to David Reisman, by the time of his 1971 Fabian pamphlet, *A Social-Democratic Britain*, Crosland was using the term 'to mean superstructure socialism that at the margin depends unashamedly on the economic success of profit-seeking capitalism'.[7]

Crosland's ideas were most clearly set out in his *The Future of Socialism*, published in 1956. Rejecting a class-based analysis and the labour theory of value, Crosland called instead for a redistribution of income to ensure the less well-off shared in the benefits of material progress and the affluent society. Crosland did not share the ascetic tendencies of many of his colleagues who had been brought up on Tawney, the Webbs and the Fabians, and saw no incongruity between high levels of consumption and socialist ideals of brotherly love.[8] Indeed, he explicitly disliked the paternalism that frequently drove the Left's anti-commercial ethic and urged the Labour Party to associate itself with riches and luxury, else it would remain identified 'in the public mind with austerity, rationing, and restrictive controls'.[9] In a period when capitalism was showing many of its benefits, Crosland expressed his faith in the post-war planners to build a better Britain, urging economic policy to encourage growth and investment so that policy-makers might focus on proposals for social welfare and social equality. In a deliberate abandonment of his own and Labour's Fabian background, Crosland advocated a mixed economy to both increase private incomes and free up personal consumption and to provide the funds for a government cultural policy that would improve collective consumption. Despite betraying his subjective preferences his picture of a 'more colourful and civilised country' symbolically distanced his social democratic politics from trade-union dominated, austere and class-based labourism:

We need not only higher exports and old-age pensions, but more open-air cafés, brighter and gayer streets at night, later closing-hours for public houses, more local repertory theatres, better and more hospitable hoteliers and restaurateurs, brighter and cleaner eating-houses, more riverside cafés, more pleasure-gardens on the Battersea model, more murals and pictures in public places, better designs for furniture and pottery and women's clothes, statues in the centre of new housing-estates, better-designed street-lamps and telephone kiosks, and so on *ad infinitum*. The enemy in all this will often be in unexpected guise; it is not only dark Satanic things and people that now bar the road to the new Jerusalem, but also, if not mainly, hygienic, respectable, virtuous things and people, lacking only in grace and gaiety.[10]

[7] D. Reisman, *Anthony Crosland: The Mixed Economy* (Basingstoke, 1997), p. 64; D. Marquand, *The Progressive Dilemma: From Lloyd George to Blair* (1991; London, 1999), pp. 166–78.
[8] C. A. R. Crosland, *The Future of Socialism* (London, 1956), p. 287.
[9] *Ibid.*, pp. 293–4. [10] *Ibid.*, pp. 521–2.

Young and Crosland's close personal relationship was sealed by the intellectual exchange that took place between them and their shared values and opinions. Both looked to Sweden and America for 'practical, egalitarian remedies' and Young's commitment to sociology and social research as the precursors to any social policy found its way into *The Future of Socialism*.[11] Both aimed to reform education, both worried about the individual in the modern state, both rejected the manipulationist school of thought and believed in the ability of individuals to engage in rational choice, and both favoured a democratic and decentralised version of political economy.[12] Writing in 1999, Young heralded Crosland as 'the greatest social revisionist of his time' and added that 'very little in *The Future of Socialism* seems wrong to me'.[13] Crosland was far from being the only social democratic reformer within the Labour Party, and was certainly not the first. Evan Durbin's *The Politics of Democratic Socialism* in 1940 was an important precursor to Crosland, and Young had contact with such figures through the Tavistock Institute and Durbin's 1945 conference on the 'Psychological and Sociological Problems of Modern Socialism', attended also by Tawney, John Bowlby, Karl Mannheim, T. H. Marshall and Harold Wilson.[14] These concerns with the psychological needs of the individual constituted a recurrent theme in Crosland and Young's conversations and would be an important influence in the latter's consideration of ordinary people's needs both in his work on consumerism, his political writings and in his sociological investigations at the Institute for Community Studies. Young's personal relationship with Crosland therefore symbolised an intellectual connection that was being made between the emerging disciplines of social science and the older economic and political goals of socialism that would produce an optimistic spirit among the professionals of the centre-ground in the 1950s and 1960s.

Young's own political development had begun with a brief flirtation with the Communist Party in the 1930s before he moved on to direct PEP during the war and then the Labour Party's research department in 1945.[15] His subsequent disillusionment with nationalisation policy and administration began in 1947 when he expressed doubts about the speed of socio-economic change. He feared that the gap between 'them' and

[11] K. Jefferys, *Crosland* (London, 1999), p. 57; Briggs, *Michael Young*, p. 98.

[12] Reisman, *Anthony Crosland*, pp. 156–8, 168–9.

[13] M. Young, 'Anthony Crosland and socialism', in D. Leonard (ed.), *Crosland and New Labour* (Basingstoke, 1999), pp. 49, 51.

[14] S. Brooke, 'Evan Durbin: reassessing a Labour "revisionist"', *Twentieth-Century British History*, 7:1 (1996), 39.

[15] T. Smith and A. Young, 'Politics and Michael Young', in G. Dench, T. Flower and K. Gavron (eds.), *Young at Eighty: The Prolific Public Life of Michael Young* (Manchester, 1995), pp. 135–42.

'us' was just as apparent, the former no longer being the capitalist class but the officials of the new state bureaucracy. According to Asa Briggs, Young's distrust of 'bigness' at this time was forcing him to reach similar conclusions to E. F. Schumacher in *Small is Beautiful*, Young adding psychology to the other's 'study of economics as if people mattered'.[16] Young's subsequent work in social research and his establishment of the Institute of Community Studies in Bethnal Green, his commitment to education and lifelong learning, the beliefs ironically expressed in *The Rise of the Meritocracy*, and his faith in the family as the basic unit of society have led others to argue that his overall project has been one of 'elemental humanism': 'people coming together in mutual support'.[17] Provided the connections were made between ordinary citizens and the state through private, voluntary and public institutions, society would be revitalised through individual enterprise and initiative. At the end of his life Young's ambitions came to fruition in his School for Social Entrepreneurs, though in 1994 he had already set out his ideal relationship between the state, society and the individual: 'The best form of economic and social organisation is one that involves small groups of freely competing individuals in pursuit of common ends, whether those groups are called family businesses, or small companies or co-operatives or clubs.'[18]

It would be entirely mistaken to over-emphasise Young's impact on modern consumerism, given the range of influences observed to have acted upon the formation of the CA in chapter 7. In any case, many have commented on the difficulties of working with Young in any one of the multitude of organisations he helped set up. He was prone to become bored with the routine administrative tasks and his dynamism caused as much confusion and chaos as it did leadership and direction.[19] At the CA, 'much time was spent appraising his proposed ventures and clearing up the debris if they failed' and the organisation's constitution itself was developed on a rather ad hoc basis.[20] In addition, his supposed 'elemental humanism' might be better described as a 'pragmatic radicalism' since some have suggested that his faith in the working classes remained coloured by earlier Fabian assumptions in the sense that education was

[16] Briggs, *Michael Young*, pp. 88–92; E. F. Schumacher, *Small is Beautiful: A Study of Economics as if People Mattered* (1973; London, 1974).

[17] G. Dench, T. Flower and K. Gavron, 'Introduction', in Dench *et al.* (eds.), *Young at Eighty*, p. ii; see also essays by Willmot, Barker and Halsey; M. Young, *The Rise of the Meritocracy* (1958; Harmondsworth, 1961).

[18] Briggs, *Michael Young*, p. 5.

[19] M. Dean, 'The architect of social innovation', in Dench *et al.* (eds.), *Young at Eighty*, pp. 105–9.

[20] J. Mitchell, 'A triptych of organisations: CA, SSRC, NCC', in Dench *et al.*, *Young at Eighty*, p. 10; Interview with Len Tivey, 7 March 2002.

a means to persuade the disenfranchised to think like the middle classes: 'his aims are classless, but his means usually bourgeois'.[21] Certainly, the philosophy of *Which?* owed as much to inculcating ideals of socially-determined rationality and discrimination as it did to objectivity and independence. But Young did bring to consumerism an intellectual leadership that positioned it as a social movement and one which was firmly rooted in the type of social democratic ideals associated with the Crosland wing of the Labour Party. In 1960, he positioned the new consumerism well beyond the realm of the individual assessment of comparatively tested goods. In a provocative call to arms to the Labour Party, *The Chipped White Cups of Dover* suggested a revolution had taken place in people's outlook on life: 'class based on production is slowly giving way to status based on consumption as the centre of social gravity . . . politics will become less and less the politics of production and more and more the politics of consumption'.[22] If Labour failed to take account of this new interest of citizens, its policies would become increasingly irrelevant and a new Consumers' Party would emerge. Crucially, however, and mirroring Percy Redfern's faith in an earlier brand of consumerism in the 1920s, Young perceived his consumers as liberal individuals who would free politics from the economic sectionalism that tied the Labour Party to the TUC and the Conservatives to the CBI. His consumers would be progressive, socially aware and committed to their duties as well as their rights as citizens. They would not be 'acquisitive and materialist', but broadminded internationalists ('for it is not as producers that we feel sympathy for Indian or Chinese peasants'), Eurocentric, benevolent and in favour of the liberal lifestyles earlier set out by Crosland, a situation eased with the immediate relaxation of the licensing laws.[23] This was a much wider vision of consumerism than could be incorporated within the CA, but it was a clear statement that Young saw in consumers a third force in society which represented a continuous thread in his work through to his joining the SDP and his subsequent publication of *The Chipped White Cups of Steel* in 1987 which reasserted his belief that the progressive party should place the consumer centre stage.[24]

Not all consumer activists shared Young's political aspirations and certainly very few of the subscribers to *Which?* But many of the most influential members of the CA Council were broadly committed to consumerism as a social movement, rooted in the dynamics of post-war British society. As if to symbolise this vision, in 1961 Young proposed moving the

[21] P. Barker, 'Michael Young', *New Society* (8 August 1968), 188; Mitchell, 'A triptych of organisations', p. 10; Interview with Rachel Waterhouse, 8 March 2002.

[22] M. Young, *The Chipped White Cups of Dover* (London, 1960), p. 11.   [23] *Ibid.*, p. 19.

[24] Briggs, *Michael Young*, p. 303; M. Young, *The Chipped White Cups of Steel* (London, 1987).

offices of *Which?* to the South Bank, reflecting the Council's view of consumerism 'as a central part of social life in Britain'.[25] Although Young had been careful to include representatives of all the political parties, the social democratic and even democratic socialist influence remained strong on the Council throughout the 1960s. Perhaps because of his chairmanship of the Independent Commission of Inquiry into the Co-operative Movement 1956–8, Crosland had avoided joining the CA Council, but he did so in 1958 and his presence was apparent even after his resignation in 1962.[26] Also prominent in the CA's first decade was the socialist lawyer, Anthony Dumont, who remained close to Crosland, the left-leaning Mary Adams, formerly of the BBC, the Fabian John Thirlwell and, most prominently, Jennifer Jenkins, Chair of the CA from 1965 to 1976.[27] She herself had sacrificed a possible political career for her husband's, having been Chair of the Cambridge University Labour Club at the beginning of the war while Roy had been Chair of the Oxford University Democratic Socialist Club. During her time in charge, the non-party political stance of the CA was aided by the axis she formed with the Conservative Director, Peter Goldman, but the concerns of the social democratic tendency still drove the CA to attempt to make *Which?* appeal to a working-class audience and to obtain better representation for the consumer throughout the official institutions of the state.

By the end of the 1960s the social-minded concerns of consumerism were promoted again by Charles Medawar. A CA staff worker from 1966, Medawar left Britain in 1971 on an exchange visit to the United States to work with Ralph Nader at the Centre for the Study of Responsive Law ('Nader's Raiders'). He returned to Britain and the CA inspired to create the Public Interest Research Centre (PIRC), which published through a non-profit body, Social Audit Ltd. Initially chaired by Young, PIRC was Medawar's vehicle for researching the social accountability of government and industry.[28] Aware that the media was turning against Nader's aggressive tactics and his apparent assumption that all actions of business were somehow dubious, Medawar emphasised his Young-like intention to 'build up a reputation on a basis of solid, accurate research'.[29] Social Audit did so with some success, informatively criticising the power structures of large firms, the social impact of marketing methods such as pyramid selling and certain questionable forms of advertising.[30] It positioned

[25] Interview with Alastair Macgeorge, 26 March 2002.
[26] Interview with Rachel Waterhouse, 8 March 2002.
[27] CA, *Which? and Consumers' Association* (1965; London, 1972), p. 8.
[28] *Ibid.*, p. 10; G. Smith, *The Consumer Interest* (London, 1982), p. 291.
[29] Quoted in *Guardian* (9 October 1971), p. 10; *Guardian* (19 October 1971), p. 10.
[30] R. Wraith, *The Consumer Cause: A Short Account of Its Organisation, Power and Importance* (London, 1976), p. 58; C. Medawar and L. Hodges, 'The social cost of advertising', *Social Audit*, 1:1 (1973), 28–52.

itself as a consumer group that asked 'why?' rather than 'which?', and sought to investigate companies by measuring their impact on consumers and the general public. Its radicalism came in the form of its acknowledged bias, in its assumption that all who exist in a centre of power – be it in government, public enterprise or private company – 'should account for the use of their power'.[31] *Social Audit*, the organisation's journal, produced articles written with a certain irreverence and in the style of investigative reporting, but the criticisms were always backed by solid research and led to one commentator labelling the PIRC 'the respectable underground'.[32] In its attempts to assess the power and responsibility of business through socially inclined criteria of performance, *Social Audit* proved an important forerunner of the radical journalism associated with the anti-globalisation movement, though Medawar himself has become increasingly concerned with the drugs industry and the promotion of products containing toxic substances.[33]

Within the workings of the CA, the more socially concerned aspects of consumerism expressed themselves in the debates over political campaigning and the relationship with citizenship discussed in chapter 9. However, from the very beginning the Council was keen to extend its services to the working classes and to increase the appeal of *Which?* to a wider audience, either through the establishment of a more popular version or through direct sale in bookshops.[34] Largely, though, the CA's efforts consisted of attempting to extend its model of consumerism across social groups, knowing full well that such a model was not always applicable. A survey conducted in 1965, for instance, concluded that discrimination, effective decision making and rational choice were affected by class, since 'a working-class woman who does not know the right questions to ask or the relevant qualities to look for, is likely to arrive at a final choice quickly and easily and feel happy that this choice represents value for money even though, to a critical outside observer, she may appear to have "thrown her money away" '.[35] The CA was unwilling to compromise its approach, however, and it did little to make its magazine more accessible, in terms of making the reports less technical or less demanding upon the reader.

---

[31] C. Medawar, *The Social Audit Consumer Handbook: A Guide to the Social Responsibilities of Business to the Consumer* (Basingstoke, 1978), p. ix.

[32] Wraith, *Consumer Cause*, p. 59.

[33] See for instance, M. Frankel, *The Social Audit Pollution Handbook* (Basingstoke, 1978).

[34] CAA 14: Social Surveys, *Which? Final Report: A National Study on Behalf of Consumers' Association* (London, 1962); Marketing Advisory Services, *Market Research Proposal to Investigate Current Attitudes Towards Consumer Protection with Special Reference to Which?* (London, 1964).

[35] CAA 14: E. Rodnight, *Attitudes to Spending Money on Consumer Goods and Services* (London, 1965).

The solution to such a problem was instead the perennial emphasis on more information, either through the CA's own literature or in collaboration with the Consumer Council. One such effort, pushed by Jenkins and Young, was for setting up street corner telephone kiosks to provide immediate consumer advice on the high street.[36] This particular idea was dropped, though the CA continued in its attempts to bring consumerism directly to the high street, advising all consumers at or slightly before the point of sale, a form of market intervention which extended well beyond the leisured rational discrimination of *Which?* reading.

In 1964, the CA began discussing the establishment of consumer advice centres, to be positioned near or in shopping centres. Earlier examples existed in experiments in Berlin from 1928 and in 1950s Vienna, the USA and the Scandinavian countries, but no such advice was available in Britain, except in pioneering trading standards offices in Sheffield and Bristol.[37] Following the failure of the Molony Committee recommendation – that CAB become the frontline for consumer complaints – and various other unsuccessful overtures to business, the Consumer Council and government to establish mobile consumer units and even a Housewives' Consultancy Service, the CA decided to go ahead with an experiment on its own.[38] In 1967, the CA's Development Unit investigated the possibility of creating a personal advisory service, to be known as a 'consumer clinic'.[39] In 1969, pilot projects were begun in Hammersmith and Croydon, though the flagship consumer advice centre turned out to be in Kentish Town in Camden. Here, the centre was located within the main shopping district and had the opportunity to provide impartial pre-shopping advice to a socially and racially mixed cohort of the population. The initial month-long experiment extended to two years, during which period it dealt with 40,000 enquiries and generated much media and national attention. A majority of its clients were middle class, but a clear minority demonstrated that the centre was reaching the working class as well, suggesting 'the consumer creed, that narrow religion of graduate wives, will be spread among the masses'.[40] In line with its primary duty

[36] Interview with Alastair Macgeorge, 26 March 2002.
[37] CAA 27: *The Need for Consumer Advice Centres* (1975), p. 6; S. Cockram, *The Development of Consumer Advice Centres in the UK* (Paper presented to IOCU, 1978), p. 1.
[38] D. Prentice, 'Local advice for consumers', in J. Mitchell (ed.), *Marketing and the Consumer Movement* (London, 1978), p. 63; Central Office of Information, *Fair Trading and Consumer Protection in Britain* (London, 1976), p. 31; S. Franks, 'Selling consumer protection: competitive strategies of the Consumers' Association, 1957–1990', MPhil thesis, University of Oxford (2000), p. 44; D. Grose, 'Citizens' Advice Bureaux', *Consumer News*, 16 (September 1964), 1–2.
[39] CA, *Annual Report, 1967–1968*, p. 5.
[40] Cited in Franks, 'Selling consumer protection', p. 63.

to its *Which?* subscribers, the CA was unable to fund a project that cost £20,000 per annum in running costs alone and it was forced to close the experiment. But Camden Council agreed to take over the running of the centre and the CA campaigned for other local authorities to assist in providing general consumer information, pre-shopping counselling and help with post-shopping complaints. Within a year, the first such Consumer Advice Centre had opened in Greenwich, followed by several other London Boroughs, plus the Scottish town of East Kilbride.[41]

The movement to open further advice centres was given a renewed impetus in the Local Government Act 1972 which enabled local trading standards authorities to create consumer advice centres within their area. Three years later the Minister for Consumer Affairs set aside £1.4 million to establish forty-nine new centres, and in 1977–8 the Department of Prices and Consumer Protection provided a further £3 million for another 120 centres, as part of a wider move to curb inflation.[42] By the end of 1975 there were seventy-four centres, including a number of mobile units operating in rural areas, and by 1979, the number of centres peaked at around 200.[43] They were assisted by the CA Advice Centre Servicing Unit which provided information, specialist knowledge and professional training for local staff in the form of a Diploma in Consumer Advice.[44]

Other specialist clinics also proliferated. Just as the number of consumer advice centres rose from one to 120 between 1970 and 1976, so too did the number of housing advice centres increase from 2 to 150 and the number of law centres from 1 to 25. Under threat, the CAB commissioned an investigation which concluded that general advice centres were more cost-effective than specialist clinics and encouraged better communication between specialist fields.[45] It was followed by a National Consumer Council report of 1977 that suggested the same, though neither expected their findings to be used by the Conservative government in 1979 as a justification for cutting an annual budget which had reached £4 million.[46] The decision of Margaret Thatcher, mirroring as it did Edward Heath's closure of the Consumer Council in 1970, marked an important end to the development of one branch of consumerism. Local authorities were unwilling to fund the centres themselves and within months fifty-six had closed.[47] Thatcher's decision was taken on grounds of cost-effectiveness, but CA workers felt the centres had not had sufficient time

[41] Prentice, 'Local advice', p. 65.
[42] Franks, 'Selling consumer protection', p. 67.   [43] Smith, *Consumer Interest*, p. 280.
[44] CAA 27: *The Need for Consumer Advice Centres*, p. 6.
[45] *Guardian* (26 July 1975), p. 18.
[46] Whincup, *Consumer Legislation*, p. 160; NCC, *The Fourth Right of Citizenship: A Review of Local Advice Centres* (London, 1977), p. 3.
[47] Franks, 'Selling consumer protection', p. 67.

to prove themselves. Alastair Macgeorge, Assistant Director of the CA at the time, argues that consumer advice was to the economy what preventative medicine was to health: a low cost method of stopping problems with goods and services ever arising.[48] In addition, the centres represented a genuine attempt to put into practice the social democratic vision of the CA's pioneers. They encouraged not simply individual empowerment according to the *Which?* model but practical market assistance ensuring, in its most idealised role, that consumers almost literally took to the point of purchasing an institutional body of expert knowledge. Emphasis was still placed on education and rational choice, but the advice centres were the main attempt by the CA to adapt its professional consumerism to the consuming outlook of other groups in society.

The National Consumer Council (NCC)

In the early 1970s, when the Conservatives performed a U-turn in consumer policy, setting up the OFT and appointing Geoffrey Howe as Minister for Consumer Affairs, the Labour Party too began to re-think its attitude to consumers. Several commentators cynically suggested Labour was merely joining a 'vote-winning bandwagon', but there were indications that the Left was developing and extending the more social and political aspects of consumerism found in sections of the CA.[49] In a period of rising inflation, consumerism was to be associated with prices as well as value for money. Just as in the First World War, a period of economic instability created a political environment attuned to both prices and wages. In Labour's anti-inflation policy wage restraint could only be urged if voters remembered their roles as consumers as well as workers.[50] The Counter-Inflation Act of 1973 had set up a Price Commission with power to control prices through a Price Code. Under the Conservatives this lacked any real power and has been described as 'the best lunch club in London'.[51] The Labour Party, therefore, added to this measure with two Prices Acts in 1974 and 1975 which enabled the government, through the Commission, to impose maximum prices on subsidised foods and to force the indication of unit prices of goods in retail shops.[52] By the end of March 1977, the Price Commission had investigated around twenty market sectors, including goods and services as diverse as motor

[48] Interview with Alastair Macgeorge, 26 March 2002.
[49] Winchup, *Consumer Legislation*, p. 7.
[50] UK Government, *Attack on Inflation: A Policy for Survival* (London, 1975).
[51] Private correspondence between Rachel Waterhouse and author.
[52] COI, *Fair Trading*, p. 16; Wraith, *Consumer Cause*, pp. 19–20; Price Commission, *A Guide to the Price Controls in Stage Four* (London, 1975).

fuel, fruit and vegetables, electrical appliances, sanitary towels and funeral charges. Although anti-inflation policy was not necessarily a pure consumer issue, the concern with prices reflected an older consumerism that was not to be divorced from the concerns of the modern consumer movement. In the 1960s, consumer representation had not extended to prices and incomes policy, but by the mid-1970s there were important links in personnel in consumer and inflation policy. More significantly, Labour's Department of Prices and Consumer Protection (DPCP), set up in March 1974, took over responsibility from the Department of Trade for the Price Commission and almost all areas of official concern for consumers. The DPCP, headed by the Minister Shirley Williams, was also responsible for the Monopolies and Mergers Commission, the Consumer Protection Advisory Committee, the National Consumer Council, the Metrication Board, competition policy and consumer advice and protection.[53] In 1977, a Price Commission Act restricted the operation of the Price Code to just the limitation of profit margins, but enabled greater powers of investigation in regard to larger companies. By the end of the 1970s, however, Labour's anti-inflation measures were considered a failure and the Conservatives reversed the prices policy. The 1980 Competition Act, introduced as a Bill almost immediately after the Conservatives came to power in 1979, abolished the Price Commission, reflecting a type of consumerism that had been seen in the removal of central funding for local advice centres.[54]

But the Labour Party's other extension of consumerism lay in the creation of the National Consumer Council in 1975. While in opposition in 1972 Labour had published a Green Paper on advertising which had criticised the abolition of the Consumer Council and proposed a replacement with further powers to test the claims made by advertisers and to implement a statutory code of advertising practice. Once the Labour Party came into power in 1974 the Advertising Standards Authority responded by strengthening its own voluntary system of regulation.[55] This satisfied many within the party though it still moved to create a National Consumer Council. *National Consumers' Agency*, published in September 1974, built on many of the ideas of Young seeking to ensure that consumers obtained a role in economic policy and 'all aspects of our national life' 'as important as that of the producer'.[56] In particular, consumerism was to extend beyond the social confines of the middle-class

[53] J. Aspinall, 'Glossary of organisations active in consumer affairs', in Mitchell, *Marketing*, pp. 260–1.
[54] Whincup, *Consumer Legislation*, p. 36.
[55] Mitchell, 'A triptych of organisations', pp. 13–14.
[56] DPCP, *National Consumers' Agency*, Cmnd. 5726 (London, 1974), pp. 4, 7.

professionals of the *Which?*-buying public and work for 'the inarticulate and disadvantaged'.[57] The NCC was established as a non-statutory, independent (though nevertheless partisan) body, in early 1975, funded by a government grant of over £300,000 (rising steadily to £2 million by 1990). Supported by equivalent Councils in Wales, Scotland and Northern Ireland, the NCC worked to represent consumers and influence all aspects of government policy in their interest.[58] The initial Council membership reflected the wider social goals of the organisation, as representatives were selected not from a balance of interests of manufacturers and trade unions but from across the voluntary sector, including such figures as Chris Holmes of the homeless charity, Shelter, and established consumer policy workers such as Rachel Waterhouse. However, in the early years, they were eclipsed by the overbearing presence of the Chair, Michael Young, who had ensured that those nominated to the Council were those whom he himself had wanted.[59] Beneath the Council, the NCC staff was able to draw on the expertise of several established consumer workers, many of whom had been attached to the CA during the 1960s. They were organised into a Consumer Policy Unit, concerned mainly with the economic and financial livelihood of consumers, and a Social Policy Unit, concerned with 'vital social matters' such as housing, health and social security. In addition, a Public Affairs Unit was created in recognition of the expansion of the NCC's work in the socio-political sphere and was headed by Eric Midwinter, Chair of the Advisory Centre for Education (another organisation established by Young).[60] The agenda of the NCC was reflected in the appointment of the first Director, a former co-operator whom Young supported. He was quickly replaced by John Hosker of the CA who left at the same time as Young in 1977, to be replaced by Jeremy Mitchell, an experienced figure who had joined the CA in 1958, moved over to the Social Science Research Council with Young in 1965 and worked for the OFT from 1974 to 1977.

In contrast to the Consumer Council of the 1960s, the NCC began immediately to develop a proactive, even aggressive, campaigning role. Roy Hattersley committed the organisation to 'righting the balance' of power between manufacturers, broadly defined, and shoppers, patients, parents, passengers and tenants.[61] Three organising principles – 'to speak up for the inarticulate'; to concern itself as much with the private as the public sector; and to press for a 'stronger voice for the consumer whenever decisions affecting his or her everyday life are taken' – were put

[57] *Ibid.*, p. 4.   [58] COI, *Fair Trading*, p. 35.
[59] Interview with Rachel Waterhouse, 8 March 2002.
[60] NCC, *Annual Report, 1978–1979*, p. 6; interview with Maurice Healy, 26 March 2002.
[61] NCC, *Annual Report, 1976–1977*, p. 3.

into effect straight away.[62] In practice, this often led to the continuation of policies first advocated by the Consumer Council. It monitored consumer complaints and the extent to which consumers sought and were able to get redress. It continued to assess developments in the legal system, such as the gaps in the laws relating to product liability and the codification of consumer rights in the supply of services. It campaigned for the relaxation of Sunday trading legislation and it made itself aware of any developments in technology which could improve the position of the consumer, such as Prestel which the NCC hoped to establish in post offices and advice centres to provide people with information about their legal rights and entitlements.[63] Finally, it pushed for greater consumer education within schools, though the OFT and the CA were to concern themselves more with this role. Importantly, however, this was not to foster a narrow individualist 'race of super-shoppers' but to promote a sense of consumer-citizenship which embraced a wider social responsibility to the community.[64]

The NCC's distinctive agenda emerged from its remit to cover the concerns of disadvantaged consumers and 'why the poor pay more', a phrase developed in the US by David Caplowitz in 1963 along with 'consumer detriment' – that the poor are unable to obtain value for money through the structural, financial and educational factors which give them a weak bargaining position in the marketplace – and which was taken up by many campaigning groups in Britain in the 1970s.[65] The concept of consumer detriment directed many of the NCC's activities in the 1970s, extending consumerism into areas forgotten about since the Co-operative movement had been at its height.[66] Credit unions, for instance, have persisted in being a central concern of the NCC's activities. These self-help systems enabled consumers to access credit cheaply and co-operatively and the NCC worked to provide the institutional framework to encourage this. Its most notable success here came in providing the secretariat for the Credit Union Steering Group which was able to influence the passage of the Credit Unions Act in 1979.[67] But a concern for the poor and the disadvantaged led the NCC into all areas of public and private life. Investigations were made into the treatment of the individual by both manufacturers of goods and providers of services, but especially the state. Food prices and fuel were early concerns, resulting in NCC interventions

---

[62] NCC, *Annual Report, 1978–1979*, p. 7.
[63] NCC, *Annual Report, 1981–1982* , pp. 12–19.
[64] NCC, *Annual Report, 1982–1983*, p. 32.
[65] D. Caplowitz, *The Poor Pay More: Consumer Practices of Low-Income Families* (New York, 1963); F. Williams (ed.), *Why the Poor Pay More* (London, 1977); NCC, *For Richer, for Poorer* (London, 1975); D. Piachaud, *Do the Poor Pay More?* (London, 1974).
[66] NCC, *Annual Report, 1976–1977*, p. 11; *1977–1978*, p. 19.
[67] NCC, *Annual Report, 1977–1978*, p. 15; NCC, *Consumers and Credit* (London, 1980).

on economic policy within the EEC, especially the Common Agricultural Policy, and on the organisation of the nationalised industries.[68] This in turn led to a consideration of conservation issues while its assessment of increased gas and electricity prices on low income households saw the production of a number of concrete policy proposals.[69] Concern over fuel raised broader questions about the effectiveness of nationalised industry consumer councils and the NCC's highly critical report built on previous consumerist critiques of these bodies.[70] Local authorities were often as bad at responding to consumer needs.[71] In council housing, rigid rent payment schemes often hurt disadvantaged consumers and a multitude of petty-minded and overbearing local authority clauses (for example, that North Dorset tenants use their baths only for the purposes intended) reflected a bureaucratic paternalism that, in the long run, served neither the interests of the consumer nor the local authority.[72] Instead, the NCC sought to give tenants a greater say in the management of their affairs, allow them to carry out their own repairs and develop their own regulations and, as with its fuel policy, provide greater flexibility in payment schemes for the impoverished.[73] The 1980 Housing Act aroused much controversy through its 'right-to-buy' provisions but, for the NCC, the principal point of this piece of the legislation was the extension of tenants' rights which it had fought to have included within it.[74]

The conversion of the tenant into the consumer reflected a wider process of the dissemination of a consumerist rhetoric into areas previously regarded as beyond the market. Even in business, the NCC extended the meaning of the consumer to include not only the end purchaser but also an active agent in the running of the firm: its 1982 investigation, *Consumers in Business*, explored structural opportunities to give consumers 'a more influential voice in private industry'.[75] The NCC was interested in the development of charters, or statements of consumer rights within particular industries, be it rail, transport, education or the legal profession.[76]

---

[68] NCC, *Annual Report, 1976–1977*, pp. 9–16; *1977–1978*, pp. 19–20.
[69] NCC, *Annual Report, 1981–1982*, p. 27; NCC, *Paying for Fuel* (London, 1976), p. 114.
[70] NCC, *Consumers and the Nationalised Industries* (London, 1976).
[71] M. Healy, 'What are local government services for?', *Local Government Studies* (November/December 1985), 12–14; J. Gyford, *Citizens, Consumers and Councils: Local Government and the Public* (Basingstoke, 1991).
[72] NCC, *Tenancy Agreements Between Councils and their Tenants* (London, 1976); NCC, *Soonest Mended* (London, 1979); NCC, *Cracking Up* (London, 1982).
[73] NCC, *Annual Report, 1976–1977*, p. 17; *1978–1979*, p. 19; NCC, *Behind with the Rent* (London, 1976).
[74] NCC, *Annual Report, 1981–1982*, p. 22.   [75] *Ibid.*, p. 21.
[76] NCC, *Annual Report, 1976–1977*, pp. 18–19, 26–7; British Railways Board, *The Commuters' Charters: The Foundation of a Progressive Community served by a Dynamic Railway* (London, 1981); Welsh Consumer Council, *Within Reach? Planning Public Transport and Accessibility* (Cardiff, 1982).

The National Health Service, though long the focus of 'patient's rights', was a particular concern for the NCC and investigations were launched into issues such as the access of the old and the very young to primary health care, the ability of community health councils to take up individual patient-consumer's complaints, and the opportunities for collaboration with such bodies as MIND (the National Association for Mental Health, established in 1946) and the Patients' Association (established in 1963).[77] Europe too became an arena for both the further extension of consumer rights within an international context and the establishment of the consumer at the centre of any new policy development.[78] Even unemployment was constructed as a consumer issue, the lack of access to the means of production provoking a parallel lack of access to the means of consumption. Guides were published on *How to Survive Redundancy!*, offering advice on debt counselling and money management, and criticisms were directed at means-tested benefits as claimant-consumers were shown to be given a poor deal as they were not made aware of their full range of entitlements.[79]

The NCC's aim in spreading the language of consumerism was never to impose an *a priori* ideological assumption about the benefits of the free market within the public sector. Instead, the goal was to empower individuals within a range of institutions whose bureaucracies and internal procedures seemed to have forgotten the people to whom their work was supposedly directed. The purpose here reflected once more the long-term concerns of Michael Young who set out the working philosophy of the NCC almost entirely on his own prior to 1977. Much of this was encapsulated in his stress on education and information, two services said to constitute 'the fourth right of citizenship' and thus complementing T. H. Marshall's three civil, political and social rights.[80] While Marshall would have included education and information within his formulation of social rights, Young believed them so crucial to the 'lifeblood of democratic government' that they warranted separate recognition especially since 'without the right to education and information the other three sets of rights are liable to be hollow shams'.[81] Young therefore emphasised the

---

[77] NCC, *Annual Report, 1977–1978*, pp. 28–9; *1978–1979*, p. 20; *1981–1982*, pp. 24–5; C. Ham, 'Power, patients and pluralism', in K. Barnard and K. Lee (eds.), *Conflicts in the National Health Service* (London, 1977), pp. 99–120; NCC, *Patient's Rights* (London, 1982).

[78] NCC, *Annual Report, 1976–1977*, p. 26; *1977–1978*, p. 22–3; *1978–1979*, p. 17.

[79] NCC, *Annual Report, 1981–1982*, p. 19; *1976–1977*, pp. 22–3; *1977–1978*, pp. 27–8; NCC, *Means Tested Benefits* (London, 1976).

[80] NCC, *Fourth Right*; T. H. Marshall, *Citizenship and Social Class* (Cambridge, 1950).

[81] NCC, *Fourth Right*, p. 6; M. Young, 'Foreword', in M. Minogue (ed.), *A Consumers Guide to Local Government* (London, 1977); NCC, *Annual Report, 1977–1978*, p. 24.

institutional provision of information, though this was not simply to be the data of comparative testing, but whatever gave the individual freedom to act and to choose. And information was not to be passively presented, waiting to be viewed by already educated, informed, discriminating shoppers, but was to be taken to the public at large through existing advice centres and welfare rights agencies in forms that corresponded with the day-to-day realities of different sectors of the population. For Young and the NCC, the right to information was 'as much a prerequisite of democracy as freedom of speech, the right to vote and the right to justice'.[82] Aspects of state and society which prevented access to information were therefore to be opposed and the NCC found itself campaigning against official secrecy and for the re-establishment of advice centres after the Conservative government had stopped central funding in 1979.[83]

Young assumed the NCC ought to reach down to the ordinary consumer, enabling him or her to play an active role in society, while at the same time reaching up to the highest official institutions in order that the consumer voice was placed at the heart of government. Developing his mutual aid principles, Young established a Bulk Buy Bureau within the first year of the NCC, 'to promote the growth of bulk purchase groups among disadvantaged consumers' and had moved to encourage the development of credit unions through the Credit Union Steering Group.[84] His belief in mutual aid was apparent in his earlier publications stretching back to the 1950s, but after leaving the NCC in 1977 he put it into more obvious practice with the creation of the Mutual Aid Centre. This organisation oversaw such ventures as the Milton Keynes OK Service Station, which enabled motorists to carry out their own repairs, the Brain Train, a study club for rail commuters, Brass Tacks, a co-operative workshop based in Hackney, and numerous bulk buy clubs, housing co-operatives, pre-school play groups, and greater parent–teacher co-operation.[85] It also led to the creation of the College of Health in 1983 which encouraged patients to discuss their experiences as 'consumers of health care', while publishing *Healthline* and *Waiting List Clearing House*.[86] Its aim was to 'help people help themselves', fostering projects that were 'small, local and on a human scale', and deliberately extending organised consumerism beyond comparative testing as the willing members of the NFCG were enrolled into the Mutual Aid Centre's projects.[87]

[82] NCC, *Annual Report, 1977–1978*, p. 24; *1976–1977*, p. 23.
[83] NCC, *Annual Report, 1981–1982*, p. 17; R. Delbridge and M. Smith (eds.), *Consuming Secrets* (London, 1982).
[84] NCC, *Annual Report, 1976–1977*, pp. 20–1.
[85] Briggs, *Michael Young*, pp. 292–4; *NFCG Newsletter* (February 1979), p. 252.
[86] M. Rigge, 'Self-help and empowerment in health', in Dench *et al.* (eds.), pp. 39–41.
[87] *NFCG Newsletter* (October 1977), p. 6.

In 1977 he set out his ideas with Marianne Rigg, drawing upon an extensive labour movement history which included G. D. H. Cole, the Webbs and especially Robert Owen and Prince Kropotkin. Young's 'new consumerism' was to provide an updated version of a nineteenth-century social fabric that had consisted of trade unions, working men's clubs, the Co-operative Society, the Methodist chapel, the Friendly Society, and the football club. In the late twentieth century, the groups Young placed under the umbrella of mutual aid consisted of the CA and the NFCG, health and social support groups (this varied from Alcoholics Anonymous to Weight Watchers to the Self-Help Organisation for Prisoners), amenity groups (here, the National Trust, Friends of the Earth and the Conservation Society were placed of at the end of a lineage that stretched back to William Morris' Society for the Protection of Ancient Buildings), housing co-operatives and associations, and single-issue pressure groups such as Gingerbread and the Child Poverty Action Group. At the centre of all of this 'blend of idealism and practicality' would stand a revived Co-operative movement, for which he established the Co-operative Consumer Campaign to 'bring back to a selfish society some vital elements of mutual aid and some vital elements of altruism'.[88] Young's unabashed idealism was the culmination of the logic of his persistent critiques of the power of the little man in the modern state. He was assisted by other like-minded colleagues in the NCC who also attempted to connect new forms of small-scale co-operation with the established Co-operative movement.[89] In further works on producer co-operation and the principles of mutualism, Young extended his thoughts on consumerism and citizenship to suggest a vision of society in which the politics of affluence was intricately bound up with the politics of necessity and grass-roots activism.[90]

At the other end of Young's state–society spectrum, the consumer was to be placed at the heart of government. Young accepted the chair of the NCC only on the condition that he was also given a seat on the National Economic Development Council, one of the three central pillars of 1970s corporatism. Here, he hoped to act as a powerful consumer advocate, forging a third way between the power blocs of the workers and the manufacturers. This was vital, the NCC felt, since employers and trade unionists were thought too often to link together to keep the

[88] M. Young and M. Rigge, *Mutual Aid in Selfish Society: A Plea for Strengthening the Co-operative Movement* (London, 1979), p. 42.

[89] J. Mitchell, 'Co-operatives and the new consumer movement', *Society for Co-operative Studies Bulletin*, 34 (1979), 83–90.

[90] M. Rigge and M. Young, *Building Societies and the Consumer* (London, 1981); M. Young and M. Rigge, *Revolution from Within: Co-operatives and Co-operation in British Industry* (London, 1983).

benefits of increased productivity to themselves rather than passing them on to consumers.[91] Instead of worker directors of companies, the NCC proposed consumer directors. The NCC fought against the exclusion of consumers' interests in economic policy and urged a greater voice in inflation and incomes policy.[92] Representation was formulated as a 'right' for consumers and was therefore to be increased, with consumer advocates being given a clear role and constituency, along with expert advice in support.[93] Such policies were not without problems. At the micro-level, not all grass-roots consumers could be relied upon to provide the energy and commitment necessary to start up mutual aid projects and it is clear that even of those consumers attached to the CA and the NFCG, most were unaware or else in disagreement with Young's vision. And at the macro-level, Young's consumerism was not always effective as he himself struggled to provide constructive consumer suggestions at all times: his bargaining position that consumers would prefer wage increases to be zero per cent fell only on the astonished deaf ears of manufacturers and trade unionists.[94] A later consumer representative on the NEDC, Rachel Waterhouse, has explained that she often had difficulty in formulating the consumer view in its meetings and that there were problems in attracting the attention of the chair. That Waterhouse was able to contribute was due to effectiveness of the CA and NCC research teams stood in support behind her, but without this, the consumer, sitting as an individual, was often likely to have little to say.[95]

The main initiative through which Young planned to bring about his version of consumerism while at the NCC, however, was not through supporting small-scale ventures, but through creating a consumer constituency that could rival the power of the trade unions or the employers' organisations. The Consumer Congress was first held in September 1975, bringing together representatives from over 100 organisations concerned with the consumer movement, from CA officers, local consumer group representatives, nationalised industry consumer council officials and interested parties from single-issue pressure groups whose range of activities sometimes coalesced with certain consumer campaigns. Young and the NCC imagined the Congress as the basis for a 'powerful third force balancing the influence of management and labour in the development of government policy'.[96] It was held to represent 'the determination of

[91] NCC, *Annual Report, 1976–1977*, p. 27.
[92] NCC, *Annual Report, 1977–1978*, p. 18; *1978–1979*, p. 14.
[93] NCC, *Annual Report, 1977–1978*, pp. 15, 19.
[94] Interview with Len Tivey, 7 March 2002.
[95] Interview with Rachel Waterhouse, 8 March 2002.
[96] NCC, *Annual Report, 1975–1976*, p. 14.

consumers to play a full part in public affairs, . . . to achieve recognition that there should be four partners to the setting of national policies – government, labour, management and consumers'.[97] Unlike business-men and trade unionists, though, consumers were 'highly fragmented': the Congress was to be the first step 'towards the creation of a genuinely national, democratically-controlled, consumer movement'.[98] The NCC organised the Congress with increasing support and funding from the CA throughout the 1980s and it certainly appeared that it acted as a rallying point for many disparate groups. The Congress held in 1985 at the University of Sussex attracted delegates from organisations as varied as Age Concern, the Association for Housing Aid, the Association for Neighbourhood Councils, the Claimants and Unemployed Workers Union, the Council for the Protection of Rural England, the Department of Health and Social Security, Friends of the Earth, the Social Democratic Party, the Ramblers' Association and the Trade Union Action Association.[99]

The Congress has been regularly criticised, even by its strongest supporters such as the NFCG, for its very diversity, the sheer weight of contrasting interests producing 'bland and unexciting, even boring' Congress resolutions.[100] For instance, when discussing privatisation in 1986, a Congress workshop concluded that there were too many contrasting opinions to formulate a specific policy; the only resolution that could be passed was for the need for greater consumer representation in the privatisation process.[101] The openness of the Congress has enabled organisations such as the Advertising Standards Authority, the BSI and the Automobile Association to attend, groups which were elsewhere being criticised as subject to industry control.[102] Former consumer activists often look back upon the Congress with little nostalgia. One described the meetings as 'dreadful' while another complained that meetings were too divided, the whole process weakened by groups of amateurs being insufficiently informed of matters of expertise or organisations as diverse as CAMRA (the Campaign for Real Ale) which were not felt to be a part of the 'real' consumer movement.[103] Between some groups there was even 'hatred and bitterness', 'rivalry and bitchiness', a feeling not helped by an early NCC report to Congress on the ineffectiveness of the nationalised industry consumer councils which split feeling amongst the floor. It is likely that in the history of the Congress 'the actual substantive output of it was zero' and by the 1990s it had arguably become a 'drinking club for trading

---

[97] NCC, *Annual Report, 1976–1977*, p. 28.   [98] NCC, *Annual Report, 1977–1978*, p. 31.
[99] CAA 21: *Consumer Congress Handbook 85*.
[100] *Ibid.*, p. 7; *NFCG Newsletter* (8 October 1978), p. 154.
[101] CAA 21: *Consumer Congress 86*, p. 19.   [102] CAA 21: *Consumer Congress 87*, p. 13.
[103] Interviews with Rachel Waterhouse, 8 March 2002, Len Tivey, 7 March 2002.

standards officers'.[104] Finally, some even felt that the Congress symbolised the impracticality of Young's brand of consumerism, as he attempted
to weave single-issue politics into an organisation modelled on traditional
political lines.[105] Certainly, the government has hastened the demise of
the Congress, refusing to allow public funds to go to it via the grant-in-
aid to the NCC. Consequently, today, the Congress has been abolished
and attempts have been made to create a system of broad subject areas,
to which single-issue groups can be attached. Ultimately, though, this
too has failed and the remnants of the NFCG and the Congress have,
instead, merged to form the National Consumer Federation (NCF). In
September 2002, the NCF held it first annual conference which just
thirty-five consumers attended.[106]

With such obvious weaknesses, one has to be wary of issuing qualifying
statements about the impact of the Consumer Congress. Yet of those who
have criticised the Congress, one has also stated that 'I thought that it
achieved one very great thing – that it did sometime in the 1980s make all
these funny people, most of whom had never seen that there was any commonality in their work whatsoever, see that there was.'[107] The Congress
might not have been the forum for the creation of clear policy objectives,
but it established an atmosphere that fostered connections, links and campaigning networks, crucial to the future development of consumerism. It
brought a diversity to consumerism which enabled new topics and issues
to be at least brought within the ambit of the consumer cause. Workshops
at Congress could be based on such traditional consumer issues as food
labelling and bus services, but also housing, local government services,
legal aid, and the problems faced by consumers in the EEC.[108] By 1990,
Congress workshops were discussing health, housing, public utilities and
social security, establishing working principles based on rights, participation, dignity, universalism and redress.[109] The Congress Committee
reflected the new focus on networks for action rather than ideologically
driven campaigning. These groups accepted their differences, but would
embark on campaigns on single issues regardless. The Congress has become one of a number of expanding fora at which organisations can establish citizenship rights through a consumerist rhetoric, as well as adding
to the range of issues included within the consumer interest. In addition to topics such as social security, privatisation, credit unions, housing
and health, the consumer movement has expanded into the protection

[104] Interview with Maurice Healy, 26 March 2002.
[105] Private correspondence between Rachel Waterhouse and author.
[106] Private correspondence between Jeremy Mitchell and author.
[107] *Ibid.*   [108] NCC, *Consumer Congress 85*, p. 11.
[109] NCC, *Consumer Congress 1990*, p. 8.

of the countryside, freedom of information and ethical purchasing and investment.[110] In itself, then, the Congress was far from being a success, especially when compared to the activities of the Trade Union Congress as was Young's original intention. But if it did not result in a social movement in the fullest sense of the term, it did produce a political language and contributed to a political technique ideally suited to a set of organisations claiming to represent everybody and which have consequently had to avoid any dogmatic statement of their political philosophy.

Young's consumerist vision was taken up by his successor in 1977, Michael Shanks, a journalist and economist who had served in the previous Labour Government's Department of Economic Affairs. Although committed to the virtues of choice in the market – he often repeated that 'competition is the consumer's best friend' – he shared with Young a dislike for the institutions of class and privilege that made Britain 'stagnant' and was committed to solving national economic problems through a concurrent consideration of social problems.[111] Strongly opposed to authoritarian or communist control of industry he likewise criticised the potentially 'lethal' social and economic consequences of a narrow monetarist policy. His third way solution was for a 'stakeholder' society, a 'Rational Society' in which the straitjacket of the 1970s corporate state would be loosened as groups other than trade unions and employers' organisations would sign a new 'social contract' with the state. What he feared most was that Britain would drift 'willy-nilly into the sclerosis of the corporate state'.[112] His project was distinctly Habermassian in the sense that he rejected government based on the negotiation of organised private interests ('the conflict of competing groups') and supported instead 'a consensus based on rational discussion and debate'. Such a reappraisal of state and society was crucial in this 'twilight of dying ideologies' where efforts to forge social cohesion were necessary if Britain was to 'survive the death of ideology and the vacuum of religious faith'.[113]

Shanks also shared a desire to create a cohesive philosophy for consumerism: almost as soon as he entered office, the first question he asked his staff was, 'what's the theory?'[114] His main interest was in the management of the economy, and his attitude to consumers was that they ought to be at 'the heart of economic policy and industrial practice': Adam Smith's

[110] NCC, *Consumer Congress 1986*, p. 27; NCC, *Consumer Congress 1992: Breaking Down Barriers*, p. 23.
[111] M. Shanks, *The Stagnant Society: A Warning* (Harmondsworth, 1961).
[112] NCC, *Annual Report, 1977–1978*, p. 4.
[113] M. Shanks, *What's Wrong with the Modern World? Agenda for a New Society* (London, 1978), pp. 157–9.
[114] Interview with Maurice Healy, 26 March 2002.

famous axiom, he claimed, 'should be hung in every boardroom and trade union headquarters in the country'.[115] The NCC offered a means to construct this new society, and he drew on the earlier rhetoric of Young and possibly even of co-operative idealists such as Percy Redfern, to argue that the consumer interest was 'not a narrow or sectional one' and could, theoretically, provide the basis for a new engaged citizenship: 'we are partisan only for the general interest of everyone as consumers'.[116] He expected the NCC to have a central say in all aspects of national life. In 1979, the NCC followed up their discussion of inflation policy set out in *Real Money, Real Choice* (1978) with an outline of the relationship between *The Consumer and the State* which looked 'through consumers' eyes at the structure and problems of the public sector, of public spending and taxation' – a study of 'economic policy as if consumers mattered'.[117] Now consumerism was defined as a concept which could include proposals attacking inflation and unemployment, encouraging competition in a mixed economy, allocating public resources to measures designed to strengthen the economy and ensuring the maximum degree of participation by all the interests concerned, consumers as well as producers: 'the concept of the consumer as an atomic, self-seeking individual out to maximise his own individual well-being no longer corresponds to the facts. Consumerism is an integral part of society, with broad social objectives and a growing international framework'.[118]

Such a participatory form of consumerism, based not on a specific economic interest, could only succeed if the alliances and campaigns of different groups which were increasingly being referred to as the consumer policy network were effective. Unity was required else the NCC would be 'a pressure group without a proper lobby behind it', threatening to bring about the age-old problem of consumerism: that its high-minded rhetoric could dissolve into nothing or its individual empowerment focus could be captured, restricted and re-directed along more narrow policy channels.[119] For instance, just as Shanks addressed the Consumer Congress in 1981 on the need for a strong consumer input into the formal channels of economic policy, so too did Geoffrey Howe draw upon those less ambitious feelings within the consumer movement, applauding their reticence about getting involved in politics and praising instead a consumerism that supported 'an economy directed to the fulfilment of our

---

[115] M. Shanks, speech to Consumer Congress, Swansea (4 April 1981), p. 3 (Janet Upward's private papers).
[116] M. Shanks, 'Foreword', in NCC, *Real Money, Real Choice: Consumer Priorities in Economic Policy* (London, 1978), p. ix.
[117] NCC, *The Consumer and the State: Getting Value for Public Money* (London, 1979), p. 1.
[118] M. Shanks, *The Consumer in Europe* (Brussels, 1979), p. 14.
[119] *Guardian* (13 September 1978), p. 12.

needs as individuals'.[120] Indeed, Howe's comments reflected a political backlash against consumerism, and Shanks and the NCC allowed their pro-competition message to eclipse their earlier stakeholder principles. From the early 1980s, the Council clearly restrained itself from making grandiose pronouncements about a new consumer-led socio-political order, finding a government more ready to listen only to its arguments for greater choice and less protectionism.[121] Moreover, although the government had not formally warned the NCC off from the directions set in Shanks' earlier publication, Ministers nevertheless made manifest their strong disapproval of these activities.[122] Consumers were now to act as 'constructive critics' and the NCC was to intervene only in response to research conducted by the Consumer Concerns Survey, rather than acting on behalf of consumers in advance of any empirical investigation.[123] By 1983, Shanks seemed to be deliberately arguing against his earlier vision of the role of consumers in government, as well as putting to an end Young's notion of the NCC: 'We have never been, have never sought to be and could not be the same kind of body as the CBI or the TUC. We have never aspired to become an institutional colossus. Our mission has rather been to help consumers *as individuals* to get a fairer crack of the whip in our complex, institutionalised society.'[124] Consumerism was to move away from its social democratic traditions and respond instead to the new political environment, Thatcher's 'individualism and self-expression' (posited against centralisation) being praised as 'ideology to which consumers . . . can respond'.[125]

Shanks' reversal in attitude was just as likely a product of his own disillusionment with the ability of consumers to take up the position within civil society which he had ascribed to them, than a political manipulation of the NCC's activities. The membership of the Council was not subject to overtly political appointments in the early 1980s and the balance between professional, voluntary and consumer representatives was maintained. Under the articles of association, governments were allowed to instigate two NCC investigations in any given year, but even here the NCC found no real problem. For instance, it was clear that it had been asked to research such issues as the banking sector, the Common Agricultural Policy and air transport regulation because 'civil servants knew that what we [the NCC] were likely to produce would not be unsympathetic

---

[120] G. Howe, Speech to Consumer Congress, Swansea (5 April 1981), p. 27 (Janet Upward's private papers).
[121] NCC, *Annual Report, 1981–1982*, pp. 2–3.
[122] Private correspondence between Jeremy Mitchell and author.
[123] NCC, *Annual Report, 1981–1982*, p. 11.
[124] NCC, *Annual Report, 1982–1983*, p. 1.   [125] *Ibid.*

to the then government'.[126] But this also enabled the NCC to comment on areas which it had previously been unable to even research, opening doors which might otherwise have been closed. The only overtly political direction taken by the government was a negative decision not to appoint a chair as pro-active or as challenging as Young and Shanks had initially been. Although a known supporter of the Labour Party, Shanks' successor, Michael Montague, was supported by Norman Tebbit for his credentials as a self-made millionaire businessman and his almost complete lack of prior knowledge of the consumer movement. Montague was 'not really interested in theory', lacked any clear political values and seemed more concerned about improving the respectable appearance of the NCC to Ministers and the media, as well as securing himself a peerage.[127] He avoided, or was incapable of, making any statements on the principles of consumerism, preferring instead to simply list the specific achievements of the NCC.[128] In 1987, rather than setting out the aims and objectives of the NCC, he finished his report on the year with a minor complaint about the speed of drivers on the road, while elsewhere the NCC reverted to an older consumerism in stating that 'self-help is the best protection for consumers'.[129]

But by the time of the appointment of Montague to the chair, the initiative at the NCC had firmly shifted from the Council members to the salaried staff and such veteran consumer policy workers as the two directors in the 1980s, Jeremy Mitchell and Maurice Healy. This is crucial because by the end of the decade more political appointments were being made to the Council and John Major's office was felt to provide 'no positive agenda for the public sector at all'.[130] NCC staff therefore began to develop their own operating philosophy, beginning in 1984 with Healy's setting out of a number of 'working principles'. Building on the rights-based model of consumerism which had dominated international groups since the early 1960s, Healy explored the relationship between consumerism and citizenship. While careful to maintain a distinction between the two, it was acknowledged that once one explored the various means by which to solve 'market breakdown' – that is, the multitude of instances where the fictional ideal of perfect competition was seen not to work in practice – the solutions involved a necessary engagement with the public sphere which broke down the boundaries between purely consumer issues and political issues. Organising the NCC's

---

[126] Interview with Maurice Healy, 26 March 2002.
[127] *Ibid.*; private correspondence between Jeremy Mitchell and author.
[128] NCC, *Annual Report, 1984–1985*, p. 2; NCC, *Annual Report, 1985–1986*, pp. 1–2.
[129] NCC, *Annual Report, 1986–1987*, pp. 2, 10.
[130] Interview with Maurice Healy, 26 March 2002.

working principles around access, choice, information, redress and safety, Healy added equity, an early concern of Shanks that sought to campaign against 'arbitrary discrimination' between consumers based on characteristics unrelated to their roles as consumers. Access also could involve broader issues if it was generally agreed that the state had a duty to provide a service equally to all consumers. While some issues such as the decision for war clearly fell within the realm of pure citizenship, questions about taxation, public spending, representation and power blurred the line between consumerism and politics. The role of the NCC, therefore, was not to 'bring to decisions about consumer issues the pre-dispositions that we have from other parts of our lives', but to try and judge each issue according to its own merits and to elaborate carefully upon the specific consumer interest in any given situation.[131]

This appears at first hand a rather vague formula, but it follows the practical political approach adopted by the early activists of the modern consumer movement. The NCC's development, both in the 1980s and through to the present, therefore follows that incremental development which sees the gradual expansion of consumerism in various areas of local and national political life. Major successes for the NCC included its contribution to the opening up of the banking system and air transport, the extension of shop trading hours and its criticisms of the legal system that saw further developments in the small claims courts (where consumers could seek redress on an individual basis for relatively minor complaints) and in alternative dispute resolutions, such as the introduction of the ombudsman to the private sector. No ideological opposition was voiced against issues such as privatisation during the 1980s and 1990s as the NCC felt it could not adopt a political stance either for or against public ownership. Instead it focussed more on ensuring that the system of consumer representation within the mechanisms of an independent regulator were more appropriate policies to pursue for the collective mass of consumers. Today, despite some uncertainties as to its role in the mid to late 1990s, the NCC continues to work to educate consumers, regulate markets in the consumer interest, tackle issues of exclusion for those on low incomes, increase consumer representation and develop consumer protection measures as and when the need arises. Its working principles are still based around access, choice, safety, information, redress, representation and fairness (what was formally termed equity) and many of its main policy issues remain the same: the relationship between the consumer and the citizen; the definition of the consumer

---

[131] NCC, *Some Working Principles for Organisations Representing Consumers* (1984, revised 1987), Healy's private papers.

interest; the constituency of the NCC as a representative body; and the ability to maintain an independent voice.[132] This latter point has recently provoked fierce criticism from George Monbiot who has attacked the NCC for its Friends scheme which enables corporations to contribute to NCC funds through the payment of an annual £10,000 subscription. Even those within the consumer movement aware of the checks to ensure that the NCC will remain independent are irritated by such a scheme, since any such association with commerce can only lead to the sullying of the NCC's reputation in the public mind.[133] The NCC has disputed the implied corrosion of its independence and so far, as it continues to intervene on topics such as food policy, competition law (the Enterprise Bill) and pensions, it would seem to have countered Monbiot's claims as its political interventions maintain its traditions of lobbying on specific items of reform.

The Left in Britain has been commonly held to have failed in its strategies to respond to the demands of an increasingly affluent population.[134] This was a persistent culture from the 1950s to the extent that demands still had to be made of the mainstream Labour Party to embrace consumerism and a politics of consumption in the late 1980s.[135] John Beishon, Director of the CA, argued that it was not until 1989 that the Labour Party resolved the worker/consumer friction within its ideology, despite its initial commitment to the NCC.[136] Labour's *Consumer Choice and Quality of Life* committed the party to a 'powerful' Department of Consumer Affairs, a Food Standards Agency and a Consumers' Charter in which the boundaries between consumerism and citizenship were blurred: the former was defined as 'the aspiration of users and consumers for greater control over both their immediate environment – and the wider social and economic forces which shape it'.[137] The culmination of this redeveloped Labour Party strategy was the espousal by Tony Blair of Anthony Giddens' *The Third Way*. This important text urged social democrats to embrace a system which took account of two fundamental aspects of the 'post-materialist' age: the desire for greater personal freedom and personal choice, together with the growth of non-traditional

---

[132] NCC, *What is the National Consumer Council* (London, 2002); private correspondence between author and Anna Bradley, 8 January 2002.
[133] Letter from Jeremy Mitchell to Deidre Hutton [NCC Chair], 4 December 2002.
[134] L. Black, *The Political Culture of the Left in Britain, 1951–1964: Old Labour, New Britain?* (Basingstoke, 2003); S. Fielding, 'Activists against "affluence": Labour Party culture during the "Golden Age", circa 1950–1970', *Journal of British Studies*, 20 (2001), 241–67.
[135] F. Mort, 'The politics of consumption', in S. Hall and M. Jacques (eds.), *New Times: The Changing Face of Politics in the 1990s* (London, 1989), pp. 160–72.
[136] J. Beishon, 'Empowering consumers', *New Socialist* (June/July 1989), 16–17.
[137] *Ibid.*, p. 16; Labour Party, *Consumer Choice and Quality of Life* (London, 1989).

politics such as ecology, animal rights, sexuality and consumerism. The overall aim of third way politics is to 'help citizens pilot their way through the major revolutions of our time: globalisation, transformations in personal life and our relationship to nature'.[138] It is to utilise a programme made up of what have become New Labour buzzwords: the radical centre, the new democratic state, an active civil society, a democratic family, a new mixed economy, equality, inclusion, positive welfare, the social investment state and so on. In a sense, these proposals are hardly radical and they appear to build on many ideas to which Young and Crosland have been attached, suggesting that third way politics could consist of organised consumers, joined in forces through various campaigning networks, fighting to improve individual liberty while at the same time aiming to ensure that such freedoms were enjoyed by all.[139] Organisations such as the NCC were and are crucial to this form of political culture, with its promotion of the interests of the socially and economically excluded and its ability to bring together disparate voices, none of whom are motivated by a grand narrative of their historical or political legitimacy.

Social consumerism, as found within the objectives of the early CA Council and institutionalised within the NCC, was an important precursor to third way politics, Shanks' faith in consumers as rational citizens seeming to epitomise the desire to find a new basis for political action outside of the unions and the employers' organisations. Yet as a precursor, social consumerism shares with the third way many of its problems and weaknesses. It has had the ability – seen especially in the Consumer Congress – to bring together new social and political groups and to provide a sense of unity to an otherwise disparate set of interests. New Labour has apparently persisted in legitimising this form of politics and ascribed an important future role for the NCC in the government economic policy document, *Modern Markets: Confident Consumers*. Yet not all consumers can be expected to have the energy of a Michael Young, constantly attempting to create the links between grass-roots activism and mutual assistance practices and the higher institutions of power and bureaucracy often held to have divorced themselves from the lived realities of people's consuming actions. Instead, social consumerism has the danger of repeating the long-established circularity of consumer politics. Just as it draws strength from its ability to take on new causes and its incremental expansion into new policy spheres, so too does it become ever distant from the specific concerns of consumers at the point of purchasing and from a set of firm policy goals that make it a recognisable social movement.

---

[138] A. Giddens, *The Third Way* (Cambridge, 1998), p. 64.
[139] Smith and Young, 'Politics and Michael Young', p. 142; Leonard, *Crosland and New Labour*.

As one recent NCC survey found, consumers have proved reluctant to get involved in the promotion of their own interests as they feel it can be a waste of time. Third way politics might have resulted in an explosion of information and referral systems for consumers, but often this information is of the wrong kind and the consumer-focus of public and private institutions does not extend beyond its own rhetoric.[140] Despite all the developments in what has been termed the 'consumer revolution', even consumer activists themselves have questioned their practical impact on government and business and the degree of consumer empowerment that actually took place, especially in the 1980s.[141] Yet the irony is that without the active engagement of the mass of consumers on a regular basis, consumerism has had to develop its ambit as it has adopted a social role in speaking *for* consumers who are unwilling to speak for themselves. It is this that has enabled broad social agendas to emerge which have taken consumerism well beyond the realm of value-for-money purchasing. As consumerism has attached itself to the concerns of single-issue pressure groups on topics such as housing policy, credit unions and more recently the environment, it has even come to develop a set of policies more usually associated with anti-consumerist campaigning groups. Single-issue politics has enabled the CA and the NCC to appear at once radical and conservative, at the same time friends with business and with political protest. As will be seen in the next chapter, this is even more apparent within an international framework. Globalisation has produced a series of challenges for organised consumerism which has taken the politics of consumption well beyond the initial aims of the CA, and many organised consumer groups now find themselves supporting specific policy demands not too distant from the slogans on the banners of the street.

[140] NCC, 'Consumers say getting involved is a waste of time', *NCC News* (15 March 2002).
[141] R. John (ed.), *The Consumer Revolution: Redressing the Balance* (London, 1994).

11   Affluence or effluence: globalisation and ethical consumerism

The critique of luxury remains as strong as ever it was in the eighteenth century. While specific objects, especially psychoactive substances and commodities associated with youth culture, continue to give rise to moral discourses and government regulation, general unease about modern forms of luxury have persisted, whether it be in exposés of the excesses of corporate capitalism or the play on liberal guilt invoked by Galbraith, Packard, Mitford and their successors. In a recent *Philosophy Today* article Philip Cafaro outlined the elements of the ancient philosophers' virtue ethics that urged limited material accumulation and the disciplining of consuming desires.[1] He concludes that less is, in fact, more, in the sense that a rejection of the dismal life of consumption will lead to a greater focus on the spiritual and the intellectual. To this critique we might add a recent Christian assessment of the consumer society or even a range of anti-globalisation critiques.[2] But a more interesting observation of this ongoing discussion of luxury is the belief shared by many commentators that consumers themselves, rather than their self-appointed moral guardians, are beginning to feel a similar sense of unease with material abundance. If the problem facing affluent consumers in the 1950s was the inability to make informed choices, the problem facing affluent consumers today is one of too much choice. As with the ass in Jean Buridan's allegory, so confused are we by the array of brands and images for identical goods placed before us, that we are prone to starve through our inability to choose between two equally attractive piles of hay. According to a report commissioned in 2000, US-style commercialism in Britain 'has failed to enrich our lives but has caused confusion and anxiety as people struggle with the mind-boggling array of options available'.[3]

Such sentiments have been taken as evidence of a growing consumer resentment of corporate culture and a disenchantment with the branding

---

[1] P. Cafaro, 'Less is more: economic consumption and the good life', *Philosophy Today*, 42:1 (1998), 26–39.
[2] J. Benton, *Christians in a Consumer Culture* (Ross-Shire, 2000).
[3] *Guardian* (24 April 2000), pp. 7, 17.

of the global economy. According to John Vidal, 'consumers are on the march', reacting against the power of the multinationals and scoring important victories against, for instance, Shell's decision to dump its old oil rigs at sea or Barclays Bank's financial stake in the apartheid regime of South Africa.[4] In June 1999, the Women's Institute voted to join with groups such as the CA, Greenpeace, Friends of the Earth and seventy other consumer, environmental and single-issue pressure groups to oppose any further increase in the cultivation of genetically modified (GM) crops. Together, these traditional voluntary groups and NGOs have formed, according to Vidal, a powerful third sector of consumers, forming a 'civil society' which has sought to check the transference of power from governments to multinationals. He went on to predict that consumer power would realise its potential on the streets of Seattle in early December 1999 as a myriad of groups prepared to join forces in protest against the World Trade Organisation.[5]

Shortly after the Seattle demonstrations, however, activists were apparently to find a new guidebook and leader. Naomi Klein's *No Logo* has been heralded as the '*Das Kapital* of the anti-corporate movement', its uncovering of the economic abuses and exploitation which lie behind the corporate brand clearly capturing the imagination of a generation.[6] Klein's book is a brilliant piece of investigative journalism, at its best in its vivid accounts of the conditions of the workers in the factories and sweatshops of Nike, Diesel and The Gap. But it is far from being a manifesto for the growing numbers of anti-globalisation groups she recounts in her later chapters. Indeed, it contains almost no theoretical observation whatsoever, nor any statement of the ideological unity between the various strands of protest, and perhaps what has therefore been the most interesting aspect of the book has been its reception. In the perceived absence of a radical, post-Marxist understanding of the dynamics of the global economy, protestors have been eager to latch on optimistically and even blindly to *No Logo* as the most relevant exposition of the new political-economic environment. Even the Socialist Bookstore in London featured *No Logo* as its main display for several months, despite Klein's only conceptual link to an older politics of dissent being a rejection of the identity issues which dominated campus politics in the late 1980s and early 1990s and a bald assertion that consumers need to remember the economic structures that give rise to western affluence.

---

[4] J. Vidal, 'Power to the people', *Guardian [G2]* (7 June 1999), pp. 2–3.
[5] *Guardian* (27 November 1999), p. 15.
[6] N. Klein, *No Logo* (London, 2000); *Observer Review* (12 November 2000), p. 3; K. Viner, 'Hand-to-brand combat', *Guardian Weekend* (23 September 2002), pp. 12–21.

It is not that Klein's work requires a theoretical exposition of globalisation and she is in many ways correct to argue that the strength of the new protestors lies in the very absence of a manifesto. Single-issue politics, as in the field of organised consumerism, has drawn strength from its diversity and its ability to incorporate incrementally new agendas and issues. But some attempt nevertheless needs to be made to understand the relations between forms of protest and the consumer society within which they operate. What appears below is an attempt to locate the consumer movement within the rise of modern-day single-issue global politics. From almost the very beginning of the life of the CA, attempts were made to collaborate on international projects. The first part of this chapter therefore focuses on the development of such international bodies as the Bureau Européen des Unions de Consommateurs (BEUC) and, in greater detail, the International Organisation of Consumers' Unions (IOCU). The second half examines, in contrast, the rise of ethical consumerism in Britain and the concerns it shares with much of the global resistance movement.

While these different strands of consumerism have almost no crossover in terms of personnel or institutional support, they are examined together here because of the similarity of many of their concerns. Although funded mainly by comparative testing organisations, IOCU has expanded into the developing world and today involves itself in campaigns to maintain standards of living among poorer nations and to limit the ability of multinational corporations to exploit consumers rich and poor alike. Furthermore, many of the IOCU's initiatives have focussed on issues such as pollution and the environment, human rights and forms of government protection, all areas which have motivated the rise of ethical consumerism and the politics of the consumer boycott. What is apparent in this chapter is that the language of rights which has dominated post-Second World War consumer movements has also come to take on board a series of consumer duties within an international context, thereby replicating many of the concerns of 'consumers' at the end of the nineteenth century. Consumer and anti-consumer are thus treated as one within this chapter, though this is not only a means to demonstrate the similarity in the concerns of an older organised consumerism with a wave of modern single-issue protests. An ongoing theme of this chapter will be to follow through the implications of a recent scholarship which claims that not only our social and cultural, but also our political, life has come to be shaped by the world of goods. Whether one subscribes to *Which?* or to the *Ethical Consumer*, then, one develops political opinions about the world through an understanding of the meaning of the commodities we choose, or do not choose, to consume. Whether consumers feel they have obtained a position from which they can bargain with business and the state within a global capitalist framework, will dictate the moderation or extremism of their responses.

The global consumer movement

The spread of US-style comparative-testing consumerism was not just restricted to Britain in the post-Second World War period. The CA had been preceded by such organisations as the Union fédérale de la consommation in France (1951), the Nederlandse Consumentenbond (1953) and the Belgian Association des Consommateurs (1957), as well as several state-sponsored bodies such as the Norwegian Forbrukerrådet (1953) and the Swedish Statens Konsumentråd (1957).[7] With the development of the Common Market, these organisations increasingly recognised the need for a European perspective on many consumer issues. Consequently, in February 1962, the BEUC was formed to co-ordinate the activities of the independent consumer groups from the then six EEC member countries. For its first ten years the BEUC aimed to assist members with product testing and to influence the development of EEC policy, as well as holding regular meetings to discuss other matters of mutual interest and to develop contacts with consumer groups in countries outside of the EEC.[8] Financed largely by the subscriptions paid by its non-profit-making members, the BEUC expanded its scope alongside the growth of the EEC itself. In 1972, Eirlys Roberts of the CA was made Director of the BEUC in anticipation of the UK's entry into Europe the following year and, with the extra income obtained with the membership of such a comparatively robust organisation, the BEUC was able to set up a permanent office in Brussels in May 1973.

Although the BEUC has launched prominent campaigns for lead-free petrol and against the use of hormones in beef, most of its activities have been based around developing consumer policies within the EEC, monitoring the complicated processes of legislation from the European Commission through to the Council of Ministers and later the European Parliament. Originally, the Council of Europe had set out a Consumer Protection Charter, based around the five established consumer movement concerns of protection, redress, information, education and

---

[7] IOCU, *The Consumer and the World of Tomorrow: Report of the Second Conference of the IOCU* (The Hague, 1962), p. 1; see entries on Belgium, France, Norway, Sweden and the Netherlands in S. Brobeck, R. N. Mayer and R. O. Herrmann (eds.), *Encyclopaedia of the Consumer Movement* (Santa Barbara, 1997).

[8] J. Murray, 'Bureau Européen des Unions de Consommateurs', in Brobeck *et al.* (eds.), *Encyclopaedia*, pp. 73–6.

representation, which influenced the establishment of the Consumers' Consultative Committee (CCC) in 1973. Working in close collaboration, the CCC and BEUC drew up a draft programme which, subject to the various amendments made by the numerous institutions of the EEC bureaucracy, was finally ratified by the Council of Ministers in 1975 as the first Programme for Consumer Protection and Information. Subsequently, the Programme came to be referred to as the Consumer Charter of the Community and its five areas of action were framed within the language of rights, providing a crucial reference point for the harmonisation of European consumer legislation within which the British system was broadly in line.[9]

British consumer activists have always played a prominent role in Europe, with many leading advocates gaining their first experience in the CA and the NCC. Their actions have been assisted by the formation of the UK Consumers in the European Community Group which helped co-ordinate policy initiatives prior to negotiation at European level.[10] Michael Shanks, as Chairman of the NCC, saw in Europe the danger of replicating the productivist bias of the corporate state as, for instance, in the UK's NEDC or West Germany's 'Concerted Action'. Noting that there was no direct mention of consumer protection in any of the treaties establishing the European Communities, Shanks worried in 1979 that consumerism was to be, along with social policy, environmental protection, regional development and overseas aid, a mere tactic to provide Europe with a 'human face'. In the discussions over the second Programme for Consumer Protection, he urged, as in his early plans for the NCC, not just more legislation but the implementation of structures that created a 'consumer-oriented society', moving the consumer 'out of the ghetto' and into a 'horizontal' type of policy-making: for example, by placing the consumer centre-stage, the Common Agricultural Policy (CAP) would become a food, rather than a farm, policy.[11]

As with consumerism in Britain, Shanks' aim to make consumers fully integrated partners within the corporate state was never realised, though the EEC and later the EU have continued to be at the forefront of

---

[9] L. Maier, 'Consumer policy in the European Union', in Brobeck *et al.* (eds.), *Encyclopaedia*, pp. 248–51; H. W. Micklitz and S. Weatherill, 'Consumer policy in the European Community: before and after Maastricht', *Journal of Consumer Policy*, 16:3–4 (1993), 285–322; M. A. Orsini, 'Consumer policy and the European Economic Community', in E. S. Maynes (ed.), *The Frontier of Research in the Consumer Interest* (Columbia, MO, 1988), pp. 510–21; R. Wraith, *The Consumer Cause: A Short Account of its Organisation, Power and Importance* (London, 1976), pp. 62–6; J. Aspinall, 'Glossary of organisations active in consumer affairs', in J. Mitchell (ed.), *Marketing and the Consumer Movement* (London, 1978), pp. 273–4.

[10] NCC, *Annual Report, 1978–1979*, p. 17.

[11] M. Shanks, *The Consumer in Europe* (Brussels, 1979).

consumer protection measures. Additional Programmes on Consumer Protection were adopted throughout the 1980s and, from 1989, three year action plans have been set out. Article 129a of the 1992 Maastricht Treaty entitled the European Commission to ensure a high level of consumer protection in three of Europe's five fundamental consumer rights: health and safety, protection of economic interests and information and education. Today, institutions exist for the articulation of the consumer interest at a range of different levels. Within the European Parliament there is a Committee on Environment, Public Health and Consumer Affairs. A sub-committee on consumer affairs exists within the Economic and Social Committee which advises directly the Council of Ministers. Since 1989 there has been a Commissioner for Consumer Affairs and in 1995 the Consumer Policy Service was upgraded to a Directorate General (XXIV), with the responsibility for assessing all aspects of EU policy that impacted upon the consumer, though it has come to have an increasing emphasis on food and health. Finally, the increased status of consumer affairs within Europe was apparent in the upgrading of the Consumer Consultative Committee into a full Council in 1990. However, comparative-testing style organisations were dissatisfied with the inclusion of trade union and co-operative movement members and, as has so often been the case, this attempt to unite two different politics of consumption, or two very different branches of a much more broadly conceived consumerism, failed and the Council became the Consumer Committee in 1995, consisting once again (as with the original CCC) of representatives of the fifteen national consumer bodies. For organisations such as the CA and the BEUC, the restriction of consumer representation to specific consumer organisations has helped focus European consumerism on issues around the established rights, but it has restricted its extension into areas of traditional concern for the labour movement and also the IOCU.[12] And for some critics, European consumer policy has remained a populist measure, a rhetoric which appears to respond to the concerns of the people but which is ultimately a top-down programme. Here, an institutionalised consumerism which is careful in its selection of the groups to speak for the consumer offers only a limited 'culture of complaint' rather than a wholly 're-energised' society.[13]

Other international organisations have also attempted to speak for the consumer, adopting a similar rights-based language which as much pre-empts rather than responds to a grass-roots consumer movement. The Organisation for Economic Co-operation and Development

[12] Maier, 'Consumer policy in the EU', p. 250; CAA 66: A. Bradley, 'The role of consumer associations' (June 1990).
[13] A. Burgess, 'Flattering consumption: creating a Europe of the consumer', *Journal of Consumer Culture*, 1:1 (2001), 93–117.

(OECD) appointed its own Committee on Consumer Policy in 1969 which has constantly monitored the types of national consumer protection policies which are compatible with the OECD's main function of fostering international trade and achieving 'the highest sustainable economic growth'.[14] The United Nations has worked more closely with consumer groups, especially in the areas of unethical marketing (for example, Nestlé's infant milk formula) and product safety, resulting in the publication, from 1982, of a UN Consolidated List of Banned Products. Within the UN, the IOCU has Category I status, enabling it to speak as a national delegation (though it cannot vote), and a set of Guidelines for Consumer Protection were created in 1985. Again, consumerism in this document is defined through a series of rights, or government responsibilities, in regard to product safety, consumers' economic interests, quality standards, the distribution of essential goods and services, redress and education and information.[15] The Guidelines have acted as an important reference for the development of consumer protection legislation in Asian, African and South American states, thereby ensuring that the principles of organised western consumerism have provided the models for the development of nation-specific politics of consumption. However, the Guidelines also made reference to food and other essential goods and services, reflecting the politics of necessitous consumption which is still most relevant to the majority of nations. By the mid-1990s, the UN Commission for Sustainable Development and the UN Economic and Social Council were urging the inclusion of guidelines on the promotion of sustainable consumption, placing duties as well as rights on consumers to think further than the boundaries of rational self-interest contained within the comparative testing model.[16]

But the principal means by which western consumerism has been spread around the globe has been the IOCU. In the mid-1950s, French, Italian and American activists began to discuss the establishment of an international body,[17] but following a visit made by Elizabeth Schadee of the Dutch Consumentenbond to Caspar Brook of the CA in early 1958,

[14] OECD, *Annual Report on Consumer Policy, 1975* (Paris, 1975); E. Linke, 'OECD Committee on Consumer Policy', in Brobeck *et al.* (eds.), *Encyclopaedia*, p. 419; OECD, *A Global Marketplace for Consumers* (Paris, 1995); OECD Committee on Consumer Policy, *Consumer Policy During the Past Ten Years* (Paris, 1983).

[15] United Nations, *Guidelines for Consumer Protection* (New York, 1986); D. Harland, 'The United Nations Guidelines for Consumer Protection', *Journal of Consumer Policy*, 10 (1987), 245–66.

[16] A. Peterson and J. M. Halloran, 'United Nations Consumer Protections', in Brobeck *et al.* (eds.), *Encyclopaedia*, pp. 581–3.

[17] C. E. Warne, 'Consumer organisations: an international conference?', *Cartel*, 7:1 (1957), 2–5; speech by Warne made in 1959 reprinted in F. G. Sim, *IOCU on Record: A Documentary History of the IOCU, 1960–1990* (Yonkers, NY, 1991), pp. 13–19.

moves were made to carry out joint comparative tests. They approached Colston Warne of the US Consumers' Union who pledged financial support to any such venture, having already received expressions of interest from Michael Young and even the International Co-operative Alliance, though the latter was not to play a role in the future development of the IOCU. The First International Conference on Consumer Testing met at the Hague from 30 March to 1 April 1960, with delegates from seventeen organisations in fourteen countries, and led to the establishment of a Technical Exchange Committee to supervise joint product testing and the IOCU to act as a clearing house for the exchange of information. With an initial annual budget of £5,000 (including £2,000 from the US), the IOCU was created with an office in the Hague, a journal entitled *IOCU Bulletin*, and a Council consisting of the Dutch, British and American sponsors of the conference, plus the Belgian Association des Consommateurs and the Australian Consumers' Association.[18]

The growth of the IOCU is a testament in itself to the global importance of organised consumerism since the 1950s. By the time of its third meeting, in Norway in 1964, the IOCU was clearly an international movement. The Japanese Consumers' Association alone sent thirty-two delegates and the range of 'observers' reflected an interest well beyond the comparative testing organisations that formed the IOCU's core: manufacturers' organisations sent several delegates but so too did the Co-operative movement, the Supreme Co-operative Council of Poland, and the Soviet Union.[19] In 1970 the Council still consisted of the core of the five founding members, but also five co-opted members (Stiftung Warentest of West Germany and the national consumer bodies of the UK and the Scandinavian countries) and four elected members from Austria, New Zealand, Israel and Canada. A further sixteen Associate members and twenty-three Corresponding members ensured that organised consumerism now reached into Asia, Africa and Latin America, if only into the richest nations of these areas.[20] By 1990, however, the IOCU had extended well beyond the affluent West and an Executive had been formed which included South Korea and Mauritius and had as its President Erna Witoelar of the Yayasan Lembaga Konsumen, Indonesia.[21] Today, the IOCU is called Consumers International, and in November 2000

---

[18] Sim, *IOCU*, pp. 26–7; S. Brobeck, 'Consumers International', in Brobeck *et al.* (eds.) *Encyclopaedia*, pp. 175–9.
[19] IOCU, *Consumers on the March: Proceedings of the Third Biennial Conference of the IOCU* (The Hague, 1964), pp. 139–43.
[20] IOCU, *Knowledge is Power: Consumer Goals in the 1970s. Proceedings of the Sixth Biennial World Conference of the IOCU* (The Hague, 1970), pp. 115–17.
[21] IOCU, *Consumer Power in the Nineties: Proceedings of the Thirteenth IOCU World Congress* (The Hague, 1991), p. 113.

it held its 16th World Congress in Durban, South Africa. Its headquarters are in London, but there are thriving regional offices in Africa, Asia and Latin America. Incredibly, in 1999 there were 253 members from 115 different countries which ranged from all the states of the western world to post-communist Eastern Europe and a whole collection of developing states (China, Chad, Guatemala, El Salvador, Gabon, Nigeria, Malawi and Burkina Faso) that, on first instinct, one might suppose had other interests that needed defending than those of consumers.[22]

This expansion was by no means inevitable since western and especially British consumers have dominated the IOCU's history (for instance, Peter Goldman acted as Treasurer for several years, was President from 1970–5 and was about to become Director-General before he died in 1987[23]) and private comparative testing bodies have been the movement's backbone. The IOCU originally took as its *raison d'être* the four consumer rights first articulated by President Kennedy in his speech to Congress in March 1962 – the right to safety, to be informed, to choose and to be heard. These offered a model for the potential Americanisation of consumerist agendas around the world as various interests would be articulated through the language of US constitutional liberalism. And in the first decade of its existence at least, IOCU consumerism was centred around the faith in rational choice as a means to improve competition and raise standards of living around the world.[24] According to Eva Preiss of the Austrian Verein für Konsumenteninformation, production had been rationalised in the early twentieth century: now it was up to the 'brotherly' consumer organisations to rationalise consumption on behalf of the individual shopper who too often cried alone in the wilderness.[25] For Peter Goldman, the IOCU represented the opportunity to awaken a 'sleeping giant'. Whereas trade unions had been set up to rectify the balance of power between capital and labour, consumerism had emerged to rectify the balance of power between the ignorant consumer and the fully informed manufacturer. The solution was simple: 'Wissen ist Macht. Knowledge is power'.[26] Henry Epstein of the Australian Consumers' Association took the historical awareness and missionary zeal still further and ascribed an almost utopian end-goal to the movement, in which consumption and purchasing would become entirely logical. In attempting to achieve this, the 1962 IOCU meeting was 'a kind of second Internationale' and subsequent institutional developments within the IOCU

---

[22] Consumers International, *Annual Report, 1999*, pp. 37–41.
[23] CA, *Annual Report, 1987–1988*, p. 5.
[24] IOCU, *The Consumer and the World of Tomorrow: Report of the Second Conference* (The Hague, 1962), p. 7.
[25] IOCU, *Knowledge is Power*, p. 8.   [26] *Ibid.*, p. 106.

have been designed to promote education, representation, standards and the policing of dangerous goods through a Consumer Interpol.[27]

Yet for other consumers none of these activities and ideas provided the IOCU with a specific rationale. As Michael Shanks argued in 1978, the IOCU had been in a position to lead the world but had failed to find an 'overall ideology' with which to unite a global citizenry. The IOCU was in a position, he claimed, to break from its middle-class roots, acquire a social conscience and begin a social revolution which would tackle the issues of multinational capitalism, population growth, economic imbalance and the whole range of questions facing the modern world citizen. Although the priorities of the consumer would always be with safety, choice, information and redress, it was time to build on the grass-root aspects of consumerism as a movement and begin to have a direct and influential role in global affairs.[28] Shanks' indictment of his colleagues for their lack of a grand narrative or a theoretical justification of their existence was unfair and was perhaps ignorant of some of the developments which had been occurring in the IOCU over the last seventeen years. As the organisation had expanded throughout the 1960s it had been forced to confront issues facing consumers not imagined by the enthusiasts of comparative testing, expanding incrementally the definition of the consumer interest. Firstly, in the Scandinavian countries where it was felt the population was too small to sustain an effective comparative testing organisation based on private subscription, state organisations had been created to represent all consumers. These bodies had attended IOCU meetings but, as non-private bodies, were not permitted to sit on Council. This resulted in a potential split which was only resolved by 1968 when a new constitution was adopted which shifted power from the original Council to the General Assembly, made up of Associates which were 'active exclusively on behalf of consumers'.[29] The IOCU was therefore made more democratic, with the Council being elected, paving the way for the emergence of European state-sponsored organisations such as the Statens Konsumentråd of Sweden and the Arbeitsgemeinschaft der Verbraucherverbände of West Germany which had no individual members but was made up of fifteen constituent regional bodies. What such state-sponsored bodies brought to the IOCU was a far greater concern with regulation, participation, the economy and citizenship, issues which in

---

[27] IOCU, *Consumer and World of Tomorrow*, p. 77; IOCU, *A World in Crisis: The Consumer Response: Proceedings of the Ninth IOCU World Congress* (The Hague, 1978); IOCU, *Consumer Policy 2000: Seminar Report* (The Hague, 1986), pp. 33–4; K. Gillman, *The Consumer Interpol* (The Hague, 1981); International Organisation for Standardisation (ISO), *Consumer Standards Today and Tomorrow* (London, 1976).
[28] IOCU, *World in Crisis*, pp. 16–20.   [29] Sim, *IOCU*, p. 42.

turn provided comparisons and stimuli to different national agendas and made the IOCU leaders regard themselves as 'humanists' campaigning to create a 'consumer civilisation'.[30]

Secondly, and still more significantly, were the efforts of the Development Committee to establish consumer organisations around the world, which gradually focussed the work of the IOCU on disadvantaged consumers and those without the ability to obtain the information necessary for individual discrimination. It also made the IOCU aware of the very different problems facing consumer activists, such as when seven prominent members of the Greek movement were arrested and imprisoned without trial during the events following the political uprising of 1973.[31] In April 1963, the IOCU had been granted consultative status by the Economic and Social Council of the UN resulting in a greater concern for non-affluent consumers at the 1964 biennial conference. Even Colstone Warne, a prominent advocate of comparative testing urged the consumer movement to be 'not only attentive to the problems of choosing automobiles, air conditioners and refrigerators, but . . . also with the day to day issues of those in countries which have not yet attained an advanced technology'.[32] As a consequence, the IOCU began to work more closely with the UN in the 1960s, to upgrade its efforts to help set up new consumer groups and to make efforts to collect data on the kinds of problems facing poorer consumers.[33] One early investigation, undertaken by RICA, urged economic development policy to take account of the consumer else risk making the same mistakes as 'doctrinaire Marxism or laissez-faire capitalism', though its own recommendations for greater local voluntary action among consumers did not detract too far from the *Which?*-brand of consumerism.[34] Such vague platitudes have been followed up in later decades with more concrete action on foreign debt relief, inappropriate baby foods and assistance with food production and distribution to ensure adequate supplies to consumers.[35] Yet in the early 1960s, many of the IOCU discussions smacked of a well-meaning philanthropic humanitarianism that was not really overcome until emerging non-western consumer groups began to speak at the meetings and workshops of the IOCU.

Rational choice was increasingly acknowledged to be a far less important concern for many of the world's consumers. In 1969, for the first time, the IOCU held a meeting in what it identified as a developing nation,

---

[30] IOCU, *Consumers on the March*, pp. 14–19.
[31] IOCU, *Report for 1972–1974* (The Hague, 1975), p. 1.
[32] IOCU, *Consumers on the March*, p. 6.   [33] Sim, *IOCU*, pp. 57–9.
[34] RICA, *New Nations: Problems for Consumers* (London, 1964), p. 45.
[35] IOCU, *World in Crisis*, p. 6; IOCU, *Consumer Solidarity: For a Better World: Proceedings of Twelfth Congress* (The Hague, 1987), pp. 30, 82–3.

in Kingston, Jamaica, while Florence Mason of the CU continued to write to nascent consumer activists across the world such that she had corresponded with organisers in over 140 countries by 1980.[36] In the 1970 biennial meeting, Persia Campbell, the committed internationalist, UN worker and former first New York State Consumer Counsel (1955–8), led a discussion on 'the consumer in the developing countries' and, in 1974, the theme for the Sydney conference was the cost of living, enabling discussion of the problems of both inflation within the affluent west and everyday getting and spending for the poor.[37] Here, the IOCU was able to expand its sphere of protest to include a sustained critique of 'big business' which drew on an intellectual trajectory which stretched back to Galbraith's 'countervailing powers' and looked forward to alliances with the anti-Reaganite actions of campaigners like Ralph Nader.[38] But as well as seeking to curb the power of multinationals through UN-sanctioned codes of conduct and other measures to keep down the cost of living, the IOCU has also turned to the quality of life, the right to a clean environment being added to the original list of four fundamental consumer rights. Taking the view that consumerism must ask itself, 'how much is enough?', the IOCU set up a Working Group in 1970 which soon presented its declaration on 'The Consumer and the Environment' to the UN's own conference on the subject.[39] The consumer interest in the environment was initially conceived as the need for collective action on, for instance, the abolition of dangerous chemicals and rising rates of energy consumption.[40] It has drawn heavily on the agenda of Rachel Carson and expanded into more general environmental issues such as ozone layer depletion and hazardous technologies which present dangers for workers exposed to unnecessary risk through inadequate health and safety regulations.[41] The Bhopal gas leak tragedy in December 1984 was a defining moment for the IOCU as it has subsequently moved to combat 'corporate callousness in exposing consumers and communities to highly

---

[36] Sim, *IOCU*, pp. 60–1.
[37] IOCU, *Report for 1972–1974*, p. 2; IOCU, *Knowledge is Power*, pp. 77–92.
[38] M. Green, 'The mega-corporation versus consumers', speech at 1986 conference reprinted in IOCU, *Consumer Policy 2000*, pp. 18–21.
[39] A. Durning, 'An environmentalist's perspective on consumer society', in L. B. Glickman (ed.), *Consumer Society in American History: A Reader* (Ithaca, 1999), pp. 78–81; IOCU, *Biennial Report, 1970–1972* (The Hague, 1972), pp. 11–15.
[40] IOCU, *The Quality of Life: 1972 World Congress Handbook* (The Hague, 1972), pp. 21–3.
[41] R. Carson, *Silent Spring* (1962; Harmondsworth, 1999); IOCU, *Consumer Solidarity*, 77–81; IOCU, *Five Billion Consumers: Organising for Change Proceedings of Eleventh World Congress* (The Hague, 1984), p. 52; T. Gips, *Breaking the Pesticide Habit: Alternatives to Twelve Hazardous Pesticides* (Penang, 1990); S. Rengam and K. Snyder, *The Pesticide Handbook: Profiles for Action* (Penang, 1991); IOCU, *Pests at Home: A Consumer Guide to Safer Pest Control* (Penang, 1993).

hazardous products' and the ability of corporations to fabricate misinformation which is accepted by governments 'apathetic' to the interests of ordinary citizens.[42] A logical development of this policy has been a concern with nuclear safety and more recently biotechnology and GM foods, all of which were identified as early as 1970 as part of a broader shift to a humanitarian form of consumerism in which the IOCU was to be concerned with a 'general welfare policy with the object of promoting the physical, psychological and social well-being'.[43]

Even though the source of funding for the IOCU ultimately came from the pockets of subscribers to test magazines concerned mainly with the purchasing of better refrigerators, it is clear that as early as 1964 the IOCU was becoming a forum for the articulation of more radical consumerist agendas. It was then that Henry Epstein of the Australian Consumers' Association, a keen advocate of rationality and individual consumer action, asked whether organised consumerism did not 'intend to march around in a circle to a tune played with one finger on a cash register' and suggested instead that activists focus on 'needs' as well as 'pleasures'.[44] It was then also that Michael Young questioned the achievements of the modern consumer movement and called for a range of other questions to be addressed, thus beginning a trend as trade unionists and co-operators, although not allowed to join, were at least invited to speak at IOCU meetings in the 1960s and spread consumerism beyond 'literate upper middle class women'.[45] He launched into a broad commentary on the state of organised consumerism. The IOCU, he claimed, had to take account of the social costs of consumption and perhaps even the Marcusean anti-consumerist attacks being led by students, hippies, beatniks and dropouts. Consumerism had to acknowledge that 'the affluent society is also the effluent society', that it must take into account issues of deforestation, pesticides, recycling and the suffering of the poor, and that testing organisations had to move away from helping consumers as individuals to regarding consumers 'as members of a society which collectively has to bear the costs' of increased spending.[46] His expansion of the IOCU's role was followed by frequent conference discussions on 'the limits of consumption', inequality and 'the quality of life' and he returned to his theme in 1978, casting aside the self-interested complaining that appeared on Esther Rantzen's TV programme, 'That's Life', and embracing instead a 'third sector' which saw much greater links with

[42] IOCU, *Consumer Solidarity*, p. 79.
[43] IOCU, *Knowledge is Power*, p. 10.   [44] IOCU, *Consumers on the March*, p. 130.
[45] IOCU, *Knowledge is Power*, p. 17; IOCU, *World in Crisis*, p. 11.
[46] IOCU, *Knowledge is Power*, pp. 30–6.

the Co-operative movement, as he took inspiration from the Rochdale Pioneers, the 'active democracy' of the Mondragon Co-operative in Spain, the Israeli kibbutzim and his own Mutual Aid Centre.[47]

By the early 1980s, the consumerism of the IOCU was firmly defined as a movement which had a major contribution to make in all the problems of the world, including both the economic and the physical environment: 'it stresses the importance of international solidarity which must assure that the basic needs of consumers *all over the world* are reasonably satisfied'.[48] By 1984 campaigns ranged from food supply, tobacco control, pharmaceutical medicines, protectionism, the power of transnational corporations, working women and breastfeeding, banned products, environmental disasters such as Bhopal, the problems facing disabled and young consumers, international codes of practice, energy policy, nuclear power and access to information technology.[49] The first World Consumer Rights Day was launched on 15 March 1983 and, one year later, the IOCU had added to Kennedy's four rights, the right to redress, the right to consumer education and the right to a healthy environment. Consumerism was still defined through rights, but they were also human rights, and interpreted according to a broad view of liberalism which harked back to the notions of duty within the nineteenth-century thought. The consumer right was therefore 'the right not to be exploited either by individuals or by social and economic systems'.[50]

The principal advocate of such a global vision of consumerism within the IOCU was Anwar Fazal from the Malaysian consumer movement, whose own rise to prominence symbolised the greater power afforded to the non-western consumer groups by the 1980s. In classic civil rights rhetoric, Fazal spoke of the need for 'solidarity', 'spirit' and 'the strength of many voices together'. Quoting 'we shall overcome' he adopted a more aggressive tone to those businesses and governments which denied consumers their freedoms and he ended with a self-confessed 'romantic' call to arms that demanded 'access to a dignified and fuller life. We are a force for human rights, we are a force for social justice, and we are a force for a better, a kinder and a happier world. We rise from one ocean, we drink one water, we breathe one air, we share this earth.'[51] The *Consumer Manifesto 2000* likewise called for a 'just and fair society' and listed a set of demands which included the implementation in all countries of the

[47] IOCU, *World in Crisis*, pp. 31–3, 37–9; IOCU, *Five Billion Consumers*, p. 52; IOCU, *Quality of Life*, pp. 21, 25.

[48] IOCU, *World in Crisis*, p. 3.   [49] IOCU, *Five Billion Consumers*, pp. 52–6, 62–7.

[50] CAA 24: Miscellaneous papers on World Consumer Rights Day, leaflet.

[51] IOCU, *Consumer Policy 2000*, p. 13.

UN Guidelines for Consumer Protection, the full implementation of a Code of Conduct on Transnational Corporations, regulation of the international food supply, the removal of trade barriers and the international prohibition of trade in dangerous substances.[52] Crucially, the manifesto also stated the IOCU commitment to 'promoting the fulfilment of basic needs of consumers, in particular of the poor, low income and disadvantaged.' This was a remarkable addition and was soon to become the eighth consumer right of the IOCU.[53] In fact, it implied less a right and more a duty, given that the ultimate source of funding for the IOCU was the pockets of affluent consumers in Europe and the United States who had probably largely forgotten or never experienced either poverty, disadvantage or the struggle to meet basic needs.

As closer links were established between the IOCU and green and ethical consumerism (symbolised by the keynote address of 1990 given by Ralph Nader[54]), the constitution was again changed to facilitate greater parity between North and South. And, to mark the IOCU's commitment to both rich and poor, it changed its name in 1994 to Consumers International (CI), thus removing any remaining symbolic association with straightforward comparative testing consumerism.[55] Today, issues of food standards and safety, consumer health, the regulation of global trade, sustainable consumption, consumer representation and national consumer protection regimes continue to dominate its work. But greatest attention is given to sustainable consumption and the whole range of questions arising from globalisation, making many of CI's main campaigning efforts indistinguishable from other forms of global resistance. Significantly, CI staff joined a myriad of representatives from other NGOs on the streets of Seattle to campaign against aspects of the World Trade Organisation in 1999.[56] For an older generation of consumer activists, there is a worry over the scope of this CI vision. It is feared that many activists 'are not particularly interested in consumerism' and that 'things are being done in the name of consumers which are really being done in the name of something else', such as environmentalism, anti-colonialism, or the protests against GM foods.[57] Yet it has been the ability of IOCU to make itself such a broad umbrella that has also clearly provided much of the impetus for its continued expansion. There might still be no coherent consumerist ideology at work, but it is one institution which has made

---

[52] *Ibid.* p. 7.
[53] IOCU, *Consumer Solidarity*, p. 85; IOCU, *Biennial Report, 1970–1972*, pp. 25, 29.
[54] IOCU, *Consumer Power in the Nineties*, pp. 1–16.
[55] Brobeck, 'Consumers International', p. 179.
[56] Consumers International, *Annual Report, 1999*, p. 18.
[57] Interview with Maurice Healy, 26 March 2002.

a definite attempt to link a politics of affluence with a politics of necessity. In its campaigns against the exploitative profits of multinationals, it
draws on an anti-colonial and anti-profiteering rhetoric that establishes
links all the way from J. A. Hobson and Sidney Webb to Naomi Klein
and George Monbiot. And, in its concerns for the problems faced by
developing world women consumers, it has reinvoked a feminist politics
of consumption long since forgotten, at least in Britain. In a poem contained in the 1985 Filipino Women's Manifesto, reproduced in an IOCU
investigation into women and consumption, the line, 'We are the housewives who can barely make ends meet because of the dwindling value
of the peso and spiralling prices', points to a common experience which
motivated the political interventions of a Teresa Billington Greig and a
Margaret Llewelyn Davies.[58]

Unity for the IOCU has come not through a theoretical abstraction
on the links between milk and microprocessors, but through a pragmatic
focus on the politics of networks. Just as British consumerism began to
operate within policy networks from the late 1970s, so too did the IOCU
combine with other NGO's and supra-national institutions to formulate campaign strategies on single issues. By 1986, IOCU seminars and
workshops were focussing on networks as the way forward for future campaigning. Pointing to successful ventures such as the International Baby
Food Action Network (IBFAN), the Pesticide Action Network (PAN)
and the Health Action Network (HAN), Jean Halloran of the US Consumers' Union argued that networks focussed expertise, attention and
resources on single issues, developed concern and solidarity among par-
ticipants and provided a global dimension to otherwise local issues.[59]
Many examples exist of how, by the 1990s, the IOCU's activities could
rely on well-established networks of personnel, materials and institutional
support. It has meant the original unity which existed between the comparative testing organisations that created the IOCU in 1960 has long
been lost, but the range of questions the international 'consumer' is able
to answer is theoretically boundless, precisely because its network-based,
single-issue politics has never been directed by ideology over experience.
The irony is, of course, that many aspects of the consumer society which
gave rise to the organised consumer movement are now being opposed
by the IOCU and the stance it has taken on certain topics has made it indistinguishable from the apparently more radical organisations which are
opposed to globalisation, favour ethical consumption and which might
be more appropriately be termed anti-consumerist.

---

[58] T. Wells and F. G. Sim, *Till They Have Faces: Women as Consumers* (Penang, 1987), p. ii.
[59] IOCU, *Consumer Policy 2000*, p. 49

Ethical consumerism

Ethical consumerism is recognisable as a social movement of the last three decades, as firstly 'green' or environmental issues and then human and animal rights issues have been brought to bear upon aspects of personal consumption. Yet unloading a wider political baggage on to goods can hardly be described as a recent phenomenon and surely stretches as far back as one wishes to take a history of material culture. If ethical consumerism is therefore to be identified as a movement specifically bound up with contemporary society, then some broader understanding of the role of consumption needs to be made. It is now a commonplace within consumption studies to discuss the extent to which material culture is used to explore individual identity. In an arguably post-industrial, postmodern, disorganised or 'late capitalist' society, exchange values are alleged to have given way to sign values, substance to form, and reality to image. As individual identities are no longer rooted within an economic structure based around production, they have become agents operating instead within a culture of consumption, defining themselves and their relations to the world through the symbolic expression afforded by goods. So much is familiar, but so too is it likely that the more the commodity dominates the individual's consciousness, the more probable it is that material culture will form the basis through which knowledge about the world is obtained and learned: as greater importance is attached to consumption, the more it is likely that political action will begin first through our roles as consumers. Yet while some scholars have begun to turn more to the politics rather than the culture of consumption, examining issues of regulation, social movements and citizenship, few have tried to make deliberate links between the politics of consuming identity and the politics of societies more traditionally understood. Ethical consumerism, however, provides just such a case study for this type of intellectual link.

To do this, one has to reject Michael Young's claim that information represents the fourth right of citizenship and suggest instead that the whole field of culture is the final corner to Marshall's civil, political and social rights. 'Cultural rights' acknowledge the increased emphasis placed on consumption in the affluent west and emerge within the liberal tradition from the right to explore one's social and political identity through the culture of consumption. Thus, for example, new gendered identities are often first explored through alternative uses of consumption, either for the individual to express difference or allegiance to a recognised subculture. Consumption helps make real the explored identity, the expression of which is then defined as a right. Consumption, as the foremost tool within everyday life, enables new social forms to be developed, which are in turn positioned as rights – rights which need protecting by the state, but which are actually lived through and demonstrated to the world through consumption. Similarly, the modern consumer movement itself began with the development of a new social habitus based around affluent goods. While some might dismiss the *Which?*-buying public as props to materialistic individualism, it is clear that their culture of consumption ultimately gave rise to the articulation of further rights and a number of attempts to extend liberal citizenship. Once these individual rights were converted into the broader liberal duty to ensure that others enjoy the same such rights, consumerism, at least in the work of the IOCU, became a global political movement. Ethical consumerism can also be seen as the means by which social and individual identities – be it vegetarian, environmentalist, feminist, humanist – have first been explored and expressed through consumption, translated into rights and then become the basis of political action usually through single-issue politics.

If consumption is the site for the development of individual and collective identity, then it must follow that the politics of consumption has the potential to be as broad and as varied as humanity itself. This is seen no more so than in the history of consumer boycotts. Strikes against commodities have ranged from eighteenth-century nationalist movements in the United States and Ireland to the sugar boycott of the anti-slavery movement and on to the avoidance of retail stores which did not sell trade union-approved goods.[60] In recent decades, in Britain alone, there have been boycotts against lead in paint (1984), against an amusement park because of its captured whales and dolphins (organised by Greenpeace, 1984), against Tarmac and MAN-VW over their links with cruise missiles (organised by CND, 1983) and against Schweppes for using non-returnable bottles (organised by Friends of the Earth, early 1970s).[61] Famous international campaigns have included the boycott of Barclays for its activities in apartheid-era South Africa, Nestlé for its marketing of baby-milk substitutes and of Douwe Egberts for processing coffee from Angola. At present, the *Ethical Consumer* magazine maintains a list of around forty companies being boycotted, ranging from oil companies such as Esso, Texaco and Shell, clothes stores such as Gap, Nike and Marks & Spencer and perceived perennial offenders such as McDonald's

---

[60] T. H. Breen, 'An empire of goods: the Anglicisation of colonial America, 1690–1776', *Journal of British Studies*, 25 (1986), 467–99; T. H. Breen, ' "Baubles of Britain": the American and British consumer revolutions of the eighteenth century', *Past & Present*, 69 (1988), 73–104; S. Foster, 'Consumer nationalism in eighteenth-century Dublin', *History Today*, 47:6 (1997), 45–51.

[61] N. C. Smith, *Morality and the Market: Consumer Pressure for Corporate Accountability* (London, 1990), pp. 299–309.

and Philip Morris. Added to this list are several countries included for
their abuses of human rights, including China, Turkey, Burma and Israel,
as well as the United States through the 'boycott Bush' campaign.[62]

There is no strict coherence to boycotts as a form of general consumer protest. Campaigns have been inspired for the defence of human
rights, for and against ethnic minorities, to defend workers, to support
particular religions, to protect the environment and to save money for
the consumer.[63] Often these might even be contradictory, such as the
National Anti-Hunt Coalition's campaign against the John Lewis Partnership for its encouragement of animal hunting by its workers on company
outings, a form of company welfare that might otherwise have encouraged other consumers to shop at its stores in support of its treatment of
its staff.[64] While boycotts themselves might be as diverse as the range
of political opinions consumers bring to their consumption decisions,
Monroe Friedman argues that early boycotts, such as the protests over
food prices or the white label campaigns of the Consumers' Leagues,
tended to be 'marketplace-oriented', involving direct protests outside
shops or of picket lines against boycotted stores. Today, boycotts tend
to be 'media-oriented', aimed just as much at 'embarrassing their targets
by exposing their objectionable behaviours in the news media' as they do
at hurting the companies financially.[65] Their success or otherwise (empirically extremely difficult to test) still depends on the ability to concentrate
either the target, the market activity, or the social, economic, ethnic or
geographical characteristics of the protestors, but it is clear that modern
boycotting rests very much on the institutions of the information society. Boycotting reflects the increased information consumers now have
at their disposal, information which means their acts of consumption
often become the starting point for a process of political awareness, either through the boycott itself or what Friedman also refers to as the
'buycott': the targeted purchase of goods and services to reward particular firms for behaviour in accord with the activists' wishes.[66]

Buycotts, though, are only a specific action of a more general trend towards ethical consumer behaviour. Arising out of the boycott movement
and the growth of single-issue political groups since the 1960s, green

[62] See website: http://www.ethical consumer.org/boycotts/boycotts_list.htm.
[63] M. Friedman, *Consumer Boycotts: Effecting Change through the Marketplace and the Media* (London, 1999).
[64] *Ethical Consumer*, 53 (1998), 31; *Ethical Consumer*, 70 (2001), 26.
[65] M. Friedman, *Consumer Boycotts*, p. 226; M. Friedman, 'American consumer boycotts in response to rising food prices: housewives' protests at the grassroots level', *Journal of Consumer Policy*, 18 (1995), 55–72.
[66] M. Friedman, 'A positive approach to organised consumer action: the "buycott" as an alternative to the boycott', *Journal of Consumer Policy*, 19 (1996), 439–51.

consumerism was seen to have come of age with the publication of *The Green Consumer Guide* in 1988.[67] Aimed at 'a "sandals-to-Saabs" spectrum of consumers', rather than those committed to a 'hair-shirt lifestyle', the *Guide* attempted to build on previous green consumer victories, such as the shift to unleaded petrol and the greater use of biodegradable products.[68] It shared the same optimism and principles of the early CA and it drew strength from a survey of environmental organisations, 88 per cent of which believed that individual consumer choice could have a major impact on the direction of the economy. Friends of the Earth's *Good Wood Guide* supported not a state-directed control of the logging industry, but offered information for consumers acting by themselves to switch their preferences in the marketplace away from hardwoods grown in tropical forests to sustainable alternatives. Green consumerism was therefore shifting away from the ascetism, self-denial and anti-materialism of the austere Left and building instead on the growing number of 'lifestyle' shoppers so apparent in the consumption studies literature. For these consumers, green consumerism was just as much a projection of identity as any subcultural *bricoleur*, though the *Guide* hoped that the focus on lifestyle would be equally important for society as well as the self. By the early 1990s, companies were embracing some degree of green consumerism within their marketing strategies and notable achievements included the declining manufacture of CFC-propelled aerosols and the abandonment of animal testing by several cosmetics manufactures.

The trend is best encapsulated with the emergence of the Ethical Consumer Research Association (ECRA). This might be regarded as just one of a large number of institutions which today promotes alternative visions of the consumer society, but it warrants further study in itself because of its direct parallels with the CA, focussing as it does on rational choice and appealing to a particular section of society or habitus. ECRA began in 1987 as a research group collecting information on company activities, but began publishing the bi-monthly *Ethical Consumer* in March 1989. Although never as successful as the CA (there were just 5,000 subscribers at the end of its first year), it has drawn on a committed subscriber membership, many of which were able to provide ECRA with a £40,000 collective loan in 1991 to finance its expansion.[69] *Ethical Consumer* has drawn on a whole range of political beliefs, committing itself to the promotion of universal human rights, environmental sustainability and animal welfare. While the magazine itself informs consumers of these issues in relation

---

[67] Earlier, less successful, efforts had also been made. For example, J. Holliman, *Consumer's Guide to the Protection of the Environment* (London, 1971).

[68] J. Elkington and J. Hailes, *The Green Consumer Guide* (London, 1988), p. 2.

[69] ECRA, *Ethical Consumer Briefing Pack* (Manchester, 1997), p. 2.

to particular goods, ECRA has also continued to research into company affairs. It has maintained a database called Corporate Critic made up of collected publications which are critical of specific company activities and it continues to undertake research projects for other organisations on corporate responsibility and environmental impact analysis, as well as campaigning on specific subjects.

Within the magazine, testing is done on common household goods in the same manner as *Which?*, though because of resource limitation there is a tendency to focus on cheaper branded items. Instead of 'blobs' indicating effective performance, durability and value for money, however, *Ethical Consumer* tables indicate company performance under the categories of environment (pollution levels, stated environmental policy, use of nuclear power), animals (involvement in animal testing and factory farming) and people (collusion with oppressive regimes, workers' rights and use of irresponsible marketing methods). Further columns refer to the companies' political donations, whether a boycott has been called and an 'alert' indicating other perceived unethical practices such as land rights for indigenous peoples, involvement in Third World debt, unusual corporate structure, excessive directors' remuneration or support for genetic engineering.[70] *Ethical Consumer* acknowledges the problems in assessing these criteria objectively. On workers' rights, for instance, it often has to rely on companies' Codes of Conduct which it knows, in the absence of their own sustained research, may differ substantially from actual practice.[71] The consumer is therefore left to decide for him or herself which brand to choose, factoring in his or her own attachment to each of the column criteria. As with the CA, then, ECRA's consumerism must necessarily place limits on its forms of assessment in order to make worthwhile points for comparison, and questions of taste, aesthetics and, in this case, quality and value for money, have to be excluded.

Ethical Consumer, however, has avoided the accusations of prescriptive advice that have sometimes been directed at *Which?*. 'Best Buys' are often broken down into three areas, so that the consumer can make a choice depending on the relative importance attached to corporate responsibility, the environment or animal welfare. Often, the best buy selected is not even included in the test, as for instance in an assessment of branded clothing, which ultimately decided that best buys consisted of items chosen from the *Green Clothing Directory's* list of smaller suppliers.[72] Articles on products are usually followed by a more general discussion, which points to alternatives, the wider political issues involved and occasionally

---

[70] *Ibid.*, p. 7; *Ethical Consumer*, 56 (1998–9), 33.
[71] *Ethical Consumer*, 65 (2000), 33.   [72] *Ethical Consumer*, 50 (1997–8), 7.

even the need for a campaign. The magazine makes it clear that ethical consumerism is just as much about politics as it is about individual choice: subscribers are encouraged to act both as discriminating consumers and as informed citizens at one and the same time. But such a style is necessary given the acknowledged absence of ideological unity among *Ethical Consumer* readers. While all might agree that animal and workers' welfare are damaged by many aspects of consumer capitalism, not all would attach equal importance to the two. Examples of outright division do occur. An article discussing the relative merits of personal equity plans, for instance, might invoke the ire of a consumer who believes all forms of share purchasing to be wrong.[73] Similarly, while the Co-operative movement has generally done well in comparative tests and is seen as an ally in modern ethical consumerism, another allied group, People for the Ethical Treatment of Animals, was calling for a boycott of the CWS in 1998 because the Co-operative's insurance arm held a 1 per cent shareholding in an animal testing laboratory.[74] As a small publishing concern, ECRA is able to contain potential disparate elements within its general aim of raising consumer awareness. Were it to expand, it would face the same issues that the CA faced when entering political debate: to fight one campaign too strongly might provide ECRA with a political identity too focussed and divisive for a general body of ethical consumers concerned with a whole range of issues.

Given this potential for division, there is nevertheless a general scepticism of consumer capitalism and a commitment to raising ethical and political awareness within the pages of the magazine. The January 1994 issue was devoted entirely to anti-consumerism, with articles on how to reduce consumption and the problems of GATT for the developing world.[75] This has been followed up with similar pieces, such as advice on how to avoid the 'rat race'.[76] The magazine has regular updates about current boycott campaigns, encouragement being given to consumers through the listing of successes, a favourite citation being the reduction of Barclays' share of the student market from 27 per cent to 15 per cent forcing the bank to withdraw from South Africa.[77] A similar feature on 'campaign news' also updates readers on the wider political background and a Corporate Watch feature has run exposés on the activities of such global companies as Philip Morris, Disney, Premier Oil, Wal-Mart and DuPont, as well as powerful families such as the Wallenbergs of Sweden and individuals ranging from Rupert Murdoch to George W. Bush, the latter for having abandoned the Kyoto global warming agreement soon

---

[73] *Ethical Consumer*, 51 (1998), 18.   [74] *Ibid.*, p. 5.   [75] *Ethical Consumer*, 27 (1994).
[76] *Ethical Consumer*, 49 (1998), 31.   [77] *Ethical Consumer*, 66 (2000), 19.

after entering office.[78] *Ethical Consumer's* articles have reflected the diversity of a movement ECRA has attempted to head and which at one point it suggested mobilising through local ethical consumer groups.[79] Pieces have appeared on subjects as varied as pollution, child labour, green electricity, organic meat, car sharing, the Common Agricultural Policy, oppressive régimes, the social economy, the World Trade Organisation, sweatshops, human rights and the jewellery trade and the recycling policies of local authorities. It is clear that this is not a consumerism that has the consumer's economic interest at heart, but a consumerism which uses knowledge about consumption as the first point of entry into wider debates concerning citizenship.

And this is a citizenship that is dependent upon links and connections, forming networks which occasionally overlap with those of the CA and IOCU. ECRA supported the two defendants in the *Mclibel* trial and has encouraged the spread of credit unions and Local Exchange Trading Schemes (LETS), supporting the New Economics Foundation in 1997 in its parliamentary campaign to 'win an exemption from loss of benefits for people using LETS'.[80] It has welcomed the attempts to create better links between rural producers and urban consumers through farmers' markets and has reviewed the increasing number of ethical stores on the internet.[81] It fosters links with anti-corporate culture groups and individuals such as Adbusters and the comedian Mark Thomas, as well as single-issue pressure groups such as Greenpeace and Friends of the Earth and the equivalents of ECRA around the world.[82] It has added to the range of protestors at international anti-globalisation demonstrations, delaying the publication of its sixty-seventh issue in late 2000 as most of its staff were late returning from the Prague meeting against the World Bank and International Monetary Fund (IMF).[83] The downside of such diversity has been the inability to provide a coherent ethical consumer ideology to match its growth. As it has expanded it has failed to address some issues such as the conditions of workers in the UK, preferring instead to highlight the plight of the poor in developing nations. It is clear from the letters pages that animal welfare motivates many of its subscribers, most of whom occupy a relatively affluent or highly educated position which has made ECRA aware of its lack of success in attracting poorer consumers.[84] This concern with the spread of its message across a wider social spectrum

---

[78] *Ethical Consumer,* 57 (1999), 31–2; 58 (1999), 30–1; 60 (1999), 32–3; 61 (1999), 36–7; 65 (2000), 36–7; 66 (2000), 34–5; 70 (2001), 28–9.
[79] *Ethical Consumer,* 47 (1997), 5.
[80] *Ethical Consumer,* 50 (1997–8), 13; 48 (1997), 30.
[81] *Ethical Consumer,* 70 (2001), 16–18; 71 (2001), 21.
[82] *Ethical Consumer,* 75 (2002), 32–3; 71 (2001), 5; 66 (2000), 36–7; 67 (2000), 29.
[83] *Ethical Consumer,* 67 (2000), 5.   [84] *Ethical Consumer,* 48 (1997), 26–30.

mirrors the efforts of the CA in the 1960s, but so far ECRA has not really expanded its publishing efforts beyond *Ethical Consumer*, publishing only *The Ethical Consumer Guide to Everyday Shopping* in 1993.[85] In its campaigning it has had to act more as a whistleblower rather than a sustained critic, perhaps failing to tackle coherently some of the wider issues concerning the World Trade Organisation and globalisation. And while it might have consistently pressed for greater consumer representation and corporate accountability, on some issues, such as mergers and takeovers, it has shown some indecision on the relative merits of economies of scale versus corporate power, mirroring the tensions within social democratic thought over the efficiencies of nationalisation at the expense of diversity in consumption.[86]

Recently, however, ECRA has attempted to present a more coherent elaboration of ethical consumerism. It has worked to develop a European network of organisations and researchers in the hope of becoming an effective lobbying presence for responsible consumption within the EU and in 2001 it published its *Manifesto for Change*. The *Manifesto* focussed ethical consumerism into a movement for corporate accountability, providing yet further links between the concerns of ethical consumers and the aims of earlier organisations such as Social Audit. It calls for a stimulus to ethical consumption to be provided by government purchasing and for greater regulation of recycling as well as the setting of minimum standards for corporate use of energy, environmental impact and animal welfare. Import duties on externally-verified fairly traded goods are to be scrapped while taxes on pollution, carbon energy use and transportation are to be introduced. It also adopts the usual consumerist demand for greater information, with labels identifying country of origin, ingredients, energy use and original manufacturer, while companies' ethical claims are to be regulated by the Ethical Trading Initiative, along the lines of the NCC's work on regulating green claims. Further information is also to be disclosed on social and environmental reporting, on directors' pay and on the workings of the financial sector, transforming the principle of 'commercial confidentiality' into one of a consumer's 'right to know'. Finally, a series of radical measures to control corporate power are also proposed: a 'right to reply' to TV advertising; the reform of the libel laws so that companies – as with governments – cannot sue their critics; the abolition of advertising to children less than twelve years of age; greater power to shareholders to raise questions at AGMs; requirements to make companies legally accountable to 'stakeholders' other than shareholders; the change of the UK Human Rights Acts to prevent firms

[85] ECRA, *The Ethical Consumer Guide to Everyday Shopping* (Manchester, 1993).
[86] *Ethical Consumer*, 64 (2000), 5.

being given the same rights as individuals; the abolition of the WTO, life patents and tax havens; and the introduction of a 'Tobin Tax' on currency speculation.[87]

The *Manifesto* develops the consumerism of the CA and the NCC in that it aims to provide institutional frameworks for consumers to hold in check the power of big business while at the same time improving the position of the individual shopper through greater knowledge provided by the marketplace. It establishes a link between *Ethical Consumer* and the range of other services within ECRA, from Corporate Critic to a Consultancy Service, a Shareholder Analysis report and a Company Screening facility. And it further connects the work of ECRA to that of countless other organisations, from anti-consumer groups such as Enough, the human rights campaigners at Amnesty, the environmentalists at Greenpeace, the social economists at the think tank the New Economics Foundation, charity workers at Christian Aid and the Co-operative stores' ethical business ventures.[88] Several of these – CAFOD, Christian Aid, New Consumer, Oxfam, Traidcraft and the World Development Movement – came together to create the Fairtrade Foundation, a body which administers the Fairtrade Label in Britain (it began in the Netherlands in 1988). Its mark, found on coffee, tea, cocoa, honey, bananas, mangoes, orange juice and sugar, signifies a better deal for developing world producers, of which there were 350 Fairtrade certified producer groups operating in thirty-six countries in 2002. The Fair Trade movement draws upon the philanthropic traditions within consumerism, receiving support from the National Federation of Women's Institutes and the Townswomen's Guilds (as well as a number of experienced Christian groups such as Tearfund), while its certified products are promoted within *Ethical Consumer*. Rob Harrison, a founding director of ECRA and an editor of its magazine, is keen to stress the links between such groups and recognises the importance of speeches made by IOCU figures such as Anwar Fazal who, in 1986, stressed the responsibility of consumers to 'the conditions under which products are made'.[89]

The impact of such ethical and global concerns on actual consumers is difficult to measure. On the one hand, the existence of 1 million vegetarians in the UK signifies a substantial form of politicised consumption at the most mundane, everyday level.[90] And a series of surveys reviewed by

[87] 'The ECRA 2001 Manifesto for Change', *Ethical Consumer*, 72 (2001), 32–5.
[88] See web pages: http://www.enough.org; www.neweconomics.org; www.fairtrade.org.uk; http://www.co-op.co.uk.
[89] Cited in R. Harrison, 'A new movement?', unpublished paper kindly sent by Harrison to the author, June 2002.
[90] Smith, *Morality and the Market*, p. 2.

ECRA over the last decade shows that around 50 per cent of consumers participated in some form of ethical purchasing on a regular basis, from simply buying fairly traded goods to the outright politicised boycott of certain companies.[91] This trend shows no signs of dissolving and, indeed, sales of organic produce are booming, recycling is more common and human rights issues have become increasingly prominent, following the high-profile campaigns against The Gap and Nike.[92] The Co-operative Bank's Ethical Trading Index calculates that ethical purchasing increased by 18 per cent from 1999 to 2000, a figure substantially higher than general economic growth.[93] Since then, 1999 has been taken as the baseline for the EPI (Ethical Purchasing Index) which now stands at 125, or an increase in sales of £2 billion in two years.[94] However, the higher prices of ethical produce also deter many younger consumers who are perhaps most likely to become the movement's future lifestyle shoppers and ethical consumerism has not been able to reach beyond the educated professionals often working in the voluntary sector which *Ethical Consumer*'s reader profiles suggest form the core of its subscribers.[95] Furthermore, care needs to be taken in measuring the rise in ethical purchasing. Although some products, such as Freedom Food eggs, energy-saving lightbulbs and Forest Stewardship Council wood have obtained a market share of 20 per cent, the Co-operative Bank still refers to the 30:3 syndrome, 'the phenomenon in which a third of consumers profess to care about companies' policies and records on social responsibility, but ethical products rarely achieve more than a 3% market share'.[96] And fair trade products have to be placed in the reality of a wider economic picture. Buying a bunch of five fair trade bananas pales into insignificance alongside the tens of thousands of people employed along the supply chain for plantation bananas, which in turn will only constitute less than 1 per cent of a UK consumer's weekly food bill.[97] And research into ethical consumers' behaviour demonstrates such a variety of individual motivations that it is difficult to make any conclusions about the coherence of this social phenomenon, apart from the rising trend towards positioning

---

[91] Harrison, 'A new movement?', p. 1; *Ethical Consumers*, 50 (1997–8), 24.
[92] M. Rayner, 'Product, price or principle?', *Ethical Consumer*, 76 (2002), 32–4.
[93] T. Newholm and D. Shaw, 'Ethical consumers', in J. R. Miller, R. M. Lerner, L. B. Schiamberg and P. M. Anderson (eds.), *Human Ecology: An Encyclopaedia of Children, Families, Communities and Environments* (Santa Barbara, forthcoming).
[94] S. Williams and D. Doane, *Ethical Purchasing Index 2002* (London, 2002), p. 2.
[95] *Ethical Consumer*, 50 (1997–8), 26–8; 51 (1998), 25; R. Cowe and S. Williams, *Who are the Ethical Consumers?* (London, 2000).
[96] *Ethical Consumer*, 76 (2002), 34; 67 (2000), 29.
[97] I. Cook, 'Commodities: the DNA of capitalism', at http://apm.brookes.ac.uk/exchange/texts/index.htm.

everyday purchasing as the site of moral considerations, previously located elsewhere.[98]

However, while actual ethical purchases might still be limited in scale,
it is clear that there has been an increased interest in the factors which lay
behind affluent consumption. The huge success of Naomi Klein's *No Logo*
has given rise to a publishing sector witnessing an increasing crossover
between academic and commercial texts. The concerns of George Ritzer
with McDonaldisation have been followed by a number of more popular
reactions against global consumer culture and the questioning of whether
the west, or Americans in particular, shop too much.[99] A number of
British equivalents of *No Logo* have been published, including George
Monbiot's series of essays on the collusion of business and New Labour
and Noreena Hertz's study on the influence of multinational corporations
on global democracy, though the latter descends into neo-Thatcherite
praise for the welfare services offered by enlightened entrepreneurs, a conclusion perhaps unexpected from an author who unblushingly writes of
her role in developing capitalist organisations in the former Soviet Union
and the Middle East.[100] There has further been a growth in interest in
anti-capitalist groups such as Adbusters, though its more recent magazine
images tend to provide inspiration for the marketing strategies it seeks to
condemn, and especially the new forms of protest citizen-consumers can
make outside of the traditional political process.[101] A recent best-selling
exposé of the fast food industry has become the latest equivalent of Upton
Sinclair's examination of the turn-of-the-twentieth century meat-packing
business and Jessica Mitford's exploration of the US funeral industry.[102]
The global nature of many local market disputes has been exemplified
by the surge of interest in the trial of José Bové, a French farmer who

[98] T. Newholm, 'Understanding the ethical consumer: employing a frame of bounded rationality', Ph.D. thesis, Open University (2000).

[99] G. Ritzer, *The McDonaldization of Society* (London, 1995); G. Ritzer, *Enchanting a Disenchanted World* (London, 1999); J. de Graaf, D. Wann and T. H. Naylor, *Affluenza: The All-Consuming Epidemic* (San Francisco, 2001); J. B. Schor, *Do Americans Shop Too Much?* (Boston, MA, 2000); J. B. Schor, *The Overspent American: Why We Want What We Don't Need* (New York, 1998); R. Nader, *Cutting Corporate Welfare* (New York, 2000); T. Frank, *One Market Under God: Extreme Capitalism, Market Populism and the End of Economic Democracy* (London, 2001).

[100] G. Monbiot, *The Captive State: The Corporate Takeover of Britain* (London, 2000); N. Hertz, *The Silent Takeover: Global Capitalism and the Death of Democracy* (London, 2001).

[101] K. Lasn, *Culture Jam: The Uncooling of America* (New York, 1999); *Adbusters*, various editions, 2000–2; J. Elkington and J. Hailes, *Manual 2000: Life Choices for the Future You Want* (London, 1998); G. McKay (ed.), *DiY Culture: Party and Protest in Nineties Britain* (London, 1998).

[102] E. Schlosser, *Fast Food Nation: What the All-American Meal is Doing to the World* (Harmondsworth, 2001); J. Mitford, *The American Way of Death* (London, 1963); U. Sinclair, *The Jungle* (1906; Harmondsworth, 1965).

led a protest against McDonald's in Millau in the Roquefort-making region of southern France.[103] And Arundhati Roy, highlighting the human consequences of dam-building projects in India, further links the east to the west. Her book's title, *The Cost of Living*, at one and the same time refers to the economic language of purchasing, while making explicit the social costs of production that go into capitalist advance.[104]

The connections between much of this anti-globalisation politics and the consumer movement are not direct or obvious. To add to the confusion, 'anti-consumerism' employs a very different meaning of the term (acquisitive, materialist) than that found in the self-empowerment movement of organised consumerism. And the institutional links between the NCC, the CA and bodies such as ECRA have been limited, though by the 1990s the CA was beginning to publish regularly on environmental issues.[105] But the agendas at the global level have become increasingly similar. In the protests against the World Trade Organisation at Seattle in November 1999, particular issues included air pollution, hormone-treated beef, food labelling, the Multilateral Agreement on Investment (which restricted the ability of nation states to regulate currency and investment), deforestation, competition policy within national contexts which went against WTO rules, and the legal and political obligations attached to long-term loans by the IMF to developing countries.[106] These are all topics upon which global consumerism has offered its voice. In the year in which the Seattle demonstration took place, Consumers International had been campaigning on GM foods, for greater food labelling, for greater accountability within the WTO, on international trade regulations and the support for developing nations, plus a whole variety of measures designed to improve sustainable consumption. At Seattle, while anarchists, labour organisations, marxists, environmentalists, ethical consumers and representatives from a multitude of NGOs demonstrated on the streets, thirty delegates from Consumers International attended the WTO meeting, bringing to the negotiations many of the same concerns that were being heard outside.[107]

What much of the popular literature on globalisation and the responsibilities of the western consumer has failed to do is outline the structures of a global society within which the activist operates. At its weakest, one is simply told that action will lead to change: in the absence of a

---

[103] J. Bové and F. Dufour, *The World is Not for Sale: Farmers Against Junk Food* (London, 2001).

[104] A. Roy, *The Cost of Living* (London, 1999).

[105] CAA 66: S. Locke, 'Future directions for consumerism and their applications for business' (23 May 1991).

[106] Working Group on the WTO, *A Citizen's Guide to World Trade Organisation* (USA, 1999).

[107] Consumers International, *Annual Report, 1999* (London, 2000).

general theoretical framework, at odds with his own more effective interventions on single issues, George Monbiot's closing words in *Captive State* are, 'Only one thing can reverse the corporate takeover of Britain. It's you.'[108] Possibly this is a fair assessment of the situation, though as a blueprint for action it is rather inadequate. At the other extreme, Hardt and Negri have attempted to delineate the contours of world politics and unite within a new grand narrative the disparate groups and agendas of the anti-globalisation movement. In *Empire*, they adapt Foucauldian concepts of biopower, transferring this amorphous regime of governance to the supranational level, arguing that power is no longer located within the nation state, nor within a specific group of multinational corporations, but is spread through the nexus of discourses, institutions, governments and companies which collectively control production and in turn seek to engage in the production of social life itself. This will result, however, not in the creation of identities harmonious with 'empire', but in a 'dialectic of exploitation', replacing the old marxist dialectic of modernity.[109] Biopolitics has within it the seeds of dissent and of its own destruction and, Hardt and Negri insist, subjugated groups will first subvert the hegemonic languages of global capitalism and then create new systems of 'ethico-political' behaviour. The 'new singularity' between many diverse groups will come through a realisation that they 'are all in fact against Empire', and disregard the false consciousness of nationalist and ethnic agendas. While the authors might be correct to highlight the de-centred nature of much economic and political power today, and here they follow the lead taken by figures such as Daniel Bell and Alain Touraine, they offer little as to what precisely will constitute the 'new singularity' of opposition. Realising their responsibility to do so, they spend a few final pages insisting that all workers must have equal rights to full citizenship, must be entitled to a social wage, and must see themselves – 'the multitude' – as a telos, recognising their autonomy and their right to re-appropriate social forms and create new modes of living.

It is unlikely such a vague blueprint for action will unite the 18,000 consumer, anti-consumer, trade union, Christian, charity and single-issue pressure groups. Instead, one needs to understand not so much the unity of interests between the groups but the structures of the socio-political system within which they operate. Manuel Castells has argued that capitalism and the global economy has moved into an informationalist age. Again, power is no longer located within centralised economic institutions but is found within the system of information flows which now

---

[108] Monbiot, *Captive State*, p. 360.
[109] M. Hardt and A. Negri, *Empire* (2000: Cambridge, MA, 2001), p. 43.

marks out the 'network society'. Whereas in the industrial age of capitalism, productivity rested on the ability to find and distribute new forms of energy, today, 'in the new, informational mode of development the source of productivity lies in the technology of knowledge generation, information processing, and symbolic communication'.[110] There is thus more power in the actual flow of information than there is in any one site. Capitalism therefore seems increasingly divorced from its economic reality, as it becomes reduced to the flow of information on an electronic network, whose nodal points have become the great international cities of the world. Those unable to participate in the flow of information become excluded from the network society, while those who succeed are the ones most likely to be able to switch from one network to another. Forms of cultural identity, especially those based on religious fundamentalism, nationalism and ethnic or territorial identities, have been on the rise among those groups excluded through their ability to produce or catch hold of the flow of information within the network.[111]

If the work of the IOCU and ECRA forms a civil society of consumption, then it will only continue to do so if they operate within the network society. While the existence of the network creates divisions between the information rich and the information poor, between the financier and the marginalised ethnic minority member, consumerism is significant because of its attempts to operate within and beyond the network society. As a movement produced by affluence, organised national consumer movements have sought to ensure that consumers have not been excluded from the production and distribution of information about the end results of capitalism. In this, they have achieved some success, though their access to information is still not as equal as that of the manufacturers, but the international consumer groups have attempted to reach out of the network and bring in those consumers who would otherwise be excluded. This has required a reinterpretation of the 'consumer', first by arguing that those who survive on a minimal diet are still consumers and, secondly, by using the language of consumerism in order to attempt to achieve degrees of citizenship within the global society for those poor workers and consumers outside Europe and the United States. Thirdly, though, the meaning of the affluent consumer has also expanded, such that the responsibilities of the citizen are increasingly being focussed through the act of consumption, as information about goods is used as the first point of entry into the network society for many western consumers. Consumer activists have long recognised that their ability to overcome 'the division into people

[110] M. Castells, *The Rise of the Network Society* (1996; Oxford, 2000), p. 17.
[111] M. Castells, *The Power of Identity* (1997; Oxford, 2000).

and countries who are information-rich and people and countries who are information-poor will be the challenge' of future years.[112] But a challenge too will be for the activists of Consumers International and the seemingly anti-consumer groups such as ECRA to work together and be able to transfer networks as and when the pressure of single-issue politics demand. Within the institutions of the civil society of NGOs, links have been established, especially in consumer concerns over environmental issues. The next stage will be the development of networks over questions of human rights and social justice and the ability of such groups to make effective the flow of information on these issues.

[112] N. Sargant, 'Consumer power as a pillar of democracy', in G. Dench, T. Flower and K. Gavron (eds.), *Young at Eighty: The Prolific Public Life of Michael Young* (Manchester, 1995), p. 197.

Conclusion: the quantity or the quality of choice

In a recent interview, Sheila McKechnie, the Director of the CA, was emphatic that her organisation did not represent a movement of either a social or a political kind.[1] Her statement represents a remarkable end to a history of consumerism that has been precisely about the search for just such a movement. Yet McKechnie's statement stands in sharp contrast to the clear ideals of many consumer activists – concerned with either necessity or affluence – who have attempted to use the politics of price as the starting point for the basis of a rejuvenated and active social democracy, if not socialist democracy. In the public proclamations of the First World War Consumers' Council, the writings of co-operative demagogues such as Percy Redfern, the policy formulations of organisations such as Political and Economic Planning, the activities of 'social entrepreneurs' such as Michael Young and in the key speeches of consumer policy workers such as Michael Shanks, consumerism has been positioned as a middle way between the vested interests of trade unions and employers that not only aimed to establish a new universalist rhetoric but sought to engage the public in a plethora of institutions associated with civil society.

McKechnie's statement too had the additional purpose of distancing the current work and agenda of the CA from both its own past and the activities of other consumer organisations, be it the NCC, the OFT, the NFCG or even Consumers International. According to McKechnie, the economic, social and political context within which consumers act has profoundly changed. Whereas in continental Europe consumers still find themselves within a 'social solidarity' model – that is, they can expect a number of intermediaries between the individual and the state to articulate their concerns – in Britain, she argues, the effects of privatisation, deregulation and the neo-liberal market reforms of the 1980s have produced new criteria for consumer action. Global economic changes, too, have resulted in the retreat of the state and the creation of 'gatekeeper organisations' which 'increasingly bypass government and determine what

[1] Interview with Sheila McKechnie, 11 December 2002.

329

consumers will and will not receive'.[2] In addition, demographic changes have eroded the norm of the traditional family unit and there is a cultural legacy, linked to the explosion of the quantity, type and channels of information, which has resulted in the decline of 'deference' so that individuals are less willing to place their fate entirely in the hands of the expert. The main consequences of this for consumerism have been the continued move to an increasingly complex world and the transition from a 'high trust to a low trust environment'.[3] That is, on one side of the state–individual relationship, consumers are less willing to believe that official organisations will protect their interests, while, on the other, cutbacks in government provision (together with the greater power handed to supranational economic organisations) ensure that the state cannot meet the public's expectations of what it sees as a sufficient level of consumer protection.

The appropriate response for the CA to this situation, though, is not the re-creation of a social movement. Consumers are felt to be far too busy managing the complexity of everyday life, work and politics to devote themselves as citizens to the consumer cause. But some changes are thought necessary. From the 1950s to the 1970s a degree of unity existed between the CA as a provider of economic information and its political campaigning role. The ideals of the CA 'pioneers', together with the thousands of consumers connected through the NFCG, provided a clear indication that there was something which could readily be labelled a 'consumer movement'. The reforms of the late 1980s, introduced by John Beishon and Rachel Waterhouse, however, have resulted in an increasing divide – captured within an institutional framework – between the CA's commercial and campaigning roles. This has not resulted in a decline in the CA's intervention in the political sphere and, indeed, it became increasingly prominent throughout the 1990s as the voice of the consumer in the media and in government as it was frequently called upon to represent the consumer interest. But there has been growing concern within the CA that its *Which?* subscribers are insufficiently connected to the wider goals of the CA. Furthermore, the CA's focus on single issues has prevented an ongoing examination of its more general principles and it is felt that the CA has not made best use of its political muscle in the new socio-economic environment created in the 1980s and consolidated in the 1990s.

Consequently, McKechnie and others have advocated a more 'tough market' consumerism in which CA adopts a more interventionist

[2] S. McKechnie, 'The new consumerism', Lothian European Lectures (22 November 1999), p. 2.
[3] Interview with McKechnie.

approach so that consumers can use their economic power to effect change. It means the CA has recently adapted its role from one of a research-based think-tank type of campaigning group to one which simply states, 'let's sort this out folks'.[4] The principle of the 'new consumerism' is that the CA acts as an organising body for the mass of consumers which uses its collective economic power to either force the market structure itself to change or for the state to intervene to reform that market. There are thus no limits placed on the extent of individual consumer power, and the self-interested actions of individual consumers are aligned with the wider political objectives of the CA's campaigning side. It also means that the CA can focus its work on a number of big 'signature' campaigns which capture the interest of its members and results in a more prominent media discussion which in turn forms a platform for political reform. The clearest example of this type of consumerism is the attack on the automobile industry which began in September 1999 when the CA urged motorists not to buy new cars in the UK until prices fell. When this was felt not to have worked, the CA launched carbusters.com in March 2000 (complete with a vehicle painted in the Union Jack and featuring the licence plate, 'GB RIP OFF'), actually entering the market itself to ensure consumers could obtain the cheaper prices available to motorists in the rest of Europe.[5]

This type of consumerism is a response to the perceived limitations of individual action in bringing about change and, to some extent, follows the earlier points of entry of consumer groups into politics. Yet this is not simply a continuation of an older CA activity since it seeks to bring the consumer and his or her representative into agreement over a single issue. Rather than fighting for all consumer issues, then, while the individual only looks after his or her own interests, the CA focuses on a prominent topic one after another. If this coalesces with the campaigning style of other single-issue pressure groups, the CA maintains that it nevertheless remains distinct. In a reluctantly used expression, McKechnie has described current CA campaigning as 'postmodern', in the sense that its sequential nature enables it to jump from one major campaign to the next and, significantly, it backs up traditional political activities such as lobbying and direct action with the economic power of consumers. Consumers themselves can either follow the CA's lead by re-directing their purchasing in the market, else support the campaign initiatives through various forms of protest to back up the CA's own lobbying activities. The consumer is therefore not expected to be involved either at every stage or in every campaign and the CA can rely on its critical mass of

---

[4] *Ibid.*   [5] For further details on this and other examples see http://www.which.net.

Which? subscribers to always provide a substantial body of support to each consumer cause.

This is a campaigning style which is far from perfect since there are important questions to be asked as to which issues are selected to obtain the greatest attention, but it at least moves consumerism from the economic act of purchasing to the wider social concerns of citizenship. This has been regarded as an important point for the CA as it has feared it may lose its prominence as an activist organisation in the light of the developments outlined in chapter 11 and it certainly raises some of the social democratic concerns so central to the agendas of the CA Council members in the 1950s and 1960s. It forces the CA to look beyond the individual and to recommend, depending on the particular case, that it speaks for all consumers, that the solution warrants a collective response or that the state should intervene to restructure the provision of the good or service. For instance, where individual responses have been clearly inappropriate, such as in the BSE crisis, it has campaigned for the setting up of the Food Standards Authority. It has monitored consumer concerns over GM foods and advocated better labelling regulations and, while its campaigns over food policy in Europe have been long standing, it launched 'Scrap the CAP' in December 2001. Whereas in pharmaceutical policy it has sometimes favoured direct advertising to consumers as a means of promoting individual choice it is now concerned more generally that the major drugs firms are putting profits before both the NHS and the patient. Too often, the CA has realised that its policies have only favoured the middle classes and has therefore recommended financial advice be made available to all – 'Advice for Life' – so that scandals such as the mis-selling of personal pensions in the 1980s do not occur again. On this issue, although it has shied away from straightforward demands for greater state pensions, it has acknowledged that the subject cannot just be an individual one and has come out in favour of a collective pension scheme based on some degree of compulsion. Finally, in a shift away from an earlier focus on educating individuals on how to complain, the CA has pushed for inclusion within the Enterprise Bill a clause which gives it a special status as a 'super-complainer'. This provides the ultimately private organisation with an official public position comparable to some of the functions of the OFT and the NCC and acknowledges that the CA sees itself as representing all consumers whether affluent or disadvantaged.

This extension of the CA's role highlights the problems facing the consumer policy network today as the CA appears to seek to eclipse the functions of other consumer organisations. But it also recognises the fact that no such consumer movement has emerged, at least in the sense imagined by Michael Young during his time at either the CA or the NCC, and that some new form of political action is required if the agendas of ordinary consumers are, nevertheless, to be heard and acted upon throughout the public sphere and in the official institutions of government. The CA is again attempting to take the lead, as it has done so often before, in defining consumerism while other consumer groups remain concerned with issues such as independence, representativeness and the definition of the consumer interest, issues which have shaped and influenced just about every organisation related to consumer affairs throughout the twentieth century. Today, though, the CA's attempt to set out a new campaigning framework and a new style of consumerism is particularly relevant in the light of some of the problems facing other consumer groups. While the CA has claimed it is no longer a movement, the decline of the NFCG would seem to confirm this. With the loss of support of an aged class of professionals who dominated the local groups in the 1960s and 1970s, the overall membership of the CA has also declined. The vast majority of these are not concerned with the CA's wider campaigning role and it is their existence which has prompted many to regard the CA as a movement without an ideology save that of promoting individual acquisitiveness. Opportunities have arisen for the CA to respond to the agendas of an emerging generation of activist consumers, but these have, instead, drifted to single-issue campaigning groups and the approach to consumerism found in *Ethical Consumer* magazine. But this organisation, too, has its limits. It maintains a Ruskinian idealism in its focus on the responsibilities rather than the rights of consumers, but altruism is rarely a force for sustained political development. Clementina Black's criticisms of her own Consumers' League in the late nineteenth century are still relevant and it has usually been the case that boycotts, although often a powerful political tool, are mainly successful when there is a clear non-consumer issue at stake or when a specific cohort of consumers can be mobilised: for example, when middle-class women boycotted sugar, the blood-stained produce of the slave trade. The Co-operative movement's recent inroads into ethical consumerism could bring a large institutional framework in support of such a style of consumerism, though many consumers still need to understand its role as more than a shop. The CA, too, has never made any significant overtures to the Co-op, and for too much of its history an element of snobbery seems to have led the CA to regarded the CWS as a scruffy, if well-meaning, working-class relative who is now well past their prime and who ought to step aside to allow in the real professionals. The CA has, however, continued to support Consumers International and the many ethical issues found in that organisation's stance on the international marketplace, but globalisation itself continues to present challenges to consumers that are far from being resolved. A recent example is again that of Naomi Klein whose collection of journalism published since she wrote *No Logo* still demonstrates an inability to produce both concrete and general political solutions to the problems and inequities identified within global capitalism.[6]

This diversity of consumerism re-creates an older problem as to who it is that speaks for the consumer. Potential divisions within the consumer voice – which there will always be given that consumerism attempts to speak for everybody – are exacerbated when non-consumer groups step into the debate. One of the main issues that has always faced consumers is their independence from business. The OFT, for instance, has achieved notable successes in its defence of the consumer against monopoly, collusion and unfair trading practices, but it is an organisation that firmly sees the consumer interest in the successful operation of business, competition and the free market. When Deirdre Hutton became Chair of the NCC in 2000 she pledged her partisan think tank to the established aim of Young and Shanks; that is, making the consumer voice 'as influential as the CBI and the TUC'.[7] Subsequently, the corporate Friends scheme, launched in 2001, has instead sought to develop partnerships with business and industry with companies such as Barclays, Coca-Cola and BT donating £10,000 each year and others such as Sainsbury's and Prudential funding research projects by the NCC. No matter what the number of safeguards introduced to protect the NCC's independence, such a relationship can only sully its independence in the public mind.[8] The same too can be argued of the CA which has increasingly attempted to become a direct player in the market as with cars and financial services. This has attracted much criticism, especially when the CA has found it has made commercial partnerships which have resulted in the CA not having a full control on a market they intended to run in the consumer's interest. The CA has come to realise, though, that its 'family silver' is its reputation for honesty, objectivity and independence. It is likely, then, that the CA will retreat from the sort of commercial ventures that have attracted bad publicity in the newspapers from whose readers it draws its support.[9]

At times, the consumer comes across as an entity used only to support the interests of others, be it the politician, the businessman or the trade union. The rhetoric of consumerism is invoked as a tool of political populism with few real powers being granted to him or her. Instead, the role

[6] N. Klein, *Fences and Windows: Dispatches from the Front Lines of the Globalization Debate* (London, 2002).
[7] NCC press release, 13 December 2000.
[8] NCC, *Making the Difference* (London, 2002), pp. 15–16.
[9] *The Times* (5 December 2002), p. 3; interview with McKechnie.

of the consumer is narrowed to the extent that scholars in the US have spoken less about consumerism and more about 'customer-citizenship'. Areas of consumer concern might therefore be fenced off, as in the traditional British policy of regarding the cinema as a trade product rather than a cultural artefact as it is in other countries. And state consumerism can limit the consumer's role as a supporter of industry rather than as an active citizen who determines for him or herself the extent of their influence. Thus, whereas the Minister for Consumer Affairs had full Cabinet status in the 1970s, the current Labour government has continued the Conservative restriction of this area of political action. Melanie Johnson is now only a Parliamentary Under-Secretary within the Department of Trade and Industry and her position is allied to business through her title as Minister for Competition, Consumer Affairs and Markets. The position is necessarily compromised as she cannot act as a consumer champion independent of the concerns of other interested parties.

Despite the worry that consumer interests remain firmly eclipsed by others within government, and the response of the CA to create a new form of activism that deals with this, many of these weaknesses ought not to detract from the overall achievements of the consumer movement. Indeed, in the longer historical perspective, affluent consumerism at least has obtained many successes for itself. Most notable, is the presence of consumer organisations in public life. The NCC continues to comment on the range of issues outlined in chapter 10 and it remains committed to the task of defending 'disadvantaged' consumers. There might still be problems with the Food Standards Agency relating to its representation of the consumer voice both on its Council and in wider state circles, but it does at least exist. The Department of Trade and Industry (DTI) continues to imagine the consumer as the individual customer of a good or services, but it provides a variety of support mechanisms for this role. It has overseen the Competition Act of 1998 and the Enterprise Act of 2002 which have increased the powers of the OFT and enabled consumers to seek damages for anti-competitive practices as well as extending the consumer protection measures more generally. The DTI provides a Consumer Gateway to enable consumers with access to the internet to find quickly the organisations and sources of help to deal with particular problems. And the new Consumer Support Networks, although they do not commit funds to reviving the local consumer advice centres of the 1970s, do at least help co-ordinate the activities of various advice agencies from Citizens' Advice Bureau to Age Concern and Trading Standards Offices. More generally, in addition to the established consumer bodies, consumers can turn to private organisations to register complaints, to voluntarily created industry bodies overseeing a particular sector and to government ombudsmen in the legal and financial sectors.[10]

Speaking today, consumer activists from the 1950s and 1960s all emphasise the extent to which consumerism actually put consumers on the map, both in political and economic terms. From the 1968 Trade Descriptions Act to current competition law, consumer organisations have been consulted as crucial agents in policy formation. They have successfully lobbied MPs on numerous specific acts of legislation and the NCC and the CA sit as consumer representatives on countless official bodies and committees. In its impact upon the economy, activists consistently point to the absence of a consumer-minded approach of business in the immediate post-Second World War period. Classic examples of consumer oversight include the inappropriate height of kitchen furniture for housewives and the range of product testing measures which were designed from the engineer's rather than the user's point of view. Although it is difficult to assess the precise impact of *Which?* reports on demand a recurrent concern of the CA has been the motorcar. This has led to accusations that comparative testing consumerism led to the decline of the British car industry, but more likely is it that management consistently failed to respond to the needs and criticisms of consumers: the success of foreign manufacturers, instead, has been attributed to not only absolute advantages in the costs of production, but the ability of engineers to adapt their designs to consumer demand. Such effects of consumerism are difficult to measure, and more research is required in this area, but it is certainly felt today that business can only succeed if it gives consumers what they want: organised consumerism has played a central role in this shift in attitudes among manufacturers.

More difficult to quantify still is the extent to which consumer education has created more rational and discriminating shoppers. The idealised *Which?* reader – so scientific in his or her approach that equality is gained in the bargaining relationship with the manufacturer – largely remains a mythical figure but, thanks to the large amount of information now available, at least the consumer does have the choice as to when and where to exercise his or her rationality. The impact of consumerism upon the language of commerce and politics is equally difficult to trace. Everywhere, it seems, the consumer interest is invoked to justify a policy measure or market action. Here, the consumer appears to be rendered empty of meaning but it is undeniable that consumerism has been used by consumers themselves to defeat the power relations inherent within systems

---

[10] See various websites, especially http://www.consumer.gov.uk; http://www.csnconnect. ork.uk; http://www.dti.gov.uk/ccp/.

of provision. Not all of this has been welcomed. Businesses have derided the nagging complaints of so-called fanatical shoppers, and public sector workers have bemoaned the greater attention given to the consumer/user in education, health, local government and the social services. Too often it appears that the language of consumerism is used to legitimate other agendas, be it the desire to cut funding, to improve efficiency, to lower wages or to perpetually modernise, while the actual consumers themselves do not receive any greater choice or improved service. But it has to be remembered that consumer organisations entered these arenas out of frustration at the lack of attention given to the individual patient, tenant, pupil and ratepayer. Consumerism, at least in the 1970s in the work of the NCC, seemed to offer a form of empowerment for consumers too often overlooked in a set of economic and political relations dominated by the interests of workers and employers.

It is in this attempt to create a new basis for social democracy that we can see the dominant narrative within this history. Undoubtedly, the preceding chapters have demonstrated the importance of consumerism to the history of the twentieth century. They have corrected a common oversight and shed light on how the language of consumerism which pervades all aspects of politics today came into being. They have demonstrated the diversity within consumerism and reasons why some consumer political models have won out over others. This history of the politics of consumption has also emphasised related points too. For instance, Part A showed how working-class politics was often dominated as much by price as by pay and that the everyday attention given to spending was a crucial stimulus to political allegiance. Consumption has also been an arena for women to enter the political sphere, either in the radicalism of many working-class women's organisations in the first half of the century, or in the more conservative inclinations of an expanding number of middle-class women's groups in the middle decades of the century. But always this consumerism has been a point of entry to construct a third way in politics, freeing the notion of citizenship from the anti-democratic shackles alleged to be cast upon it by the vested interests of the capitalist and the trade unionist. Co-operators, planners, professionals, campaigners and theorists have all attempted to position the consumer as a new force in society with the power to revive civil society and active democracy and to restructure the state and the economy in the interests of the people.

Yet here lies the problem of consumerism. If an intellectual rationale has been constructed at varying points for the creation of a socio-political movement, it has had either to open its agendas to the myriad interests of consumers or has become so vague in its operating principles that it has opened itself up to capture by other political forces. Co-operative ideologues may well have celebrated the utopian goal of the Co-operative Commonwealth, but without a finely articulated relationship to capital, the state and the worker it failed to obtain the initiative within the practical politics of the labour movement. When consumerism has focussed instead on a specific aspect of the debate it has captured the allegiance of thousands, and sometimes millions, but it has lost too its force as a social democratic goal. When others within the Co-operative movement held it to be just another form of trading, that is what it remained: a shop with little revolutionary potential. And when post-Second World War consumerism concentrated purely on value for money and the point of purchasing, its apparent radicalism was lost as its agenda rapidly equated with the models of liberal economics. But all this is not to deny the constant attempts to create a social movement and it is here that consumerism has offered the most potential, both in the ideas it has generated and in the reforms it has inspired. Consumerism has been most successful as a middle-way ideology when it has clearly used the consumer as the starting point for a rejuvenated citizenship and when it has mixed a pragmatic political ideology with an economic interest for its individual supporters. Except in the First World War, when the Consumers' Council tied the consumer to agendas of the state socialist worker, consumerism has had most impact when it has occupied a broadly social democratic or democratic socialist middle ground. It is then that the consumer has had the potential at least to direct the affairs of state, politics, society and economy without resorting to narrower sectionalist interests.

Thus, when Teresa Billington Greig positioned consumerism as an overtly feminist agenda she urged women to use consumption and domestic issues as the means to transform the nature of political debate and action, thereby forging a new direction for citizenship amidst what she saw as the producer-oriented and masculine world of the early twentieth century. She was unsuccessful as her consumerism was purely theoretical and lacked an outline of the practical steps required to support her movement. But she also failed to combine her politics with the economic interests of the individual and her ideas could therefore never hold as much appeal as those of Margaret Llewelyn Davies' did to the rank of women co-operators throughout the Guilds. Co-operation owed its success to its ability to mix idealism and self-help, but it also combined the identity of the consumer with that of the worker and thus became a central part of the labour movement. That it did not succeed according to its own criteria as a political ideology was due to the tensions over its relationship with the state after the First World War, and the Fabians instead set out the socialist vision, with the Co-operative input being increasingly marginalised from the position of parity it obtained with workers and citizens in the Webbs' *Socialist Commonwealth*. The Fabian view also dominated the Labour Party leadership and resulted in the exclusion of alternative consumer-oriented politics in the inter-war decades, be it the ILP's concept of the living wage, the campaigns over the cost of living led by Labour women and in the inadequately conceptualised Consumer Council Bills proposed in the 1930s. But this general consciousness of price and consumption, beyond either profits or wages, inspired a more centrist response in the work of PEP which hoped to use consumption as a more rational means of socio-economic planning than what it felt to be the sectionalist interests of the trade unions and the employers. PEP's importance also lays in its bridging of the gap between goods defined as necessities and those defined as comforts, and its investigations into food councils and comparative testing bodies provides an important link between the two sections of this book. Its social democratic vision, to be implemented by civic-minded professional experts, was a clear inspiration to the post-Second World War generation of planners who dominated the early Consumers' Association and who again saw in consumerism the means to correct both the imbalances of the economy and of politics. While the 1960s Consumer Council appears to have been, in comparison, an attempt to contain consumerism within a narrowly defined role, the rediscovery of poverty in that decade led to the creation of the NCC which firmly located the consumer at the centre of a new social democratic order. Although it was not a vision shared by all, it is clear that many of the early NCC Council members hoped the consumer would come to share as prominent a role in public life as the TUC and the CBI. Finally, consumerism as a wide-ranging social philosophy has been most persistently articulated in the work of IOCU, as the concerns of third world producers have been located institutionally alongside the interests of global consumers.

Consumerism, then, has offered the most potential not when it has confined itself to obtaining value for money at the point of sale, but when it has sought an active relationship with the wider concerns of citizenship. It means that broader questions have to be asked of consumer issues. For instance, is the consumer interest in the railways only one of ensuring that the particular service scrutinised provides the best value for money for the rail user? Or should the consumer be an active participant in the wider debates about the railways, helping to determine such issues as the superiority of either public or private provision, the reforms necessary to ensure passenger safety and the role of organisations such as the Strategic Rail Authority? Comparative testing consumerism might point to the better value of some goods and the ease of shopping provided by supermarkets, and certainly affluent *Which?* readers have been happy to load up their cars at out-of-town shopping centres. But between 1995 and 2000 around 30,000 local retail outlets were closed in the face of such competition, and another 28,000 closures are predicted by 2005.[11] Does the consumer interest lie in individual convenience at the expense of ripping the heart out of small and medium-sized communities? Or should the consumer be engaged in a wider citizenship debate about the appropriate balance between larger and smaller stores and the need to introduce measures to maintain communities through the protection of pubs, post offices, banks and grocers? In the area of broadcasting, should consumerism merely conclude that the consumer interest lies in greater choice in TV programming? Can its comments on the BBC, for instance, be restricted to a demand for it to be open to competition? Or should con- sumerism avoid the lowest common denominator of private choice and argue instead that the BBC's system of collective provision offers the best means of offering a real choice to the range of marginal interests of all kinds of TV viewer?

Many other examples of this kind could be given, often revolving around whether 'choice' is a quantitative or qualitative issue. If the former, then consumerism is to be restricted to the act of individual economic transactions in the marketplace. If the latter, then consumerism will en- ter the arena of citizenship. What is significant is that the CA is aware itself that its own brand of consumerism needs to take into account the wider issues if it is to maintain its lead as a forward-thinking activist or- ganisation. In September 2002 it set out to 'stretch the consumer/citizen boundary'.[12] Responding to problems such as the privatisation measures which too often failed to transfer power to consumers, and the growth of other activist organisations in a global civil society, the CA has felt the need to recapture the public imagination: there is a fear that there is 'a lack of focus in our work and poor communication about our priorities and the way we reach them'.[13] For too long it has concentrated on individ- ual empowerment solutions to economic problems and has insufficiently investigated the ways in which collective responses might be sought. It acknowledges the strengths of its pragmatic and incremental approach to wider social and political issues but recognises the need to set out some general principles as to its relationship to citizenship. Accordingly, the CA has attempted to broaden its own definition of consumerism. This is not to include such clear citizenship issues as the decisions for war and the type of electoral system to be adopted, but it is to include topics such

[11] *Guardian*, 16 December 2002, p. 7.
[12] M. Childs, A. Asher and S. McKechnie, 'The consumer–citizen divide', internal CA document (September 2002), p. 1.
[13] *Ibid.*, p. 3.

as the distribution of resources within society, 'the need to ensure that we all have a healthy and comfortable old age; the need to ensure that we are not exposed to greater risk than necessary without means of assessment and control; the need to ensure that we are all aware of our impact on the environment and our fellow human beings'.[14]

Ultimately, though, the CA has not resolved this tension between consumerism and citizenship – there is no 'magic bullet in the citizen-consumer debate' – just as others have failed to do so also. Consumerism as a social movement accepts that people do not act or think of themselves as consumers all the time in the same way that they might do as citizens. It is therefore appropriate for the CA to adopt the campaigning strategies which McKechnie refers to as the 'new consumerism' and which build on its long tradition of suggesting specific solutions to specific problems, its expansion dictated more by pragmatic than theoretical considerations. In the near future, then, the CA will focus on issues such as health, identifying the extent to which the consumer voice is heard and the ability of all consumers to exercise real choice through being able to 'exit' the particular system of provision. And other issues will include public sector broadcasting, welfare services, the long-term care of the elderly and personal finance. These are all, however, extensions into the interests of its middle England membership and there is a certain lack of courage in entering into a dialogue with new consumer concerns. There is a greater tendency, for instance, to focus on the problems of the public sector, perhaps because it is easier to obtain results here, rather than issues related to private corporations whose activities at executive and worker level provoke greater divisions within the CA membership. Instead, the CA has devoted some of its energies to exploring models of 'social capitalism' and 'corporate citizenship'. These are far different from Shanks' earlier calls to include within economic policy a concern for social issues as well, and involves instead regarding the corporation as a citizen which will respond to the values of the people it deals with: shareholders, managers, employees, customers. It is the creed of Blair, Clinton and Schröder and involves a faith placed in companies – based on the evidence of the activities of a tiny number of civic-minded corporations and against the evidence of decades of corporate malpractice – to attract customers by investing in the social issues that they will find attractive. Thus, the firm's 'social capital' will be built up, as will its 'brand equity'.[15] Despite employing a vocabulary which flies in the face of the plain-speaking commitments of an earlier generation of consumer activists, the CA's exploration of

[14] *Ibid.* p. 11
[15] M. Willmott and P. Flatters, 'Corporate citizenship', internal CA document (1999).

'corporate citizenship' appears to avoid the real issues facing consumers' relationship to private companies. Furthermore, it exhibits a remarkable degree of trust in a set of organisations which the CA elsewhere believes has caused a growing cynicism and distrust among consumers to commerce. Perhaps the collapse of concerns such as Enron will put paid to the idea that profit-making capitalist organisations will see it in their interests to provide welfare services to its fellow 'citizens' and the CA will ignore in the future such a Panglossian social philosophy.

The challenge for the CA is to make connections with an expanding range of consumer groups who are tackling more seriously issues of corporate responsibility, state intervention and the global market. Yet although it has involved itself with GM foods, responsible consumption and the discussion of 'food miles', it has consistently avoided any close contact with the Co-operative movement and the *Ethical Consumer* magazine. Indeed, the Council 'has expressed a desire to distance CA from groups like Greenpeace'.[16] This is a clear example of timidity since single-issue politics, and ethical consumerism in particular, are hardly radical movements any longer. Even the Women's Institute is content to join a network of such groups in supporting restrictions on the development of GM foods and the Ethical Purchasing Index demonstrates a clear desire by many consumers for greater information in this area. But the CA continues to tread tentatively, fearing to step too far beyond what it believes are the concerns of its members and it has avoided making strong statements on issues such as transport policy and its reporting on companies has not extended beyond the tests on their goods. The CA has decided to stick to its traditional methods of 'identifying the wider consumer interest, participating in dialogue with industry and government, and providing trusted information to consumers'.[17] But if it is to address the issues of citizenship it has set out in other documents, it must decide whether it is to 'give more consideration to collective rather than individual forms and levels of consumption, or to become a resource for networking and collective action between consumers.'[18]

These are the issues which are the concerns of a new generation of consumers. The interests of these groups and individuals who wish to focus not only on the rights but also the responsibilities of consumption would seem to mark out an important shift in consumerism. Yet the socially aware shoppers of today are the inheritors of a consuming tradition stretching back across the twentieth century and which came most into focus in the 1950s and 1960s. The CA would do well to make better links with these new groups, not least because they are dealing

[16] CA, 'Ethical issues', internal CA document (2001), p. 5.   [17] *Ibid.*   [18] *Ibid.*

with issues of fundamental similarity. Michael Young ought here to have the final word. His involvement in consumerism stretches back to PEP in the Second World War, to the Labour government of 1945, the birth of the CA in 1956, the establishment of the NCC in 1975 and in his own attempts to link comparative testing consumerism with earlier co-operative traditions in his Mutual Aid Centre in the late 1970s and 1980s. The title of his 1949 pamphlet, *Small Man: Big World: A Discussion of Socialist Democracy,* encapsulates the sense of alienation individuals and consumers can feel from the institutions of the state and the private and public corporations of the marketplace. This sense of consumer disenfranchisement explains the nature of consumerism adopted by many of the organisations outlined in this book. But it can also refer too to the desire by today's consumers to make links between their consuming lives and the other dimensions of global citizenship. This might not be done in the form of a socio-political movement usually associated with trade unions or suffrage campaigners, but consumerism as a movement will have to build on the policy of creating alliances between the CA, Consumers International and a whole host of NGOs and official bodies. As ever, consumerism will continue to be reinvigorated through the campaigning links it makes and will only reduce the no man's land between the individual and the 'big world' through effective participation in the network society. Only then, as Young put it, will individuals 'be made to matter'.[19]

---

[19] M. Young, *Small Man: Big World: A Discussion of Socialist Democracy* (London, 1949), p. 4.

Bibliography

1. ARCHIVAL AND UNPUBLISHED SOURCES

ARCHIVE OF THE CONSUMERS' ASSOCIATION, LONDON

CAA 12: CA Reports (various) 1973–85
CAA 13: RICA Reports (various) 1963–93
CAA 14: Reports by other bodies commissioned by the Consumers' Association
CAA 21: IOCU publications
CAA 22: Various publications
CAA 23: Various publications
CAA 24: Various publications
CAA 25: IOCU publications
CAA 26: In-house newsletters; interviews
CAA 27: Historical internal documents; various speeches and papers
CAA 28: CA publications
CAA 28: Other organisations' material
CAA 30: CA's annual reports
CAA 31: RICA publications; CA reports (e.g. campaigning, policy and survey)
CAA 66: Various miscellaneous CA publications and leaflets
CAA 67: CA book/reports
    [Plus various other internal documents]

BRITISH LIBRARY OF POLITICAL AND ECONOMIC SCIENCE

Violet Rosa Markham Papers
Political and Economic Planning Archive
Leonard K. Elmhirst Papers

BRITISH STANDARDS INSTITUTION LIBRARY, LONDON

OC/11: Minutes of Consumer Committees
Thompson, M. S., *The History of the Women's Advisory Committee of the British Standards Institution* (1975).
WAC Reports
    [Plus various miscellaneous materials]

MODERN RECORDS CENTRE, UNIVERSITY OF WARWICK

MSS 292: Trade Union Archive

PUBLIC RECORD OFFICE, KEW

Consumer Advisory Council (1950–51)
BT 258/352–355: Consumer protection policy
CAB 124/2749: Consumer Advisory Centre
PREM 8/1183: Relations between government and industry
PREM 11/1542: Distribution and Marketing Committee

Consumer Council, 1963–70
AJ 1–10: Consumer Council papers
BT 258/1492–4: Proposed Consumer Council
BT 258/1524–6, 2103: Consumer protection
BT 296/119: Appointments
PREM 11/4527: Decision to set up Consumer Council
T 224/1356: Consumer protection policy

Consumers' Council Bills, 1930s
BT 63/25/1: Consumers' Council Bill, 1939
POWE 26/183–4, 203: Consumers' Council Bill, 1930
T 161/299: Treasury Committees: Consumers' Council, 1929–31
T 163/61/8: Consumers' Council Bill, 1931

Consumers' Council, First World War
MAF 60/150: Sale of Food, 1918–22

Consumers' Councils, Agricultural Marketing Acts
MAF 34/28: Agricultural Marketing Regulations
MAF 34/719: Consumer Committee Reports
MAF 194/815: Consumers' Councils

Food Council
MAF 69/6: Minutes
MAF 69/8–9: Membership
MAF 69/10: Consumer research in the USA
MAF 69/11: Trade Unions
MAF 69/12: Powers to obtain information

Nationalised industries
CAB 124/5: Public accountability
POWE 17/82: Working Party on Consumers' Councils
POWE 28/26: Proposed Consumers' Councils

Second World War control of goods
BT 64/1976–7: Consumer Needs Department
BT 131/33: Board of Trade wartime controls

Short weight and adulteration
BT 101/697: Standard Weights and Measures Office

DSIR 26/247–251: Food adulteration
HO 45/5338: Frauds

Committee on Consumer Protection (Molony)
BT 258/878: Minutes
BT 258/879–895: Committee Papers

NATIONAL LABOUR HISTORY ARCHIVE, MANCHESTER
Consumers' Council archive [Marion Phillips papers]

NEWSPAPERS AND PERIODICALS

Adbusters
Birmingham Consumer
Bulletin of the RTSA
Cartel
The Consumer
Consumer News [Monthly Bulletin of RICA]
Dictionary of National Biography
Direct Buying Magazine
Ethical Consumer
Focus
Guardian
News of the World
NFCG Newsletter
Northern Star
Parliamentary Debates, House of Commons
Planning
Shopper's Guide
Social Audit
The Times
Trader and Consumer
Watch Dog
Which?

UNPUBLISHED THESES

Beauchamp, C., 'Consumer interest and public interest', M.Phil. thesis, University of Cambridge, 2000.
Beaumont, C., 'Women and citizenship: a study of non-feminist women's societies and the women's movement in England, 1928–1950', Ph.D. thesis, University of Warwick, 1996.
Franks, S., 'Selling consumer protection: competitive strategies of the Consumers' Association, 1957–1990', M.Phil. thesis, University of Oxford, 2000.

Hilson, M. K., 'Working-class politics in Plymouth, c.1890–1920', Ph.D. thesis, University of Exeter, 1998.

Mertens, M., 'Early twentieth-century youth movements: nature and community in Britain and Germany', Ph.D. thesis, University of Birmingham, 2000.

Newholm, T., 'Understanding the ethical consumer: employing a frame of bounded rationality', Ph.D. thesis, Open University, 2000.

Whitworth, L., 'Men, women, shops and "little, shiny homes": the consuming of Coventry, 1930–1939', Ph.D. thesis, University of Warwick, 1997.

WORKING-CLASS AUTOBIOGRAPHIES, MANUSCRIPT COLLECTION, UNIVERSITY OF BRUNEL

Armitage, J., *The Twenty Three Years. Or the Late Way of Life – and of Living*, 1974.

Austin, V., *[Untitled]*, n.d.

Ayre, J., *The Socialist*, 1980s.

Hughes, G. C., *Shut the Mountain Gate*, 1980s.

2. PRIMARY BOOKS AND ARTICLES

Acland, R., D. Bruce, B. Castle, R. Crossman, H. Davies, L. Hale, T. Horabin, M. Lipton, I. Mikardo, S. Swingler, G. Wigg and T. Williams, *Keeping Left: Labour's First Five Years and the Problems Ahead*, London, 1950.

Addison, C., *Why Food is Dear*, London, 1925.

Advance Democracy (1938), on *The People's Cinema: The Films of the Co-operative Movement* (National Co-operative Film Archive).

Anderson, G. G., *The Call for Protection in the Interest of the Consumer*, London, 1925.

Association of Scientific Workers, *Spotlight on Shopping: Consumer Research*, London, 1951.

Attlee, C., *Labour Keeps Its Word*, London, 1946.

Attlee, C., *What Labour Has Done*, London, 1946.

Barker, P., 'Michael Young', *New Society* (8 August 1968), 188.

Barnard, K., and K. Lee (eds.), *Conflicts in the National Health Service*, London, 1977.

Barton, E., *Through Trade to the Co-operative Commonwealth*, London, 1930.

Barton, E., *Women: In the Home, the Store and the State*, Manchester, c.1928.

Baynes, M., *Advertising on Trial: The Case for the Consumer*, London, 1956.

Beishon, J., 'Empowering consumers', *New Socialist* (June/July 1989), 16–17.

Benn, E., *Producer vs. Consumer: Thoughts on Difficulties*, London, 1928.

Benn, E., 'The curse of collectivism', *National Review*, 118 (1942), 359–63.

Beveridge, W. H., *British Food Control*, London, 1928.

Birmingham Consumer Group, *Annual Reports, 1963–1975*.

Black, C., *The Consumers' League: A Proposal that Buyers Should Combine to Deal only with Employers who Pay their Workers Fairly*, London, 1888.

Black, C., *A Natural Alliance*, London, 1892.

Black, C., *Sweated Industry and the Minimum Wage*, London, 1907.

Black, C., *The Truck Acts: What They Do, and What They Ought to Do*, London, 1894.

Blake, J. *Memories of Old Poplar*, London, 1977.

Board of Trade, *Monopolies, Mergers and Restrictive Practices*, Cmd. 2299, London, 1964.

Board of Trade, *A Statement on Resale Price Maintenance*, Cmd. 8274, London, 1951.

Bondfield, M., *The Meaning of Trade*, London, 1928.

Braddock, A. P., *Applied Psychology for Advertisers*, London, 1933.

Brailsford, H. N., *Socialism for Today*, London, 1926.

Brailsford, H. N., J. A. Hobson, A. Creech Jones and E. F. Wise, *The Living Wage*, London, 1926.

Briggs, A. (ed.), *William Morris: Selected Writings and Designs*, 1962, Harmondsworth, 1977.

British Medical Association, *Secret Remedies: What They Cost and What They Contain*, London, 1906.

British Railways Board, *The Commuters' Charters: The Foundation of a Progressive Community served by a Dynamic Railway*, London, 1981.

Brown, I., *Art and Everyman*, London, 1929.

BSI, *Annual Reports, 1946–1965*.

BSI, *Fifty Years of British Standards, 1901–1951*, London, 1951.

BSI, *Reports on the Conference of Women's Organisations*, 1956–61.

BSI, *Speaking Up for Consumers: Information about BSI and Consumer Representation*, London, 1999.

BSI, *Standards and the Consumer: First Annual Report of the Advisory Council on Standards for Consumer Goods, 1955–1956*, London, 1956.

BSI Consumer Affairs Division, *What Every Mum Should Know About British Standards*, London, 1976.

BSI Consumer Policy Committee, *Annual Report 1999*, London, 1999.

BSI, CA, Office of Fair Trading and Inner London Education Authority, *Suzie and the Supershopper*, London, 1974.

Burns, C. D., 'The appropriate types of authority for the operation of publicly owned utility services, and the powers which they should have: the consumer and public utility services', *Public Administration*, 4:4 (1926), 318–29.

Burton, E., *The Battle of the Consumer*, London, 1954.

CA, *Ailments and Remedies*, London, 1965.

CA, *Annual Reports, 1957–2002*.

CA, *Buying Secondhand*, London, 1966.

CA, *Insurance and the Consumer*, London, 1968.

CA, *The Law for Motorists*, London, 1962.

CA, *The Legal Side of Buying a House*, London, 1965.

CA, *Pregnancy Month by Month*, London, 1968.

CA, *Radiation: Part of Life*, London, 1965.

CA, *Thirty Years of Which?: Consumers' Association, 1957–1987*, London, 1987.

CA, *The Travelling Consumer*, London, 1964.

CA, *What to do when Someone Dies*, London, 1967.

CA, *Which? and Consumers' Association*, 1965; London, 1972.

CAC, *Representing the Consumer Advisory Standards Committee*, London, n.d.

CAI, *Education for the Consumer*, London, 1935.

CAI, *The Working Class Home: Its Furnishing and Equipment*, London, 1937.

Campbell, H., *Wanting and Working*, London, 1947.
Caplowitz, D., *The Poor Pay More: Consumer Practices of Low-Income Families*, New York, 1963.
Carr-Saunders, A. M., P. S. Florence and R. Peers, *Consumers' Co-operation in Great Britain: An Examination of the British Co-operative Movement*, London, 1938.
Carson, R., *Silent Spring*, 1962; Harmondsworth, 1999.
Central Office of Information, *Fair Trading and Consumer Protection in Britain*, London, 1976.
Chase, S., and F. J. Schlink, *Your Money's Worth: A Study in the Waste of the Consumer's Dollar*, New York, 1927.
Circus, P. J., *Towards a General Duty to Trade Fairly?*, London, 1988.
Citrine, W. M., *Labour and the Community*, London, 1928.
Clay, H., *Co-operation and Private Enterprise*, London, 1928.
Clemesha, H. W., *Food Control in the North-West Division*, Manchester, 1922.
Cole, G. D. H., *A Century of Co-operation*, Manchester, 1944.
Cole, G. D. H., *Chaos and Order in Industry*, London, 1920.
Cole, G. D. H., *Guild Socialism Restated*, 1920; London, 1980.
Cole, G. D. H., *Labour's Second Term*, London, 1949.
Cole, G. D. H., *Self-Government in Industry*, 1917; London, 1919.
Cole, G. D. H., and A. W. Filson (eds.), *British Working Class Movements: Select Documents, 1789–1875*, London, 1951.
Cole, H. R., and A. L. Diamond, *The Consumer and the Law*, London, 1960.
College of Law, *Fair Trading and Consumer Protection*, London, 1973.
Coller, F. H., *A State Trading Adventure*, Oxford, 1925.
Commission of Enquiry into Industrial Unrest, *Summary of the Reports of the Commission*, Cd. 8696, London, 1917.
Committee on Consumer Protection [Molony Committee], *Final Report*, Cmnd. 1781, London, 1962.
Committee on Consumer Protection, *Interim Report*, Cmnd. 1011, London, 1960.
Committee on Resale Price Maintenance [Lloyd Jacob Committee], *Report*, Cmd. 7696, London, 1949.
Conservative Party, *Manifesto 1951*, London, 1951.
Conservative Party, *Firm Action for a Fair Britain: The Conservative Manifesto 1974*, London, 1974.
Conservative Party, *Manifesto 1979*, London, 1979.
Conservative Party, *Manifesto 1983*, London, 1983.
Conservative Party, *The Next Moves Forward: Manifesto 1987*, London, 1987.
Consumer Council, *Annual Reports, 1963–1970*.
Consumer Council, *Information for Consumer Education*, London, 1965.
Consumer Standards Advisory Committee [later the CAC], *An Introduction to the CSAC*, London, 1956[?].
Consumers International, *Annual Report, 1999*.
Consumers' League, *Prospectus*, London, 1887.
Co-operative Union, *Consumers and the Community*, London, 1961.
Cowe, R., and S. Williams, *Who are the Ethical Consumers*, London, 2000.
CPAC, *Disguised Business Sales*, London, 1976.

CPAC, *A Report on Practices Relating to Prepayment in Mail Order Transactions and in Shops*, London, 1976.

CPAC, *Rights of Consumers*, London, 1974.

CPAC, *VAT Exclusive Prices*, London, 1977.

Crosland, C. A. R., *The Future of Socialism*, London, 1956.

Curtis, H., and M. Sanderson, *A Review of the National Federation of Consumer Groups*, London, 1992.

Daniels, G. W., *Capital, Labour and the Consumer*, London, 1929.

Davies, M. L., *Co-operation in Poor Neighbourhoods*, Nottingham, 1899.

Davies, M. L., *The Education of Guildswomen*, Manchester, 1913.

Davies, M. L., *Guild Work, in Relation to Educational Committees of Co-operative Societies*, Manchester, 1898.

Davies, M. L., *Inaugural Address, 54th Annual Congress of the Co-operative Union*, Manchester, 1922.

Davies, M. L., *Life as We Have Known It*, 1931; London, 1990.

Davies, M. L., *Women as Organised Consumers*, Manchester, 1921.

Delbridge, R., and M. Smith (eds.), *Consuming Secrets*, London, 1982.

Digby, M., *Producers and Consumers: A Study in Co-operative Relations*, 1928; London, 1938.

Digby, M., *The World Co-operative Movement*, London, 1949.

Director-General of Fair Trading, *Review of UK Self-Regulatory System of Advertising Control*, London, 1978.

Douglas, C. H., *Economic Democracy*, London, 1920.

Douglas, C. H., *Social Credit*, London, 1924.

DPCP, *National Consumers' Agency*, Cmnd. 5726, London, 1974.

DPCP, *Review of the Price Code*, London, 1974.

DTI, *Modern Markets: Confident Consumers*, Cm 4410, London, 1999.

ECRA, *Ethical Consumer Briefing Pack*, Manchester, 1997.

ECRA, *The Ethical Consumer Guide to Everyday Shopping*, Manchester, 1993.

Eley, H. W., *Advertising Media*, London, 1932.

Elkington, J., and J. Hailes, *The Green Consumer Guide*, London, 1988.

Fabian Society, *Committee of Enquiry on the Control of Industry: Memorandum by the Chairman (Beatrice Webb)*, Letchworth, 1910.

Fisher, J., *The Plot to Make You Buy*, New York, 1968.

Flint, E., *Hot Bread and Chips*, London, 1963.

Food Council, *Annual Reports*.

Frankel, M., *The Social Audit Pollution Handbook*, Basingstoke, 1978.

Freeden, M. (ed.), *J. A. Hobson: A Reader*, London, 1988.

Freedman, L., and G. Hemingway, *Nationalisation and the Consumer*, London, 1950.

Fulop, C., *Competition for Consumers: A Study of the Changing Channels of Distribution*, London, 1964.

Gide, C., *Consumers Co-operative Societies*, 1913; Manchester, 1921.

Gide, C., *Principles of Political Economy*, London, 1903.

Gilboy, E., 'The cost of living and real wages in eighteenth-century England', *Review of Economics and Statistics*, 18:3 (1936), 134–43.

Gillman, K., *The Consumer Interpol*, The Hague, 1981.

Giordan, M., *The Consumer Jungle* (London, 1974).

Giordan, M., *How to be Exploited (And How to Avoid It)*, London, 1978.

Gips, T., *Breaking the Pesticide Habit: Alternatives to Twelve Hazardous Pesticides*, Penang, 1990.

Goldman, P., *Some Principles of Conservatism*, London, 1961.

Goodenough, G., *The Central Board and the Grant to the Women's Co-operative Guild*, Manchester, 1914.

Goodhart, P., *A Nation of Consumers*, London, 1965.

Goodhart, P., M. Benrose, J. Douglas, I. MacArthur, P. McLaughlin and J. B. Wood, *Choice: A Report on Consumer Protection*, London, 1961.

Greig, T. B., *The Consumer in Revolt*, London, 1912.

Grimond, J., *Better Buys*, London, n.d.

Gundrey, E., *At Your Service: A Consumer's Guide to the Service Trades and Professions*, Harmondsworth, 1964.

Gundrey, E., *A Foot in the Door: An Exposé of High Pressure Sales Methods*, London, 1965.

Gundrey, E., *Help!*, London, 1967.

Gundrey, E., *Your Money's Worth*, Harmondsworth, 1962.

Gyford, J., *Citizens, Consumers and Councils: Local Government and the Public*, Basingstoke, 1991.

Harbury, C. D., *Efficiency and the Consumer*, London, 1958.

Hargrave, J., 'The case for social credit', *Cavalcade* (8 May 1948).

Harries, J. V., *Consumers: Know Your Rights*, London, 1978.

Harris, R., and A. Seldon, *Advertising and the Public*, London, 1962.

Hartwell, R. M. (ed.), *The Causes of the Industrial Revolution in England*, London, 1967.

Healy, M., 'What are local government services for?', *Local Government Studies* (November/December 1985), 12–14.

Henderson, F., *Capitalism and the Consumer*, London, 1936.

Hilton, J., *Rich Man, Poor Man*, London, 1944.

Hilton, J., *A Study of Trade Organisations and Combinations in the UK*, London, 1919.

Hilton, J., *This and That: The Broadcast Talks of John Hilton*, London, 1938.

Hobson, J. A., 'The General Election: a sociological interpretation', *Sociological Review*, 3 (1910), 105–17.

Hoggart, R., *The Uses of Literacy*, 1957; Harmondsworth, 1973.

Holliman, J., *Consumer's Guide to the Protection of the Environment*, London, 1971.

Holyoake, G. J., *The Co-Operative Movement Today*, London, 1891.

Holyoake, G. J., *The History of Co-operation in England: Its Literature and Advocates, Volume 2. The Constructive Period, 1845–1878*, London, 1879.

Holyoake, G. J., *The Policy of Commercial Co-operation as Respects Including the Consumer*, London, 1873.

Houlton, E., *'Which?' Put to the Test*, London, 1967.

Hyndman, R. T., *The Last Years of H. M. Hyndman*, London, 1923.

International Organisation for Standardisation (ISO), *Consumer Standards Today and Tomorrow*, London, 1976.

IOCU, *Biennial Report, 1970–1972*, The Hague, 1972.

IOCU, *The Consumer and the World of Tomorrow: Report of the Second Conference*, The Hague, 1962.

IOCU, *Consumer Policy 2000: Seminar Report*, The Hague, 1986.

IOCU, *Consumer Power in the Nineties: Proceedings of the Thirteenth IOCU World Congress*, The Hague, 1991.

IOCU, *Consumer Solidarity: For a Better World: Proceedings of Twelfth Congress*, The Hague, 1987.

IOCU, *Consumers on the March: Proceedings of the Third Biennial Conference of the IOCU*, The Hague, 1964.

IOCU, *Five Billion Consumers: Organising for Change Proceedings of Eleventh World Congress*, The Hague, 1984.

IOCU, *Knowledge is Power: Consumer Goals in the 1970s. Proceedings of the Sixth Biennial World Conference of the IOCU*, The Hague, 1970.

IOCU, *Pests at Home: A Consumer Guide to Safer Pest Control*, Penang, 1993.

IOCU, *The Quality of Life: 1972 World Congress Handbook*, The Hague, 1972.

IOCU, *Report for 1972–1974*, The Hague, 1975.

IOCU, *A World in Crisis: The Consumer Response: Proceedings of the Ninth IOCU World Congress*, The Hague, 1978.

Jacks, L. P., *The Road to Enjoyment*, London, 1928.

John, R. (ed.), *The Consumer Revolution: Redressing the Balance*, London, 1994.

Johnson, H., *Religion Interferes*, London, 1928.

Jowett, F. W., *Socialism in Our Time*, London, 1926.

Kamenka, E. (ed.), *The Portable Karl Marx*, Harmondsworth, 1983.

Keynes, J. M., *The General Theory of Employment, Interest and Money*, 1936; London, 1964.

Labour Party, *Challenge to Britain*, London, 1953.

Labour Party, *Consumer Choice and Quality of Life*, London, 1989.

Labour Party, *How the Housewife Suffers*, London, 1938.

Labour Party, *Labour Believes in Britain*, London, 1949.

Labour Party, *The Labour Party and Social Credit: A Report on the Proposals of Major Douglas and the 'New Age'*, London, 1922.

Labour Party, *Let Us Face the Future*, London, 1945.

Labour Party, *Let Us Win Through Together*, London, 1950.

Labour Party, *My Family's Food Costs More and More*, London, 1937.

Labour Party, *Socialism and Social Credit*, London, 1935.

Laski, H., *The Recovery of Citizenship*, London, 1928.

Laver, E. A., *Advertising and Economic Theory*, Oxford, 1947.

Leavis, F. R., *Mass Civilisation and Minority Culture*, Cambridge, 1930.

Levett, A. E., *The Consumer in History*, London, 1929.

Levy, H., *Retail Trade Associations: A New Form of Monopolist Organisation in Britain*, London, 1942.

Levy, H., *The Shops of Britain: A Study of Retail Distribution*, London, 1947.

Liberal Party Consumer Committee, *Consumer Protection*, London, 1962.

Linton, A., *Not Expecting Miracles*, London, 1982.

Lloyd, E. M. H., *Experiments in State Control at the War Office and the Ministry of Food*, Oxford, 1924.

Lowe, R., *Sale of Goods and Hire Purchase*, Harmondsworth, 1968.

Mackie, E. (ed.), *The Commerce of Everyday Life: Selections from 'The Tatler' and 'The Spectator'*, Boston, MA, 1998.

Macrosty, H. W., *Trusts and the State: A Sketch of Competition*, London, 1901.
Mahin, J. L., *Advertising: Selling the Consumer*, London, 1914.
Mandeville, B., *The Fable of the Bees*, New York, 1962.
Marcuse, H., *One Dimensional Man*, London, 1964.
Margelius, S., *The Innocent Consumer*, London, 1967.
Marshall, A., *Principles of Economics*, 1890; London, 1961.
Marshall, T. H., *Citizenship and Social Class*, Cambridge, 1950.
Martin, E., *The Best Street in Rochdale*, Rochdale, 1985.
Medawar, C., *The Social Audit Consumer Handbook: A Guide to the Social Responsibilities of Business to the Consumer*, Basingstoke, 1978.
Methven, J., *Is the Consumer Over Protected?*, Edinburgh, 1975.
Mikardo, I., *The Second Five Years*, London, 1949.
Mill, J. S., *Essays on some Unsettled Questions of Political Economy*, London, 1992.
Mill, J. S., *Principles of Political Economy, with Some of Their Applications to Social Philosophy*, 1852; London, 1968.
Millar, R., *The Affluent Sheep: A Profile of the British Consumer*, London, 1963.
Ministry of Reconstruction, *Report of the Committee on Trusts*, Cd. 9236, London, 1919.
Minogue, M. (ed.), *A Consumer's Guide to Local Government*, London, 1977.
Mitchell, B. R., and P. Deane, *Abstract of British Historical Statistics*, Cambridge, 1962.
Mitchell, J., 'Co-operatives and the new consumer movement', *Society for Co-operative Studies Bulletin*, 34 (1979), 83–90.
Mitchell, J., 'Management and the consumer movement', *Journal of General Management*, 3:4 (1976), 46–54.
Mitford, J., *The American Way of Death*, London, 1963.
Monier-Williams, G. W., *Food and the Consumer*, London, 1935.
Monopolies and Restrictive Practices Commission, *Collective Discrimination*, Cmd. 9504, London, 1955.
Morris, W., *News from Nowhere*, 1890; London, 1970.
Morrison, H., *Team Work for the Nation*, London, 1947.
Nader, R., *Unsafe at any Speed: The Designed-in Dangers of the American Automobile*, New York, 1965.
Nathan, M., *The Story of an Epoch-Making Movement*, London, 1926.
NCC, *Annual Reports, 1975–2002*.
NCC, *Behind with the Rent*, London, 1976.
NCC, *The Consumer and the State: Getting Value for Public Money*, London, 1979.
NCC, *Consumer Congress Directories, 1976–1989*.
NCC, *Consumers and Credit*, London, 1980.
NCC, *Consumers and the Nationalised Industries*, London, 1976.
NCC, *Cracking Up*, London, 1982.
NCC, *For Richer, for Poorer*, London, 1975.
NCC, *The Fourth Right of Citizenship: A Review of Local Advice Centres*, London, 1977.
NCC, *Making the Difference*, London, 2002.
NCC, *Means Tested Benefits*, London, 1976.
NCC, *Patient's Rights*, London, 1982.

NCC, *Paying for Fuel*, London, 1976.

NCC, *Real Money, Real Choice: Consumer Priorities in Economic Policy*, London, 1978.

NCC, *Soonest Mended*, London, 1979.

NCC, *Tenancy Agreements Between Councils and their Tenants*, London, 1976.

NCC, *What is the National Consumer Council*, London, 2002.

Neale, E. V., and E. O. Greening, *Proposal for an International Alliance of the Friends of Co-operative Production*, Edinburgh, 1892.

Neville, R., *Co-operation*, London, 1901.

NFCG, *A Handbook of Consumer Law: A Practical Guide to Consumers' Problems*, London, 1982.

Nixon, E., *John Hilton: The Story of His Life*, London, 1946.

Northcott, J. F., *Value for Money? The Case for a Consumers' Advice Service*, London, 1953.

OECD, *Annual Report on Consumer Policy, 1975*, Paris, 1975.

OECD, *A Global Marketplace for Consumers*, Paris, 1995.

OECD Committee on Consumer Policy, *Consumer Policy During the Past Ten Years*, Paris, 1983.

OFT, *Annual Reports, 1973–2000*.

OFT, *Anti-Competitive Practices: A Guide to the Provisions of the Competition Act, 1980*, London, 1980.

OFT, *Consumer Dissatisfaction Report*, London, 1986.

OFT, *Consumer Guarantees: A Discussion Paper*, London, 1984.

OFT, *Fair Deal: A Shopper's Guide*, London, 1982.

OFT, *A General Duty to Trade Fairly: A Discussion Paper*, London, 1986.

OFT, *An Outline of UK Competition Policy*, London, 1990.

OFT, *The Work of the Office of Fair Trading*, London, 1976.

OFT Consumer Affairs Division, *Consumer Strategy*, London, 1991.

Ogilvy-Webb, M., *The Government Explains: A Report of the Royal Institute of Public Administration*, London, 1965.

Oram, A. E., *Labour's Good Housekeeping*, London, 1950.

Orwell, G., *The Lion and the Unicorn*, 1941, Harmondsworth, 1982.

Orwell, G., *The Road to Wigan Pier*, London, 1937.

Orwell, S., and I. Angus (eds.), *The Collected Essays, Journalism and Letters of George Orwell, Volume 3: As I Please, 1943–1945*, Harmondsworth, 1970.

P. P., *Citizen's Charter: Raising the Standard*, Cm 1599, London, 1991.

P. P., *Consumers' Council Bill*, Bill 20, 1938.

P. P., *Consumers' Council Bill*, Bill 177, 1930.

P. P., *Consumers' Council Bill (as amended by Standing Committee C)*, Bill 222, 1931.

P. P., *Report of the Purchase Tax/Utility Committee*, Cmd. 8452, London, 1952, p. 5.

P. P., *Report and Special Report from Standing Committee D on the Consumers' Council Bill with the Proceedings of the Committee*, 144, 1930.

P. P., *Report and Standing Committee C on the Consumers' Council Bill with the Proceedings of the Committee*, 141, 1931.

Packard, V., *The Hidden Persuaders*, 1957; Harmondsworth, 1960.

Packard, V., *The Waste Makers*, New York, 1961.

Paish, G., *Ought we to Save?*, London, 1928.

Pearson, K., *Life in Hull: From Then Till Now*, Hull, 1979.

Peel, C. S., *A Year in Public Life*, London, 1919.

Philip, A. J., *Rations, Rationing and Food Control*, London, 1918.

Piachaud, D., *Do the Poor Pay More?*, London, 1974.

Plato, *The Republic*, Harmondsworth, 1955.

Potter, B., *The Co-operative Movement in Great Britain*, 1891; London, 1987.

Price Commission, *A Guide to the Price Controls in Stage Four*, London, 1975.

Priestley, J. B., *Delight*, London, 1949.

Priestley, J. B., *English Journey*, 1934; Harmondsworth, 1987.

Priestley, J. B., *The Good Companions*, 1929; London, 1950.

Priestley, J. B., 'A new tobacco', *Saturday Review*, 144 (1927), 216–17.

Priestley, J. B., and J. Hawkes, *Journey Down a Rainbow*, London, 1957.

Pritt, D. N., L. Solley, J. Platt-Mills and L. Hutchinson, *Crisis and Cure: The Socialist Way to Prosperity and Peace*, London, 1950.

Ramsay, I. D. C., *Rationales for Intervention in the Marketplace*, London, 1984.

Redfern, P., *The Consumer's Place in Society*, Manchester, 1920.

Redfern, P., *The Story of the CWS: The Jubilee History of the Co-operative Wholesale Society Limited, 1863–1913*, Manchester, 1913.

Redfern, P., *Twenty Faces of the World*, London, 1929.

Redfern, P. (ed.), *Self and Society: Social and Economic Problems from the Hitherto Neglected Point of View of the Consumer*, 2 vols., London, 1930.

Redmayne, P., and H. Weeks, *Market Research*, London, 1931.

Rengam, S., and K. Snyder, *The Pesticide Handbook: Profiles for Action*, Penang, 1991.

RICA, *British Co-operatives: A Consumers' Movement?*, London, 1964.

RICA, *Consumer Education: Conceptions and Resources*, London, 1964.

RICA, *Elderly Consumers: The Problem Assessed*, London, 1965.

RICA, *General Practice: A Consumer Commentary*, London, 1963.

RICA, *New Nations: Problems for Consumers*, London, 1964.

RICA, *Town Planning: The Consumer's Environment*, London, 1965.

Richardson, J. J. R., *The Great Betrayal: The Impact of Nationalisation on the Worker, the Trade Union, Local Authorities, the Consumer, Management and the Taxpayer Since 1946*, London, 1950.

Riesman, D., *Abundance for What*, London, 1956.

Riesman, D., *The Lonely Crowd*, New Haven, 1950.

Rigge, M., and M. Young, *Building Societies and the Consumer*, London, 1981.

Roberts, E., 'Consumers in the common market', *European Studies*, 22 (1975), 1–4.

Rogers, J. E. T. (ed.), *Speeches on Questions of Public Policy by The Right Honourable John Bright*, London, 1869.

Rowe, J. W. F., *Everyman's Statistics*, London, 1929.

Royal Commission on Food Prices, *Report, Minutes, and Statements of Evidence*, 3 vols., Cmd. 2390, London, 1925.

RTSA, *The Intelligent Woman's Guide to Shopping*, London, 1935.

RTSA, *Standards of Retail Practice*, London, 1935.

RTSA, *To the Thoughtful Retailer* . . . , London, 193?.

Ruskin, J., *Munera Pulveris: Six Essays on the Elements of Political Economy* (1862–3), in E. T. Cook and A. Wedderburn (eds.), *The Works Of John Ruskin*, London, 1903–12.

Ruskin, J., *Sesame and Lilies*, 1864; London, 1907.

Ruskin, J., *Unto This Last: Four Essays on the First Principles of Political Economy*, 1862; London, 1898.

Russell, J., *The Sugar Duties: A Consumer's Protest against a Scale of Duties on Sugar*, London, 1864.

Schumacher, E. F., *Small is Beautiful: A Study of Economics as if People Mattered*, 1973; London, 1974.

Shanks, M., *The Consumer in Europe*, Brussels, 1979.

Shanks, M., *The Stagnant Society: A Warning*, Harmondsworth, 1961.

Shanks, M., *What's Wrong with the Modern World? Agenda for a New Society*, London, 1978.

Sharp, E., *Daily Bread*, London, 1928.

Sinclair, U., *The Jungle*, 1906; Harmondsworth, 1965.

Smiles, S., *Self-Help*, 1859; London, 1929.

Smith, A., *The Wealth of Nations*, 1776; Chicago, 1976.

Snowden, P., *The Faith of a Democrat*, London, 1928.

Snowden, P., *The Housewife's Budget*, London, 1924.

Stannesby, A., *Consumer Rights Handbook*, London, 1986.

Stephen, J., *Flapdoodle about "Flappers"*, London, 1918.

Stewart, M., *Consumers' Councils*, London, 1953.

Strachey, J., *Labour's Task*, London, 1951.

Street, H., *Freedom, the Individual and the Law*, Harmondsworth, 1963.

Syson, L., *Fair Trading*, London, 1964.

Tawney, R. H., *The Acquisitive Society*, 1921; London, 1945.

Tench, D., *The Law for Consumers*, London, 1962.

Thompson, W., *An Inquiry into the Principles of the Distribution of Wealth most Conducive to Human Happiness*, London, 1824.

Todd, J. *The Big Sell*, London, 1961.

Todd, M., *Snakes and Ladders: An Autobiography*, London, 1960.

Trevelyan, G. M., *Must England's Beauty Perish?*, London, 1929.

UK Government, *Attack on Inflation: A Policy for Survival*, London, 1975.

United Nations, *Guidelines for Consumer Protection*, New York, 1986.

Veblen, T., *The Theory of the Leisure Class*, 1899; Harmondsworth, 1979.

WAC, *21st Anniversary Year, 1972*, London, 1972.

Walter, K. (ed.), *Co-operation and Charles Gide*, London, 1933.

War Emergency: Workers' National Committee, *Memorandum on the Increased Cost of Living During the War, August 1914 – June 1916*, 3rd edn., London, 16.

War Emergency: Workers' National Committee, *Minutes of Executive Committee*, London, 1914–16.

War Emergency: Workers' National Committee, *Report, August 1914 to March 1916*, London, 1916.

Ward, C., *How to Complain*, London, 1974.

Webb, B., *The Discovery of the Consumer*, London, 1928.

Webb, B., and S. Webb, *A Constitution for the Socialist Commonwealth of Great Britain*, London, 1920.

Webb, B., and S. Webb, *The Consumers' Co-operative Movement*, London, 1921.

Webb, C., *The Woman with the Basket: The History of the Women's Co-operative Guild*, Manchester, 1926.

Webb, C., *The Women's Guild and Store Life*, London, 1892.

Webb, S., and B. Webb, 'The Assize of Bread', *Economic Journal*, 14 (1904), 200.

Wells, T., and F. G. Sim, *Till They Have Faces: Women as Consumers*, Penang, 1987.

Welsh Consumer Council, *Within Reach? Planning Public Transport and Accessibility*, Cardiff, 1982.

Whyte, W. H., *The Organization Man*, 1956; Harmondsworth, 1960.

Wight, R., *The Day the Pigs Refused to be Driven to Market: Advertising and the Consumer Revolution*, London, 1972.

Williams, F. (ed.), *Why the Poor Pay More*, London, 1977.

Williams, S., and D. Doane, *Ethical Purchasing Index 2002*, London, 2002.

Wilson, A. (ed.), *Advertising and the Community*, Manchester, 1968.

Women's Co-operative Guild, *The ABC of the Women's Co-operative Guild*, Manchester, 1924.

Women's Co-operative Guild, *General Rules*, Manchester, 1921.

Women's Co-operative Guild, *Woman of Tomorrow*, Manchester, 1943.

Wood, J. M., *Protecting the Consumer*, London, 1963.

Woolf, L. S., *The Control of Industry by the People*, London, 1915.

Woolf, L. S. *Co-operation and the Future of Industry*, London, 1918.

Woolf, L. S., *Socialism and Co-operation*, London, 1921.

Woolf, L. S., *The Way of Peace*, London, 1928.

Worswick, G. D. N., *The Consumer: His Place in Society*, London, 1946.

Wraith, R., *The Consumer Cause: A Short Account of its Organisation, Power and Importance*, London, 1976.

Wright, C., *Better Buying*, London, 1967.

Yamey, B. S., *Resale Price Maintenance and Shoppers' Choice*, London, 1960.

Young, M., *The Chipped White Cups of Dover: A Discussion of the Possibility of a New Progressive Party*, London, 1960.

Young, M., *The Chipped White Cups of Steel*, London, 1987.

Young, M., *Labour's Plan for Plenty*, London, 1947.

Young, M., *The Rise of the Meritocracy*, 1958; Harmondsworth, 1961.

Young, M., *Small Man: Big World: A Discussion of Socialist Democracy*, London, 1949.

Young, M., and M. Rigge, *Mutual Aid in Selfish Society: A Plea for Strengthening the Co-operative Movement*, London, 1979.

Young, M., and M. Rigge, *Revolution from Within: Co-operatives and Co-operation in British Industry*, London, 1983.

3. SECONDARY BOOKS AND ARTICLES

Aaker, D. A., and G. S. Day (eds.), *Consumerism: Search for the Consumer Interest*, 3rd edn., Basingstoke, 1978.

Aldridge, A., 'The construction of rational consumption in *Which?* Magazine: the more blobs the better', *Sociology*, 28:4 (1994), 899–912.

Aldridge, A., 'Engaging with promotional culture: organised consumerism and the personal financial services industry', *Sociology*, 31:3 (1997), 380–403.

Anderson, P., and R. Blackburn (eds.), *Towards Socialism*, London, 1965.

Andrews, M., *The Acceptable Face of Feminism: The Women's Institute as a Social Movement*, London, 1997.

Atiyah, P. S., *The Sale of Goods*, 1957, London, 1990.

Atkins, P. J., 'White poison? The social consequences of milk consumption, 1850–1930', *Society for the Social History of Medicine*, 5:2 (1992), 207–27.

Attfield, J. (ed.), *Utility Reassessed: The Role of Ethics in the Practice of Design*, Manchester, 1999.

Bailey, P., *Leisure and Class in Victorian England: Rational Recreation and the Contest for Social Control*, London, 1978.

Barker, A. (ed.), *Quangos in Britain: Government and the Networks of Public Policy Making*, Basingstoke, 1982.

Barnett, L. M., *British Food Policy During the First World War*, London, 1985.

Baudrillard, J., *The Consumer Society: Myths and Structures*, London, 1998.

Baxendale, J., ' "I had seen a lot of England's": J. B. Priestley, Englishness and the people', *History Workshop Journal*, 51 (2001), 87–111.

Bayliss, R. A., 'The Consumers' Council 1918–1921', *Journal of Consumer Studies and Home Economics*, 3 (1979), 37–45.

Bayliss, R. A., 'The Consumers' Councils Bills 1929–1939', *Journal of Consumer Studies and Home Economics*, 4 (1980), 115–23.

Begg, D., S. Fischer and R. Dornbusch, *Economics*, 4th edn., London, 1994.

Belchem, J., and N. Kirk (eds.), *Languages of Labour*, Aldershot, 1997.

Benson, J., *The Rise of Consumer Society in Britain, 1880–1980*, London, 1994.

Benton, J., *Christians in a Consumer Culture*, Ross-Shire, 2000.

Berg, M., and H. Clifford (eds.), *Consumers and Luxury: Consumer Culture in Europe, 1650-1850*, Manchester, 1999.

Bermingham, A., and J. Brewer (eds.), *The Consumption of Culture 1600–1800: Image, Object, Text*, London, 1995.

Berry, C., *The Idea of Luxury: A Conceptual and Historical Investigation*, Cambridge, 1994.

Bevir, M., 'Sidney Webb: utilitarianism, positivism and social democracy', *Journal of Modern History*, 74 (2002), 217–52.

Bevir, M., and F. Trentmann (eds.), *Critiques of Capital in Modern Britain and America: Transatlantic Exchanges 1800 to the Present Day*, London, 2002.

Bihl, L., *Consommateur: Défends-toi!*, Paris, 1976.

Birchall, J., *Co-op: The People's Business*, Manchester, 1994.

Black, L., *The Political Culture of the Left in Britain, 1951–1964: Old Labour, New Britain?*, Basingstoke, 2003.

Blaszak, B. J., *The Matriarchs of England's Co-operative Movement: A Study in Gender Politics and Female Leadership, 1883–1921*, London, 2000.

Bleaney, H. F., *Under-Consumption Theories: A Historical and Critical Analysis*, London, 1976.

Bocock, R., *Consumption*, London, 1993.

Bohstedt, J., 'Gender, household and community politics: women in English riots, 1790– 1810', *Past & Present*, 120 (1988), 88–122.

Bohstedt, J., 'The moral economy and the discipline of historical context', *Journal of Social History*, 26:2 (1992), 265–84.

Bonner, A., *British Co-operation: The History, Principles, and Organisation of the British Co-operative Movement*, Manchester, 1961.

Borrie, G., *The Development of Consumer Law and Policy: Bold Spirits and Timorous Souls*, London, 1984.

Borrie, G., and A. L. Diamond, *The Consumer, Society and the Law*, 1964, London, 1973.

Bourdieu, P., *Distinction: A Social Critique of the Judgement of Taste*, London, 1986.

Bourdieu, P., *In Other Words: Essays towards a Reflexive Sociology*, Cambridge, 1994.

Bourdieu, P., *The Logic of Practice*, Cambridge, 1990.

Bourke, J., *Working-Class Cultures in Britain, 1890–1960: Gender, Class and Ethnicity*, London, 1994.

Bové, J., and F. Dufour, *The World is Not for Sale: Farmers against Junk Food*, London, 2001.

Breckman, W., 'Disciplining consumption: the debate on luxury in Wilhelmine Germany, 1890–1914', *Journal of Social History*, 24 (1991), 485–505.

Breen, T. H., ' "Baubles of Britain": the American and British consumer revolutions of the eighteenth century', *Past & Present*, 69 (1988), 73–104.

Breen, T. H., 'An empire of goods: the Anglicisation of colonial America, 1690– 1776', *Journal of British Studies*, 25 (1986), 467–99.

Breward, C., *The Hidden Consumer: Masculinities, Fashion and City Life, 1860– 1914*, Manchester, 1999.

Brewer, J., *The Pleasures of the Imagination: English Culture in the Eighteenth Century*, London, 1997.

Brewer, J., and R. Porter (eds.), *Consumption and the World of Goods*, London, 1993.

Briggs, A., *Michael Young: Social Entrepreneur*, Basingstoke, 2001.

Briggs, A., and J. Saville (eds.), *Essays in Labour History, 1886–1923*, Basingstoke, 1971.

Brobeck, S., R. N. Mayer and R. O. Herrmann (eds.), *Encyclopedia of the Consumer Movement*, Santa Barbara, 1997.

Brooke, S., 'Evan Durbin: reassessing a Labour "revisionist" ', *Twentieth Century British History*, 7:1 (1996), 27–52.

Burgess, A., 'Flattering consumption: creating a Europe of the consumer', *Journal of Consumer Culture* 1:1 (2001), 93–117.

Burnett, J., *A History of the Cost of Living*, Harmondsworth, 1969.

Burnett, J. *Plenty and Want: A Social History of Diet in England from 1815 to the Present Day*, London, 1966.

Burton, A., *The People's Cinema*, London, 1994.

Butler, D., and G. Butler, *Twentieth-Century British Political Facts*, London, 2000.

Cafaro, P., 'Less is more: economic consumption and the good life', *Philosophy Today*, 42:1 (1998), 26–39.

Campbell, C., *The Romantic Ethic and the Spirit of Modern Consumerism*, Oxford, 1987.

Carbery, T. F., *Consumers in Politics: A History and General Review of the Co-operative Party*, Manchester, 1969.

Carey, J., *The Intellectuals and the Masses: Pride and Prejudice among the Literary Intelligentsia, 1880–1939*, London, 1992.

Carrier, J. G., and D. Miller (eds.), *Virtualism: A New Political Economy*, Oxford, 1998.

Carter, E., *How German is She? Postwar West German Reconstruction and the Consuming Woman*, Ann Arbor, 1997.

Castells, M., *The Power of Identity*, 1997; Oxford, 2000.

Castells, M., *The Rise of the Network Society*, 1996; Oxford, 2000.

Charlesworth, A., 'From the moral economy of Devon to the political economy of Manchester, 1790–1812', *Social History*, 18:2 (1993), 205–17.

Charlesworth, A., and A. J. Randall, 'Comment: morals, markets and the English crowd in 1766', *Past & Present*, 114 (1987), 200–13.

Chessel, M.-E., 'Aux origines de la consommation engagée: la Ligue sociale d'acheteurs, 1902–1914', *Vingtième siècle. Revue d'histoire*, forthcoming.

Chester, D. N., *The Nationalisation of British Industry, 1945–1951*, London, 1975.

Chinn, C., *They Worked All Their Lives: Women of the Urban Poor in England, 1880–1930*, Manchester, 1988.

Clapson, M., *A Bit of a Flutter: Popular Gambling and English Society, c. 1823–1961*, Manchester, 1992.

Clark, A., *The Struggle for the Breeches: Gender and the Making of the British Working Class*, Berkeley, 1995.

Cohen, L., *Making a New Deal: Industrial Workers in Chicago, 1919–1939*, Cambridge, 1990.

Cohen, S., *Folk Devils and Moral Panics: The Creation of Mods and Rockers*, London, 1972.

Cole, M. (ed.), *The Webbs and their Work*, London, 1949.

Conekin, B., F. Mort and C. Waters (eds.), *Moments of Modernity: Reconstructing Britain, 1945–1964*, London, 1999.

Constantine, S., *Buy and Build: The Advertising Posters of the Empire Marketing Board*, London, 1986.

Consumers' Association, *Thirty Years of 'Which?' 1957–1987*, London, 1987.

Cook, I., 'Commodities: the DNA of capitalism', at http://apm.brookes.ac.uk/exchange/texts/index.htm.

Cook, I., 'Social sculpture and connective aesthetics: Shelley Sacks' "Exchange Values"', *Ecumene: A Journal of Cultural Geographies*, 7:3 (2001), 338–44.

Cooke, P. J., and D. W. Oughton, *The Common Law of Obligations*, London, 1989.

Crawford, E., *The Women's Suffrage Movement: A Reference Guide, 1866–1928*, London, 1999.

Cross, G., *An All-Consuming Century: Why Commercialism Won in Modern America*, New York, 2000.

Cross, G., *Time and Money: The Making of Consumer Culture*, London, 1993.

Crossick, G., and S. Jaumain (eds.), *Cathedrals of Consumption: The European Department Store, 1850–1939*, Aldershot, 1999.

Crowley, J. E., 'The sensibility of comfort', *American Historical Review*, 104:3 (1999), 749–82.

Cunningham, H., *Leisure in the Industrial Revolution c.1780–c.1880*, London, 1980.

Daunton, M., 'Payment and participation: welfare and state-formation in Britain 1900–1951', *Past & Present*, 150 (1996), 214.

Daunton, M., and M. Hilton (eds.), *The Politics of Consumption: Material Culture and Citizenship in Europe and America*, Oxford, 2001.

Davidoff, L., and C. Hall, *Family Fortunes: Men and Women of the English Middle Class, 1780–1850*, London, 1987.

Davies, A., *Leisure, Gender and Poverty: Working-Class Culture in Salford and Manchester, 1900–1939*, Milton Keynes, 1992.

Davis, B. J., *Home Fires Burning: Food, Politics and Everyday Life in World War I Berlin*, Chapel Hill, 2000.

De Certeau, M., *The Practice of Everyday Life*, London, 1984.

De Graaf, J., D. Wann, and T. H. Naylor, *Affluenza: The All-Consuming Epidemic*, San Francisco, 2001.

De Grazia, V., and E. Furlough (eds.), *The Sex of Things: Gender and Consumption in Historical Perspective*, London, 1996.

De Vries, J., 'The industrial revolution and the industrious revolution', *Journal of Economic History*, 54:2 (1994), 249–70.

Dench, G., T. Flower and K. Gavron (eds.), *Young at Eighty: The Prolific Public Life of Michael Young*, Manchester, 1995.

Dover, H., *Home Front Furniture: British Utility Design, 1941–1951*, Aldershot, 1991.

Edsforth, R. W., *Class Conflict and Cultural Consensus: The Making of a Mass Consumer Society in Flint, Michigan*, New Brunswick, 1987.

Eger, E., and C. Grant (eds.), *Women and the Public Sphere: Writing and Representation 1660–1800*, Cambridge, 2000.

Elkington, J., and J. Hailes, *Manual 2000: Life Choices for the Future You Want*, London, 1998.

Ellmeier, A., and E. Singer-Meczes, 'Modellierung der sozialistischen konsumentin. Konsumgenossenschaftliche (frauen)politik in den zwanziger jahren', *Zeitgeschichte*, 16 (1989), 410–26.

Epstein, J., *The Early Days of Consumers' Association: Interviews with CA's Founders and Those Who Carried on Their Work*, London, 1989.

Ewen, S., *Captains of Consciousness: Advertising and the Social Roots of the Consumer Culture*, New York, 1976.

Featherstone, M., *Consumer Culture and Postmodernism*, London, 1991.

Fielding, S., 'Activists against "affluence": Labour Party culture during the "Golden Age", circa 1950–1970', *Journal of British Studies*, 20 (2001), 241–67.

Fielding, S., P. Thompson and N. Tiratsoo, *"England Arise!" The Labour Party and Popular Politics in 1940s Britain*, Manchester, 1995.

Fine, B., and E. Leopold, *The World of Consumption*, London, 1993.

Finn, M., *The Character of Credit: Personal Debt in English Culture, 1740–1914*, Cambridge, 2003.

Finn, M., 'Women, consumption and coverture in England, c.1760–1860', *The Historical Journal*, 39:3 (1996), 703–22.

Finn, M., 'Working-class women and the contest for consumer control in Victorian county courts', *Past & Present*, 161 (1998), 116–54.

Firat, A. F., and N. Dholakia, *Consuming People: From Political Economy to Theaters of Consumption*, London, 1998.

Fiske, J., *Understanding Popular Culture*, Boston, MA, 1989.

Fletcher, A., and J. Stevenson (eds.), *Order and Disorder in Early Modern England*, Cambridge, 1985.

Foster, H. (ed.), *Postmodern Culture*, London, 1985.

Foster, S., 'Consumer nationalism in eighteenth-century Dublin', *History Today*, 47:6 (1997), 45–51.

Fowler, D., *The First Teenagers: The Lifestyles of Young Wage-Earners in Interwar Britain*, London, 1995.

Fox, R. W., and T. J. Lears (eds.), *The Culture of Consumption: Critical Essays in American History, 1880–1920*, New York, 1983.

Frank, D., 'Housewives, socialists and the politics of food: the 1917 New York cost-of- living protests', *Feminist Studies*, 11 (1985), 255–85.

Frank, D., *Purchasing Power: Consumer Organising, Gender, and the Seattle Labour Movement, 1919–1929*, Cambridge, 1994.

Frank, T., *One Market Under God: Extreme Capitalism, Market Populism and the End of Economic Democracy*, London, 2001.

French, M., and J. Phillips, *Cheated Not Poisoned? Food Regulation in the United Kingdom, 1875–1938*, Manchester, 2000.

Friedman, J. (ed.), *Consumption and Identity*, London, 1994.

Friedman, M., 'American consumer boycotts in response to rising food prices: housewives' protests at the grassroots level', *Journal of Consumer Policy*, 18 (1995), 55–72.

Friedman, M., *Consumer Boycotts: Effecting Change through the Marketplace and the Media*, London, 1999.

Friedman, M., 'A positive approach to organised consumer action: the "buycott" as an alternative to the boycott', *Journal of Consumer Policy*, 19 (1996), 439–51.

Fraser, W. H., *The Coming of the Mass Market, 1850–1914*, Basingstoke, 1981.

Gabriel, Y., and T. Lang, *The Unmanageable Consumer: Contemporary Consumption and its Fragmentation*, London, 1995.

Galbraith, J. K., *The Affluent Society*, Cambridge, MA, 1958.

Galbraith, J. K., *American Capitalism: The Concept of Countervailing Power*, 1952; Harmondsworth, 1963.

Giddens, A., *Modernity and Self-identity: Self and Society in the Late Modern Age*, Cambridge, 1991.

Giddens, A., *The Third Way*, Cambridge, 1998.

Glendinning, A., ' "Deft fingers" and "persuasive eloquence": the "lady demons" of the English gas industry, 1888–1918', *Women's History Review*, 9:3 (2000), 501–37.

Glickman, L. B. (ed.), *Consumer Society in American History: A Reader*, Ithaca, 1999.

Glickman, L. B., *A Living Wage: American Workers and the Making of Consumer Society*, Ithaca, 1997.

Glickman, L. B., 'The strike in the temple of consumption: consumer activism and twentieth-century American political culture', *Journal of American History*, 88:1 (2001), 99–128.

Glickman, L. B., 'Workers of the world, consume: Ira Steward and the origins of labor consumerism', *International Labor and Working Class History*, 52 (1997), 72–86.

Golby, J. M., and A. W. Purdue, *The Civilisation of the Crowd: Popular Culture in England 1750–1900*, London, 1984.

Goodwin, N., F. Ackerman and D. Kiron (eds.), *The Consumer Society*, Washington, DC, 1997.

Greenberg, C., *Or Does it Explode? Black Harlem in the Great Depression*, Oxford, 1997.

Grugel, L., *George Jacob Holyoake: A Study in the Evolution of a Victorian Radical*, Philadelphia, 1976.

Gurney, P., *Co-operative Culture and the Politics of Consumption in England, 1870–1930*, Manchester, 1996.

Gurney, P., 'The middle-class embrace: language, representation and the contest over co-operative forms in Britain, 1860–1914', *Victorian Studies*, Winter (1994), 253–86.

Hall, S., and M. Jacques (eds.), *New Times: The Changing Face of Politics in the 1990s*, London, 1989.

Hall, S., and T. Jefferson (eds.), *Resistance through Rituals: Youth Subcultures in Post-War Britain*, London, 1976.

Hannah, L., *The Rise of the Corporate Economy*, London, 1983.

Hardt, M., and A. Negri, *Empire, 2000*, Cambridge, MA, 2001.

Harland, D., 'The United Nations Guidelines for Consumer Protection', *Journal of Consumer Policy*, 10 (1987), 245–66.

Harrison, B., *Drink and the Victorians: The Temperance Question in England, 1815–1872*, Keele, 1994.

Harrison, B., *Peaceable Kingdom: Stability and Change in Modern Britain*, Oxford, 1982.

Harrison, B., *Prudent Revolutionaries: Portraits of British Feminists between the Wars*, Oxford, 1987.

Harvey, D., *Spaces of Hope*, Edinburgh, 2000.

Hay, D., 'The state and the market in 1800: Lord Kenyon and Mr Waddington', *Past & Present*, 162 (1999), 101–62.

Heinze, A., *Adapting to Abundance: Jewish Immigrants, Mass Consumption and the Search for American Identity*, New York, 1990.

Hertz, N., *The Silent Takeover: Global Capitalism and the Death of Democracy*, London, 2001.

Hewison, R., *Culture and Consensus: England, Art and Politics since 1940*, London, 1995.

Hilton, B., *The Age of Atonement: The Influence of Evangelicalism on Social and Economic Thought*, Oxford, 1988.

Hilton, M., 'The fable of the sheep; or, private virtues, public vices. The consumer revolution of the twentieth century', *Past & Present*, 176 (2002), 222–56.

Hilton, M., 'The female consumer and the politics of consumption in twentieth-century Britain', *The Historical Journal*, 45:1 (2002), 103–28.

Hilton, M., 'Retailing history as economic and cultural history: strategies of survival by specialist tobacconists in the mass market', *Business History*, 40:4 (1998), 115–37.

Hilton, M., *Smoking in British Popular Culture, 1800–2000*, Manchester, 2000.

Hinton, J., *Labour and Socialism: A History of the British Labour Movement, 1867–1974*, Brighton, 1983.

Hinton, J., 'Militant housewives: the British Housewives' League and the Attlee government', *History Workshop Journal*, 38 (1994), 129–56.

Hinton, J., 'Voluntarism and the welfare/warfare state: Women's Voluntary Services in the 1940s', *Twentieth Century British History*, 9 (1998), 274–305.

Hobsbawm, E., *Age of Extremes: The Short Twentieth Century, 1914–1991*, London, 1994.

Hoggart, R., *The Way We Live Now*, London, 1995.

Hollander, S., *The Economics of John Stuart Mill, Volume 1: Theory and Method*, Oxford, 1985.

Hont, I., and M. Ignatieff (eds.), *Wealth and Virtue*, Cambridge, 1983.

Horkheimer, M., and T. Adorno, *Dialectic of Enlightenment*, 1944; London, 1973.

Horowitz, D., *The Morality of Spending: Attitudes towards the Consumer Society in America 1875–1940*, Baltimore, 1985.

Howson, S., and D. Winch, *The Economic Advisory Council, 1930–1939: A Study in Economic Advice during Depression and Recovery*, Cambridge, 1977.

Hunt, K., 'Negotiating the boundaries of the domestic: British socialist women and the politics of consumption', *Women's History Review*, 9:2 (2000), 389–410.

Hunt, K., *Socialist Women* (London, 2001).

Hutchinson, F., and B. Burkitt, *The Political Economy of Social Credit and Guild Socialism*, London, 1997.

Jacobs, M., ' "How about some meat?": the Office of Price Administration, consumption politics, and state-building from the bottom up, 1941–1946', *Journal of American History*, 84:3 (1997), 910–41.

Jarvis, D., 'Mrs Maggs and Betty: the Conservative appeal to women voters in the 1920s', *Twentieth Century British History*, 5:2 (1994), 129–52.

Jefferys, K., *Crosland*, London, 1999.

Jessop, B., 'Institutional re(turns) and the strategic-relational approach', *Environment and Planning A*, 33 (2001), 1213–35.

Johnson, P., *Saving and Spending: The Working-Class Economy in Britain, 1870–1939*, Oxford, 1985.

Jordan, B., and M. Drakeford, 'Major Douglas, money and the new technology', *New Society* (24 January 1980), 167–9.

Joyce, P., *Visions of the People: Industrial England and the Question of Class, 1840–1914*, Cambridge, 1991.

Kamminga, H., and A. Cunningham (eds.), *The Science and Culture of Nutrition, 1840–1940*, Amsterdam, 1995.

Kaplan, T., 'Female consciousness and collective action: the case of Barcelona, 1910–1918', *Signs*, 7 (1982), 545–66.

Keat, R., N. Whiteley and N. Abercrombie (eds.), *The Authority of the Consumer*, London, 1994.

Kidd, A., and D. Nicholls (eds.), *Gender, Civic Culture and Consumerism: Middle-Class Identity in Britain, 1800–1940*, Manchester, 1999.

Kimber, R., and J. J. Richardson, *Pressure Groups in Britain: A Reader*, London, 1974.

Kipping, M., and N. Tiratsoo, *Americanisation in 20th Century Europe: Business, Culture, Politics*, Lille, 2002.

Kirk, N., *Change, Continuity and Class: Labour in British Society, 1850–1920*, Manchester, 1998.

Klein, L., *Shaftesbury and the Culture of Politeness: Moral Discourse and Cultural Politics in Early Eighteenth-Century England*, Cambridge, 1994.

Klein, N., *Fences and Windows: Dispatches from the Front Lines of the Globalization Debate*, London, 2002.

Klein, N., *No Logo*, London, 2000.

Kohn, M., *Dope Girls: The Birth of the British Drug Underworld*, London, 1992.

Lacquer, T. W., *Religion and Respectability: Sunday Schools and Working-Class Culture, 1780–1850*, New Haven, 1976.

Laermans, R., 'Learning to consume: early department stores and the shaping of modern consumer culture, 1860–1914', *Theory, Culture and Society*, 10 (1993), 79–102.

Langford, P., *A Polite and Commercial People: England, 1727–1783*, Oxford, 1989.

Lash, S., and J. Urry, *The End of Organised Capitalism*, Cambridge, 1987.

Lasn, K., *Culture Jam: The Uncooling of America*, New York, 1999.

Lears, T. J., *Fables of Abundance: A Cultural History of Advertising in America*, New York, 1994.

Lears, T. J., *No Place of Grace: Antimodernism and the Transformation of American Culture, 1880–1920*, Chicago, 1994.

LeMahieu, D. L., *A Culture for Democracy: Mass Communication and the Cultivated Mind in Britain Between the Wars*, Oxford, 1988.

Leonard, D. (ed.), *Crosland and New Labour*, Basingstoke, 1999.

Liddle, P. H. (ed.), *Home Fires and Foreign Fields: British Social and Military Experience in the First World War*, London, 1985.

Lih, L. T., *Bread and Authority in Russia, 1914–1921*, Los Angeles, 1990.

Lipsey, R. G., and K. A. Crystal, *Positive Economics*, 8th edn., Oxford, 1995.

Loeb, L. A., *Consuming Angels: Advertising and Victorian Women*, Oxford, 1994.

Longmate, N., *The Breadstealers: The Fight Against the Corn Laws, 1838–1946*, London, 1984.

Lury, C., *Consumer Culture*, Oxford, 1996.

MacCord, N., *The Anti-Corn Law League 1838–1946*, London, 1958.

Mackenzie, J. M. (ed.), *Imperialism and Popular Culture*, Manchester, 1986.

Maguire, P. J., and J. M. Woodham (eds.), *Design and Cultural Politics in Postwar Britain: The Britain Can Make It Exhibition of 1946*, London, 1997.

Maier, C., *Recasting Bourgeois Europe: Stabilisation in France, Germany, and Italy in the Decade after World War I*, Princeton, 1975.

Malcolmson, R. W., *Popular Recreations in English Society, 1700–1850*, Cambridge, 1973.

Marchand, R., *Advertising the American Dream: Making Way for Modernity, 1920–1940*, Berkeley, 1985.

Marquand, D., *The Progressive Dilemma: From Lloyd George to Blair*, 1991; London, 1999.

Marwick, A., 'The Independent Labour Party in the 1920s', *Bulletin of the Institute of Historical Research* 35:91 (1962), 62–74.

Marwick, A., 'Middle opinion in the thirties: planning, progress and political "agreement" ', *English Historical Review*, 79 (1964), 285–98.

Marwick, A., *The Sixties*, Oxford, 1998.

Maynes, E. S. (ed.), *The Frontier of Research in the Consumer Interest*, Columbia, MO, 1988.

McCracken, G., *Culture and Consumption: New Approaches to the Symbolic Character of Consumer Goods and Activities*, Bloomington, 1988.

McKay, G. (ed.), *DiY Culture: Party and Protest in Nineties Britain*, London, 1998.

McKendrick, N., J. Brewer and J. H. Plumb, *The Birth of a Consumer Society: The Commercialisation of Eighteenth-Century England*, London, 1982.

McKibbin, R., *Classes and Cultures: England 1918–1951*, Oxford, 1998.

McKibbin, R., *The Ideologies of Class: Social Relations in Britain, 1880–1950*, Oxford, 1990.

Melling, J., *Rent Strikes: People's Struggle for Housing in West Scotland, 1890–1916*, Edinburgh, 1983.

Melman, B., *Women and the Popular Imagination in the Twenties: Flappers and Nymphs*, New York, 1988.

Mercer, H., *Constructing a Competitive Order: The Hidden History of British Anti-Trust Policy*, Cambridge, 1995.

Micklitz, H. W., and S. Weatherill, 'Consumer policy in the European Community: before and after Maastricht', *Journal of Consumer Policy*, 16:3–4 (1993), 285–322.

Midgley, C., *Women against Slavery: The British Campaigns, 1780–1870*, London, 1992.

Miles, P., and M. Smith, *Cinema, Literature and Society: Elite and Mass Culture in Inter-War Britain*, London, 1987.

Miller, D. (ed.), *Acknowledging Consumption: A Review of New Studies*, London, 1995.

Miller, P., and N. Rose, 'Mobilizing the consumer: assembling the subject of consumption', *Theory, Culture & Society*, 14:1 (1997), 6.

Millward, R. and Singleton, J. (eds.), *The Political Economy of Nationalisation in Britain, 1920–1950*, Cambridge, 1995.

Mitchell, J. (ed.), *Marketing and the Consumer Movement*, London, 1978.

Monbiot, G., *The Captive State: The Corporate Takeover of Britain*, London, 2000.

Morgan, K. O., *Consensus and Disunity: The Lloyd George Coalition Government, 1918–1922*, Oxford, 1979.

Morgan, K. O., *Labour in Power, 1945–1951*, Oxford, 1986.

Nader, R., *Cutting Corporate Welfare*, New York, 2000.

Newholm, T., and D. Shaw, 'Ethical consumers', in J. R. Miller, R. M. Lerner, L. B. Schiamberg and P. M. (eds.), *Human Ecology: An Encyclopaedia of Children, Families, Communities and Environments* (Santa Barbara, forthcoming).

O'Connell, S., *The Car in British Society: Class, Gender and Motoring, 1896–1939*, Manchester, 1998.

Offer, A., *The First World War: An Agrarian Interpretation*, Oxford, 1989.

Parkin, M., M. Powell and K. Matthews, *Economics*, 4th edn., London, 1998.

Parssinen, T., *Secret Passions, Secret Remedies: Narcotic Drugs in British Society, 1820–1930*, Manchester, 1983.

Pelling, H., *A History of British Trade Unionism*, 1963; Harmondsworth, 1971.

Perkin, H., *The Rise of Professional Society: England since 1880*, 1989; London, 1990.

Phillips, J., and M. French, 'Adulteration and food law, 1899–1939', *Twentieth Century British History*, 9:3 (1998), 350–69.

Phillips, J., and M. French, 'The pure beer campaign and arsenic poisoning, 1896–1903', *Rural History*, 9:2 (1998), 195–209.

Pickering, P., and A. Tyrell, *The People's Bread: A History of the Anti-Corn Law League*, London, 2000.

Pinder, J. (ed.), *Fifty Years of Political and Economic Planning: Looking Forward, 1931–1981*, London, 1981.

Poster, M. (ed.), *Jean Baudrillard: Selected Writings*, Oxford, 1988.

Poster, M., 'The question of agency: Michel de Certeau and the history of consumerism', *Diacritics* (Summer 1992), 94–107.

Pugh, M., *Women and the Women's Movement in Britain, 1914–1959*, Basingstoke, 1992.

Pugh, M., 'Women, food and politics, 1880–1930', *History Today*, 41 (1991), 14–20.

Putnam, T., R. Facey and V. Swales (eds.), *Making and Unmaking: Creative and Critical Practice in a Design World*, London, 2000.

Randall, A. J., and A. Charlesworth (eds.), *Markets, Market Culture and Popular Protest in Eighteenth-Century Britain and Ireland*, Liverpool, 1996.

Randall, A. J., and A. Charlesworth (eds.), *The Moral Economy and Popular Protest: Crowds, Conflict and Authority*, Basingstoke, 2000.

Rappaport, E., *Shopping for Pleasure*, Princeton, 2000.

Reisman, D., *Anthony Crosland: The Mixed Economy*, Basingstoke, 1997.

Reisman, D., *The Economics of Alfred Marshall*, London, 1986.

Richards, J., *The Age of the Dream Palace: Cinema and Society in Britain, 1930–1939*, London, 1984.

Richards, T., *The Commodity Culture of Victorian England: Advertising and Spectacle, 1851–1914*, London, 1991.

Riddel, N., 'Walter Citrine and the British Labour Movement, 1925–1935', *History*, 85:278 (2000), 285–306.

Ritschel, D., *The Politics of Planning: The Debate on Economic Planning in Britain in the 1930s*, Oxford, 1997.

Ritzer, G., *Enchanting a Disenchanted World*, London, 1999.

Ritzer, G., *The McDonaldization of Society*, London, 1995.

Roberts, E., *Consumers*, London, 1966.

Roberts, E., *A Woman's Place: An Oral History of Working-Class Women*, Oxford, 1984.

Roper, M., *Masculinity and the British Organisation Man since 1945*, Oxford, 1994.

Rose, N., *Inventing our Selves: Psychology, Power and Personhood*, Cambridge, 1996.

Rowse, R. D., *Left in the Centre: The Independent Labour Party, 1893–1940*, London, 1966.

Roy, A., *The Cost of Living*, London, 1999.

Samuelson, P. A., and W. D. Nordhaus, *Economics*, 13th edn., London, 1989.

Schlosser, E., *Fast Food Nation: What the All-American Meal is Doing to the World*, Harmondsworth, 2001.

Schor, J. B., *Do Americans Shop Too Much?*, Boston, MA, 2000.

Schor, J. B., *The Overspent American: Why We Want What We Don't Need*, New York, 1998.

Scott, G., *Feminism and the Politics of Working Women: The Women's Co-operative Guild, 1880s to the Second World War*, London, 1998.

Searle, G., *Morality and the Market in Victorian Britain*, Oxford, 1998.

Self, R., 'Treasury control and the Empire Marketing Board: the rise and fall of non-tariff preference in Britain, 1924–1933', *Twentieth Century British History*, 5:2 (1994), 153–82.

Sekora, J., *Luxury: The Concept in Western Thought, Eden to Smollett*, London, 1977.

Shammas, C., *The Pre-Industrial Consumer in England and America*, Oxford, 1990.

Sim, F. G., *IOCU on Record: A Documentary History of the IOCU, 1960–1990*, Yonkers, NY, 1991.

Sivanandan, A., *A Different Hunger: Writings on Black Resistance*, London, 1982.

Skidelsky, R., *Politicians and the Slump: The Labour Government of 1929–1931*, London, 1967.

Sladen, C., *The Conscription of Fashion: Utility Cloth, Clothing and Footwear, 1941–1952*, Aldershot, 1995.

Slater, D., *Consumer Culture and Modernity*, Oxford, 1997.

Sloman, J., *Economics*, 4th edn., London, 2000.

Smart, J., 'Feminists, food and the fair price: the cost of living demonstrations in Melbourne, August–September 1917', *Labour History*, 50 (1986), 113–31.

Smith, G., *The Consumer Interest*, London, 1982.

Smith, N. C., *Morality and the Market: Consumer Pressure for Corporate Accountability*, London, 1990.

Stewart, R., *Design and British Industry*, London, 1987.

Susman, W., *Culture as History: The Transformation of American Society in the Twentieth Century*, New York, 1984.

Stevenson, J., *Popular Disturbances in England, 1700–1870*, London, 1979.

Stevenson, J., *Social History of Britain*, 1984, Harmondsworth, 1990.

Storch, R. D., 'Popular festivity and consumer protest: food price disturbances in the Southwest and Oxfordshire in 1867', *Albion*, 14 (1982), 209–34.

Strasser, S., C. McGovern and M. Judt (eds.), *Getting and Spending: European and American Consumer Societies in the Twentieth Century*, Cambridge, 1998.

Sussman, C., *Consuming Anxieties: Consumer Protest, Gender and British Slavery, 1713–1833*, Stanford, 2000.

Sussman, C., 'Women and the politics of sugar, 1792', *Representations*, 48 (1994), 48–69.

Swagler, R., 'Evolution and applications of the term consumerism: themes and variations', *Journal of Consumer Affairs*, 28:2 (1994), 347–60.

Tebbut, M., *Making Ends Meet: Pawnbroking and Working-Class Credit*, London, 1984.

Thompson, D., *The Chartists*, London, 1984.

Thompson, E. P., *Customs in Common*, London, 1993.

Thompson, E. P., 'The moral economy of the English crowd in the eighteenth century', *Past & Present*, 50 (1971), 79.

Thompson, E. P., 'Time, work discipline and industrial capitalism', *Past & Present*, 38 (1967), 59–91.

Thompson, F. M. L. (ed.), *Landowners, Capitalists and Entrepreneurs: Essays for Sir John Habakkuk*, Oxford, 1994.

Thompson, F. M. L., *The Rise of Respectable Society: A Social History of Victorian Britain, 1830–1900*, London, 1988.

Thompson, N., 'Hobson and the Fabians: two roads to socialism in the 1920s', *History of Political Economy*, 26:2 (1994), 203–20.

Thompson, N., *The Market and its Critics: Socialist Political Economy in the Nineteenth Century*, London, 1998.

Thompson, N., *Political Economy and the Labour Party: The Economics of Democratic Socialism, 1884–1995*, London, 1996.

Tiersten, L., 'Redefining consuming culture: recent literature on consumption and the bourgeoisie in Western Europe', *Radical History Review*, 57 (1993), 116–59.

Tivey, L., *Nationalisation in British Industry*, London, 1973.

Tomlinson, J., *Government and Enterprise since 1900: The Changing Problem of Efficiency*, Oxford, 1994.

Tomlinson, J., 'The limits of Tawney's ethical socialism: a historical perspective on the Labour Party and the Market', *Contemporary British History*, 16:4 (2002), 1–16.

Tosh, J., *A Man's Place: Masculinity and the Middle-Class Home in Victorian England*, London, 1999.

Townshend, J., *J. A. Hobson*, Manchester, 1990.

Trentmann, F. (ed.), *Paradoxes of Civil Society: New Perspectives on Modern German and British History*, Oxford, 2000.

Trentmann, F., 'Wealth versus welfare: the British Left between Free Trade and national political economy before the First World War', *Historical Research*, 70:171 (1997), 70–98.

Van der Linden, M., 'Working-class consumer power', *International Labour and Working-Class History*, 46 (1994), 109–21.

Vernon, J., *Politics and the People: A Study in English Political Culture, c.1815–1867*, Cambridge, 1993.

Vincent, D., *Poor Citizens: The State and the Poor in Twentieth-Century Britain*, London, 1991.

Waites, B., *A Class Society at War: England 1914–1918*, Leamington Spa, 1987.

Warde, A., and J. Gronow (eds.), *Ordinary Consumption*, London, 2001.

Waters, C., *British Socialists and the Politics of Popular Culture, 1884–1914*, Manchester, 1990.

Weatherill, L., *Consumer Behaviour and Material Culture in Britain, 1660–1760*, London, 1988.

Whincup, M. H., *Consumer Legislation in the United Kingdom and the Republic of Ireland*, London, 1980.

Whiteley, N., *Design for Society*, London, 1993.

Williams, D. E., 'Morals, markets and the English crowd in 1766', *Past & Present*, 104 (1984), 56–73.

Williams, K., *Get Me a Murder a Day! A History of Mass Communication in Britain*, London, 1998.

Williams, R., *Communications*, Harmondsworth, 1962.

Williams, R., *Culture and Society, 1780–1950*, London, 1958.

Williams, R., *Keywords*, London, 1976.

Williams, R., *The Long Revolution*, London, 1961.

Williams, R. H., *Dream Worlds: Mass Consumption in Late Nineteenth-Century France*, 1982, Los Angeles, 1991.

Wilson, J. F., *British Business History, 1720–1994*, Manchester, 1995.

Winch, D., *Riches and Poverty: An Intellectual History of Political Economy in Britain, 1750–1834*, Cambridge, 1996.

Winch, D., and P. O'Brien (eds.), *The Political Economy of British Historical Experience, 1688–1914*, Oxford, 2002.

Winstanley, M., *The Shopkeepers' World*, Manchester, 1983.

Winter, J. M., *Socialism and the Challenge of War: Ideas and Politics in Britain, 1912–1918*, London, 1974.

Woodham, J. M., 'Managing British design reform II: The film *Deadly Nightshade* – an ill-fated episode in the politics of "good taste" ', *Journal of Design History*, 9:2 (1996), 101–15.

Woodward, C. D., *BSI: The Story of Standards*, London, 1972.

Working Group on the WTO, *A Citizen's Guide to World Trade Organisation*, USA, 1999.

Wright, A. W., *G. D. H. Cole and Socialist Democracy*, Oxford, 1979.

Yeo, E. J. (ed.), *Radical Femininity: Women's Self-Representation in the Public Sphere*, Manchester, 1998.

Yeo, S. (ed.), *New Views of Co-operation*, London, 1988.

Zweiniger-Bargielowska, I., *Austerity in Britain: Rationing, Controls and Consumption 1939–1955*, Oxford, 2000.

Zweiniger-Bargielowska, I., 'Bread rationing in Britain, July 1946 – July 1948', *Twentieth Century British History*, 4 (1993), 57–85.

Zweiniger-Bargielowska, I., 'Rationing, austerity and the Conservative Party recovery after 1945', *Historical Journal*, 37 (1994), 173–97.

Index